THE FONTANA ECONOMIC HISTORY OF EUROPE

General Editor: Carlo M. Cipolla

There is at present no satisfactory economic history of Europe—covering Europe both as a whole and with particular relation to the individual countries—that is both concise enough for convenient use and yet full enough to include the results of individual and detailed scholarship. This series is designed to fill that gap.

Unlike most current works in this field the *Fontana Economic History of Europe* does not end at the outbreak of the First World War. More than half a century has elapsed since 1914, a half-century that has transformed the economic background of Europe. In recognition of this the present work has set its terminal date at 1970 and provides for sixty contributions each written by a specialist. For the convenience of students each will be published separately in pamphlet form as soon as possible. When all the contributions have been received they will be gathered into six volumes as The Fontana Economic History of Europe. A library edition will also be available.

THE FONTANA ECONOMIC HISTORY OF EUROPE

The Fontana Economic History of Europe

The Emergence of Industrial Societies Part Two

Editor Carlo M. Cipolla

Fontana/Collins

First published in this edition 1973
Second Impression September 1975
Third Impression October 1976
Fourth Impression September 1977

Made and printed in Great Britain by
William Collins Sons & Co Ltd Glasgow

Contents

7. The Industrial Revolution in the Nordic Countries*

Lennart Jörberg

A SURVEY OF ECONOMIC DEVELOPMENTS

During the nineteenth-century economic developments in Denmark, Finland, Norway and Sweden—the Nordic countries, or, as they are more loosely called, Scandinavia —exhibited a number of common traits. At the same time there were a number of obvious differences in their individual circumstances and in the components of their economic growth.

Over the centuries, the countries of Scandinavia have often shared a common history, and not only in the form of internecine warfare. For long periods in the Middle Ages they were joined in a single political union, under Denmark's leadership. When the Middle Ages came to an end, Norway remained in this union, while Finland remained united to Sweden. Up to the mid-seventeenth century the southernmost parts of what is today Sweden belonged to Denmark. In 1809 Sweden ceded Finland to Russia, and up to 1917 Finland remained a grand duchy of the Russian Empire. In 1814 Norway changed her union partners, Denmark being forced to yield her to Sweden, under whose crown the two countries were united up to 1905.

During the latter part of the century a certain community of economic interests began to make itself felt. From the mid-1870s up to the First World War a Scandinavian monetary union was in force. By mid-century all four countries had lost their international political importance and were only slowly being affected by economic changes that had been taking place in Europe during the first half of the century. Denmark excepted, the Nordic

* The author wishes to express his gratitude to Professor C. M. Cipolla and Dr. C. A. Nilsson for commenting upon an earlier version of this chapter.

countries must have been among the poorest of Western European nations.

Today, all four are highly industrialised. Their per capita national incomes are among the highest in the world. In the mid-nineteenth century the economic expansion which led up to this transformation was accelerated; and before the outbreak of the First World War (although Finland's development was less striking) it had turned Denmark, Norway and Sweden into fairly prosperous nations. Sweden's industrial development, indeed, probably occurred more swiftly than any other European country's at that time, while Denmark's and Norway's economic expansion was not dominated in the same way by industrial growth.

In the mid-nineteenth century the Scandinavian countries still had a predominantly agrarian structure. The industrial sector was of scant importance. Indeed, of the three countries, only Sweden had even established such a sector; namely iron and steel. In the eighteenth century Sweden, together with Russia, had dominated the European iron market, but by the middle of the nineteenth her importance had fallen off greatly as a supplier of iron to Europe. Swedish iron-mining could rely on considerable quantities of raw materials in the form of iron ore, but Sweden had no coal at all and the cost of producing pig iron using charcoal made it hard for her to compete with the cheaper coke-smelted product. Notwithstanding repeated attempts by the Swedish producers to strengthen their competitive position by improving the quality of their iron, Swedish exports of bar iron grew but slowly during the first half of the nineteenth century.

Norway's main industrial sector was her timber industry, timber exports and freight earnings being her chief source of foreign currency earnings. Finland's timber exports were inconsiderable and Denmark lacked any industrial raw materials suitable for export.

Although all four countries had a predominantly agrarian structure, their income levels were quite different. Denmark and Norway had a per capita national product perhaps ⅓ higher than Sweden's, which was higher than the Finnish. Before the First World War, however, Sweden had reached about the same level as Denmark, and Finland's income level, too, had risen relatively to the other countries.

Between 1870 and 1913 the gross national product (GNP), expressed in fixed prices, increased by 3·7% per annum in Denmark, by 2·4% in Norway, and by 3·4% in Sweden. Since Sweden's population increase was much lower than Denmark's, and somewhat lower than Norway's (1·1, 0·8, and 0·7% per annum for Denmark and Norway and Sweden respectively) per capita production rose quickest in Sweden (cf. Kuznets, 1966, tab. 6·6). No national income figures are available for Finland; but a Finnish author has roughly estimated that it must have increased by about 2·3% per capita per annum. This would mean that Finland's GNP rose more swiftly than any of the other Scandinavian countries', since her population increase was nearly 1·2% per annum (Björkqvist, 1958, p. 21).

This again would mean that during the four decades previous to the First World War, the GNP, expressed in current prices, increased by nearly 200% in Denmark, by 150% in Norway, and by more than 250% in Sweden (Table 1). This implies that, internationally speaking, Scandinavia could show one of the swiftest growth-rates of any of those countries which at the beginning of the twentieth century could be regarded as industrialised.

It is questionable whether this development was due to identical factors in all four countries, or to what extent their differing degrees of development around 1870 came to influence their expansion.

Certain common traits can easily be discerned. In proportion to their GNP, all four countries' overseas trade was large, and during the period became still larger. Again, all four were dependent upon a small range of export goods: Denmark above all on agricultural products, Norway on fish, timber products and shipping, and Sweden on timber and iron. In all four countries agricultural productivity rose: most in Denmark, least in Norway. On the other hand, industry was a smaller stimulant to economic development in Denmark and Norway than in Sweden or Finland. In Denmark, consumer products dominated the industrial sector, while in Sweden developments were led by the capital goods industry.

Norway's and Sweden's large-scale emigration, mainly to the USA, had an important effect on the total production increase, while Danish emigration remained small. In Norway, emigration absorbed about half the natural population increase, and in Norway, Sweden and Finland the population increase was a good deal smaller than the relation between their birth- and death-rates might lead one to suppose. The Scandinavian countries' growth-rate was uneven, and their periods of expansion and stagnation did not coincide until the 1890s, when all four showed a big increase in both GNP and investment.

It is to be noted, however, that the countries' rapid growth was largely due to external factors, e.g., increased foreign demand. But the products affected in each country were quite different in each case. In Denmark, it was agriculture that was chiefly affected; in Norway the service industries (i.e., shipping, while there was a fall in timber exports), and in Sweden mainly industry. Finland's exports consisted chiefly of timber products and butter. The industrial expansion of each country thus occurred on quite a different basis from its neighbours', and was dominated by quite different sectors of their economy. Thus it is an open question how far home demand was dependent upon external factors.

POPULATION GROWTH AND ECONOMIC DEVELOPMENT

About the year 1870 Denmark, Finland and Norway each had about the same number of inhabitants, viz. about 1·8 million, while the population of Sweden amounted to about 4 millions—approximately double that of each of her neighbours. Before the First World War Denmark had about 2·8, Finland 3·2, Norway 2·4 and Sweden 5·5 million inhabitants. The Danish population growth had thus been

TABLE 1: Percentage increase in population, national product and product per capita, 1866–1910[1]

| | POPULATION | | | NATIONAL PRODUCT | | | | | | PRODUCT/CAPITA | | | | | |
| | Denmark | Norway | Sweden | current prices | | | constant prices | | | current prices | | | constant prices | | |
				D	N	S	D	N	S	D	N	S	D	N	S
1866/70 to 1871/75	4·6	3·0	2·6	(20·8)	33·7	40·0	—	13·7	29·4	(15·7)	29·6	36·2	—	10·6	25·3
1876/80	5·3	5·9	4·1	2·9	5·6	9·4	7·7	9·4	10·0	−2·3	−·3	4·2	2·2	3·2	5·2
1881/85	4·9	2·8	3·5	11·5	−1·1	3·1	19·9	3·2	8·5	6·2	−3·8	·7	14·3	·5	5·9
1886/90	5·4	2·6	3·0	3·7	−1·6	−1·2	12·4	8·5	9·5	−4·7	−4·0	−4·0	6·9	5·7	6·4
1891/95	4·2	3·3	1·9	19·5	13·2	16·5	18·6	11·6	13·9	14·8	9·4	14·2	13·8	8·1	11·8
1896/00	6·2	6·3	4·1	16·8	22·4	26·5	21·7	12·4	22·7	9·8	15·4	21·3	14·5	5·6	17·7
1901/05	6·2	5·2	3·6	22·3	9·8	19·1	17·3	7·9	13·8	15·1	4·1	15·0	10·4	2·6	9·8
1906/10	6·0	2·8	3·7	18·4	19·2	30·7	14·1	12·7	21·0	11·8	15·9	26·1	7·6	9·6	16·7
1866/70–1896/00	34·8	26·3	20·8	101·7	90·4	129·8	—	74·7	136·6	49·7	50·6	90·0	—	38·3	95·5
1866/70–1906/10	51·8	36·6	29·8	192·2	149·0	257·7	—	112·3	225·7	92·7	81·9	175·7	—	55·4	150·0

Sources: Denmark: Population: Statistisk Aarbog 1920. NDP 1866/70: Cohn, 1953, p. 109. NDP 1871–1910: Bjerke-Ussing, 1958, table II

Norway: Population: Statistiske Oversikter, 1948, table 14. GDP: Bjerke, 1966, pp. 97, 130, 151

Sweden: Johansson, 1967, tables 55, 58, 59

about 50%, the Finnish about 75%, the Norwegian about 35% and the Swedish hardly 30%; (the changes [the first derivate] in population growth are shown in diagram 1).

Denmark's population growth occurred more evenly than the other Scandinavian countries', standing at about 20,000 per annum up to the 1890s, when it rose to about 30,000 per annum. The growth in the Norwegian and Swedish populations obviously fluctuated together, partly under the impact of emigration. Danish emigration was less important than Norway's and Sweden's, and in Finland emigration did not even start until about 1890, as can be seen from the fluctuations in the growth curve. At the end of the 1860s the fairly even growth curve was interrupted and their harvest failures and outbreaks of disease connected with them caused an absolute drop in the Finnish population. In the first six months of 1868 death brought losses of up to a fifth of the population of some regions of Finland (Haatanen, 1968, p. 361). A clearly discernible Malthusian positive check thus set in. But it is also possible to regard those starvation years as having been a shock which pushed Finland out of her stagnation. The need for greater diversification, above all in agriculture, had become obvious, and measures were taken to support a develop-

---

1. The calculations in constant prices are not uniformly made in the three countries. Bjerke-Ussing have converted 1913 data into 1929 prices via a cost of living index. Thereafter, the prices for 1870-1913 were adjusted to the relation they had in 1913, i.e. data for 1870-1913 still reflect all the price fluctuations during this period (op. cit. p. 126f.). Further, the national income up to 1920 is based on income tax returns, adjusted for tax-exempt incomes. The Norwegian material is based on 'index numbers calculated with the aid of prices for a specific year' (Bjerke, 1966, p. 22). Different weighing methods with weights for 1865, 75, 85 and 1900 show no great variation in the growth-rate. The annual information, however, is based on interpolation between a number of interjacent years when production statistics are found. The Swedish series are based on production statistics and are deflated with different indices for the various sectors, which makes them more reliable, although a better price material could change the relations somewhat. Because the Swedish statistics for agriculture are most unreliable and overestimate the upward trend after 1870, a revision will lead to some reduction in the growth.

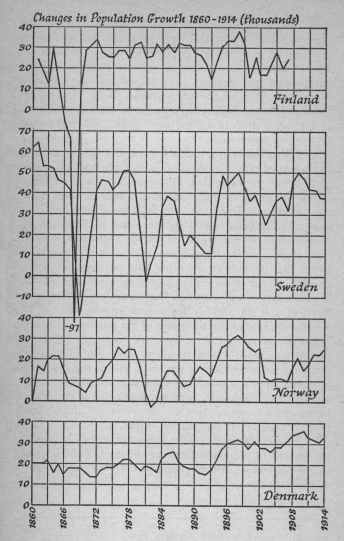

Changes in Population Growth 1860–1914 (thousands)

Finland

Sweden

Norway

−97

Denmark

Diagram 1.   Sources, see page 382.

ment to the economy. During those years, Sweden, too, experienced a drop in her population, due in part to crop
failures and the ensuing big increase in emigration. Failed
harvests do not seem to have caused an interruption in
Denmark's population development. Both Finland and
Sweden were marked by their pre-industrial economies and
as a result a drop in agricultural yield could still cause a
decrease in population.

The Scandinavian countries, generally speaking, had a
birth-rate of rather more than 30 ‰,[1] Finland with about
36 ‰ being the exception. Around 1880 these birth-rates
began to fall in all four countries, fastest in Sweden and
most slowly in Denmark. Death-rates of less than 20 %
were already being noted in the 1820s in Denmark and
Norway and all the countries except Finland had death-
rates of 20 ‰ or less from the mid-nineteenth century on,
lower, that is, than in any other European countries. This
meant that the natural population increase after 1880, as
has been noted, was larger in Denmark than in Norway or
Sweden, and the Danish population growth was also less
affected by emigration than that of the other Scandinavian
countries, as can be seen from the fact that Denmark's
population growth was stronger than the other Scandinavian countries during the later half of the nineteenth
century. The wave-like movements, discernible in the
population growth-rate, were not solely due to emigration.
Long waves in population development can quite clearly
be seen even before emigration began.

In Sweden, as in the other three countries, there was a
big growth in population during the period 1810-25, and
this is something which cannot wholly be explained by
earlier variations in population growth. As to Sweden it has

1. ‰ signifies per thousand.

Sources: Denmark: Statistisk Aarborg, 1920
       Finland: 1860-1870, Statistisk Årsbok för Finland, 1936
                  1871-1907, Sundbärg, 1908
       Norway: Statistiske Oversikter, 1948
       Sweden: Historisk statistik, part 1, 1955

TABLE 2: Annual population growth 1801-1910 (per 1000)

	Denmark	Finland	Norway	Sweden
1801/20	8·2	6·8	5·7	4·8
1821/30	9·3	13·3	14·7	11·2
1831/40	7·3	5·2	9·7	8·4
1841/50	9·9	12·5	11·7	10·4
1851/60	12·3	6·5	14·0	10·3
1861/70	10·0	1·3	7·9	7·7
1871/80	9·6	15·4	10·1	9·1
1881/90	9·4	13·2	4·1	4·7
1891/1900	11·4	11·1	11·3	7·1
1901/10	11·0	10·8	5·7	0·8
1801/50	8·6	14·4	9·3	7·9
1851/1900	10·5	10·4	9·5	7·8
Total increase per cent				
1801/50	53	97	59	48
1851/1900	69	62	60	47
1801/1900	159	219	154	119

Source: Sundbärg, 1908, tables 11 and 12 and statistical year-books for each country.

The Finnish population statistics do not exclude emigrants, which means that the original figures are overstated. Sundbärg corrected these errors and later revisions at the end of the 1940s by the Finnish Central Bureau of Statistics confirm Sundbärg's estimates, within a few decimal points.

been pointed out that there was, at that time, an unprecedented increase in potato cultivation. In earlier periods an existing agricultural organisation had been capable of absorbing an increase in population. Production methods had remained largely unchanged. But now, because of the steady growth in population, the limit of what this old agricultural system could yield was reached The only way of breaking with the earlier structure was to carry through a radical improvement in productivity, and the only way to do this was by introducing a new type of crop. This increase in potato output also helped to release grain for export. It is therefore probable that the grain exports from Sweden which began in the 1830s were partly due to an increased consumption of potatoes and not to any great productivity improvement in grain growing.

The big increase in population during the period 1810-25 is reflected in a sharp rise in the rate of population growth in the 1850s and again in the 1870s and 1890s These were also the periods of maximum economic growth. There can hardly be any obvious correlation between an increase in the population growth-rate and the growth of the economy, at least not in such a way that the one variable is caused by the other The causality is mutual. But of course the number of individuals of working age, the formation of families and fertility do affect the economic situation. In periods where a great many households are being formed, demand is accentuated: and the creation of these households is, on the one hand, a result of a change in economic activity, and, on the other—through multiplier and accelerator effects—leads to increased demand for dwellings and other consumer and investment goods.

The great increase in the population in the 1870s as well as the increase in external demand which made itself felt in the form of exports contributed to accelerate and also helped to prolong by several years the boom conditions which had prevailed internationally only until 1873. The rising waves in population growth which occurred in all the Scandinavian countries during the 1890s also coincided with an economic expansion. Whether these increases in internal demand had as great an influence on the boom conditions of the 1870s and 1890s as had been exerted by the more easily discernible increases in external demand is something that still calls for research. Where Finland is concerned, the lack of major population waves until the 1890s can perhaps in part explain the character of her economic expansion.

In other words, in Norway and Sweden, above all, rising per capita incomes conformed with rising population growth: or, to express the matter in another way, the rise in total production was larger than the increase in population during periods of increased population growth. This population growth also conformed with a strong internal migration, above all in the form of greater urbanisation.

TABLE 3: Degree of urbanisation in the Scandinavian countries. Per cent

	Denmark	Finland	Norway	Sweden
1860	23	6	15	11
1880	28	8	20	15
1890	33	10	24	19
1900	38	13	28	22
1910	40	15	29	25

Movement to the cities was stronger when population growth was at its maximum. Since it is usually younger age-groups who migrate to the cities, there is a tendency for more new families to be established. So both migration and the creation of new households contribute to increase the rate of economic growth and change the structure of the economy.

The degree of urbanisation is a fair indication of the countries' economic level at the beginning of this period, and the growth in urban population is also a rough index of their economic development.

Further, in a pre-industrial society, a relatively low population growth must be considered an advantage. If the population is to remain at the same income level, a higher rate of growth will call for a high level of investment. Therefore a substantial growth rate, which is yet not so great as to absorb the total rise in income level is favourable to such a society's economic growth. This, not merely because the working sector of the population will exceed that of a society with high population growth rate, but also because the need for savings will not become so great that it will prevent any increase in per capita income. Most countries in the earliest stages of their economic expansion show rather insignificant capital formation, and this is more easily achieved if population growth is moderate.

At quite an early stage the Scandinavian countries invested considerably in popular education. As early as the end of the eighteenth century Denmark had a compulsory school system, Norway had one by 1827, Sweden by 1842, and Finland by 1866. By the middle of the nineteenth century it was estimated that all Norwegian adults under the age of 50 could read, and in the year 1900 almost all persons of more than 15 years of age in Finland could both read and write. That is to say, before the onset of the industrial revolution, an event which by its nature called for a re-schooling of the population, this Scandinavian educational investment had already produced a literate population. This must have facilitated the changeover to industrial methods and been a factor contributing to economic growth. It must also have greatly facilitated the introduction of new techniques and helped physical and human capital to complement each other in a balanced way. Such investment, in turn, must have been made easier by a population growth of about 1% per annum, or less. Fairly good education and, compared with more advanced countries, a low death-rate, had positive effects on income development.

Per capita income in the Scandinavian countries increased greatly during the period 1870-1910. In fixed prices the changes were as follows:

	Denmark	Norway	Sweden
1870	100	100	100
1875	107	114	110
1885	127	113	128
1890	148	126	137
1895	162	129	150
1910	214	161	231

There is a clear difference in the individual countries' rates of development. Between 1870 and 1890 per capita income in Denmark rose by 48% and between 1890 and 1910 by 45%. In Norway this increase was 26% and 28% respectively, and in Sweden 37% and 69%. In Sweden the rate of increase accelerated powerfully during the two later

decades, while in Denmark and Norway there was no substantial difference between the periods (see also table 1). It
was only during the later period that there was any notable
levelling out of income as between the countries. It is also
obvious that Norway's per capita income development
differed from Sweden's, and—albeit to a lesser extent—
from Denmark's. In Norway, between 1870 and 1875, per
capita income rose more swiftly than in any Scandinavian
country, falling off during the following decades. The rise
after 1885 did not bring it back to the 1875 level until the
end of the 1880s.

The Danish income growth during the first half of the
1870s was moderate, and remained at the level it had then
reached, without any notable changes until 1885, thereafter
rising more or less steadily until 1905. During the five years
following there were only insignificant rises.

In Sweden, the growth-rate was very strong, almost
equal to the Norwegian during the first half of the 1870s.
Then, up to 1890, it remained largely stationary, to
accelerate again, almost as notably as before, between 1890
and 1895. That Swedish per capita income had reached
much the same level as the Danish and Norwegian before
the First World War was therefore due to these short
periods of very swift growth. When analysing the Scandinavian development it is therefore just as important to try
and explain these jerky short period movements in income
growth as to explore the reasons for the weak growth of
the Norwegian economy during the period 1875-1900, or
the more continuous growth of per capita income in Denmark between 1885 and 1905.

As has already been pointed out, there is a clear correlation between periods of stronger economic growth and the
growth of the population of working age. In Norway the
15-64 age-group grew by 10% between 1865 and 1875,
while the population as a whole only grew by 6·7%.
Between 1880 and 1890, while the Norwegian per capita
income stagnated, the total population grew by about 5%,
while the working-age population fell by 1%.

In Sweden the working age population rose by 9·3%

between 1870 and 1880. This was a faster rate of growth than in any subsequent decade previous to 1914. In Denmark, on the other hand, with a relatively weaker growth than in the other two countries during the 1870s, the total population grew faster than the labour force, or by 10% as against 7·8%. During the following decades, on the other hand, the rise in the labour force was more accentuated in Norway and Sweden, while at the same time Denmark experienced a steady rise in per capita income. In Sweden, too, during the 1890s and the first decade of the twentieth century, the growth in the size of the 15-65 age-group was stronger than total population growth (Sources: see table 1).

Naturally, an increase in the working age population is in itself no guarantee of increased output. If work cannot be found for the extra workers, the result will merely be under-employment or unemployment. Rising employment, however, even without any increase in productivity per individual worker, leads to a larger gross product. Since the labour force increased more swiftly during periods of international boom, the result was a large increase in output. This conformity between the supply of labour and international demand was characteristic of the 1850s, 1870s and 1890s in Sweden. A further factor, which must be taken into account, is that domestic demand, as has been mentioned before, was also stimulated by increased household formation; which in turn must still further have accelerated the increase caused by foreign demand.

In Denmark, this congruity between the two components making for increased demand was lacking in the 1870s. In Norway, between 1880 and 1890, stagnation in the number of individuals of working age, together with falling per capita real income, indicates that, at a time when both Denmark and Sweden succeeded in compensating for a falling growth-rate in their labour forces by productivity-stimulating measures, there was no improvement in productivity per gainfully employed person.

In the initial stages of the industrial era in Scandinavia, about four-fifths of Finland's population was engaged in agriculture and ancillary work. In Denmark this figure was somewhat more than half. In Norway and Sweden, about 70% were occupied in that sector. In the two latter countries there was a greater fall in this respect up to 1910 than there was in Denmark, something quite natural in itself, inasmuch as the agrarian sector in Denmark was considerably smaller at the beginning of the period. In Norway the greatest fall occurred between 1865 and 1890, with a very moderate further fall up to 1910. Between 1850 and 1900 the Norwegian population increased by about 800,000, to which figure 500,000 emigrants must be added. Of the 800,000 who remained in Norway, about half a million supported themselves by industry and crafts, while a quarter of a million were occupied in commerce and transportation (Ströme, 1956, p. 49). In Sweden there was a greater flight from agriculture during the latter half of this period than there had been in the first half, while in Finland the relative changes between 1880 and 1890 were inconsiderable, and between 1890 and 1910 were smaller than in the other Scandinavian countries.

In Denmark the industrial sector grew very slowly, while in Sweden it was swifter than in any other Scandinavian land. In Finland commerce and transportation represented a very small fraction, about 5% in 1910. In the other countries this sector was about the same size, or between 13 and 16%, and while in Sweden the service sector diminished, in the other countries, notably in Norway, it expanded.

From this survey it becomes apparent that economic developments in Denmark were different from those in Norway and Sweden. Around 1870 agriculture represented the largest segment of the gross national product of all these three countries (also, of course, in Finland, although there is no supporting information from that quarter). Although Sweden's agrarian population represented a larger segment of her total population than the other two countries', she was deriving a smaller fraction of her total production from agriculture than either Denmark

TABLE 4: Gross domestic product at current prices by sector of origin. Per cent

	Denmark					Norway					Sweden				
	1870	1875	1890	1900	1910	1865	1875	1890	1900	1910	1866/70	76/80	86/90	96/00	06/10
Agriculture, fishing, etc.	48	43	35	29	30	45	35	32	25	24	39	36	32	28	25
Mining, manufacturing, construction	52	57	65	71	70	18	22	24	28	26	19	22	22	27	33
Transport & communication						10	14	12	11	11	4	5	6	6	7
Other						27	29	32	36	39	38	37	40	39	35
Total GDP	100	100	100	100	100	100	100	100	100	100	100	100	100	100	100

(For Denmark, the Mining, manufacturing, construction and Transport & communication rows are combined by a brace into a single figure: 52, 57, 65, 71, 70.)

For Norway, the calculations are based on the number of workers in various branches of industry and the calculations presume the same relation between gross national product per worker in each branch of industry as in 1910

Sources: Denmark: Bjerke-Ussing 1958, p. 144
Norway: Bjerke 1966, p. 25
Sweden: Johansson 1967, p. 150

or Norway. That is to say, Denmark's agricultural productivity was greater, and its role in her economic development was of quite another order from what it was in Sweden or Norway, and even as late as 1910 Denmark's agriculture was more important to her economy, measured in terms of her total product, than Norway's or Sweden's were to theirs. How the changes in other sectors in Denmark looked is impossible to determine. But in Norway and Sweden the industrial segment of the GNP had outstripped the agricultural by about 1900.

There is nothing particularly original about such a course of development. A structural change of this sort is quite simply what is meant by industrialisation. A major increase in non-agrarian productivity is a consequence of, among other things, changing demand and income elasticity. A factor worth remarking would seem to be the minimal number of individuals in 'other sectors' in Sweden, and the discrepancy between this number and their share of the GNP. More research in this area will be required if this discrepancy is to be explained.

Industrial expansion initially demands a certain level of efficiency in one or more sectors outside the industrial area; a supply of labour, capital adequate to modern industrialisation, a sufficient demand for industrial products, and management modern enough to make long-term decisions and avail itself of technical or other types of innovations. Therefore, to assess the Scandinavian countries' industrial development, it is important to consider the efficiency of their agriculture and transportation systems, the size, distribution, mobility and education of their labour forces, the functional adequacy of the capital market, the response of industrial management to changing market situations, both internally and externally, and the distribution of investments, in respect both of labour and capital.

TABLE 5: Population, by occupation. Percentages

DENMARK	1870	1880	1890	1901	1911	Change 1870-1911
Agriculture, fishing	55	54	49	44	36	−19
Manufacturing & handicrafts	26	26	28	30	28	+2
Commerce, transport	7	8	10	11	14	+7
Other	12	12	13	15	22	+10

FINLAND		1880	1890	1900	1910	Change 1880-1910
Agriculture		75	73	68	66	−9
Manufacturing & handicrafts		7	8	11	12	+5
Transport & communications		2	2	3	3	+1
Commerce		1	1	2	2	+1
Other		16	16	16	16	±0

NORWAY	1865		1890	1900	1910	Change 1865-1910
Agriculture, forestry, fishing	69		51	44	43	−26
Manufacturing, mining	16		22	26	25	+9
Commerce, transport	10		15	15	16	+6
Other	5		12	15	16	+11

SWEDEN	1870	1880	1890	1900	1910	Change 1870-1910
Agriculture, forestry, fishing	72	68	62	55	49	−23
Mining, manufacturing & handicrafts, construction	15	17	22	28	32	+17
Commerce, transport	5	7	9	10	13	+8
Other	8	8	7	7	6	−2

Data for Norway are not wholly comparable as between 1865 and the following years, and for Denmark the classification is not uniform between 1911 and the previous years. The numbers therefore must not be regarded as other than an approximation of a development tendency

Sources: Denmark: Bjerke-Ussing 1958, p. 10
       Finland: Statistisk Årsbok för Finland, 1936, table 24
       Norway: Statistiske Oversikter 1948, p. 36 f.
       Sweden: Statistisk Översikt 1919, p. 7

THE EXPANSION OF AGRICULTURE

With agriculture constituting so great a share, fluctuations in this sector dominated Denmark's total GNP up to the beginning of the 1880s. During that decade Denmark's agricultural contribution, relatively speaking, fell, and the country's income growth was progressively influenced by the other sectors of the economy. However, during short periods, agriculture still occasionally dominated developments. From 1888 on, agricultural incomes rose sharply, and this led to a swifter growth in the GNP than during the earlier part of the decade. Between 1888 and 1891 agricultural incomes rose by 41% while other sectors of the economy only showed a 17% increase. At the end of the 1890s and for a few years afterwards growth in agricultural income accelerated. Thereafter, up to the First World War, all sectors developed more or less parallel.

In Sweden, too, there was a strong correlation between agricultural income and gross product up to the end of the 1880s. After that date industrial income accelerated and, with the exception of a recession at the beginning of the 1890s, the rate of growth in the industrial sector was much greater than in the agricultural; only during the pre-1907 boom does Swedish agriculture show a rate of growth comparable to that of Swedish industry.

In Finland income development in agriculture was more even than in Denmark and Sweden. For the period 1878-1914 the increase for agricultural income has been calculated at 2·8% per annum. The biggest deviations from the general trend are to be found in the early 1880s, when the increase exceeded the trend value, and at the end of the same decade, when the trend lay higher than the real growth (Björkqvist, 1958, p. 99 et seq.). As mentioned before, no statistics are available for Finland's national income during this period. It is therefore impossible to determine how far income growth was influenced by agriculture. Nor are there any data on annual changes in these sectors in Norway.

DENMARK

In spite of the fact that around the year 1870 Denmark was
employing fewer individuals, both relatively and absolutely,
in agriculture than the other Scandinavian countries,
agriculture nevertheless came to exert a very much greater
influence on her economic development than it did on
theirs. Analysis of the changes in Danish production, structure and productivity reveals that agriculture played the
same role in developing the Danish economy as industry
did in Sweden, as shipping did in Norway, and timber
products in Finland. Agriculture became specialised, production assumed an ever more industrial scale, and exports
of agricultural products became the chief earners of foreign
currency. Further, the growth in agricultural labour productivity and the growth in income following therefrom
came to be the main driving force behind the creation of
Danish industry, and furthermore, proved decisive, for the
structure of Denmark's industrial output.

From the 1830s up to the 1870s, Danish agriculture went
through a period of steady growth, interrupted only by
insignificant reverses. Price trends were also favourable.
Prices for rye rose by almost $\frac{2}{3}$, for livestock, meat and dairy
products by even greater amounts, and for pork by nearly
150%. The production growth was caused by improving
productivity, increased acreage, and the employment of a
larger labour force. The acreage growth, however, was quite
modest, about 20%, while production volume rose by
about 80% (Cohn 1957, p. 302). It also transpires from
these price changes that the 'terms of trade' as between
vegetable and animal products were in the latter's favour,
the only exception being during the first half of the 1850s,
when grain prices were influenced by the rise in demand
during the Crimean War. Between the end of the 1850s and
the end of the 1880s the terms of trade for meat and dairy
products as against vegetable products were improved by
about 60% (calculated in terms of the relation between rye
and pork prices).

This tendency—even stronger, for instance, for the relation between wheat and butter—led Danish farmers to change over progressively to livestock rearing, so that as early as about 1870 exports of meat products outstripped grain exports. During the 1870s and 1880s this favourable situation for livestock products improved still further, and the biggest improvement in their terms of trade occurred at that time.

Between the beginning of the 1870s and the first five years of the twentieth century, total agricultural output rose by about 140%. Total crop output on the other hand only rose by about 50%, at the same time as crop production for marketing fell by almost half, i.e., farmers were now using an even greater part of their output for further processing in the form of livestock. This is apparent from the fact that, while grain output rose by no more than 20%, root crops multiplied by twenty. From the 1880s Denmark was a net importer of grain. At the same time her meat and dairy products more than doubled (Bjerke-Ussing, 1958, p. 52). This growth occurred on a largely unchanged acreage and with an increase in labour force of just over 10%. This change of production in the direction of an ever greater specialisation in meat and dairy products was in part due to increased British demand for such products; in part to increasing competition from Russian and American producers on the European grain market.

The invention of the milk separator, at the end of the 1870s, also changed the technical basis of dairy farming. Butter productivity rose sharply, a change facilitated by the growth of the Danish co-operative movement. As late as 1880 there were still no co-operative dairies in Denmark. But in 1890 there were 679 of them and in 1913 they numbered more than 1100 (Skrubbeltrang-Hansen, 1945, p. 432).

One factor strongly promoting the growth of co-operatives was the smaller farmers' fear of exploitation by their larger colleagues who, having more capital, were able to purchase separators. In addition to co-operative dairies and slaughterhouses, the farmers set up co-operative societies to purchase raw materials necessary to their own production and to market their finished products, and formed export associations, etc.

TABLE 6: Denmark: Production of some important agricultural items, 1870-1914

	1 Milk	2 Butter	3 Pork	4 Grain*	5 Root crops*	6 Milk/ cow	7 Butter/ cow
	1000 tons					kilogrammes	
1870/74	1150	38	50	20223	846	1000	31
1880/84	1425	47	72	22509	1762	1350	44
1890/94	2030	68	100	23686	3888	1600	54
1900/04	2770	97	137	24776	9180	2000	74
1910/14	3340	110	210	27431	17301	2750	109

*In 1000 'units of fodder'. One unit is equivalent of 100 kilogrammes barley

Sources: Col. 1-5: Bjerke-Ussing, 1958, pp. 40 and 49
　　　　　Col. 6-7: Hansen, 1924-32, vol. III, p. 572, quoted by Olsen 1962, Table VIb

The co-operative movement's success is said to have been partly due to the existence of 'folk high schools'. Started in the 1840s, these colleges represented both a movement towards enlightenment and a general rise in the level of knowledge among the farmer class and also provided a political platform from which farmers could make their demands heard by society. But they gave no technical training. Thanks to the swift growth in the number of such schools, however, it had become possible by about the year 1880 for the agricultural population in almost every parish in Denmark to attend one. The schools came to exert a widespread influence on farmers, strengthening their self-awareness as a class and their political influence (Cf. Youngson, 1967, App. 1).

Butter production came to dominate this agrarian transformation. Between 1870 and 1900 output per cow was doubled thanks to improvements in butter-making techniques and there was an even greater rise in the quantity of butter which could be produced per kilo of milk.

These developments also influenced pork production. The skimmed milk which the dairies returned to the farmers was used for pig rearing, and increasing pork production led to the establishment of slaughterhouse co-operatives. Between the beginning of the 1870s and 1914 pork output was quadrupled.

Changed price relationships within the livestock and dairy produce industry also had a stimulating effect on the change in the production trend, which occurred at that time. Not only did pork prices fall in relation to butter prices; the relation between the market price of live pigs and pork also altered. One reason for this was Germany's ban on live pig imports, in 1887, which led to a complete cessation in Danish pig exports. The implementation of new marketing techniques which this necessitated—a change to sales of packed pork and the redirection of exports, above all from Germany to Britain—fell to the lot of the co-operative movement. During the first half of the 1890s pork exports rose from about 40,000 tons to more than 100,000 tons about 1910, while during the same period butter exports rose from about 90,000 to 180,000 tons. In the beginning of the twentieth century, pork prices also improved in relation to butter, one reason being increased competition on the British market from such countries as Finland.

This, then, was how Danish agriculture met the international agricultural crisis of the 1880s: by restructuring her production in the direction of meat and dairy produce, whose prices proved more stable than those for grain; by greater concentration on the output of butter than of pigs (butter prices improving in relation to pig and pork prices); by standardising butter production; by increasing productivity per unit of acreage and worker; and by taking advantage of the low grain prices on the world market to import cheap grain and fodder, thus lowering production costs. The agricultural crisis *may* have hastened on this transformation of Danish agriculture into a highly special-

ised and efficient industry—indeed, it probably did; but it
was not its cause. As early as 1870, as has already been
noted, exports of meat and dairy products had already outstripped grain exports. The trend was already evident.
Although Denmark, like Britain, retained her free trade
policy, this did not mean the end of her agriculture as an
important factor in economic development, as was the case
in Britain.

During the 1870s Denmark's agriculture earned about
80% of all export income, a percentage which by the turn
of the century had risen to about 90% (Table 13). Thanks
to the re-distribution of agricultural production it was
possible to prevent a serious deterioration in Denmark's
terms of trade with foreign countries. In the 1870s, 60% of
her agricultural exports consisted of meat, butter, eggs and
cheese. Before the First World War this share was not less
than 87%, of which, about the year 1900—when that share
was at its peak—butter constituted almost half.

Agricultural protectionism on the Continent led Denmark to concentrate her agricultural exports on Britain,
which absorbed about 39% in 1880, and in 1900 no less
than 59%. It was Germany's share, above all, which had
shrunk (Henriksen-Ølgaard, 1960, p. 43).

Denmark's agricultural sector was thus her biggest earner
of foreign currency, and income growth in agriculture contributed to an increasing demand for non-agricultural
products.

Both within the country and in her harbours, Denmark's
concentration on meat and dairy products necessitated a
comprehensive transport network capable of handling
perishables. Concentrating so heavily on exports, Danish
agriculture placed ever greater demands on merchants,
banks and insurance companies, almost all of which were
concentrated in Copenhagen, and whose profits were reinvested in various sectors of the economy. Naturally, it is
hard to determine to what extent other branches' development was dependent upon agriculture, or how far income

growth in agriculture enabled industry—for instance by import substitution—to lay the basis of its own further growth. This problem will be considered when we come to study Denmark's industrialisation. It is nonetheless a fact that during the latter half of the nineteenth century the non-agrarian sectors expanded more rapidly than agriculture, and their share, both of population and GNP, grew. Even so, it is an open question whether Danish agriculture did not contribute even more to the country's economic transformation than appears from these statistics.

FINLAND

Of the Scandinavian countries, Finland was the most completely agrarian. About 1870 more than 80% of her population was dependent upon agriculture and allied occupations, and as late as 1910 the figure was 66% (see Table 5). Despite this drop the agricultural population, absolutely speaking, increased by nearly 400,000 individuals between 1880 and 1910. In the latter year only 12% of the population, or about 350,000 people, were dependent upon industry, while 5% were dependent on commerce and transportation (*Statistisk Årsbok för Finland*, 1936, Table 24).

During the first half of the nineteenth century Finland came progressively to concentrate on grain production. Since there were no changes in agricultural techniques, this increase in grain output occurred at the cost of livestock-rearing. More and more meadows and pastures were put under the plough, thus forcing farmers to reduce their stocks of cattle. In the great starvation year of 1867, with its bad harvest, this lop-sidedness proved catastrophic. In the following year 8% of the population, or 137,000 people, died, reducing the Finnish population by nearly 100,000 persons (Jutikkala, 1963, p. 340).

Nor was the position of Finnish agriculture improved by ever-growing competition from Russia, which could export to Finland without paying any customs duties. Finnish agriculture plunged into a crisis. During the 1870s, grain production was reduced by an increased production of meat and dairy products. Butter output expanded and butter exports rose from something over 4,000 tons in the early 1870s to more than 13,000 tons about 1910, or by nearly 3% per annum (Mammelin, 1912, p. 30). Since prices for butter also rose, simultaneously, this represented an increase in value of 4·3% per annum (Björkqvist, 1958, p. 63). Up to 1914 butter exports constituted between 8% and 18% of total Finnish exports, reaching their maximum share in 1897.

TABLE 7: Finland: Production of grains, potatoes and milk 1860-1914
(1000 tons)

	Rye	Corn	Oats	Potatoes	Milk
1860/64	177	77	23	154	434
1870/74	234	105	32	232	557
1880/84	211	88	41	270	703
1890/94	232	84	50	303	987
1900/04	218	72	26*	355	1287
1910/14	212	71	14	400	1598

*4 year average – no data for 1903

Source: Viita 1966, appendix 1

This re-structuring made Finland ever more dependent on her grain imports. Almost her entire wheat consumption was imported, and in about 1910 her rye imports were equal to her own output.

As in Denmark, but a good deal later, a co-operative movement came into being. Nor was it at all so comprehensive. In 1909 co-operative dairies constituted hardly half their total number, or about 400; but these were responsible for nearly four-fifths of Finland's butter output. In 1905 the farmers also set up an organisation to take care of exports.

The introduction of more modern production methods, new equipment and better buildings all demanded a great deal of capital. If they had relied wholly on agricultural yield Finnish farmers could hardly have come by this capital. Instead they acquired it to a great extent from sale of forests and timber. The steadily increasing timber exports led to a rise in the value of the forests, earlier regarded as more or less worthless. And since the forestry companies owned a smaller share of the acreage than they did, for instance, in Sweden, the peasants were the chief beneficiaries (Jutikkala, 1963, p. 386).

Another remarkable phenomenon is the way in which, throughout the period, the Finns continued to break new soil. One reason for this was that the number of backwoodsmen and farm hands was high in proportion to the landowning peasantry. The number of daily hands, expressed as a percentage of the total number of agricultural workers, was generally more than 40%: in some parts of the country over 50% (Jutikkala, 1963, p. 386). And it was from among this category that the urban workers were recruited. But it was also these farm labourers who tried to get a living by breaking new soil, whether their own property or farmed out to them by forestry companies or peasants.

As can be seen, however, from the rise in imports, even all this new soil did not contribute much to the nation's support. Developments can only be explained in terms of large-scale overpopulation in proportion to available resources.

Even if emigration, flight to the towns and the breaking of new soil all contributed to ease the pressure.[1] The population situation in the countryside around the year 1910 was nevertheless obviously a precarious one. Nor was there any change in the structure of the Finnish economy before 1914. Finland remained Scandinavia's most strikingly agrarian country, with a per capita income a good deal lower than her neighbours. Socially, the problem of the backwoodsmen and the unpropertied labourers—all these pioneers, who

1. This can be seen from the housing situation in the countryside. In 1901, 18% of households, or 200,000 persons, had no dwelling of their own, but were forced to live in shacks and sheds, e.g., 'sauna' bath houses, or in a corner of someone else's dwelling (Haatanen 1968, p. 363).

were Finland's chief breakers of new soil, but who, often totally dependent on the landowners for their continued existence as farmers, lived at a very low economic level and under most insecure conditions—continued to dominate. It was a problem which became acute during the World War, and was one of the reasons why the Finnish Civil War of 1918 was a clash between social classes with entirely different economic and social attitudes.

NORWAY

In spite of the primitive techniques used by the Norwegian peasantry—primitive even by comparison with Sweden, not to say Denmark—Norwegian agriculture developed swiftly during the first half of the nineteenth century. When the century opened, the Norwegian peasants were still not even using two or three-year rotation methods, but sowing the same seed year after year on the same field, until it became useless, after which it would be turned into fallow (Smith, 1875, p. 6 et seq.). About 1800, 40% of Norway's grain consumption was being imported (Johnson, 1938, p. 414). By breaking new ground and establishing schools for agricultural workers, the Norwegian authorities tried to influence developments; and up to 1850 an ever greater share of the nation's consumption was being produced within the country. This was followed by a further increase in imports. Norwegian peasants rarely came into contact with new agricultural ideas and, notwithstanding their relatively swift increase in output, remained largely self-supporting. One reason for this was the difficulty of establishing modern communications in Norway, where every valley remained a more or less isolated unit. Further, the peculiar mode of agriculture may have contributed to hold up any modernisation. Enclosure movements were less important than the splitting up of farms. In many parts people went on with collective farming, at the same time as the farms were being divided up into even smaller units by inheritance.[2]

2. For a discussion of the Norwegian land distribution system and the influence of the inheritance laws on agriculture, see e.g. Bjørkvik, The

TABLE 8: Norway: Grain, potato and milk production 1871-1914
(1000 tons)

	Wheat	Rye	Corn	Oats	Potatoes	Milk
1871/75	7·5	25	104	155	587	837
1886/90	7·1	24	97	166	591	865
1900/04	7·4	22	57	135	536	885
1910/14	10·1	23	74	174	698	1038

Source: Statistiske Oversikter, 1948, Tables 48 and 55. The figures for milk are from 1875, 1890, 1900 and 1907, respectively.

Obviously, Norway's agriculture contributed almost nothing to her economic development. Unlike her neighbours, Norway never produced any surplus for export—on the contrary, she was hardly able to support her own growing population. The peasants may have been self-supporting, but the non-agrarian population had to be supported by imports except for milk products. The swift growth of an agrarian proletariat became the reservoir from which many other branches of the economy drew their labour reserves.

However, the agricultural population was not solely dependent on the soil for its support. Many farmers were also fishermen, and fisheries played a more important part than agriculture in Norway's economic development. During the period 1866-1900, the value of the catch varied between 20 and 30 mill. kroner and the number of persons engaged in fisheries usually amounted to more than 100,000 (Statistiske Oversikter, 1948, Table 86 and 80), that is to say, about 10% of all persons in the agrarian sector over 15 years of age.

Fish products were also the most important export item up to the end of the 1860s, when they constituted about 45% of the value of all commodity exports. Even in the years immediately preceding the First World War they still con-

Farm Territories (Scand. Ec. Hist. Rev. vol. IV p. 33-61, Frimannslund R., Farm Community and Neighbourhood Community, idem, vol. IV 1 pp. 62-81 and Holmsen, A., The Old Norwegian Peasant Community, idem, vol. IV 1.

stituted about $\frac{1}{8}$ of all goods exported, being only exceeded by timber products (Statistiske Oversikter, 1948, Table 113). Fishing was also of immense importance to the Norwegian food-stuffs industry, and its exports became steadily more highly processed.

SWEDEN

Between 1770 and 1870, the agricultural section of the Swedish population sank from about 80% to 72%. But great changes in the agricultural classes lie hid behind this rather small change. The number of owner-peasants was only increasing very slowly, while the numbers of the so-called lower classes were growing very rapidly indeed. At the same time a widespread enclosure movement came into being which broke up the old villages, and new soil began to be intensively cultivated. Just how much new soil was cultivated it is hard to say exactly, since the Swedish agricultural statistics for that period are wholly unreliable. But it is clear that most of it had been broken before the 1870s. The reclamation of land was facilitated by loans both inside and outside the country, above all in the form of mortgage loans. In 1858 the bond debts of the mortgage institutions amounted to 72 mill., of which 52 mill. kronor were placed abroad (Finanskomiténs betänkande, 1863, p. 83). Repayment was in turn facilitated by a swift rise in agricultural surplus. During the 1850s, above all, grain exports grew swiftly, and remained important even as late as 1890. During the decades around 1850 oats, together with timber and iron, were Sweden's chief export items.

This export surplus was created not only by an increase in cultivated acreage and higher productivity. It was also a result of a change in consumption. Potato-growing expanded, and it is probable that this changeover from grain consumption to potato consumption freed grain for export. The relatively swift population rise may also have been partly due—to say the least of it—to the increased source of subsistence provided by potatoes. Nothing comparable to the Irish situation arose, however. The potato never achieved the same dominance in Sweden as it did in Ireland. Yet it was unquestionably an important complement, and owing to the redistributed consumption pattern which gradually assumed even greater importance, it led to a growth in grain exports most important to Sweden's economy. Such exports made it easier to amortise or repay the loans and made possible a transformation of agriculture before industry's need for capital became more urgent.

TABLE 9: Sweden: Changes in the occupational distribution of population. Numbers (1000) and per cent

	Agriculture		Industry & Crafts		Commerce & transport		Others	
	No.	%	No.	%	No.	%	No.	%
1870/1890	−62	−2	+454	+75	+216	+102	+8	+2
1890/1910	−270	−9	+726	+69	+320	+75	−39	−11

Source: Statistisk översikt, 1919, p. 7

In 1910 48% of Sweden's population were dependent upon agriculture for their subsistence, as against 32% on industry. A falling number of agricultural workers thus came to support an ever greater population. The change in consumption is reflected in a sharp increase in wheat harvests and a slight increase in rye harvests. Despite this increase Sweden became ever more dependent upon her imports of grain. During the period 1880-1910 about half the supply of wheat and a fifth of the supply of rye were being imported. At the same time, as has been noted, the exports of oats fell, to cease entirely about 1890. As in Denmark, these rises in imports can be regarded as a proof of the peasantry's increasing concentration on meat and dairy produce. Butter exports rose sharply, and up to about the year 1900 exports and imports of farm produce remained balanced—a balance which gave place to an import surplus in the early years of the present century.

In Sweden, where the matter has been much discussed, the 1880s and 1890s are regarded as having led to poorer agricultural conditions. Yet it is also possible to point to an improvement in agriculture's terms of trade in relation to industrial goods and to the fact that meat and dairy prices did not fall as fast as those for grain; and to the protectionist policies shielding Swedish agriculture in the late 1880s. As in the international discussion of such matters, it has been price developments for grain which have drawn most attention Falling grain prices—above all prices for wheat, since these fell much more than e.g., for oats—have been regarded as implying a deterioration in agricultural conditions as a whole. But, at least as far as Sweden is concerned, there is every reason to be sceptical of such a way of writing history. It is also possible that the so-called lower classes had to bear a disproportionate share of the costs involved in such a transformation and that the emigration reflected social dissatisfaction in the agrarian sector. But the problems have not been properly studied, and the results of such a study cannot be taken for granted.

THE INDUSTRIAL DEVELOPMENT

DENMARK

Denmark's industrial development differed in several ways from her Scandinavian neighbours'. In Finland, Norway and Sweden export industries exerted an important influence on developments, and thus came to set their stamp on those countries' industrial structures. In Denmark, on the other hand, an industry developed which was not aiming at export, but was concentrated on the needs of the home market Before the 1890s there was virtually no export of industrial products. The problems of Danish industry were therefore obviously of another kind than her neighbours'. Industrial growth depended on income growth within Denmark and its expansion was due either to fresh demand or to important substitutes. Changes in Danish income growth, on the other hand, were to a considerable extent dependent upon agricultural export capacity.

Thus it is possible to see Denmark's industrialisation as derived from that country's relations with Britain, her greatest outlet for agricultural products. The British market determined income growth for her agriculture, and her agriculture's demand for industrial goods determined the country's industrial structure.

Industrial development accelerated in the 1860s. One reason for this may have been that in the early 1860s Denmark lost the duchies of Schleswig and Holstein to Prussia. These areas had reached a higher stage of industrial development than the rest of Denmark and their competition is regarded as having delayed the country's industrial growth. It is not yet really known, however, just how important this change was to the Danish home market. It has been pointed out that the 1850s can also be characterised as a period of swift industrial expansion (Willerslev, 1952, p. 237).[3]

It seems reasonable to suppose that the prosperity which as a result of sharp rises in agricultural exports, developed in Denmark during the 1850s and 1860s must have influenced the industrial sector. The balance of trade was positive, there was a big increase in savings and for a few years (in the early 1870s) Denmark even became a creditor nation. It has been calculated that in 1872 Danish net assets vis-à-vis other countries amounted to about 130 mill. D.Kr. (Nielsen, 1933, p. 512). Half these assets were placed in Sweden and Germany. During the decades up to 1870 the Danish interest level was one of Europe's lowest (Willerslev, 1952, p. 243). Rising incomes and a low rate of interest had a positive influence on investment and Danish industry, like the Danish railways, began to be developed without being notably affected by the international crises of the 1860s and early 1870s. Not until the mid-1870s was Denmark affected by the international depression and then

3. Owing to lack of continuous industrial statistics during the nineteenth century, all statements can only be more or less hypothetical. Our information from 1855 and 1872 is incomplete, and it is not until 1897 that we have a complete industrial census, repeated in 1906 and 1914. Developments between those dates can only indirectly be determined, e.g., by means of import statistics for raw materials and half-finished goods.

chiefly because of changing world market prices for agricultural products. It is not clear, however, how great a part
of the increased savings of the 1850s and 1860s was transformed into industrial investment. Most of the new capital
was probably invested in agriculture. The industrial expansion, occurring at that time, related chiefly to consumer
goods production, and such developments were probably
more concentrated in Copenhagen than in other parts of
the country. In 1850, 4,400 workers were being employed
by Copenhagen industries. In 1872, the number had grown
to nearly 14,000, an annual increment of 12·5%. Altogether,
in 1872, about 35,000 workers were being employed in
Denmark as a whole.

Characteristic of the first half of the 1870s was the large
number of firms then being founded. Between 1850 and
1870, only six industrial firms had been incorporated. In
1872, alone, the number was sixteen; and the years 1873-75
saw the birth of a further sixty-nine (Willerslev, 1952, p.
211 et seq.). Many of these limited companies, however,

TABLE 10: Denmark: Number of industrial workers 1872-1914
(1000's)

	Copenhagen	Other towns	Countryside	Total
1872	14	13	8	35
1897*	25	30	18	73
1897**	32	27	14	73
1906	38	34	19	90
1914	47	39	22	108

*Industrial enterprises with more than 4 workers.

**Industrial enterprises with more than 5 workers. The 1897 data
for Copenhagen also comprehend suburbs later incorporated in the
capital

Source: Willerslev, 1954, p. 247

---

were in reality conversions and incorporations of older
firms. The man behind many such company formations

was C. F. Tietgen, the head of the Privatbanken in Copenhagen, which acted as an industrial bank, along German
lines. One of Tietgen's main tasks seems to have been to
merge smaller companies together, thus trying to create a
monopoly for one large concern (Willerslev, 1952, p. 228 et
seq.).

Tietgen exploited the ready availability of money in the
early 1870s to interest the public in the share market. By
founding companies, subscribing their shares and selling
them at a premium rate, the bankers were able to earn a
considerable founder's profit, and it seems probable that this
opportunity for making a profit was a powerful stimulus to
the boom in the incorporation of new companies which
occurred at the beginning of the 1870s (Willerslev, 1952,
p. 231).

But the majority of these newly started firms were not
mere speculations, in the sense that they after a while went
bankrupt. Of the 83 companies which came into being
between 1872 and 1876, only 20 were dissolved before 1883
(Willerslev, 1952, p. 214 et seq.). The easy money market
cannot have been the decisive factor in their creation. The
fact is, Denmark's economy had developed to a stage where
the demand for consumer goods was rising, and in which
firms providing substitutes for imports could successfully
compete. This period of new company foundations in the
1870s, however, contributed to change the size structure of
Danish industry. Even in the early stages of industrial expansion the larger firms became increasingly dominant. In
1855 only five Copenhagen factories were employing more
than 100 workers. In 1872 the number was 37, and these
were employing about half the total number of the capital's
industrial workers (Willerslev, 1952, p. 248).

On the other hand it was characteristic of Denmark that
those branches which developed swiftly were those which
had a strong craft element. There was very little mechanisation; women and children were widely employed in production—a production predominantly aimed at consumption. Thus it was the clothing, glove and tobacco industries which employed most workers. Most of the other

industries developed during this time, such as cement, brick making, mills, breweries, fertiliser manufactures and sugar refineries, were all typical home-market industries.

The cotton industry, on the other hand, which had grown up in the early stages of European industrialisation, found it harder to gain a foothold. Low customs barriers made it impossible for cotton spinning mills to compete with foreign industries, and it was not until the 1890s that such firms came into being in Denmark. On the other hand, in 1872, cotton weaving mills were employing about 1,700 workers and were among the most mechanised industries in the country. Their development had occurred in the 1860s. As late as about 1850 this branch had been chiefly run on the putting-out system. By about 1880 only highly mechanised factories remained.

TABLE 11: Denmark: Imports of cotton, wool, iron and fuels 1870-1914

	cotton tons	cotton thread tons	woollen thread tons	woollen weaves tons	iron & steel 1000 tons	fuels (units of coal) 1000 tons
1870/74	—	—	123	1268	30	(390)
1880/84	—	2576	435	1660	45	(729)
1890/94	325	3542	1003	1753	55	(1146)
1900/04	3203	2429	1565	1930	94	2295
1910/14	5418	1639	1795	1831	172	3420

Up to 1900 coal used to be measured in barrels.
The calculation in tons is approximate

Source: Bjerke-Ussing, 1958, Table XII, XIII, XIV

This development can be seen from Table 11. It was in the 1890s as the Danish cotton spinning industry became capable of competing with foreign mills. There is a sharp fall in cotton thread imports, one reason being the import of cotton spinning machinery of high productivity, higher than the average British machines'. At the same time, price relations between spun thread and raw cotton changed in such a way that it became profitable to manufacture the thread within the country. Thus, between the 1870s and the 1890s, prices for raw cotton fell by more than 50% while the drop in thread prices was not nearly so great. The only industries of any importance to concentrate on capital goods were iron foundries and engineering firms. In 1872 they employed about 5,000 workers.

TABLE 12: Denmark: Distribution of the population by occupation, 1840-1901 (per cent)

	Agriculture	Industry & Crafts	Commerce	Others
1840	56·1	23·5	4·3	16·1
1860	53·3	26·4	5·9	14·4
1880	51·1	26·0	7·7	15·2
1901	41·4	29·5	11·3	17·8

Source: Warming, 1913, p. 91

Despite relatively big developments in the 1850s and 1860s, Danish industry still hardly occupied any very prominent position by the beginning of the 1870s. Altogether it was employing 35,000 workers in factories with five or more employees, the greater number in branches producing for immediate consumption. Up to 1872 developments were dominated by Copenhagen, while the industrial development of the rest of the country was probably more sluggish. In 1897, when statistics first permit a distinction between industry and crafts, the industrial workers constituted 41% of the total number of employees in the two sectors, or 73,000 (Willerslev, 1954, p. 258). This relation would seem to have been even lower during the 1870s, which means that at the beginning of that decade, at most 10% of the population can have been dependent on industry. Further, as has been mentioned before, even the dominant industrial branches were those which had the strongest craft element. Industry cannot have been a very major force before 1872.

Between 1880 and 1910 the agricultural labour force grew from 510,000 to 540,000, or by 6%. Other sectors of the

TABLE 13: Denmark: Distribution of exports, various commodities 1874-1914

	Agricult'l products		Industrial products		Other goods		Total	
	mill. kr.	%	mill. kr.	%	mill. kr.	%	mill. kr.	%
1874	129	82	21	13	7	5	157	100
1880/84	128	79	22	13	13	8	163	100
1890/94	173	84	15	7	18	9	206	100
1900/04	287	89	16	5	18	6	321	100
1910/14	529	87	47	8	32	5	608	100

Before 1890 industrial exports consisted predominantly of milled grain

Source: Bjerke-Ussing, 1958, Table VII

economy increased from 503,000 to 811,000, or by 61% (Bjerke-Ussing, 1958, Table 1). In the latter group the industrial increase was greater than the average. Between 1872 and 1897 the number of industrial workers rose by 110% or by 38,000, and between 1897 and 1914 by 48% or by 35,000. Even up to as late as 1906, industrial expansion characteristically occurred outside Copenhagen, while during the years preceding the First World War developments in Copenhagen were considerably greater.

TABLE 14: Denmark: Annual percentual increase in number of industrial workers

	Copenhagen	Other towns	Countryside	Total
1855/72	12·5			
1872/82	1·0 ⎫	5·2	4·7	4·3
1882/97	4·4 ⎭			
1897/1906	1·9	2·9	3·8	2·6
1906/14	3·2	1·9	2·2	2·5

Source: Willerslev, 1954, p. 250

The agricultural population stagnated. The number of town-dwellers, above all, was on the increase. Between 1880 and 1900 Denmark's total population rose by 480,000, while its urban population rose from 28% to 38% of the whole. Naturally, this influenced industrial developments in many ways. The construction industry, and with it brick and cement, made great progress.

Nevertheless, Denmark's industrial development continued by and large along the lines opened up in the 1870s. The home market industry was completely dominant, and industrial exports remained insignificant. In all branches production became more heavily capitalised, as can be seen from the fact that while the number of workers rose by 17% between 1897 and 1906, industry's horsepower rose by 135%.

Import statistics give an idea of how Danish industry had improved its competitiveness. There was a relative drop in imports of consumer goods and it has been calculated that immediately before the First World War about 70% of all industrial products consumed in Denmark were being manufactured within the country (Munch, 1942, p. 592). At the same time, owing to the changeover to bacon, butter and other meat and dairy products, agriculture's demands for import goods rose sharply, as did industry's demand for raw materials.

Denmark's industrialisation was stamped by few of the dramatic traits characteristic of the other Scandinavian countries. The growth of her industries can be seen as a function of the rest of her economic development, above all in agriculture. Her industries grew up in order to supply a growing home market, and in competition with foreign countries were gradually able to supplant earlier imports of finished products. Another characteristic trait is the great

TABLE 15: Denmark: Imports by main categories. Per cent

	Raw materials to agriculture	Raw materials & half-finished goods to other production	Fuels	Consumer goods	Capital goods	Total mill. kr.
1874/94	12	44	8	31	5	263
1895/1914	21	42	9	22	6	506

Source: Bjerke-Ussing, 1958, p. 24

importance which crafts continued to enjoy alongside industry—yet another indication of the predominance of the
home market.

TABLE 16: Denmark: Number of industrial and craft workers, 1897
and 1914 (in thousands)

	1897	1914	change in %
Industry	73	108	48·5
Crafts	104	125	20·5
	177	233	31·7

Industry comprises firms with 5 or more workers

Source: Willerslev, 1954, p. 258

Another reason why industry should be regarded as a derived and not as a positive force can be seen in the extent
and distribution of investments. During the period, the
gross investment share of GNP increased from about 8% to
13% ,while the distribution of construction and equipment,
on the one hand, and machinery and transport equipment
on the other, underwent no very notable change. The latter
constituted about 40% of gross investments (Bjerke-Ussing,
1958, Table 51 and 53).

So much new capital could not be raised, as had been the
case up to 1870, on a purely domestic basis. There was a
tendency for the balance of payments deficit to rise on the
upswing of the trade cycle; but at the same time there was
also a tendency for raw material prices to fluctuate more
than prices for finished products. Export prices, that is, rose
more slowly than import prices.

The price development trend, however, was favourable
to Denmark, whose terms of trade improved at the same
time as invisible income rose, primarily thanks to a boom in
shipping.

It has been estimated that the Danish net debt to foreign
countries increased from something over 200 mill. kroner in
1899 to more than 850 mill. kroner in 1912 (Nielsen, 1933,
p. 579). The State, the mortgage banks and the City of

Copenhagen all sold bonds abroad, and certain industrial concerns also seem to have placed their shares there. During the decade prior to the First World War the deficit in the balance of payments corresponded to about 20% of the value of gross investment (Bjerke-Ussing, 1958, pp. 21 and 86). Developments show that, owing to changed competitive conditions, price developments, and a new opening for extensive new agricultural investment during the 1890s and the first decade of the twentieth century, Danish agriculture was unable to go on financing its own and other sectors' investments out of big surpluses. Thus it is clear that Denmark's economic development was not deeply marked by the growth of her industries. Agriculture and services were much more crucial to the growth of national income. The lack of an industrial exports sector was to some extent compensated for by the 'industrialisation' of agriculture. But around the turn of the century imports were about 50% bigger than exports, and Denmark's balance of payments deficit was about 40 mill. kroner a year. Only thanks to loans from the international market was it possible to cover this deficit and keep investments at the level necessary to further growth. But developments were to show that Denmark could not go on concentrating so exclusively on her agricultural sector. Thanks to conditions during the First World War she was able to repay most of her foreign debt. But the balance of payments problem has been troublesome all through the twentieth century.

FINLAND

The industrialisation of Finland must be seen against the background of that country's utterly agrarian structure in the mid-nineteenth century; also in connection with her relationship to Russia (as has been mentioned, Finland was a grand duchy of the Russian Empire between 1809 and 1917); and lastly, against the background of her great forests, which came to play the same role in the Finnish economy as agriculture was playing in the Danish.

In the middle of the nineteenth century about 80% of Finland's population was occupied in agriculture. Industry was almost non-existent. In 1836 exports of timber products amounted to about 2 mill. marks, or a quarter of all exports. Thirty years later the export value of her timber had risen to 15 mill. marks, or half the total value of all exports. But this increase had taken place without any industrial expansion to speak of. The timber was shipped in more or less crude condition and the timber trade can be regarded as having been more or less ancillary to agriculture.

Industry in the true meaning of the word was dominated by textiles, or, to be more exact, by cotton. The textile industry had been started in the 1820s by a Scottish immigrant, who manufactured the machines and sold the output of cotton thread to the peasantry. Altogether, it is typical that foreigners should have been the initiators of Finland's industrial expansion, and it was thanks to the immigration of foreign mechanics that several cotton spinning mills and engineering works came into being.

In the mid-1850s the production value of the Finnish cotton industry was hardly 2 mill. marks, and its labour force just over 900 men.

At the end of the 1850s, however, Finnish industry found itself in a new situation. By a decree of the Tsar the customs duties on Finnish goods exported to Russia were reduced or abolished, and the limit on the value of the factory-made goods which could be imported duty-free into Russia was raised. Thus Finnish exports came to enjoy a privileged status on the Russian market. But at the same time Russian goods were given unlimited duty-free access to the Finnish market and the customs privileges enjoyed by the Russians were always greater than those enjoyed by the Finns in the Russian Empire. This did not at first constitute a threat to Finland's embryonic industrialisation.

This customs relief led to a fairly important expansion within the Finnish cotton industry; but in 1885, with the downturn of the trade cycle in the 1880s and the introduction of protectionism, the Russians annulled the 1859 agreement. Although Finland still enjoyed special treatment on the Russian market, Finnish exports to Russia again became dutiable.

On the eve of the rescinding of the Russo-Finnish trade agreement, the Finnish cotton industry's output had been about one-third greater than total domestic consumption (Mathelin, 1927, p. 23) and for quite a few years during the 1860s and 1870s two-thirds of that industry's products were exported.

In 1870 Finland had five cotton mills, and sawmills and the iron works apart, these answered for one-third of both total production and all factory employees. The largest factory, Finlayson et Comp,, employed 2,300 workers and the value of its output was 3·5 mill. marks. One other factory was of almost the same size (Översikt av Finlands ekonomiska tillstånd, 1866-70, p. 20). As late as 1880 there were still no more than eight factories all told, with an output-value of over one million marks. Of them, three were textile mills, two were sugar refineries, and two were pulp and paper mills. Only 6·4% of the population was dependent upon industry for a living.

It was not only to the textile industry that the Russian market was important. Up to the mid-1880s Finland's ironworks, too, were mostly engaged in export. In the 1860s and 1870s there was great expansion. But in 1886, after the re-imposition of customs dues by the Russians in the previous year, Finnish iron exports dropped by one half (from 26,000 to 13,000 tons). As long as the Russian market had been open to Finnish industry, a number of specialist firms had grown up, chiefly aiming at exports, and Finland's textile firms were the largest in Scandinavia. Obviously, the lack of domestic purchasing power could be compensated by exports to Russia. On the other hand, it is an open question how far the free import of Russian goods had the effect of delaying Finland's industrial development. Up to 1885 Russia's industries were but little developed, and the Finnish market was extremely limited; so the mutual 'free trade' had probably been more to Finland's advantage than Russia's.

In 1886 this export-based economy, however, was wrecked, and Finnish firms had to try and find their market either at home or else attempt to redirect part of their exports. Since those products which had earlier been exported to Russia were often of a rather simple kind, and of poor quality, the latter method proved unsuccessful.

It has been pointed out, however, that the new state of affairs did have a positive effect on Finnish industry (Översikt av Finland ekonomiska tillstånd, 1880-85, p. 83). For one thing, Finland's dependence on a single foreign market was reduced, and with it her specialisation in a few products that could have led to an 'enclave' economy. For another, the Finnish textile companies—above all—were obliged to try and improve their products in order to compete with those of foreign firms, both at home and in the export market.

In connection with the abrogation of 'free trade' with Russia, certain measures were taken by the Finnish state. One was to grant loans for the modernisation of Finnish industry (op. cit., p. 83).

Even after 1885, however, Russian duties on Finnish products remained lower than the duties on other countries' products. Finland's advantage, however, was limited inasmuch as the lower customs dues only applied to certain restricted quantities of goods. On the other hand, Russian goods could no longer be imported duty-free into Finland, which meant less competition from Russian firms. But this weakened competition in the home market proved less important to Finnish industry than its earlier easy access to the Russian market.

Simultaneously, however, the Finnish home market's potential had improved and its purchasing power had risen, and this made import substitution a feasible way out for a number of branches of Finnish industry. This change was connected with the growth of a sawmills and pulp industry. In 1857 the sawmills had been permitted to use steam for their saws, thus freeing them from their earlier dependence on water-power, which had tied them to rivers and streams. More important, regulations and export duties were also removed during the 1860s (Rinne 1952, p. 26 et seq.). The result was that exports rose from ten million marks in the 1860s to fifty million marks in the 1870s.

So it was in the 1870s, when their export value was tripled, that timber exports made their break-through. Even allowing for inflationary prices—between 1870 and 1874 the average price rose by more than 50%—this resulted in exports doubling in volume in 7 years (Rinne, 1952, p. 15). The obstacles to the Finnish timber trade were removed in time for the country to be in a condition to take advantage of the international boom at the beginning of the 1870s, a boom which also had considerable effects in the other Scandinavian countries.

TABLE 17: Finland: Number of workers and production value of the sawmill, pulp and paper industry, 1885-1905

| | SAWMILLS | | PULP AND PAPER INDUSTRY | |
	number of workers (1000's)	*production value* (mill. marks)	*number of workers* (1000's)	*production value* (mill. marks)
1885	7·3	22·0	2·6	10·2
1890	10·6	33·9	3·7	13·8
1895	12·1	40·7	4·8	18·1
1900	22·0	79·5	7·1	29·9
1905	21·6	79·0	9·9	43·2

No reliable statistics on sawmill production are available prior to 1885

Source: Översikt av Finlands ekonomiska tillstånd. 1885-1905

In the 1860s, too, the Finns began to experiment with pulp manufacture and the boom of the 1870s led to the establishment of 9 mechanical pulp mills. In 1880 the first sulphate pulp mills were added, and in 1885 the first mill producing sulphite. Between 1871 and 1883 the sawmill and pulp industry saw the establishment of 42 new corporations (Schybergson, 1964, p. 70).

Quantitatively speaking the growth of the pulp industry was nevertheless not particularly swift. In 1885 the paper and pulp industry as a whole was only employing 2,200 persons and the value of its output was about 9 mill. marks. The same year 7,300 men were working in the sawmills (to which should be added an unknown number of fellers, log-drivers and hauliers). This may be compared with the total number of workers in industry in 1885: 36,000, with an output to the value of 108 mill. marks.

The sawmills were a good deal more labour intensive than the pulp and paper industry, therefore production value per worker was considerably lower. No notable change in these branches' relative share of the total number of in-dustrial workers or production value occurred until the beginning of the twentieth century, which means that the rest of Finland's industrialisation coincided with the growth of these export industries (see Table 19).

Timber products and pulp and paper industry output were responsible for an ever greater part of Finland's total exports. During the 1870s the share was 47% of the value of total exports, but by 1910-14 it had risen to more than 70%. Timber exports were concentrated on Britain and Western Europe, while paper was predominantly shipped to Russia, or between 60% and 90% for the years 1890-1910 (Björkqvist, 1958, p. 173).

The only branch to change its position much in relation to total industrial output was metal and engineering. In a short period, from 1885 to 1890, this branch increased its share from about 7% to 15%, and thereafter on the whole kept this relative position up to 1905.[4]

After 1885, the ironworks having been deprived of their growing share of the Russian market, the dynamic factor in this development can only have been the engineering in-dustry. Yet it is obvious that, even if exports to Russia did not actually increase, up to the turn of the century the Finnish metal industry was protected by Russian customs

4. Owing to a rearrangement of Finnish statistics in 1909, the figures for the years after 1908 are not comparable with those for earlier years.

barriers. About 1900 a change occurred in the relative position. By then the Russian iron industry had grown to a point where it could oust its Finnish rival, not only in Russia, but also in Finland. Russia could sell at prices lower than Finnish production costs (Björkqvist, 1958, p. 200). The Finnish iron industry had come into an unnatural position. Up to 1900, Finland had been able to meet her own needs largely by imports; while her own cheaper and poorer quality iron was exported. In 1897 pig iron output amounted to 31,000 tons, the highest figure it reached, and thereafter fell to 9,000 tons on the eve of the World War (Pihkala, 1964, p. 138 et seq.). At the same time exports to Russia fell from 22,000 to 4,000 tons. On the other hand, exports of machinery had risen from 1,000 tons to 3,000 tons. This was a structural change which had been going on continuously since the 1880s, and around the turn of the century the metals and engineering industries were employing about 20,000 workers.

TABLE 18: Finland: Distribution of exports by product, 1870-1914(%)

	Timber Products	Paper & Pulp	Agricultural Products	Others
1870/79	43·8	3·3	22·9	30·0
1880/89	44·7	8·0	23·1	24·2
1890/99	46·1	9·3	24·3	20·3
1900/09	55·0	13·7	17·6	13·7
1910/14	51·7	19·2	17·0	12·1

Source: Halme, 1955, p. 68

The growth of engineering must be regarded largely as a result of an expanded export industry. The manufacture of sawmills and steam engines grew, while, for instance, output of equipment and machinery for agriculture fell (Översikt av Finlands ekonomiska tillstånd, 1895-1900, p. 153).

During the last years of the 1890s, there was a great expansion of industry. Between 1895 and 1900 production value rose by 80%; as before, it was the export industry

TABLE 19: Finland: The structure of industry. Percentage distribution of the different branches (W = workers, V = value)

Year	Metal and Engineering		Timber Industry Total		Sawmills		Textile		Pulp and paper		Chemical	
	W	V	W	V	W	V	W	V	W	V	W	V
1885	11·5	7·1	23·3	22·2	20·0	20·3	13·2	13·0	7·1	9·4	2·7	1·9
1890	16·9	15·0	21·6	22·7	17·9	20·2	10·8	12·8	6·2	8·3	2·9	2·3
1895	18·5	13·8	22·5	24·4	18·5	21·6	11·2	13·3	7·3	9·6	2·6	3·2
1900	18·4	15·4	26·1	26·1	22·3	23·4	11·7	10·3	7·2	8·8	2·3	2·5
1905	18·3	15·8	23·7	23·0	20·0	20·1	11·0	11·7	9·2	11·0	2·7	5·6

Year	Stone, Clay, Glass etc.		Food, Beverage etc.		Leather		Others		Total (in thousands of men and millions of marks)	
	W	V	W	V	W	V	W	V	W	V
1885	8·2	3·8	17·8	27·8	4·1	6·6	12·6	8·8	36·4	108
1890	9·0	4·0	14·2	20·8	4·4	6·6	14·1	7·4	59·2	167
1895	7·7	3·7	11·9	17·5	4·1	6·6	14·1	7·9	65·3	188
1900	7·7	3·3	11·3	22·3	3·5	4·5	11·7	6·8	98·8	340
1905	9·0	3·6	10·7	20·7	3·5	4·3	12·0	9·2	107·8	393

Source: Översikt av Finlands ekonomiska tillstånd, selected years

which led the way. The sawmills nearly doubled their production value and there was equally swift growth in metals and engineering.

Notwithstanding this swift growth in industrial output, it did not give rise to any revolutionary structural changes in the Finnish economy. Between 1890 and 1910 the number of agricultural workers went on increasing.

TABLE 20: Finland: Distribution of population by sectors of the economy, 1890 and 1910

	1890 Number (1000's)	%	1910 Number (1000's)	%	1890-1910 Number (1000's)	%
Agriculture	1779	74·7	1937	66·3	+158	+9
Industry & crafts	190	8·0	357	12·2	+167	+88
Transport	50	2·1	84	2·9	+34	+68
Commerce	29	1·2	65	2·2	+36	+124
Others	331	14·0	478	16·4	+147	+44
Total	2379	100·0	2921	100·0	+542	+23

Source: Alho, 1949, p. 120

It is clear that Finland's industrial expansion, which from the 1870s closely followed the international trade cycle, was extremely dependent upon export developments. Not only were employment and production volume correlated with exports, a significant correlation also existed between employment in exports and in the home market industries, albeit sometimes with a one-year time-lag for the latter.

It is easy to see that it is the multiplier effect of the export industry which explains the domestic expansion; but it is harder to determine exactly how this mechanism worked.

The big increase in exports during the end of the 1890s led to an even bigger rise in imports. As long as industry's import-substitution capacity was limited, a big rise in export income could lead to increased competition for the rest of industry: an effect most noticeable during the 1890s, when the home market industry's employment figures began to fall one year in advance of a fall in exports.

TABLE 21: Finland's trade 1885-1910. Percentage distribution on countries

	Russia	Germany	Great Britain	Sweden & Norway	France	Denmark	Others
EXPORTS							
1885	43	9	20	8	8		15
1890	39	6	19	8	5		23
1895	34	6	19	4	8	11	18
1900	29	8	29	4	9	8	13
1910	27	12	29	4	9	3	16
1886/90	39	8	19	9	7	3	15
1891/95	34	7	23	5	8	13	10
1896/1900	29	8	30	4	8	9	12
IMPORTS							
1885	45	26	12	8	0		9
1890	36	31	16	8	1		8
1895	34	30	12	6	1	3	14
1900	37	33	13	5	2	5	5
1910	29	42	12	5	2	5	5
1886/90	42	29	14	8	0	2	5
1891/95	37	32	13	7	2	3	6
1896/1900	35	33	15	6	2	4	5

Source: Översikt av Finlands ekonomiska tillstånd, quinquennial report, 1885-1900

The picture is complicated by the fact that, at the end of the 1890s, there was a big fall in butter exports. Butter exports, which in 1896 had amounted in value to 18% of total exports, had fallen to only 10% in 1912 (Björkqvist, 1958, p. 66). This fall may have influenced the home market's demand for native products even more than it was influenced by changes in industrial export income, despite the fact that export industries were employing 35% of the total labour force. Even these, however, were a negligible few, compared with that part of the agricultural population directly or indirectly affected by fluctuations in butter exports (Korpelainen, 1964, pp. 36-42). On the other hand, the domestic consumption of butter increased, thus partly offsetting the fall in exports.

The earlier export boom conditions had been borne up on a parallel increase in exports of both industrial and agricultural products. This had an obvious effect on the boom in the home market industry. When, at the end of the 1890s, agricultural exports dropped, this decline, together with a big increase in imports, was enough to interrupt the expansion of the home market industry. The connection between exports of industrial products and the expansion of the home market is more complex than might be assumed from a simple correlation analysis. Finland mainly exported to Russia and Britain, which during the period 1885-1910 together absorbed about 60% of Finnish exports. Paper, iron, textiles, and, until the 1880s, butter mostly went to Russia, while sawmills exports and—later—butter went to Great Britain and Western Europe (see Table 21). Imports were also dominated by Russia while during the whole period Germany's share was about twice as great as Great Britain's. The continuous reduction in the Russian share of Finnish foreign trade was also caused by factors related to the weakness of the Russian market.

Trade cycle fluctuations in Finnish exports to Russia were noticeably smaller than fluctuations in her exports to Western Europe. One reason for this was the preferential tariffs—albeit for a limited quantity of goods—enjoyed by the former up to 1900. By then Russia's share of total Finnish exports had sunk to about 30%, and there was ever closer congruence between total exports and exports of timber products.

NORWAY

As was the case in Sweden and Finland, Norway's industrial development was greatly influenced by the growth of her export industry. Again, exports of merchandise were concentrated to a few countries, chiefly Great Britain. Unlike the other Scandinavian countries, however, Norway's export of services was her chief earner of foreign currency, or about 40% of the value of total exports. Such income was derived mainly from freight and, contributing to domestic saving, had an important effect on income development. Norwegian shipping developed out of the freight trade which had grown up in connection with the export of timber products during the eighteenth and nineteenth centuries. When the British Navigation Acts were repealed, free competiton led to a swift growth in tonnage. At the same time Britain also introduced free trade, leading to a rapid growth in Norwegian exports of timber products. Between 1840 and 1861 such exports rose by 714,000 cu. m., a rise which in absolute figures was greater than that which occurred in Sweden during the same period (Sweden's increase stopped at about 700,000 cu. m.). In the Scandinavian countries' competition for the British market, freight rates gave Norway a definite advantage, as freight charges were an important element in the sale prices.

A the same time the Norwegian merchant marine grew by 1,700 vessels and 420,000 net tons. This increase continued until, in 1870, her tonnage totalled more than a million tons and, in 1879, more than $1\frac{1}{2}$ million tons, remaining at that level up to the World War. There was a noticeable shift, however, in the balance between sailing vessels and steam, thus greatly increasing capacity (see Table 31). This development was also favourable to the shipbuilding industry, which occupied 6,000 workers in the 1870s in more than 200 shipyards (Holst, 1963, p. 374) and reached its pre-war maximum in 1913, occupying at that time 10,000 workers. As steamships came to constitute an ever greater share of the merchant marine, this branch stagnated. From the 1880s, however, Norway competed with foreign shipyards and more than half the tonnage was built by Norwegian shipyards in 1900 (Rugg, 1954), p. 224).

A characteristic trait of the Norwegian economy was the very poor contact, and bad communications between the various regions within the country, making it easier to import goods from abroad than to send them from one part of Norway to another. The result was a lopsided development as between countryside and the towns. Norwegian merchants financed imports for consumer goods with their profits from the sale of export goods. The volume of exports, together with rising prices, permitted an increase in imports, which in turn led to a rising standard of living in the towns. About 1850, Norway's economy by and large was an 'enclave' economy, in which the towns benefited from increasing trade and rising income from freight, while the countryside remained more or less unaffected.

The increasing export of timber products had also tended to bring about a sharp drop in return freight rates from abroad. To Norway's iron industry, earlier concentrated on export, this meant that foreign countries swiftly proved more than a match for the small and inefficient Norwegian ironworks, which lacked coal; as a fuel domestic charcoal could not compete in price with coal. Imports of bar iron rose from 7,000 tons in 1866 to 23,000 tons in 1900, while domestic production more or less came to an end (Statistiske Oversikter, 1948, Table 118).

On the other hand, Norway's engineering works were small and highly decentralised. And—unlike her ironworks—required little capital. Foreign competition did not prove overwhelming, and the engineering industry's size in 1850—12 factories employing about 200 workers—shows how limited the market was for its products.

Simultaneously a textile industry grew up. After the end of the British ban on exports of machinery in 1842, six cotton spinning mills came into being in the late 1840s. The textile industry grew behind the ramparts of a strong protectionism and the following free trade period, after 1858, had a retarding effect on the cotton industry.

The boom of the 1850s increased the total number of industrial workers by 5,000, of whom 2,000 were employed in sawmills and 1,500 in the textile industry. In 1860 just about 20,000 men were being employed in Norwegian industry.

Imbalance in Norway's industrial structure during the period of development, however, retarded expansion. Real industry was largely concentrated in two branches; engineering and cotton. But the former was dependent upon the growth of other industries, and the textile industry was held back by lack of purchasing power, above all in the country-side. To this was added foreign competition, which explains to some extent Norway's inability to expand industrially in a diversified way.

Industrialisation therefore occurred in surges, during periods when export income was particularly great and domestic income development made possible the establishment of import-substituting branches. Between these periods the industrial sector more or less stagnated.

The years 1871-75, 1886-89 and 1896-1900 may be selected as Norwegian industry's expansive periods. They were closely correlated with variations in freight income, which in turn were to some extent dependent upon fluctuations in exports. But $\frac{4}{5}$ or more of such income was earned from freight between foreign ports. It is also characteristic of this development that import volume rose more swiftly than export volume, and that the former increase was greatest during the periods of swift expansion. A contributory reason was that, relatively to the domestic price level, import prices fell, and import volume rose a good deal more quickly than GDP (Bjerke, 1966, p. 26).

In an economy like the Norwegian, with a relatively large foreign trade, changes in export and import volume and in production will obviously be connected. Exports lead to increased production, which in turn demands increased imports, both of consumer goods, industrial goods and raw materials. It has been calculated that during the years 1865 to 1895 elasticity in import volume in relation to production volume was around 1·5 (Bjerke, 1966, p. 58). This increase in imports could occur thanks to earnings from shipping and improved terms of trade. From 1865 and for thirty years thereafter, export prices remained largely constant, while prices of imported goods fell. Above all, it was steady commodity export prices which contributed to the high import elasticity. Prices for services did not develop so satisfactorily (Bjerke, 1966, p. 63).

The composition of Norwegian export goods changed little between the 1860s and the turn of the century. In 1866 more than 90% of total exports of goods consisted of products from ironworks, fishing, and forests. As late as the year 1900 these groups of merchandise still represented 75% of total export by value. But within these groups a change occurred symptomatic of a change in Norwegian industrial structure as a whole.

As in the other Scandinavian countries, the international boom of the 1870s had a great effect on Norwegian industry. Between 1870 and 1875 the number of industrial workers increased by 14,000, or nearly 50%. An entirely new branch of the timber products industry came into being. Twenty mechanical pulp works were founded, one sulphate pulp works and four paper mills. This refinement of timber production continued during the 1880s, when 35 more pulp factories and 8 paper mills were established. During the period 1865 to 1875, 325 new firms with more than 20 workers came into being, an expansion which was never repeated during the rest of the nineteenth century (Holst, 1963, p. 374f.).

During the 1870s the sawmills industry also expanded. Thereafter, however, and for the rest of the nineteenth century, there was stagnation, due to increasing competition from Sweden, Finland and Russia.

It seems probable, however, that the Norwegian export industry was working at a low level of labour productivity, i.e., that its techniques called for high labour intensity. If such techniques were to be changed, the level of capital investment would have to be greatly raised. But the little capital to be had was relatively expensive, while labour was relatively cheap. A study of conditions during the 1930s and 1940s shows that the timber products industry was working with relatively fixed, but low, capital-labour ratios (Wedervang, 1964, p. 49 et seq.). It is probable that the same conditions prevailed during the nineteenth century, which would mean that Norway's competitiveness on the world market was poor, due both to these circumstances and to the raw materials base of her timber exports being so small compared with those of her competitors abroad.

Thus the structural change in Norwegian industry occurred in Norway's traditional export branches, not only

TABLE 22: Norway: Composition of exports at current prices. Percentage distribution. Selected years

	1865	1875	1885	1895	1905	1915
1. Fishing & whaling products	21·8	20·1	16·4	17·4	15·6	14·6
2. Timber, wood, pulp, paper	23·6	19·0	19·7	20·4	21·9	14·0
3. Mining, metals & chemical products	2·9	3·3	3·2	2·4	3·4	11·7
4. Other industrial products	5·3	6·7	9·2	11·0	9·7	13·7
5. Gross freight earnings from ocean shipping	41·4	45·2	43·3	38·9	32·5	39·9
6. Other	5·0	5·7	8·2	9·9	16·9	6·1
Total	100·0	100·0	100·0	100·0	100·0	100·0
7. Total commodity exports (Mill. Kr.)	68*	104	102	137	218	677
8. Gross freight earnings by vessels in foreign trade (Mill. Kr.)	53	91	83	93	116	475

* 1866

Sources: line 1-6: Bjerke, 1966, p. 64; line 7: Statistiske Oversikter, 1948, Table 109, 112; line 8: ibid, Table 142

her largest, but also her chief earners of foreign currency. Her economic growth continued to be dependent upon exports of fish, timber and income from shipping. No heavy industry developed during the period.

Partly, this was due to lack of capital, which prevented any thorough mechanisation; and partly to lack of technically trained personnel. No engineers could be educated in Norway, for lack of schools. It was only in 1914 that the first technical college came into being.

The Norwegians tried to offset lack of capital by imports.

Their railways were largely built with foreign capital, which also played an important role in industry. About 1870, more than half the mining industry was owned by foreigners (Holst, 1963, p. 377). But capital for industrial purposes was not imported to any great extent until after 1895.

One important factor bearing on Norway's industrial development was the establishment of a customs union with Sweden in 1873. This instantly tripled the Norwegian home market. Between 1814 and 1905, as has been noted, Norway and Sweden were under one crown. Certain relaxations in trade barriers between the two countries had been made as early as 1815; for instance, a 50% reduction in customs tariffs on grain, fish and foodstuffs transported by sea, and no duties at all if by land.

In 1827 Norwegian shipping was given free access to Swedish harbours, and could carry Swedish goods unhindered by the Swedish navigation laws. Though the agreement became an obstacle to the development of Swedish shipping, it certainly facilitated an expansion of the Norwegian merchant marine. Finally, in 1873, virtually all trade barriers between the two countries were removed (Betaenkning, 1895, pp. 3-34).

In this way a much wider domestic market came into being and undoubtedly was a great advantage to both countries' industries. The Norwegian textile industry grew rapidly and began to export extensively to Sweden. When Sweden abandoned free trade in 1888 and adopted a protectionistic trade policy for her agriculture and, somewhat later, for her industry, the competitive situation became even more favourable for the Norwegians, who remained free traders. Norwegian industry could freely import goods dutiable in Sweden and in this way undersell Swedish industry in the common market. In 1897, the Swedes annulled the agreement and introduced customs dues for Norwegian goods. This fell rather heavily on the Norwegian textile and clothing industries, while the effect on Swedish industry was less noticeable. In this connection Norway also abandoned her free trade policy and customs tariffs were imposed to protect the Norwegian economy.

When assessing the importance of industry to the Norwegian economy it can be useful to compare employment in industry with shipping and fisheries. In 1860, for example, 18,000 men were employed in industry, as against 33,000 in the merchant marine. Not until 1890 were the industrial workers more numerous than the crews of Norwegian ships.

In the mid-1880s between 120,000 and 130,000 persons were engaged in cod and herring fisheries, but a great part of these were without a doubt part-time fishermen, who got most of their livings from other sources. By 1913, however,

---

TABLE 23: Norway: Number of industrial workers. Percentage distribution

Industry groups	1850	1860	1870	1879	1890	1900	1910
Clay, stone	12·1	12·9	9·2	13·2	7·4	8·4	7·9
Metal & machinery	9·6	8·3	21·1	18·4	21·5	21·7	22·2
Chemicals	0·0	1·1	2·1	5·2	4·5	2·3	3·9
Textiles	10·4	15·4	11·5	11·4	12·8	12·0	10·4
Pulp & paper	1·3	·7	1·0	3·2	7·7	8·8	14·0
Wood	28·8	31·8	30·2	26·2	21·6	21·9	14·0
Food, beverage	19·7	15·3	12·3	14·0	12·3	12·8	15·2
Clothing & shoe industries	—	0·0	0·0	1·4	3·0	2·8	4·5
Mining	13·4	10·4	7·3	4·3	4·0	3·9	5·1
Other industries	4·6	4·0	5·0	2·8	5·1	5·3	2·7
Total	100·0	100·0	100·0	100·0	100·0	100·0	100·0
Number of workers	14200	19300	33900	43100	63500	77300	98000

The number of workers in 1900 and 1910 has been reduced by those occupied in printing etc., as they are not included in earlier years.

Furthermore, the data for 1890 are not exactly comparable with early years. The data for 1910 are calculated on 'work years' and include those industries under compulsory accident insurance. Thus, the data for 1910 are not exactly comparable with earlier years.

Source: Statistiske Oversikter, 1948, Table 89 and 92

64,000 had fishing as their main occupation, a figure which can be compared with the number of industrial workers, at that time 120,000. Until the great industrial surge around the turn of the century, that is, industry was of lesser importance as an employer of labour than shipping or fisheries.

On the other hand, fisheries and shipping had weak linkage effects on other branches of the economy; i.e., from the point of view of development industry was considerably more important than might appear from a comparison of the figures. For the greater part of the period, too, fishing was carried out from primitive boats and with primitive tackle, and the capital-labour ratio must have been considerably lower than it was in industry.

A definite change was brought about in Norway's industrial development by the introduction of hydro-electric power. Norway had plenty of waterfalls, and was therefore in a favourable position. Foreign interest in investing in Norway grew, and Norwegian inventions contributed to the development of new industries.

The wave of investment in the new hydro-electric industry started about the turn of the century (Olsen, 1955, p. 120) and was followed by a positive explosion in the exploitation of water-power. In 1900 the output was 110,000 KW. In 1905, more than 850,000 KW (Holst, 1963, p. 381). The basis for this expansion was the production of calcium nitrate using German and American inventions. But it was only when inventions by the Norwegians Sam Eyde and Kristian Birkeland were put to use, that the industry assumed real importance. The manufacture of fertilisers, so-called Norwegian saltpetre, assumed considerable dimensions. In 1909 there were seventeen electrochemical and electrometallurgical factories, employing more than 2,000 workers. Production of calcium carbide was 50,000 tons, 20% of the entire world production. By 1913 exports had reached as much as 180,000 tons, to a value of 33 mill. kroner, or a sum equal to the export value of Norwegian timber products (Holst, 1963, p. 383).

This investment in capital-intensive concerns was made possible by large capital imports. The import surplus between 1901 and 1912 was a notable complement to domestic savings and during certain years in this period covered between 8% and 31% of the gross capital formation (Stonehill, 1965, p. 19).

The capital for Norsk Hydro Elektrisk Kvaelstof A/S, which produced fertilisers by means of Eyde's and Birkeland's inventions, chiefly came from Swedish and French banks (Gasslander, 1955, ch. XXIV). Aluminium production was begun in 1907 by British Aluminium Ltd.

The world market's demand for copper, sulphur and iron ore created the necessary conditions for the exploitation of Norway's pyrites and iron ore resources. These industries also required a rather advanced technique and considerable quantities of capital. Again, these were obtained abroad.

TABLE 24: Norway: Distribution of capital stock by type of activity and owner as of 31 December 1909

Branch	Total capital Million kroner	Foreign capital	Foreign capital in % of total capital
Mines	31·1	25·0	80·3
Metals	7·0	2·3	32·5
Chemicals	47·1	40·0	85·0
Heat and Light	20·8	9·7	46·7
Textiles	14·7	1·2	8·1
Paper, Leather and Rubber	72·4	32·1	44·3
Others	101·7	4·2	4·1
Total	294·8	114·5	38·8

Source: Statistisk Sentralbyrå, Fabrikstaellingen 1909, Kristiania 1911 quoted by Stonehill, 1965, p. 36

In 1909 foreign firms were employing 13·6% of the total industrial labour force, i.e., 2·6% of Norway's economically active population. The number of individuals indirectly dependent upon them must therefore have been considerably larger. Besides being larger, the foreign concerns were also more heavily capitalised than the Norwegian. In the foreign-owned firms 164 workers were employed on an average per place of work as against 41 in the Norwegian-owned. Those of mixed ownership also had more employees than those in pure Norwegian ownership. Furthermore, in the foreign-owned firms, almost 10,000 kroner were invested per worker, as against 3,000 in the Norwegian-owned (Stonehill, 1965, p. 33 et seq.). Foreign capital was concentrated in four export-orientated sectors, namely chemical pulp and paper, electricity (which supplied power to the export firms) and the mining industry (see Table 24). In 1909 there were 300 limited companies owned by foreign interests in Norway, mostly British and Swedish, and they held 80% of the stock (Holst, 1963, p. 384).

This state of affairs gave rise to alarm in Norwegian circles, and in 1907 the Storting, or Parliament, passed legislation forbidding the free establishment of foreign firms in Norway. But since these laws were not to be retroactive, foreign interests remained powerful. During the First World War quite a few were bought out with the growing Norwegian income from freight (Stonehill, 1965, p. 42).

It is difficult to assess what this hectic wave of investment meant to the Norwegian economy. It is self-evident that such investments must have had a certain multiplier effect. The Norwegian engineering industry developed swiftly and after 1905 the per capita GNP, which had remained stationary at the beginning of the twentieth century, grew swiftly. This must have produced a market situation favourable to the home market industry, since at the same time imports were impeded by customs tariffs that had been imposed after the joint Swedish-Norwegian legislation had been rescinded in 1897.

On the other hand, Norwegian industry's level of technical development was not high enough for the engineering industry to be able to take on projects demanding great investment. Electrical machinery had to be purchased in Sweden and Germany. It is also true that, in order to find an outlet for their products, those countries' electrical industries were obliged to invest in Norwegian industry. The lopsidedness in the electrical investment block had to be compensated by the electrical engineering industry's own investments in electric power. Another factor was that both the hydro-electric and the chemical industries were capital-intensive, while the number of their workers remained relatively insignificant. During the pre-war period, Norwegian industry could only profit indirectly from the advantage implied by the establishment of these new industries for the economy as a whole, and export income only partially made up for a sharp rise in imports.

TABLE 25: Norway: Annual rate of growth in percentage of GNP, 1900-15

	GNP	GNP/capita	GNP/individual aged 18-64
1900/05	0·7	0·0	−0·1
1905/10	3·5	2·9	2·8
1910/15	4·3	3·4	2·8

Source: Nasjonalregnskap 1900-1929, 1953, p. 73

Capital per capita rose by about 2% per annum after 1900, compared with 1·2% for the period 1877-1899 (Bjerke, 1966, p. 32). After 1904, capital accumulation was more rapid than population growth, something unprecedented in Norway's economic history. Of the traditional industries, the wood-processing industry was the one which grew most, nearly tripling its production between 1900 and 1915; the iron and metals industry almost doubled its output; while the textile industry increased its production by about 50% (Holst, 1963, p. 387). Since no official production data are available for this period, these statements must be regarded as only approximate.

At the same time, fisheries underwent a certain mechanisation. Internal combusion engines began to be used in the fishing fleet, the manufacture of herring oil was begun, and the fish canning industry, which in 1900 was still only employing about 1,500 workers, had more than doubled the number of its employees to 3,700, in 1910.

The increased capital accumulation after 1900, however,

does not explain the overall increase in production. Nor can the rest of the explanation be found in population growth. According to one calculation, the growth of the GNP during the period 1865-1919 can progressively be explained by 'technique' (organisation). Of the growth between 1865-74 and 1885-94 44% is attributed to improved techniques and 53% for the period 1885-94—1910-19 (Bjerke, 1966, p. 58). This expression 'technique' does not merely comprise better technical equipment (which after all also implies a growth in investment, and better economic knowledge) but also greater worker and management efficiency and the use of more efficient equipment and machines, such as can achieve higher output capacity without any corresponding increase in production costs for such machinery.

Two other factors just as important as industrial development in explaining growth in the GNP may have been the reduced self-sufficiency of an agriculture ever more concentrating on dairy products, and rising income from shipping. As late as 1910, agriculture's and fisheries' share of the GNP were almost as large as industry's, or about one-fourth each, while the transport system answered for 11% (Bjerke, 1966, p. 55). At the same time the gross output per active individual was evened out. In 1865 this figure for the services sector had been four times as great as for agriculture, forestry and fisheries. In 1910 the ratio was only 2·5. This means that before the First World War the 'enclave' economy, typical of Norway in the mid-nineteenth century, which partially explains subsequent developments, had broken down. This integration of Norwegian society must be seen as both a factor influencing its development and a result of its economic growth.

SWEDEN

Sweden's economic growth accelerated during three short, discontinuous periods.

The first was in the 1850s, the second in the 1870s, and the third in the 1890s. Of these the first was in high degree influenced by agriculture's grain exporting capacity, grain then being internationally in high demand. As has been noted before, Sweden, prior to the 1830s, had been a grain-importing country. Despite a rising population, however, her agriculture had been able to increase its output, exports during a brief period after the mid-nineteenth century being as high as exports of iron and timber products. During this period there was also a strong increase in timber exports. In the 1870s again, there was industrial expansion, quantitatively more thorough-going than before. This was in high degree the consequence of increased foreign demand while the expansion in the 1890s to an even greater extent reflected the domestic market's increased demand for industrial goods.

While agricultural yield rose after 1830, it is also possible to discern traces of industrial expansion. Between 1830 and 1860 iron mining, pig iron and bar iron production rose by about 3% per annum. Textiles were being progressively produced in factories, imports of cotton rose from about 300 tons in 1834 to over 8,000 tons in 1860. The textile industry's output of cotton thread was multiplied more than 20 times over, while output of cotton and linen weaves increased by about 20% per year. The number of factory workers rose—according to the industrial statistics—by 3·4% per year and the value of production by about 10% per year; and since during this period—1834-60—price changes were moderate, this means that productivity was considerably improved (Finanskomiténs betänkande, 1863. Tables in appendix).

The industry whose development was similar, but which at that time was not included in industrial statistics, was sawmills. During the period 1830-50 they increased their exports of sawn merchandise from 30,000 to 90,000 stds.[5] To this must be added exports of large and small square timber, which during the same period rose from about 10,000 to about 50,000 stds. (Söderlund, 1951, p. 36 et seq.).

However, the sawmills were not mechanised to any great extent before 1850. Not until 1849 was the first steam en-

5. stds.=St. Petersburg standards, still the regular unit of measurement in the trade.

gine installed, all sawing up to then having been done by water-power. But this mechanisation resulted in production being more capital-saving than before. The sawmills no longer had to be situated beside waterfalls, and the seasonal influence on sawing was reduced. This in turn could reduce storage at the sawmills; also the number of workers per unit of sawn timber.

During the first half of the 1850s, the increase in exports of timber products amounted to 50 to 60% (Söderlund, 1951, p. 68). Between the beginning of the 1860s and the beginning of the 1870s, increases in exports of sawn timber products were even greater, or from about 200,000 stds. to about 500,000 stds. (Söderlund, 1951, p. 166).

In the mid-1860s the number of industrial workers amounted to between 60,000 and 65,000. Of these, about 14,000 were employed in ironworks, about 10,000 in the sawmills industry, 11,000 in textiles and about 5,000 in engineering.

Sweden's industrial development was in high degree a process of adaptation to events outside the country's frontiers. Only to a lesser extent was it an independent process of economic expansion.

The iron industry was competing against increased international competition and had great difficulties in adapting itself so as not to lose contact with the foreign market. The result was a moderate increase in volume. Production of pig iron, for example, rose from 142,000 tons in 1850 to 300,000 tons in 1870, of which less than 10% was exported. The bulk of exports still consisted of bar iron.

To a great extent, the sawmills industry's expansion was a result of increased international demand, due to industrial development on the Continent and the simultaneous boom in building caused by rising urbanisation.

The export industry dominated the capital goods sector, and sawmills and ironworks answered for the greater part of that sector's production value. Owing to the multiplier effect this growth resulted, in turn, in an expansion within the consumer goods industry. Foreign demand for Swedish products made it possible for exporters and producers alike to extend and cheapen production. Investment therefore also influenced other branches of industry, which, as exports rose, increased their output.

In a society like the Swedish, with low per capita income and poor communications, it was also easier for the export industry to expand than for the home market industry. Expansion in the export sector could precede any extension in social overhead investments. For the development of an integrated market, investments in communications would have been necessary in the initial stages of industrialisation, but since the demand for industrial goods came from abroad, industry could begin to expand before any such investments had been made. The industrial surge of the 1870s coincided, in fact, with a hasty development of the internal communication network.

Nor was there any need in the initial stages for the export industry, which was the first to develop, to compete with

TABLE 26: Sweden: Percentual changes in GNP, industry and crafts

	GNP current prices	Industry & crafts	The share of industry and crafts in GNP %
1861/65 to			13
1866/70	8	19	14
1871/75	40	28	13
1876/80	9	0	12
1881/85	3	16	14
1886/90	—1	8	14
1891/95	14	32	17
1896/1900	26	48	20
1901/05	19	24	24
1906/10	31	29	27
1911/15	29	27	28

Source: Johansson, 1967, Table 6 and 55

the home market industry for labour and capital. A further factor was that sawmills, above all, could expand swiftly without excessive investment.

Later, competition between the two sectors acted as a

stimulus, chiefly to the consumer goods industry, which forced through innovations likely to increase its own productivity.

The industrial expansion which took place prior to 1870 only affected certain parts of Swedish society. Agriculture's dominance remained unbroken. Industry's share of the GNP was low, and did not change before the 1890s. In spite of this, industrial expansion of the 1870s may be said to have been of great importance. There was a marked acceleration in development, a break in the previous trend and the whole structure was altered both institutionally, in the shape of its enterprises, and in production.

During the 1870s extensive investment occurred in virtually all sectors of industry, as also in housing and railway construction. Agricultural exports expanded sharply, particularly during the latter half of the 1870s, when the industrial trade cycle had stagnated. This agricultural export occurred, that is, during the so-called agricultural depression, which is alleged to have affected all of Europe's agriculture. This 'depression', however, was for the most part limited to production of wheat, while prices for oats, for instance, which constituted the major part of Swedish exports, did not fall anything like as much (see p. 404). In industry, the capital goods industry's production value rose by more than 100% up to 1875, and total industrial investments by more than 80%. The GNP, measured in fixed monetary values, rose by more than 30%; twice as big an increase as during any five-year period up to 1914.

Economic expansion was stimulated by a very keen foreign demand for Swedish export goods, and the export industry's growth-rate exceeded that of the home market industry. The inflationary price rise at the beginning of the 1870s created large profits for enterprises, which to a great extent utilised them for further investments. Further, the money market was characterised by low rates of interest, a situation typical of the Swedish capital market during the later decades of the nineteenth century, due to the export industry's profits being passed on to the capital market. Furthermore, the development of the railways during the

TABLE 27:   Sweden: The share of the industrial groups in the total number of workers and the total gross value of production. Per cent (W=Workers, V=Value)

	1869/78 W	1869/78 V	1879/88 W	1879/88 V	1889/98 W	1889/98 V	1899/08 W	1899/08 V
Food, beverage* and tobacco industries	5·8	23·2	6·0	21·3	7·4	25·6	9·2	17·0
Textile industry	14·8	12·2	12·9	10·6	12·9	11·6	12·8	11·3
Leather, fur and rubber industries	2·2	1·9	1·8	1·4	2·2	1·9	3·0	3·3
Wood industries	17·4	21·1	19·9	23·0	20·8	18·2	17·5	13·2
Pulp, paper and printing industries	4·0	2·7	4·5	3·3	7·7	5·6	8·4	7·7
Stone, clay, gravel, etc. industries	6·0	2·0	7·7	2·5	11·3	3·7	13·4	4·7
Chemical industries	4·5	3·6	4·9	4·6	4·2	3·9	3·6	3·8
Mechanical engineering etc. industries	11·7	8·3	13·5	8·6	15·8	10·7	18·9	13·6
Iron & Steel works	16·5 }	23·5	15·1 }	20·1	9·6 }	17·2	5·7 }	13·9
Iron Mines	5·7 }		4·7 }		3·7 }		3·3 }	
Unclassified industries	6·4	1·5	5·7	4·6	3·2	1·6	3·1	11·5
Total Number of Workers (000)	100·0		126·0		207·6		306·4	
Total Gross Value of Production (mill. Kr.)	345·2	414·8			716·4		1372·2	

*Excluding mills and dairies.

Source: Jörberg 1961, p. 51. To make the series homogeneous, certain assessments have been made for the time before 1896. This refers especially to the sawmill industry for which there are no production data prior to 1896. The milling industry has been excluded from the group Food, Beverage & Tobacco because of the difficulty in separating in the statistics the industrial mills from the mills that produced for domestic use. For further details, see *op. cit.*, p. 50 f.

1870s was unquestionably of importance to industrial development. Transport charges fell considerably, the development of communications altered firms' costs, reduced stocks and freed capital for more productive purposes; marketing became easier, and lower transport costs meant cheaper raw materials. This in turn reduced the prices of products, which again contributed to reduce the cost of building railways.

Since the railways were often being built out through thinly populated areas, investments were made in the new railway communities which were springing up. Such investments both had the effect of increasing income for other sections of the economy, and also led to a strong geographical population movement. This transfer, by moving the working population from less productive to more productive activities, may have been at least as important as the direct effects of railway investments.

Sweden's State Railways were almost exclusively financed by foreign loans, freeing capital for other sorts of investment. During the period 1855-60, State allocations for railway construction amounted to nearly 34 mill. kronor (Finanskomiténs betänkande, 1863, p. 118). But it was not until the 1870s that railways were built on a really large scale. During that decade the length of track increased by 14% per annum, that is to say was more than tripled, reaching a length of 5,000 km., while the subsequent rate of growth up to 1914 was only about 3% per annum.

Industrial production came to demand more and more capital, and since investment was particularly heavy in the capital goods sectors this had consequences within other sectors of industry, too. In the early 1870s the iron and steel industry made big investments. The Bessemer process became established and other technical changes, too, made for cheaper production. Timber floatways were extended, which reduced stocks at the sawmills, etc. These investments had a profounder effect on the production structure than cost-reducing measures in the consumer goods industry, which, thanks to these investments in the capital goods industry, was able to improve its output and productivity. During the 1870s industry's annual gross value amounted on an average to 354 mill. kronor. During the first decade of the twentieth century this value was about 1,370 mill. kronor, an increase of 280%, while the number of workers rose by more than 200%, or from about 100,000 to 306,000.

In the 1870s, too, it was the iron, steel and mining industries which were the leading group, employing about a quarter of the industrial labour force. Next came the timber products industry, employing a fifth; that is to say, these two groups were then together employing about 45% of the total industrial labour force. During the 1890s, however, the timber products industry came to outstrip the iron industry in this respect, only to be outstripped in its turn by metals and engineering during the first decade of the twentieth century.

The diversification which took place during industrialisation was caused by innovations being made within the new branches. The paper and pulp industry more than doubled its share of the total labour force, the stone, clay and glass industries more than doubled their share, and the leather and rubber industry increased by one third. The textile industry's share, on the other hand, remained more or less stationary, while iron mining's share was sharply reduced.

The relation between the timber industry, on the one hand, and the paper and pulp industry, on the other, may be compared with the corresponding relation between iron and steel and engineering. Those groups which did not process their products to any great degree—e.g., the timber industry—lost in importance, while those branches above all which were involved in refining their products, but which based their production on the same raw materials, expanded. That the textile industry could retain its share was due to the expansion within the clothing and woollens branch, a refinement, that is, of the products of the cotton and wool industry.

In each industrial group some branches had a greater effect on growth than others. The growth of the pulp industry was a condition for the expansion of the paper and pulp industry as a whole, the shoe industry led to a development of the leather industry, match manufacture and superphosphates were the driving forces behind the chemical industry and from the turn of the century onwards the electrical industry was the most expansive of all engineering branches. By contrast, the sawmills industry—owing to its slow growth at the end of the 1890s, which held up the expansion of the timber processing industry—came to exert an opposite influence.

TABLE 28: Sweden: Annual percentual changes in gross production value during the period 1867/69-1892/95 and 1896-1912

	1867/69-1892/95	*1896-1912*
Paper pulp & printing industry	6·1	11·0
Stone, clay, glass, etc.	6·0	5·3
Foodstuffs	5·1	4·0
Chemicals	4·5	7·3
Metals & engineering	3·7	7·0
Timber industry	3·7	2·0
Iron, steelworks & mines	3·2	3·3
Textiles	2·6	5·6
Leather & rubber	1·7	10·0
Capital goods	5·2	6·2
Consumer products industry	3·3	6·1

Source: Jörberg, 1961, pp. 61 and 63

One reason for this was growing Finnish and Russian competition. In the same way, Norwegian industry, suffering from Swedish competition, had earlier found it hard to keep up.

After the first real trade cycle crisis in Swedish history—at the end of the 1870s—had been overcome, Swedish industry expanded at a rate which internationally speaking was unusually even. The fluctuations in the trade cycle followed the international pattern, but the amplitude of the swings in the Swedish cycle was smaller.

From the mid-1880s up to 1914 Sweden's export volume increased by 150%. At the same time exports to some extent came to be re-structured. The old staple goods became less important. Exports of grain came to an end, and were partially replaced by meat and dairy products, above all by butter. As has been mentioned already, the timber goods share fell, and was replaced by pulp and paper. But, from the 1890s on a new raw material—iron ore—becomes an important item of export. Iron ore exports, together with engineering exports, were the swiftest to expand.

TABLE 29: Sweden: Percentual distribution of exports by groups of merchandise. 1881-1913

	1881/85	1891/95	1901/05	1911/13
Timber products	40·4	37·1	38·5	26·1
Iron & Steel	16·2	9·5	10·2	9·3
Grain	11·7	4·7	0·4	0·3
Butter	6·3	12·0	8·9	6·0
Paper and Pulp	4·6	8·3	12·9	17·6
Iron ore	—	0·4	5·0	8·0
Engineering products	2·6	3·1	6·7	10·5
Others	18·7	22·8	17·6	21·6
Foodstuffs	24	26	13	12[*]
Raw materials	43	42	53	53[*]
Industrial goods	33	32	34	35[*]

[*]1906/10

Source: Fridlizius, 1963, p. 31 et seq.

Throughout almost the entire pre-1914 period, Sweden's terms of trade improved. During the 1870s they were strongly in Sweden's favour. Up to 1875 Swedish export prices rose a good deal more swiftly than import prices. During the last years of the 1880s, owing to stable export prices and falling import prices, the terms of trade improved by about 20%—an improvement which applied both to raw materials and finished products. The raw materials which Sweden was exporting were predominantly of a type necessary to international industrialisation, which explains the favourable price developments.

For the greater part of the nineteenth century the Swedish price level was on the rise, and this may also have facilitated

Sweden's economic expansion. Profit developments in industry, however, were not so satisfactory during the 1880s as they had been previously, or as they were to be later; but, measured in volume, Sweden's industry showed a definite expansion. While the investments of the 1870s and —in even higher degree—of the 1880s, were extensive in character—that is to say they widened the area in which capital was used—later developments led to its more intensive use: i.e., to more capital per worker. The number of workers rose a good deal more slowly than, for example, the amount of industrial horsepower. But the growth in horsepower per worker was slower during the 1880s than it had been during the preceding decade. During the third expansion period, in the 1890s, the home-market industry expanded at the same rate as the export industry and was responsible for about half of the production value before the First World War, i.e., the same share as around 1870.

It seems probable that, during the period up to the 1890s, the limited domestic market was an obstacle to Sweden's industrial expansion. The spread of innovations within industry may have been hindered by too limited a market. To be economically profitable, certain of these innovations demanded a market larger than Sweden could offer. In the initial stage of industrialisation this was probably the case in several branches of mechanical engineering. During the 1890s, the engineering industry, whose expansion was based in many cases on such Swedish inventions as the milk separator (invented in the 1870s, but widely developed during the 1890s), turbines, internal combustion engines, electrical machinery, gas accumulators and ball bearings. In this way, the engineering industry came to lose its uniform structure. One powerfully expanding sector was aiming at international markets for its products; the other, growing slowly and simultaneously, was aiming at regional outlets, and furthermore was not very specialised. The export of engineering products increased by 50% per five-year period after 1889; imports rose only half as swiftly.

Another example of Swedish industry's import substitution capacity at that time is textiles: more particularly woollens, which between 1890 and 1910 increased their production value three and a half times over. While at the end of the 1880s Swedish consumption was to 65% met by domestic output, on the eve of the First World War the home industry was in a position to supply 80% of the home market's needs.

The Swedish economy's expansion is reflected in a great increase in investment. While in the 1880s gross fixed capital formation had been about 130 mill. kronor per annum, about 1900 this rose to 300 mill. kronor per annum, and in 1913 was more than 500 million (Johansson, 1967, Table 45). In the same period the investment share in relation to GDP rose from about 10% to 13%. This was only exceeded in the boom of the 1870s.

Compared with other foreign loans, foreign loans for industrial investment seem to have been relatively insignificant. Of the total bonds issued (3,500 mill. kronor up to 1910), almost 1,800 mill. kronor had originally been placed abroad, of which more than 900 million were redeemed before 1909. Of the industrial companies' bonded debt of 598 mill. kronor, only 5% had been placed abroad. The State, for its part, had placed 83% of its 900 mill. kronor in foreign countries (Flodström, 1912, p. 223).

During the 1870-1914 period industrial production rose on an average by 4·4% per annum, while the rise in the GDP was no more than 2·8%, i.e., industrial production was doubling itself every sixteen years as against every twenty-sixth year for the GDP. This production increase can be compared with investment activities, which rose by 5% per annum, while investment in machinery rose by 4%. Since the number of industrial workers was increasing more slowly than output per worker, there was a certain increase in productivity. Between 1896 and 1912, output per worker rose by 1·6% per annum; and if we further take into account the reduction in working hours, which then occurred, we arrive at an improvement in productivity of about 2% per annum (Fastbom, 1949, p. 23).

In the mid-1890s industry's share of the GDP had increased to the point where it exceeded agriculture's contribution. Changes in the population also reflect the process of industrialisation. After 1870 the industrial population grew by, on an average, 30% per decade, while after 1880 agriculture's share of the population fell by about 5% per decade.

Around 1910, even so, the agricultural population still constituted about half the population. This share was bigger in Sweden than in Denmark and Norway, even though the Swedish industrial sector was also larger than those countries'; which means that Sweden's tertiary sector represented a smaller share than it did in Denmark and Norway. The growth of the Swedish economy was thus based on a big increase in commodity output, while in Denmark and Norway the service sector was more important. This may help to explain why Sweden's economic growth was swifter, at the same time as it also reveals how, in certain respects, her economic structure differed from her neighbours'.

It remains to analyse the similarities and differences which characterised industrial development in the various Scandinavian countries, and the factors behind it.

AGRICULTURE AND INDUSTRIAL DEVELOPMENT

One of the problems most discussed in connection with developing countries' potential economic expansion has concerned the proper balance between expansion in agriculture and in other sectors, chiefly industry. Obviously, industrialisation implies a dynamic transformation, which will profoundly contribute towards changing any economy's traditional structure. At the same time, it is pointed out that industrial expansion is dependent upon agriculture's ability to produce a surplus to support a growing population in the non-agrarian sectors. Those who would give agriculture priority maintain that its modernisation and mechanisation are a necessary pre-condition of freeing labour for industrial development. They also assert that it is relatively easier to increase agricultural yield without any great accumulation of capital, and that the agricultural sector can simultaneously develop without excessive investments in such infrastructure as housing construction, roads, social or hygienic measures. Furthermore, to develop the agricultural sector is the simplest method of creating a surplus for exports, or to reduce the need for imports. Finally, agriculture can expand without any previous or simultaneous industrial development (see e.g., Papanek, 1954, 193-6, Mellor-Johnston, 1961, p. 571). There is a certain risk, however, that such a transformation will not produce these results. If agriculture is more or less collective, as was the case in some parts of Norway, for example, during the greater part of the nineteenth century—when for lack of any thorough land reform, agriculture was split up into a great number of units—the low productivity cannot increase yield beyond what is sufficient to support a growing agricultural population. Improved productivity does not lead to general economic growth; but since there will only be a small difference in wage levels between agriculture and industry, due to only a small part of the increased production reaching the market, improved productivity can be an obstacle to labour being released from agriculture. Behind this line of reasoning lies the view that agricultural wages are not determined by marginal productivity, but by the average productivity in village communities (Gutman, 1957). In Scandinavia, within both agriculture and industry, agricultural productivity created the needful surplus and contributed to support an increasing population. In Denmark and Sweden this was clearly and definitely the case. In Norway the results were not so clear. But Norwegian agriculture had an important secondary occupation, namely fishing, which occupied about one tenth of the population, and whose output was partly merchandised within the country, but above all exported.

Increased productivity in agriculture, particularly if income is unequally distributed, can lead to capital accumulation which will be transmitted—directly or indirectly—to other sectors. In Denmark up to the mid-1870s internal savings were adequate to create investments, and not only in agriculture. Exports of agricultural products passed through the hands of middlemen, in Copenhagen for instance, and by these services created extra income which could be invested in other sectors. The same state of affairs arose in Sweden, where grain exports led to increased income for middlemen; and also in Norway, where exports of fish had the same effect.

Increased productivity in agriculture can also lead to a reduction in the agricultural population and to a transference of labour from agriculture to other sectors, i.e., to generally even more productive branches of the economy. And this can be a considerable gain for society. Further, increased agricultural income can create purchasing power in the agrarian sector, and this can be a condition of any expansion in the home market industry.

Such a development can, in simpler form, be seen as an interplay between two sectors: on the one hand agriculture, and on the other, other branches of the economy, above all industry.

In Denmark, the agrarian sector played a leading part. In Sweden its role was as important as that of industry. In Norway, where there was a big service sector, both agriculture and industry played a smaller part in developments, while in Finland agriculture had only a minor effect on economic development.

Denmark excepted, industrial expansion occurred on the basis of demand from abroad, with the result that industry's demand for labour increased. The reason why production went on rising within the agricultural sector, despite its labour losses, can only be that marginal productivity, totally speaking, must have been low. Another aspect of the matter is that agriculture was not homogeneous in its structure. There was one group, consisting of estates and farms of relatively high productivity, which also drew off labour from the smaller farms whose productivity was low and of merely marginal importance.

As industry increased its demand for labour and there was simultaneously a great deal of emigration—e.g., from

Sweden and Norway during the period after 1870, and from Finland somewhat later on, and to a much less significant extent from Denmark—this led to a rise in marginal productivity for the agricultural labour force. Also to a rise in wage levels. This could have been caused by a change in income distribution within the agricultural sector, owing to the fact that losses of workers within that sector, without any fall in production, led to a per capita rise in income for those who remained. Another way of expressing the matter is to say that, due to increased acreage and to increased mechanisation and increased output per worker, the commercial sector within agriculture got a relatively greater per capita rise in income than other groups. Nor was there any transfer to industry from this sector; on the contrary, commercial agriculture was in competition with industry for labour from the non-commercial agricultural sector. The upshot of this tendency, however, was that industry had to raise its wages in order to be able to go on attracting labour away from agriculture. As far as industry was concerned, since the supply of labour to be obtained from agriculture was elastic, increased foreign demand in the initial stages of industrialisation led to rising profits; which meant that industry could increase its demand for labour before it led to a rise in wages. The increased profits from industry were saved and invested, which led to a further demand for labour, and so to a continued rise in profits. Only when the agricultural labour force had fallen greatly did this lead to a rise in marginal productivity within the *whole* agricultural sector, on the one hand and, on the other, to a rising wages share in industry.

In Denmark, agriculture was so severely rationalised that production was able to rise sharply on the basis of a fairly stationary agricultural population. In Denmark, too, commercial agriculture had attracted to itself a large part of the non-commercial agricultural population even before any industrial expansion had got under way. Since industry in Denmark was not primarily export-orientated, any increase in demand for its products had to come from the home market, and this, the market being limited, may have led to Danish industry's productivity increase being a relatively low one. The strong position of crafts in Denmark would seem to confirm this supposition. Not until the 1890s did the craftsman's relative share of the economy begin to fall, which indicates that industry's demand for workers sharpened the competition for labour as a whole, which forced the crafts—like agriculture—to release their less productive labour.

In Finland the situation was quite different. The fact that so large a segment of the population was engaged in agriculture, and that this segment continued to increase its absolute numbers throughout the entire period may have meant that industry could recruit labour without any considerable rise in wages. In which case the result must have been that industrial expansion occurred more as a result of capital widening than of its deepening. This again may explain the insignificant structural changes in Finnish industry. Thanks to the access of labour obtainable from agriculture, the profit trend, within industry's traditional branches, could be kept at a satisfactory level, emigration from Finland not being of any size until the 1890s.

In Norway industry had to compete for the available labour both with fisheries and with the merchant marine, while at the same time a considerable amount of emigration had begun. This, on the one hand, led to swift losses of agricultural population; on the other to a rise in industrial wages. Since wages were predominantly used for consumption and the profits were reinvested, often in activities with only weak linkage effects on the economy as a whole, the wage rise had the effect of damaging the balance of payments; and this led to a major import of capital, since at the same time profits probably fell.

During the boom of the 1870s Swedish industry's labour force grew considerably; and even during the 1880s, when emigration reached its peak, the industrial labour force continued to grow at about the same rate as during the 1870s. This would indicate that marginal productivity was low, above all in the non-commercial sector of agriculture;

or, in other words, that the situation in the agricultural sector was one of under-employment.

Owing to the extent of emigration, however, industry was not able to attract labour on the same terms as it could have, had there been no such emigration. As wages had to be raised in order that industry could compete with the commercial agricultural sector for surplus population, profits fell. The reaction of management to this change seems to have been to introduce innovations to reduce costs, viz., increase the investment share, among other ways by taking up short-term foreign loans. Such was the case in the 1880s. But the same mechanism seems to have functioned later, too. The improved wage situation may have contributed to reduce emigration during the boom of the 1890s, with the result that real wages rose more slowly, which in turn improved industry's profit situation.

Such a development is confirmed by the wages share within industry. During the 1880s, when emigration was at its height, the wages share in industry rose, to fall during the 1890s and the early years of the nineteenth century. In agriculture, on the other hand, it remained fairly steady up to the beginning of the nineteenth century, when it began to fall, right up to the First World War, as is reflected by the fact that the number of wage-earners in agriculture dropped more than the number of peasants owning their own land (Jungenfelt, 1966, diagrams, II:4 and II:6).

Obviously, industry's recruitment of labour was not always—perhaps not even predominantly—at the direct expense of agriculture. Expansion in the tertiary sector was of similar significance to industrial expansion, but this does not alter the mechanism underlying the whole development. A further complication is that the Scandinavian countries were not on the same level of economic development. The more backward a country is, the harder it is to recruit workers to industry, since this always involves a change which may prove problematic to individuals used to the irregular rhythms of agriculture.

Thus, for example, Finnish agriculture was more backward than the other Scandinavian countries'; and one reason for Finnish industry's difficulties in meeting foreign competition in the domestic market may have been its workers' poor training. A result of this was that industries which did not change to capital intensive production—as the textile industry did—ran into difficulties because of the low productivity of their labour force. If recruitment of industry was not made direct from agriculture, but from among persons who had already left the land and were engaged on railway construction, or had become unskilled labour in the towns or had similar occupations, the change-over to industrial routine was easier. In Denmark, above all, this type of recruitment by stages seems to have been common, but we do not have any detailed studies on the origins of the industrial labour force from any Scandinavian country.

A further aspect of agriculture's role in the industrial development may be obtained by studying the part played by agricultural exports in earning foreign currency. During the whole period, exports of agricultural products were the chief source of foreign currency earnings in Denmark. In Sweden, during the whole period 1850 to the 1880s, they, together with timber products, played the same role. In Finland, butter exports constituted an important part of total exports. And in Norway fish, together with timber products, was the chief export item throughout the period.

The reasons for this development naturally pointed in two directions. If improved productivity in the agrarian sector is a condition of industrialisation, industrialisation in its turn leads to an increased demand for agricultural products. Urbanisation, the growth of foodstuffs industries, improved communications, all increase the market; and an increased demand for such products stimulates the growth of a commercialised agriculture and modern farming methods. If the industrial development leads to the absorption of a sufficient number of agricultural workers, wages in the agrarian sector will rise as the number of workers diminishes. Increased wages lead to a more capital-intensive production and increased output per worker. This in turn leads to rising incomes. A broader market enables the home

market industry to expand and compete with foreign products which had earlier been imported. Since agriculture's
transformation began prior to the industrial development,
investments came to be spread out in time; the surplus from
agricultural exports could be invested in the agrarian sector
before very severe competition for capital arose from the
industrial sector.

In Norway, agriculture played a smaller part than it did
in the other Scandinavian countries. But Norwegian
fisheries can, to a certain extent, be seen as a part of this
sector's foreign currency earnings with only weak linkage
effects however, on the rest of the economy. As has been
noted, the numbers employed in Danish agriculture were
relatively lower than in other Scandinavian countries, while
their productivity was higher. The initial Danish capital was
accumulated from domestic savings, while Swedish agriculture borrowed extensively abroad. Both in Denmark and
in Sweden, however, the state took an active part in agriculture's transformation by introducing various land reforms and granting loans. In Norway, where division into
smaller farms dominated, agricultural productivity remained low. Nor were any agricultural co-operatives
formed in Norway, on the Danish pattern. Co-operative
dairies existed, however.

As in all other countries which went through a process of
industrialisation, there was, in the Scandinavian countries,
a relative fall in the agricultural population and in agriculture's share of the gross national product. Since the
agricultural labour force formed a lower percentage in
Denmark than in any other Scandinavian country, the
relative level of per capita income at the beginning of the
period was lower in these countries than in Denmark.

Only in Sweden was there such a major increase that the
level rose at a rate comparable with Denmark's. In view of
the difficulties which Finnish and Norwegian agriculture
had to contend with, this is hardly surprising.

Danish and Swedish agriculture seem to have been more
swiftly transformed than was usual in Europe at that time.
It would not be correct, however, to describe Sweden's and

Denmark's transformation as revolutionary, but Norway's and Finland's as evolutionary. Nevertheless, the structural tensions which arose in Denmark and Sweden were considerable; which also in part explains their swifter economic growth. But in all four countries agriculture grew simultaneously with other sectors, a factor which also contributed to their swift industrialisation and urbanisation.

Agricultural exports contributed to earn foreign currency, and since the countries' share of the world market was small and the demand was relatively elastic, the risk of a sharp drop in prices was slight inasmuch as both price and income elasticity in the importing countries were relatively high and at the same time agriculture was sufficiently flexible to switch from exports of grain to meat and dairy product export whenever these elasticities threatened to fall.

The dominating role played by agriculture in all the Scandinavian countries up to 1914 was such that it must constantly be taken into consideration when analysing their industrial development. It is also a well-known fact that no country went through a process of industrial development before 1914 without first or simultaneously increasing its agricultural productivity.

A COMPARATIVE ANALYSIS OF INDUSTRIAL DEVELOPMENT IN THE SCANDINAVIAN COUNTRIES

The economic development of the Scandinavian countries reveals a number of similar features, and was influenced by a number of interacting variables, with many common origins.

In all four countries, incomes outside the industrial sector rose before, or simultaneously with, industrial expansion. In Denmark, during all periods of growth, agricultural exports were strongly correlated with rises in income. In Finland, at all such periods, timber exports dominated. As for Norway, her upward surge in the 1850s was dominated by exports of timber products and rises in shipping income. The same was true in the 1890s, a decade which also saw the appearance of paper pulp exports and an embryonic export from the electrochemical industry. In Sweden, the 1850s were dominated by agricultural exports, timber products and iron, which also remained in the foreground during the 1870s. The 1890s, on the other hand, showed a relative stagnation in timber product exports, compensated by a rise in pulp, engineering products and iron ore exports.

As has several times been noted, all four countries were in high degree dependent upon income from exports. One result of this dependency was that their industrial expansion occurred during periods of increased international demand. Thus the 1850s, 1870s and 1890s, in all the countries, were the decades during which industry passed through a major development.

TABLE 30: Merchandise: Exports' and imports' share of the GNP Per cent

	DENMARK		NORWAY		SWEDEN	
	Export	Import	Export	Import	Export	Import
1865/69	—	—	14	19	15	15
1875/79	23	31	14	22	18	19
1885/89	20	32	16	22	21	22
1895/99	23	34	16	28	21	22
1905/09	28	37	17	28	18	23

Sources: Denmark: Bjerke-Ussing, 1958, p. 92
       Norway: Export: Statistiske Oversikter, 1948, Table 112
                 Import: Idem, Table 110
                 GDP: Bjerke, 1966, p. 97 and Stoltz, 1954, p. 58
       Sweden: Johansson, 1967, Table 49, 51, 55

The introduction of free trade in Britain in the 1840s and later in one European country after another opened up an important market for the Scandinavian countries' exports. Simultaneous growth in population widened the market for agricultural products and rising incomes in Western Europe led to increased demand for raw materials for industry and housing construction. Income elasticities for imports from Scandinavia were high, one reason being changes in the Scandinavian economies' exports, due to new commodities replacing them when the elasticities fell. Demand was rather elastic, at the same time as supply elasticities in Scandinavia were also relatively high; all of which together led to an improvement in those countries' terms of trade. This facilitated their imports and at the same time raised their income level.

Even at the start of industrialisation, the Scandinavian countries had fairly modern sectors, with international contacts. Entrepreneurs of varying degrees of international insight existed. In Norway and Sweden, these were in the iron industry and commerce; in Denmark chiefly in commerce. In Norway, too, the merchants in the coastal towns, like the Swedish iron exporters and commercial houses, were clearly aware of the international market's requirements. Denmark's international contacts were facilitated by her proximity to Hamburg and the British market, and her merchants were in a position to assess the possibility of increasing her export of domestic products. A further factor was that, before the countries' internal communications network had been built out, it was often easier to find a market abroad than to look for demand in domestic markets which were strictly regionalised. This is above all true of Finland, Norway and Sweden.

The agricultural reforms carried out in Denmark and Sweden during the latter half of the eighteenth century and later, together with the improved terms of trade for agricultural products that arose before the 1870s, facilitated the commercialisation of agriculture. All contributed to a rise in income. Increased income from agriculture made it easier for Denmark and Sweden to finance their infrastructure and in Norway, even if fisheries and to some extent shipping had weak linkage effects on the rest of the economy, they must have facilitated capital accumulation. In Denmark the banks, notably Privatbanken, were able to participate actively in the establishment of enterprises with the communications sector and also in industry. In Finland, on the other hand, the situation was less satisfactory, partly because industry was linked with the not very expansive Russian market, partly because the economy was more backward than the other Scandinavian countries. But in Finland, too, shipping played a certain part in income rises up to the 1870s, when falling freight rates and the change-over to steamships, too costly for Finnish shipowners, contributed to the shipping industry's decline.

TABLE 31: Size of the merchant fleets (1000's of net tons)

| | DENMARK | | FINLAND | | NORWAY | | SWEDEN | |
	Steam-ships	total	Steam-ships	total	Steam-ships	total	Steam-ships	total
1852	2	103				320		204
1870	10	178	4	209	13	974	27	346
1889	94	271	6	257	168	1611	135	504
1900	247	394	54	340	505	1508	325	614
1914	434	520	86	478	1214	1784	750	901

Sources: Denmark: Warming, 1913, p. 400, Nielsen, 1933, p. 548
　　　　　Finland:　Översikt, 1890, P. 98, Statistisk Årsbok för Finland
　　　　　　　　　　1920, p. 170
　　　　　Norway:　Statistike Oversikter, 1948, Table 126
　　　　　Sweden:　Statistisk översikt, 1919, p. 72

In the initial period industrial finance seems to have been dependent, to a varying extent, on foreign capital. To begin with, the establishment, for instance, of a sawmill required only a small amount of capital; and the high profits, above all during the booms of the 1870s, were ploughed back into the concerns. Short-term foreign loans, however, were available, though their size in most branches is not known (cf. Fridlizius, 1957, chap. 11). Further, the income rise in agriculture was such that agriculture became independent of the domestic capital market, and when meat and dairy products replaced grain exports this transformation, too, could take place without relying on foreign capital. Thanks to moderate population growth, necessary investments in the infrastructure and for housing construction were also fairly limited. The earliest population growth occurred within the agricultural lower classes, who had nothing to do with the capital market; and the timber products boom of the 1870s also had less influence on urbanisation than later development in other branches, e.g., consumer products or engineering. After 1880 housing construction was also to some extent financed by foreign loans.

To this must be added the fact that wages, both in the importing countries and in Scandinavia, were not stable; and this meant that profits were not under any great pressure during the weaker periods of the trade cycle, which again implied that importing countries did not have to compensate themselves at the expense of Scandinavian export firms. Taxes, too, were low and income distribution was lopsided, which facilitated the growth of private capital.

In other words, the Scandinavian countries showed great adaptability and were able to exploit favourable phases of the trade cycle. The greater the exports' share of the Scandinavian countries' economies, with undiminished or increased income elasticity for Scandinavian products (e.g., in Britain), the swifter could be the growth of their national incomes. Just how swift, depended on demand-and-supply elasticity. The European countries' relatively swift economic growth also made possible an increased rate of growth in Scandinavia. Furthermore, there were very few British firms which had the stature of monopolies, and among Scandinavia's export firms, which were all very small and each controlling only a very small part of the market, monopolies were out of the question. All this meant a swifter expansion in demand than could have taken place had a monopoly situation existed. The growth in demand for import goods on the continent of Europe and in Britain was a function of those countries' rising income levels. Since income rose rather swiftly, and the propensity of marginal imports remained rather high, the new Scandinavian industries too, could keep up a high rate of growth. Another reason was that demand elasticity was sufficiently high for the Scandinavian countries to be able to increase their export volume by lowering prices. Technical innovations too, affected the development of exports. In certain conditions these can lead to a deterioration in the terms of trade. Falling production costs can mean increased profits. If there is great pressure of competition, on the other hand, such falling costs can entirely be to the advantage of the importing countries. The problems are theoretically abstruse and the effect of technical innovations on development and terms of trade—just to mention a few of the complexities—depends on whether such innovations imply a saving of capital or of labour, whether they are introduced into the export industries or into the competing home market industries.

The innovations during the nineteenth century took place at a rate which allowed the firms to adapt production to such new processes over a fairly long period of time. Thus, for instance, the stagnant timber products industry was compensated in the 1890s by exports of pulp and grain exports, likewise by meat and dairy exports. Where production was stable the technical advances naturally lowered costs; or, where it was extended, and in the absence of any monopoly situation, they raised profits. This means that at any given moment the Scandinavian countries enjoyed a comparative advantage—first in point of timber and grain, later for pulp and meat and dairy products. Further, since the development was sufficiently slow for the importing countries' needs of raw materials to remain stable for long periods at a time, a situation arose which offered long-lasting comparative advantages. These advantages were not, as they are today, chiefly based on superior technique, which can swiftly alter any such comparative advantages. But the change being only gradual, the Scandinavian countries, thanks to their great adaptability, had time to learn new techniques and exploit them.

Yet another factor explaining the retardation to be noted in certain older branches of industry is that technical innovations can be of minor importance. Changes which occur in the beginning of an economic expansion have a more tangible effect on production growth than subsequent changes in the same branch. Further, those branches which grow slowly will affect their complementary branches, which could have expanded more swiftly if they had not been thus hindered in this way. Again, raw materials can become harder to come by, or more expensive, thus requiring more capital and labour for production. Yet another explanation can lie in competition on the international level; if younger and more swiftly expanding branches in other countries can produce similar commodities at lower prices, this, too, will hold up a branch's expansion.

Those parts of the Scandinavian countries' industry which were exposed to international competition—whether on the export side or via imports—obviously had to adapt their prices to the world market, at least as long as their domestic market was not screened off by customs tariffs. This required those sectors' productivity development to be stronger than other sectors'. It is clear, for instance, that the strong position of crafts in Denmark is partly explicable in terms of her industries' domestic orientation and partial protection from foreign competition. Denmark's productivity development was thus less striking than the other countries, where income growth from export enterprises was in the lead.

In Finland, the home market industry showed less power of resistance against imports than it did in the other three countries. During the upward swings in the trade cycle Finland profited by income rises, using them to some extent for increased consumption. But the consumer goods industry could not always meet this demand and imports rose sharply, leading—before the cycle reached its peak—to stagnation in the consumer goods industry. Productivity development within that industry did not keep pace with developments as a whole, and even if, thanks to a large labour reserve, wages could be kept down, this proved insufficient to keep the industry competitive. Unlike Sweden's, the Finnish export industry was an 'enclave' within the economy, with less influence on the country's development as a whole. This was partly due to Finland's low economic level, and is partly explicable in terms of the large labour reserve set up by Finnish agriculture's low productivity and ensuing concealed unemployment. Another part of the explanation lies in the fact that competition between exports and consumer goods led to disparate wage developments in those two sectors, and that agricultural exports were not large enough for agriculture's income growth to lead to the consumer goods industry exerting a stabilising effect on the trade cycle. In Denmark, Norway and Sweden, the consumer goods industry generally expanded more slowly than the export sector during the upward swing of the trade cycle; but on the other hand, since competition between the sectors forced the consumer goods industry to improve its own productivity and import-competitiveness, its power of resistance against depressive tendencies was more definite than that of the export sector.

Price developments on the world market and the export firms' productivity development led to income rises, which were distributed between wages and profits. Before 1914, however, the firms had the upper hand when it came to deciding how wages and profits should be distributed, and a larger share of income rises went to the firms, leading to ploughing back of profits and capital accumulation.

During the 1880s this capital accumulation led to only minor technical changes, which meant that the labour force was favoured when it came to distributing income, since the substitution elasticities as between labour, technique and capital were lower than one (Jungenfelt, 1966, p. 203). During the 1890s, with their swift technical changes, there was a change to capital's advantage. Capital which represented the best-used techniques could obtain a 'differential rent' in relation to poorer techniques, and as more and more workers were being employed in the industrial sectors—which used modern techniques—this led to a fall in the labour share in both industry and agriculture, and, to a lesser extent, in the transport sector. At the same time the price level was on the rise, and expanding demand was increasing the firms' ability to take measures to limit competition. In Sweden, for instance, during the 1890s, a number of cartel and price agreements were made within the home market industry. This enabled a number of firms with relatively inefficient production methods to operate without incurring a loss.

The innovations made in the export sector increased both the workers' marginal productivity and the demand for labour. This led to increased incomes for employees, and so in turn to an increased demand for goods and services, i.e., it increased the national income.

There is a close connection between productivity development and the pressure of society's demand for goods. If demand is low, this can lead to a delay in improving productivity. Since large parts of the Scandinavian countries' industry were exposed to competition—either in the export market or via imports—productivity development within these industrial sectors was stronger than in the protected portions of the economy; and since wage impulses passed from those parts which were exposed to competition to the more protected, and from industry to other sectors, the rather strong pressure of demand in the Scandinavian countries became in fact the cause of a swift rise in productivity, above all in the 1870s and 1890s: that is, the profit level was sustained not only by volume increase but also thanks to technical progress.

Of the Scandinavian countries, Denmark, to judge from that share of her GDP, was the most dependent upon her foreign trade. (For Finland we have no GDP calculations, but it is probable that the Finnish ratio was lower.) Denmark's export sector rose from something above 20%, during the 1870s, to 28% in the first decade of the twentieth century. In Sweden and Norway, too, the sector grew. In Sweden, its growth came to a halt, and at the beginning of the present century had turned into a decline, at the same time as imports increased their share, one reason being increased imports of fuel and raw materials. The very large discrepancy, in Norway, between the share taken by exports of merchandise and imports can be explained in terms of that country's large export services sector. Without income from shipping the Norwegian economy's expansion would have been severely hampered.

TABLE 32: Development of exports, 1870-1909 (mill. kr.)

	Denmark	Finland	Norway goods	goods & services	Sweden
1870/79	149*	60	102	202	181
1880/89	157	68	114	217	251
1890/99	202	99	130	258	329
1900/09	369	167	205	354	443

*1874/79

Sources: Denmark: Bjerke-Ussing, 1958, p. 154
Finland: Statistisk Årsbok för Finland, 1920, Table 103.
Marks calculated in kroner with the aid of exchange
rate in Björkqvist, 1953, Table 3
Norway: Statistiske Oversikter, 1948, Table 109
Sweden: Fridlizius, 1963, Appendix A

TABLE 33:   Changes in export volume, 1865-1910 (mill. kr.) and index
1910=100

	Denmark 1912/13 prices	index	Norway 1910 prices	index	Sweden 1913 prices	index
1865			133	28	139	22
1870			157	33	200	31
1875	157	30	175	37	199	31
1880	219	42	210	45	278	44
1885	182	35	216	46	326	51
1890	204	39	274	58	374	58
1895	329	62	268	57	438	69
1900	353	67	297	63	470	74
1905	465	88	371	79	557	87
1910	527	100	470	100	637	100

Sources: Denmark: Henriksen-Ølgaard, 1960, p. 40, divided by export
price index in Ølgaard, 1966, p. 242
Norway: Bjerke, 1966, p. 130
Sweden: Fridlizius, 1963, Appendix A

TABLE 34: Commodity terms of trade in 1865-1910 (1880/84=100)

	Denmark	Norway	Sweden
1865		66	61
1870		76	85
1875	92	85	113
1880	96	87	103
1885	101	103	106
1890	93	97	97
1895	103	115	104
1900	100	115	110
1905	115		110
1910	119	127	122

Sources: Denmark: Ølgaard, 1966, p. 242
　　　　　Norway:　Bjerke, 1966, p. 142 et seq.
　　　　　Sweden:　Fridlizius, 1963, Appendix A

During the period 1870-1910, in all four countries, export volume was tripled, with a stagnation in Denmark's development during the 1880s and a poor increase in Norway during the 1890s. Except for the above-mentioned acceleration periods, the growth in Swedish export volume during the period was relatively even. But there was also an acceleration in Denmark in the 1890s, and in Norway during the first decade of the twentieth century. In all the countries there was a considerable improvement in commodity terms of trade, which to some extent explains the differences in volume and current prices. Export development for timber products clearly shows the change which occurred in Norway's and Sweden's industrial structures at the beginning of the twentieth century, when competition from Finland and Russia increased. The latter countries had large unexploited reserves of forests while in Norway stagnation was reached as early as the 1870s, and in Sweden during the 1890s.

TABLE 35: Exports of timber products 1870-1910 (1000 stds.)

	Finland	Norway	Sweden	Russia
1870	85	447	435	(30)
1890	230	397	875	330
1910	585	267	930	1300

Sources: Norway:　Statistiske Oversikter, 1948, Table 121, 122. One
standard has been calculated at 4·7 cu. m.
Others:　Jörberg, 1961, p. 82

TABLE 36: Export of paper pulp 1880-1910 (1000 tons dry weight)

	FINLAND		NORWAY		SWEDEN	
	mech-anical pulp	chem-ical pulp	mech-anical pulp	chem-ical pulp	mech-anical pulp	chem-ical pulp
1880	6		13		10	
1890	13	—	91	21	38*	35*
1900	20	5	154	84	67	138
1910	38	50	242	165	141	510

Where mechanical pulp has been given in wet weight this weight
has been reduced by half to obtain dry weight. See Statistisk översikt,
1919, p. 209.　　　*1892

Sources: Finland:　Halme, 1955, pp. 93, 111, 128 et seq.
Norway:　Statistiske Oversikter, 1948, Table 121, 122
Sweden:　Den svenska cellulosaindustrins nationalekonomiska
betydelse, 1918, p. 77

Norway and Sweden compensated for this stagnation by a
progressive changeover to paper pulp production. The
transformation was completest in Sweden, inasmuch as the
Swedish pulp industry now began to concentrate on chemical pulp, which both needed more capital and also could
command a considerably higher price on the world market,
as it could be used for book printing or where high quality
was needed, whereas mechanical pulp was used for news-
papers, wrapping, etc.

The great demand for pulp led to a rise in Swedish ex-

Diagram 2.

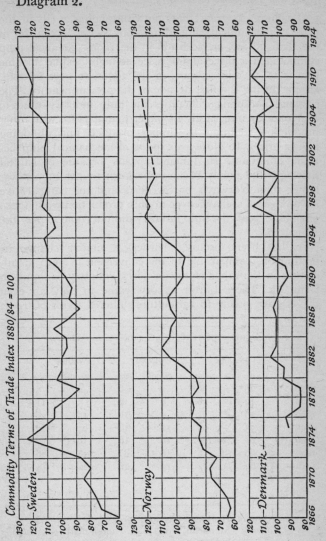

Source: see Table 34

port volume so great that, notwithstanding a fall in the price of mechanical pulp from about Sw. cr. 400 a ton in the 1870s to Sw. cr. 50 a ton in the 1890s (chemical pulp commanded a price about twice as high), export income rose from $1\frac{1}{2}$ mill. kronor, in the 1870s, to over 60 mill. kronor during the first decade of the present century. The ensuing marketing difficulties the pulp industry tried to overcome by integrating its paper manufacture with other production, refining its timber products and obtaining higher prices. In Norway, exports of mechanical pulp became dominant. In Finland, partly because of capital shortage, and partly because the sawn timber supply was larger than Norway's or Sweden's and the comparative advantages of a changeover to pulp production were not so obviously great, the pulp industry did not come to play the same role.

As has been discussed earlier, a similar change in production, comparable to the conversion to pulp manufacture in the other countries' forest industry, is found in Denmark. There butter exports came to play an even bigger part, owing to agriculture's altered terms of trade.

TABLE 37: Butter exports 1870-1910 (1000 tons, mill. kr.)

	DENMARK		FINLAND		SWEDEN	
	quantity	value	quantity	value	quantity	value
1870	15*	36*	4	6	2	5
1880	12	26	6	8	5	11
1890	43	74	7	10	15	26
1895	53	93	12	18	24	43
1900	61	120	10	16	19	37
1905	80	156	16	27	18	36
1910	89	182	12	21	22	44

*1874

Sources: Denmark: Henriksen-Ølgaard, 1960, p. 58
Finland: Mannelin, 1912, p. 31. Finnish marks calculated in kronor at current exchange rates
Sweden: Statistisk Översikt, 1919, p. 105 et seq.

Grain prices dropped, while meat and dairy produce prices kept up and butter prices from the mid-1880s to the end of the period, were on the rise. During the years immediately after the turn of the century they amounted to almost half total exports (Henriksen-Ølgaard, 1960, p. 47). This conversion led to considerable income rises for Danish agriculture.

In Finland and Sweden, too, butter exports rose. But in terms of income this rise in exports was of minor significance, above all in Finland, since the Finns could only obtain prices a good deal lower than those obtained by Danish farmers, the Finnish butter being of poorer and also uneven quality.

The Danish co-operative dairies, which had grown up in the 1880s, were able to standardise their products. This was not the case in Finland, where such co-operatives did not become important until well into the twentieth century.

However, there were large Finnish exports of butter to Denmark, which on the one hand utilised it for internal consumption and on the other repacked and re-exported it to Britain. (But the greater part of Finland's butter went to Russia.) With the growth of the margarine industry in Denmark during the 1890s, these Finnish butter exports to Denmark fell off. As the Finnish dairy industry began to expand, Finland was able to export direct to the British market, with considerable profit to Finnish agriculture as a consequence.

If the growth in export volume is compared with the rate of growth in Gross Domestic Capital Formation, obvious discrepancies appear. In Denmark the GDCF rose as much as export volume, or by about three times during the years 1870-1910. In Norway and Sweden, on the other hand, the GDCF rose by four times its initial size, compared with three times for export volume. Export volume grew relatively evenly, while the GDCF growth was concentrated on two striking periods—chiefly the first half of the 1870s and the latter half of the 1890s—with only slow growth or stagnation in between. Here Denmark is an exception. She shows a major rise in GDCF during the period 1878-1882. The reason for this would seem to be the transformation of Danish agriculture, which occurred rapidly at that time. From the 1890s on, the GDCF development, as between Denmark and Sweden, is unusually congruent. Investments in Norway remained at a much lower level, only accelerating after 1905. The effect of the great investments then being made in the hydro-electric industry on exports did not make itself felt to any great extent before 1914. The connection between changes in export volume and the investment rate is thus not unambiguous. In Sweden, agricultural exports constituted a contra-cyclical element from the 1870s

TABLE 38: Gross domestic capital formation 1870-1913. Fixed prices, 1900=100

	Denmark	Norway	Sweden
1870	34	40	36
1880	37	57	50
1890	49	74	63
1900	100	100	100
1913	113	171	153

Sources: Denmark: Bjerke-Ussing, 1958, p. 150
Norway: Bjerke, 1966, pp. 130, 150
Sweden: Johansson, 1967, p. 136 f.

TABLE 39: Gross domestic capital formation as a percentage of GDP

	Denmark	Norway	Sweden
1866/70		12·7	11·0
1871/75	12·2	14·7	14·2
1876/80	10·3	15·0	13·2
1881/85	12·1	14·9	11·7
1886/90	7·8	15·0	9·9
1891/95	8·4	16·2	10·1
1896/1900	13·8	18·0	12·7
1901/05	14·5	16·2	13·0
1906/10	11·5	17·6	12·0

Sources: Calculated from the same sources as Table 38

to the 1890s, after which total exports and exports of industrial goods came to be ever more strongly synchronised.

Naturally, variations in exports affected the trade cycle in the Scandinavian countries and partly explain the differences in GDCF already noted. Improved export prospects led to greater willingness to buy, not only within the immediately affected branches of the economy, but even in other sectors. Price rises were interpreted as heralding improvements in the business cycle. The very size of the fluctuations in exports suggests how important their influence must have been on incomes, employment and industrial activity. The purchase of new machinery and means of transport, like the extension of factories and other plant, were all equally dependent upon changes in export volume. As soon as the plants' capacity reached its limit, they were extended. On the other hand, at times when export volume ceased expanding, this could lead to a decline in the production capacity increases of the plants, and a slowing up of the rate of growth, likewise, causing a fall in the investment rate. Price prospects were also important. In the 1880s prices fell, and people expected them to go on doing so. This led to postponed investments. The need for investments accumulated, and the price rise and export volume increase of the 1890s led to an even greater rise in investments.

But profits, production volume and prices are all intimately connected in their effects, and for this reason it is hard, not to say impossible, to assess their influence on the fluctuations in investment activities; but because many branches of industry in the Scandinavian countries had a high export quota, it is evident that the connection between exports and investment was a close one.

Against this predominantly common background it will now be easier to distinguish those differences which marked industrial developments as between one Scandinavian country and another.

Finland's situation was the most peculiar. She was politically attached to, and also economically dependent upon, Russia, e.g., for her exports of textiles, iron and paper. Since, from 1859 to 1885, trade barriers were almost abolished between the two countries, some sections of Finnish production were orientated towards Russia, and this, as has been said, gave rise to a specialised type of Finnish industry, exporting low-grade goods, while the country's own needs were partly met by imports. The slow growth of the Russian market prior to 1890, however, was an obstacle to any swift expansion of Finnish industry. To some extent this had the effect of delaying conversion to a more modern type of production, such as had to be carried out if Finnish industry was to compete in the world market. Finland's iron industry found this conversion too much for it, as Norway's had earlier. Her textile industry, on the other hand, became concentrated on the home market and by import substitution to a great extent conquered it. One reason for this was that there were only a few textile firms, and these were relatively large and technically rather advanced. Industry was financed without the help of a developed banking system; fluctuations in the Finnish currency, before the introduction of the gold standard in 1878, also added to the difficulties of export firms, as did the need to give relatively long-term credit on exports to Russia, thus employing capital which could otherwise have been invested. All this meant that the structure of Finnish industry only changed very slowly.

The predominant Danish emphasis on agricultural exports, of fluctuating content, contributed to make Denmark's industrial development somewhat different in character from that of the other Scandinavian countries. Her foodstuffs industry, employing more than a fifth of the labour force, was in a considerably stronger position. In the same way the stone and quarry industry came to enjoy a prominent position thanks to such domestic raw materials as lime, which led to the establishment of a cement industry. A third important branch was engineering, which supplied Danish agriculture with its machines.

Seen exclusively in terms of the relation between the number of its employees and the total industrial labour force, the engineering industry in all four Scandinavian countries wore a very similar aspect. In Sweden, however, from the 1890s on, the branch was more export-orientated, and its production methods were also more advanced, than those of any other Scandinavian country. Its firms, only very slightly specialised, supplied the domestic market with rather unsophisticated products, while the more technically advanced were imported from abroad. The expansion in the Norwegian hydro-electric industry could not be exploited by Norwegian engineering around the turn of the century, and most of the electrical equipment had to be imported, for instance from Sweden. Sweden was the only Scandinavian country where there were important enterprises making innovations in engineering, the only exception being the manufacture of ship's engines in Denmark.

The reasons for this were that the market which in each of the countries might have provided an outlet was too small to make it worth any firm's while to introduce thorough-going innovations. Not until the 1890s was the Swedish market big enough for her engineering industry to be able to market its special products. In spite of this, many firms were working at a low level of profitability, and the risk of faulty investment was obvious. The problem of such an unbalanced development could have been solved by concentrating on exporting a firm's own innovations, or by setting up subsidiaries to use such machines in their production. In the initial stage, firms often ran into difficulties for lack of certain combinations of development and technical progress, necessary before expansion could really get started. Things could develop slowly as long as one link of a technical nature was lacking; but as soon as the development block was complete, cumulative expansion followed. These preconditions were fulfilled earlier in Sweden than in the other Scandinavian countries, with the result that Sweden's engineering industry expanded swiftly during the 1890s. This cumulative process also partly explains the differences between GDCF and export volume.

Another prerequisite for the establishment and growth of innovating firms was the availability of capital willing to take a risk. In Norway, there were large capital imports and

TABLE 40: Industrial structure, 1900. Percentual distribution of the labour force between sectors

	Denmark*	Finland	Norway	Sweden
Foodstuffs	22·5	11·8	12·5	10·1[5]
Textiles, clothing	18·5[1]	12·2[3]	13·2	12·7
Timber	—	27·1	21·3	18·9
Pulp & paper	2·7	7·4	8·6	5·2
Printing	4·9	2·6	2·9	2·3
Chemicals	6·0	2·4	2·2	6·1
Stone, clay, glass etc.	15·1	8·0	8·2	12·4
Leather, shoes & rubber	1·2	3·7	3·2	2·6
Metals & engineering	23·0	19·1[4]	21·2	24·6
Mines	—	—	3·7	3·9
Others	6·1[2]	5·6	3·0	1·2

| Total no. of workers | 73 200 | 95 100 | 79 300 | 293 500 |

*1897.

1. Including the shoe industry. 2. Including construction and timber industry. 3. Excluding the clothing industry. 4. Including the mining industry. 5. Excluding dairies.

By re-grouping the countries' industrial statistics the series have been made as homogeneous as possible. For Finland, Norway and Sweden, agreement, though not complete, is good. The Danish statistics are designed in such a way as to make any comparison with the other countries difficult. Thus e.g. parts of the construction industry, excluded from the other countries' statistics, are included. If comparison is to be exact, the percentages for 'other sectors' in the Danish statistics should be reduced, and the other sectors increased correspondingly.

Sources: Denmark: Willerslev, 1954, p. 255
    Finland: Översikt, 1904, p. 135
    Norway: Statistiske Oversikter, 1948, Table 89 and 92
    Sweden: Jörberg, 1961, appendix II

her hydro-electric industry was largely financed by foreign capital. In Denmark, where banking was most developed, the banks throughout this period took an active part in founding firms, but their chief interest, even so, lay in creating profitable mergers of existing enterprises. In Sweden, too, the banks were active, but not until the 1890s had they achieved such status that they could support such re-structuring as was necessary in face of competition on the world market. In Finland, on the other hand, shortage of capital was one of the reasons why the structure only changed slowly in the course of industrialisation. The timber products industry continued to dominate employ-ment and exports, and there was no significant import of capital. Yet another reason why the Finnish timber in-dustry was so dominant may have been that, through the 1890s, this branch's productivity went on rising. Timber product prices were on the rise, but prices for pulp and paper were falling. Since both branches were competitors for common production factors, at the same time as the productivity of the Swedish timber products industry was stagnant, this led to similar factorial terms of trade. Such competition between branches was smaller in Finland, her forests were not so fully exploited, nor her technique during the period of establishment up to the 1890s so advanced, with the consequence that productivity could be improved on the basis of relatively insignificant investment. A con-version to pulp production called for greater quantities of capital.

The development of each branch of industry is marked of course by factors which seem peculiar to the individual countries, e.g., natural resources, inventions and produc-tion methods; also, of course, by the initiative of its in-dustrialists. But it is somewhat surprising that around the turn of the century the Scandinavian countries should have shown a rather similar branch structure.

However, all countries undergoing economic develop-ment use their growing incomes in very much the same way. Expenditure on foodstuffs, clothing and housing grows more slowly than expenditure on other sorts of consumption, and in countries that are on approximately the same in-come level consumption is similarly composed.

Of course, the branch structure of industry does not directly reflect the direction of a country's consumption, inasmuch as many branches produce half-finished or capital goods, and growing mechanisation leads to increased consumption of machinery and power.

The development which the Scandinavian countries have passed through can be seen from their branch structures. With the exception of Denmark, whose development was influenced by her exceptional export structure, the other Scandinavian countries' industrial structures will be seen to be quite similar. Foodstuffs and textiles employed about the same number of workers, relatively speaking, in all three countries; and for other branches, too, the differences are relatively insignificant. Where differences do appear is in the size of the timber, pulp and paper industries, where Finland had more than one third of her labour force, while Sweden had scarcely a quarter. In return, the engineering industry plays a less prominent part in Finland; which shows that the more developed a country's industry, the smaller will be the influence of natural resources on industrial structure. Thus the distribution of raw materials has been of greater importance to the structure of international trade than to these countries' branch structure. A growing segment of commerce consists of exchanges of machines or consumer goods. Nevertheless, the structure in the Scandinavian countries reveals that, when the advantages of production on a raw material base are as great as they are in the forestry industry, branch specialisation assumes obvious importance.

In all the countries the engineering and chemical industries have assumed ever greater importance, while expansion in other branches has been slower, with constant or falling shares of total industrial production as a result.

Another interesting aspect of these countries' development, which does not directly concern industrial structure as such, though it influenced their industrial expansion, was the part played by capital formation. In general, the Scandinavian countries had a deficit in their balance of payments, which for Norway was very large and, where Denmark and Sweden were concerned, considerably so: for Denmark from the 1880s on, and for Sweden throughout the whole period. This must mean that a substantial share of capital formation was provided by foreigners, and that investment capacity grew at the same time as balance of payments problems eased. If the Scandinavian countries had followed the rule of the gold standard, they should have followed a deflationary policy and exported gold. Instead, untroubled by their balance of payments problems, and relying on the extensive capital movements which were characteristic of the pre-1914 period, they followed expansionist policies.

It is a well-known fact that economic development cannot be explained in terms of one simple cause. It is also well-known that, in the social sciences, it is hard to arrive at causal explanations, because the variables which they study are interrelated, and changes lead to complicated reactions. The explanations which have been presented here have been those which can be based on quantifiable factors. This does not mean that other, less quantifiable ones did not also play their part. As yet, however, we have no tools to carry out a more rigorous analysis of the role, certainly a most stimulating one, played by the initiative of these countries' industrialists, by the literacy of their populations, or by education in general—to mention just a few problems often discussed nowadays. It would be going too far to assert that people react mechanically to economic change. What can be asserted, however, is that those changes in economic structure which can be observed do reveal the importance of such variables.

One more thing, too, seems clear. During the latter half of the nineteenth century and up to the First World War, economic variables, however dependent upon factors beyond their control, combined in a way fortunate for the countries of Scandinavia. To put it simply, one could say that it is easy for small countries to make progress, if everyone else is making it. The crucial thing, however, is not merely to be a small country; but to be a small country with a large foreign trade, at a time when world commerce is functioning in the special way it did during the nineteenth century and up to the First World War.

BIBLIOGRAPHY

The following bibliography does not pretend to list all relevant literature on the economic development of the Nordic countries. On the other hand, the most important works are listed, a task which is fairly easy, since the books are rather few in number.

General works on the economic history of the Nordic countries are very few and mostly rather out of date. The Danish and Norwegian economic history are treated in books written in German by Bosse, Johnson and Nielsen; for Sweden the only general work is by Heckscher.

Industrial development in Denmark is treated by Willerslev; in Finland by Alho; in Norway by Holst et. al. and in Sweden by Montgomery and Jörberg.

Most works on economic history in the Nordic countries are descriptive and lack any analytical approach, one reason being that most economic historians have come to economic history from political history. The best works on Nordic economic history are written by economists, but they normally only treat the period after 1914.

Adamson, O. J. (ed.), 1952. *Industries of Norway*. Oslo.

Alho, K. O., 1949. *Suomen uudenaikaisen teollisuuden synty ja kehitys 1860-1914*. Helsinki.

Backer, J. E., 1965. *Ekteskap, fødsler og vandringer i Norge 1856-1960*. Samfunnsøkonomiske studier, 13. Oslo.

Bagge, G., Lundberg, E., Svennilsson, I., 1935. *Wages of Sweden 1860-1930*. Stockholm.

Betaenkning om mellemrigslovens indflydelse paa og betydning for Norges naeringsliv, 1895. Kristiania.

Bjerke, J., 1966., *Langtidslinjer i norsk økonomi 1865-1960* (Trends in Norwegian Economy 1865-1960.) Samfunnsøkonomiske studier, 16. Oslo.

Bjerke, K., Ussing, N., 1958. *Studier over Danmarks national-produkt 1870-1950*. Copenhagen.

Bjørkvik, H., 1956. 'The farm territories', *The Scandinavian Economic History Review*, vol. IV, no. 1.

Björkqvist, H., 1953. *Guldmyntfotens införande i Finland åren 1877-1878.* Helsingfors.

1958. *Prisrörelser och penningvarde i Finland under guldmyntfotperioden 1878-1913.* Helsingfors.

Bonsdorf, L. G., von, 1956. *Linne och Jern,* vol. I, Textiloch metallindustrierna i Finland intill 1880-talet. Helsingfors.

Boserup, E., 1965. *The Condition of Agricultural Growth.* London.

Bosse, E., 1916. *Norwegens Volkswirtschaft vom Ausgang der Hansaperiode bis zur Gegenwart.* Probleme der Weltwirtschaft, 22. Jena.

Broch, O. J., 1871. *Statistisk Årbog for Kongeriget Norge 1867-1871.* Kristiania.

Cohn, E., 1953. Håndvaerk og industri vid midten af det 19. Årh. *Nationaløkonomisk Tidskrift,* 91. Copenhagen.

1957. *Privåtbanken i Kjøbenhavn gennem hundrede aar.* Copenhagen.

1967. *Økonomi og politik i Danmark 1849-1875.* Copenhagen.

Den svenska cellulosaindustrins utveckling och national-ekonomiska betydelse 1918. Stockholm.

Derry, T. K., 1960. *A Short History of Norway.* London.

Fastbom, L., 1949. 'Några trendstudier kring Sveriges ekonomiska utveckling', *Meddeladnen från Konjunktur-institutet.* Series B, no. 10. Stockholm.

Finanskomiténs betänkande angående Sveriges ekonomiska och finansiella utveckling 1834-1860. 1863. Stockholm.

First International Conference of Economic History. Communication 1960. Paris—The Hague.

Fleetwood, E. E., 1947. *Sweden's Capital Imports and Exports.* Geneva.

Flinn, M., 1954. 'Scandinavian iron ore mining and the British steel industry', *The Scandinavian Economic History Review,* vol. II, no. 1.

Flodström, I., 1912. *Sveriges nationalförmögenhet omkring åren 1908 och dess utveckling sedan midten av 1880-talet.* Finansstatistiska utredningar utgivna av Kungl. Finans-departementet, vol. V. Stockholm.

Fridlizius, G., 1957. *Swedish Corn Export in the Free Trade Era.* Lund.

1963. 'Sweden's Exports 1850-1960', *Economy and History*, vol. IV.

Frimannslund, R., 1956. 'Farm community and neighbour-hood community', *The Scandinavian Economic History Review*, vol. IV, no. 1.

Fritz, M., 1967. *Svensk järnmalmsexport 1883-1913.* Götborg.

Gårdlund, T., 1942. *Industrialismens samhälle.* Stockholm.

Gasslander, O., 1955. *History of Stockholm's Enskilda Bank to 1914.* Stockholm.

Grotenfelt, G., 1896. *Lantbruket i Finland.* Helsingfors.

Gutman, G. O., 1957. 'A note on economic development with subsistence agriculture', *Oxford Economic Papers.* October 1957.

Haatanen, P., 1968. *Suomen amaalaisköyhälistö.* Helsinki.

Halme, V., 1955. *Vienti suomen suhdannetekijänä vousina 1870-1913.* Helsinki.

Hansen, K., 1932. *Det danske lantbrugs historie*, vol. III. Copenhagen.

Henriksen, I. B., Ølgaard, A., 1960. *Danmarks uden-rigshandel 1874-1958.* Studier fra Københavns Uni-versitets Økonomiske Institut, No. 2. Copenhagen.

Historisk Statistik för Sverige (Historical Statistics of Sweden), 1-111. 1955-1960. Stockholm.

Holmsen, A., 1956. 'The old Norwegian peasant com-munity', *The Scandinavian Economic History Review*, vol. IV, no. 1.

Holst, W., Strömme Svendsen, A., Wasberg, G., 1963. 'Industrins gjennombrudd', *Dette er Norge 1814-1964*, vol. II. Oslo.

Jensen, E., 1937. *Danish Agriculture: Its Economic Development.* Copenhagen.

Johansson, Ö., 1967. *The Gross Domestic Product of Sweden and its Composition 1861-1955.* Stockholm Economic Studies. New Series VIII. Stockholm.

Johnson, O., 1939. *Norwegische Wirtschaftsgeschichte.* Jena.

Jörberg, L., 1961. *Growth and Fluctuations of Swedish Industry 1869-1912.* Lund.

1965. 'Structural change and economic growth: Sweden in the 19th century', *Economy and History*, vol. VIII.

Juhlin-Dannfelt, H., 1925. *Lantbrukets historia*. Stockholm.

Jungenfelt, K. G., 1966. *Löneandelen och den ekonomiska utvecklingen*. Uppsala.

Jutikkala, E., 1963. *Bonden i Finland genom tiderna*. Helsingfors.

Korpelainen, L., 1957. 'Trends and cyclical movements in industrial employment in Finland 1885-1952', *The Scandinavian Economic History Review*, vol. V, no. 1.

Kuznets, S., 1960. *Six Lectures on Economic Growth*. New York.

1966. *Modern Economic Growth*. New Haven and London.

Lieberman, S., 1968. 'Norwegian Population Growth in the 19th century', *Economy and History*, vol. XI.

Lindahl, E., Dahlgren, E., Kock, K., 1937. *The National Income of Sweden 1861-1930*. Stockholm.

Lyle, A., 1939. *Die Industrialisierung Norwegens*. Probleme der Weltwirtschaft, 65. Jena.

Maddison, A., 1964. *Economic Growth in the West*. New York.

Mannelin, K., 1912. *Finlands smörexport*. Helsingfors.

Mathelin, T. G., 1927. 'Tullskydd och industriell utveckling i Finland sedan 1850-talet', *Ekonomiska Samfundets Tidskrift*, no. 10. Helsingfors.

Mellor, B. F., Johnston, J. W., 1961. 'The role of agriculture in economic development', *American Economic Review*, Sept. 1961.

Montgomery, A., 1939. *The Rise of Modern Industry in Sweden*. Stockholm.

Munch, P., 1942. 'Det danske folks livsvilkaar 1864-1914', *Schultz Danmarkshistorie*, vol. V. Copenhagen.

Nasjonalregnskap 1900-1929, 1953. Central Bureau of Statistics. Oslo.

Nielsen, A., 1933. *Dänische Wirtschaftsgeschichte*. Jena.

Nilsson, C. A., 1959. 'Business incorporation in Sweden 1849-1896', *Economy and History*, vol. II.

Ølgaard, A., 1966. *Growth, Productivity and Relative Prices*. Studier fra Københavns Universitets Økonomiske Institut, no 10. Copenhagen.

Olsen, E., 1962. *Danmarks økonomiske historie siden 1750.* Copenhagen.

Olsen, K. A., 1955. *Norsk Hydro.* Oslo.

Översikt av Finlands ekonomiska tillstånd. Bidrag till Finlands officiella statistik, II. Helsingfors 1879, 1884, 1890, 1894, 1899 and 1904.

Papanek, G. F., 1954. 'Development problems relevant to agriculture tax policy'. *Papers and Proceedings of the Conference on Agricultural Taxation and Economic Development.* Harvard Law School. Cambridge, Mass. (reprinted in Meier, G., *Leading Issues in Development Economics.* New York, 1964).

Pihkala, E., 1964. 'Finnish iron and the Russian market 1880-1914'. *The Scandinavian Economic History Review,* vol. XII, no. 2.

Rinne, H. A., 1952. *Trävaruproduktion och trävaruhandel i Björneborgs distrikt 1856-1900.* Vammala.

Rygg, N., 1954. *Norges banks historie,* vol. II. Oslo.

Samsøe, J., 1928. *Die Industrialisierung Dänemarks.* Probleme der Weltwirtschaft, 44. Jena.

Schybergson, P., 1964. *Aktiebolagsformens genombrott i Finland. Utvecklingen före 1895 års lag.* Bidrag till kännedomen av Finlands natur och folk. Utgiven av Finska Vetenskaps-societeten, no. 190. Helsingfors.

Semmingsen, I. G., 1940. *Norwegian Emigration to America during the 19th century.* Norwegian-American Studies and Records, vol. XI. Northfield, Minn.

1954. 'The dissolution of estate society in Norway', *The Scandinavian Economic History Review,* vol. I, no. 2.

Skrubbeltrang, F., Hansen, K., 1945. *Det danske lantbrugs historie.* Copenhagen.

Skrubbeltrang, F., 1953. 'Agricultural development and rural reform in Denmark', *Agricultural Studies,* no. 22 (FAO), Rome.

Smith, J., 1875. *Det norske lantbruks historie.* Kristiania.

Söderlund, E., 1951. *Svensk trävaruexport under hundra år.* (Swedish Timber Exports 1850-1950. Stockholm, 1952), Stockholm.

Statistisk Aarbog (Statistical Yearbook), Denmark.

Statistisk Årsbok (Statistical Yearbook), Finland.

Statistisk Aarbok (Statistical Yearbook), Norway.

Statistisk Årsbok (Statistical Yearbook), Sweden.

Statistiskkomiténs betänkande, vol. VI, Industristatistik. Helsingfors, 1907.

Statistisk översikt av det svenska näringslivets utveckling åren 1870-1915. Statistiska Meddelanden. Series A, vol. III, no. 1. Stockholm, 1919.

Statistiske Oversikter, 1948 (Statistical Survey). Central Bureau of Statistics. Oslo.

Stoltz, G., 1955. *Økonomisk utsyn 1900-1950*. (Economic Survey 1900-1950). Samfunnsøkonomiske studier, 3. Oslo.

Stonehill, A., 1965. *Foreign ownership in Norwegian enterprises*. Samfunnsøkonomiske studier, 14. Oslo.

Strömme-Svendsen, A., 1956. *Norsk industrihistorie*. Oslo.

Sundbärg, G., 1908. *Aperçus statistique internationaux*. Stockholm.

Svensk bergshantering år 1913. Specialundersökning av Kommerskollegium. Stockholm, 1917.

Thomsen, D. N., Oldham, J. W., Brinley Thomas, 1966. *Dansk-engelsk samhandel 1661-1963*, Erhvervshistorisk Arbog, 1965. Aarhus.

Tweite, S., 1959. *Jord of gjerning*. Kristiansand.

Warming, J., 1913. *Haandbog i Denmarks statistik*. Copenhagen.

Wedervang, F., 1964. *Development of a Population of Industrial Firms*. Bergen.

Viita, P., 1966. *Maataloustuotanto Suomessa 1800-1960*. Helsinki.

Willerslev, R., 1952. *Studier i dansk industrihistorie 1850-1880*. Copenhagen.

1954. 'Traek af den industrielle udvikling 1850-1914', *Nationaløkonomisk Tidskrift*, 92. Copenhagen.

Youngson, A., J. 1955. *Possibilities of Economic Progress*. Cambridge.

1967. *Overhead Capital*. Edinburgh.

8. The Industrialisation of Russia and the Soviet Union

Gregory Grossman

The present essay, unlike the others in this volume, does not end with the First World War. Instead, it covers a period of a little over a century for which the war is the approximate mid-point in time, and which encompasses both of Russia's great industrialisation spurts in recent history: the first, beginning in the 1860s (and especially in the mid-1880s), conducted within a capitalist framework and, at its height, under the active sponsorship of the Imperial government; the second, after 1928, under the direction of the Communist Party and within the framework of nearly complete state ownership of means of production and highly centralised planning and control. The Soviet industrialisation drive is still under way, of course.

To be sure, there are great differences between the two and it is not our intention to belittle them. But they also share important similarities and continuities, so that a simultaneous look at them may be rewarding. The Tsarist and the Soviet experiences are both outstanding examples of rapid industrialisation in a 'follower' country under conditions of great economic backwardness in relation to the aspirations of the political authorities, with active initiative and participation by the state, and with the aid of methods and institutions that would be regarded as extreme in a Western European setting. In both cases the extraordinarily swift growth of industry tended to be associated with great sluggishness — and even significant reverses — in other sectors, especially in agriculture and personal consumption; it also tended to outpace the modernisation of society, if one may be permitted the phrase.

While thus mirroring, often in a highly intensified form, some of the characteristic features of its Tsarist predecessor, the Soviet industrialisation experience could also from the start benefit from the impressive industrial achievements of the last decades of the Empire. Before the Revolution, the Bolsheviks — and especially Lenin himself [B]* — were second to none in appreciating the achievements of the capitalist boom in Russia, thereby drawing reassurance for their premise that the country was ripe for an anti-capitalist revolution given the proper political circumstances (which they found in 1917). On the other hand, when their own Five-Year Plans (FYPs) got going, for propaganda reasons they came to minimise the accomplishments of the pre-Soviet era so as to magnify their own successes. A similar bias appeared after the Second World War, when the Soviet régime and some of its foreign friends have tended to depict the USSR as an instance of successful industrialisation from a very low base and therefore a suitable model for underdeveloped countries of today. The fact is that poor and backward though it then was, Russia on the eve of the First FYP (in 1928) — or, for that matter, on the eve of the First World War — was by no means as retarded or as disadvantaged as the typical underdeveloped country in our day. Within its vast sea of poverty and backwardness there were important islands of economic strength and modernity which were later to provide invaluable *points d'appui* for the industrialisation drive after 1928, not to mention its rich natural endowment.

But to glance farther back into history: although a relative late-comer to the industrialisation scene among the major European powers, Russia had had a significant history of industrialisation for almost a couple of centuries before the spurt of the late nineteenth century. Under Peter the Great (1700–1725), a ruler of uncommon vision and inexhaustible energy, the country was forcibly modernised by means that are suggestive of methods employed over two hundred years later. Peter's chief concern — as Stalin's — was the enhancement of the internal and external power of the state, for which he required a modern economic base by the standards of the day. He initiated the establishment of many important industries, especially those neces-

---

* [B] — the works so designated are listed in the Bibliography at the end of this essay.

sary to equip his army and navy, brought in foreign specialists and know-how, and mobilised domestic resources to the utmost. The demand for the products of the new industries came chiefly from the state itself. He exploited every fiscal and financial resource to raise capital, had factories built directly by the state or offered various incentives to private interests to do so, drafted persons to found and to manage factories, and last but not least, established a form of industrial serfdom for labour. The pressure on Russian society was severe. A relapse followed Peter's death,[1] but nonetheless Russia remained the largest producer of iron in the world late into the eighteenth century, until overtaken by England going through her own industrial revolution.

In the course of most of the nineteenth century, until the last couple of decades, the Imperial government showed scant interest in industrialisation and did little directly to promote it. Still, the industrial revolution was beginning to penetrate Russia as well. Prior to 1861 — that is to say, prior to the Emancipation of the Serfs, the great turning point in Russian history of the nineteenth century — a few industries based on the new technology of the time began to appear and to spread. These were chiefly consumer goods industries — textiles, sugar — and they aimed at internal demand, enhanced as it was by the rapid growth of population. The industrial entrepreneurs of this period were notably foreigners, members of various religious minorities, and even many persons officially classified as peasants, often serfs.[2]

However, in one important respect the state acted early: it began building railroads in the middle of the century. The first major line, connecting Moscow and St Petersburg,

1. However, Professor Kahan has argued that there was more continuity in economic policy and activity between the Petrine period and the periods immediately preceding and following it than historians have generally assumed. (Arcadius Kahan, 'Continuity in Economic Activity and Policy during the Post-Petrine Period in Russia', *Journal of Economic History*, vol. XXV, No. 1, March 1965.)

2. For this period the reader is referred to William L. Blackwell, *The Beginnings of Russian Industrialisation, 1800–1860*, Princeton, 1968.

was completed in 1852. Yet by the 1860s railroad building passed mainly into private hands, though still heavily encouraged by the state. The length of track grew rapidly; from 1·6 thousand kilometres in 1860, to 10·7 in 1870 and to 22·9 in 1880. The importance of this effort can hardly be overestimated. It led the introduction of modern technical and organisational methods into the country, and paved the way for the rapid rise of international trade in the 1870s, based largely on the export of grain.

The record of economic growth between 1860 and 1913 has been re-examined and summarised by Professor Goldsmith and his associates [B]. The underlying data are skimpy, and alternative computations are attempted by the authors, but the overall picture appears to be quite clear. The rates of growth mentioned in this paragraph derive from their work. Between 1860 and 1913 the output of Russian industry (manufacturing and mining, factory and artisan production taken together) grew at an average annual rate of some 5%, a high rate for that era to be sustained for over half a century. But population growth was remarkably fast too — approximately 1·5% per year; accordingly, the *per capita* increase in industrial output averaged about 3·5% per year. Agricultural output increased at about 2% annually, or only one half of 1% per head. And because agriculture still had a predominant weight in overall output, the real national product (or national income) grew at an average annual rate of 2·5%, or only about 1% per head. The *per capita* increase of the national product is a good deal below the corresponding estimates (ranging between 2 and 3%) for Germany, United States, Canada, Sweden and Japan during the same historical period, owing in large measure — at least statistically — to the relatively fast growth of Russia's population.

However, the main industrialisation spurt in Tsarist Russia is often regarded as beginning in the mid-80s. True, the rate of industrial growth from the mid-80s to 1913 is not much higher than from 1860 to 1913, if at all. The exception is the decade of the nineties, during which the output of factory industry (including mining) grew at about 7·5%

per year (followed by stagnation in the first half of the 1900s and another spurt from 1906 on). But qualitatively the record changed after the mid-80s. The state was soon to begin playing an active and decisive role in industrialisation. Sectoral emphasis shifted in favour of the so-called heavy industries: coal-mining, petroleum extraction, mining of ferrous and non-ferrous ores, and the iron and steel industry. Much of the capital for these industries came from abroad in the form of direct investment. Similarly, rapid progress is shown by some other indicators. For instance, the literacy rate among military recruits rose from 22% in 1880 to 68% in 1913.[3]

As a result, Russia by 1913 (and the Soviet Union in 1928) disposed of the fifth largest industrial complex in the world — after the United States, Germany, Great Britain and France — although owing to the country's large population it ranked very much lower in terms of *per capita* production. Thus, industrial production per head was one-tenth or less of the American.[4] The country had attained a high rate of saving out of the national product.[5] It contained a small but significant and often high-calibre contingent of

3. A. G. Rashin, *Formirovanie rabochego klassa Rossii* (*Formation of the Working Class in Russia*), Moscow, 1958, p. 582. This, the best Soviet work on the subject, contains much quantitative data.

4. Professor Nutter [B, p. 329] has estimated the following ratios of industrial production in Russia (USSR) as % of that in the USA (the higher figure always referring to estimates at dollar prices, the lower — at ruble prices): total value added in industry, 1913 — 10·6–13·9, 1928 — 6·2–9·3; value added per person engaged, 1913 — 16·5–21·8, 1928 — 13·4–19·9; value added per head of population, 1913 — 7·4–9·8, 1928 — 5·0–7·4. For 1860–1900, Professor Bairoch places Russia at the bottom of his list of major European countries in terms of *per capita* industrial output, and near the bottom in terms of agricultural productivity (expressed as net production of vegetable-based calories per male worker in agriculture); see his essay in vol. 3 of this collection, Tables 2 and 3, p. 30. See also Prokopovich's classic calculations for *per capita* national income for several European countries in 1894 and 1913, as reproduced by Nove [B, p. 14], and Maddison's comparative data [B, pp. xvi, 31, and Appendix].

5. For 1928 the share of gross investment in gross national product, at 'factor cost', has been estimated at 20–25%; the lower figure is by Moorsteen and Powell [B, p. 364], the higher by Bergson [B, p. 282].

scientists, engineers, statisticians and other qualified specialists whose role in future Soviet industrialisation was to be crucial. The country was rapidly gaining in literacy. It had a large railroad net that could sustain much further industrial growth with only moderate additional investments in the transportation sector. And, last but not least, it had an enviable natural-resource base, either already known or to be discovered as industrialisation progressed. In sum, on the eve of the First World War (or of the Five-Year Plans), Russia had already had the benefit of several decades of rapid industrialisation and modernisation and possessed a potential for further swift growth that places it in a much more favourable circumstance than those under which most underdeveloped countries today, including Communist China, have to labour. At the same time, it was not closing the gap in industrial terms between itself and the leading powers of Western Europe and America. It was still a predominantly peasant country and a poor one.[6]

As noted, the beginning of the major industrialisation spurt in the eighties tended to coincide with a return of the state to a more active role in promoting economic development. Tariff protection led the way, beginning in 1877 and culminating in the highly protectionist tariff of 1891, the latter precipitating a serious tariff war with Germany. After 1880 the state became once again the main builder of railroads (while also purchasing some private lines). The chief undertaking in this regard was the impressive feat of construction of the Trans-Siberian Railroad during the nineties. The length of the rail net reached 50,000 kilometres by the beginning of 1900 and exceeded 70,000 when the war broke out.

The active role of the state in promoting industrialisation was particularly marked during the nineties under the leadership of a very dynamic Minister of Finance (1891–1900), S. Y. Witte.[7] Though subject to much domestic

6. For a succinct discussion of the economic condition of Russia in 1913 see Nove's economic history [B, Chapter 1].

7. The major study of Witte's ideas and policies is by Theodore H. von Laue [B].

criticism, Witte pursued a determined policy of employing the powers of the state to encourage private industry. In addition to the already mentioned policy of protectionism and the direct construction of railroads by the state, the Witte period saw a system of preferential treatment of domestic industry as a supplier of the state's needs (particularly for railroad construction and operation and for military needs) and a single-minded drive to place Russia on the gold standard in order to attract foreign capital. The gold standard was adopted in 1897. Although foreign capital had been entering Russian industry even before that, its inflow accelerated; it came to be particularly important in iron and steel, coal mining and petroleum extraction, to mention just some of the leading industries. Much foreign capital was also invested in railroad bonds, and after the turn of the century also in the big banks which, somewhat patterned on the German system, came to play a growing role in the promotion and control of industry. With foreign capital often came foreign know-how, capital goods, management and markets abroad.[8]

Of major importance to the development of the Russian economy in the nineteenth century was the great expansion of population. In the hundred years preceding the First World War the population of the Empire grew almost four-fold, or at an average rate of about 1·4% per year, and from 1860 on even somewhat faster — 1·5% per year. The absolute figures are 74 million in 1860 and 164 million in

8. By 1914 direct and indirect foreign investment in the Russian economy reached 2·3 thousand million rubles, of which 1·2 was in mining and metallurgy; among creditor countries, France led with 33% of the total, Great Britain — 23%, and Belgium — 20%. If foreign holdings of state and state-guaranteed bonds are added, the gross foreign debt of Russia amounted to some 8·5 thousand million rubles by the beginning of 1914; and, after deduction of Russian investments abroad, the net foreign debt still amounted to some 7·5 thousand million rubles. (At par, the ruble was then worth $0.51.) These figures are taken from John P. Sontag, 'Tsarist Debts and Tsarist Foreign Policy', *Slavic Review*, vol. XXVII, No. 4, December 1968, pp. 531–533, and rest mainly on estimates by P. V. Ol' and A. L. Vainshtein. Sontag's article conveniently summarises prior research on this subject and cites the relevant literature.

1913.[9] This growth was almost entirely rural; even on the eve of the war, after three (if not five) decades of swift industrialisation, the urban population still accounted for less than one-fifth of the total, and workers in mining and manufacturing (excluding the artisan sector), less than 2%. Some 80% of the population still derived its livelihood from agriculture, while a good part of the remainder continued to have close personal ties with the village. In this respect the pre-revolutionary period contrasts with the first five decades of the Soviet era when total population grew only half as fast (for reasons to be taken up later) — three-quarters of 1% per year in *comparable* territory — but the urban population rose to 55% of the total. However, in one sense the contrast turns into a parallel. The great growth in population numbers before the First World War, and especially the heavy pressure of the rural population on the supply of arable land, was doubtless a major factor in keeping peasant incomes, real wages and therefore also consumption per head very low. In other words, population pressure before the war helped accomplish what deliberate policy achieved under Stalin: it was one of the factors in a complex process that depressed consumption, thereby releasing resources for investment in industry and related sectors. Of course, under such conditions it is crucial that industrialisation should not depend primarily on internal consumer demand. This indeed was the case both during the last decades of the Empire and in the USSR.

One cannot understand this complex process without at least a quick look at what was the key question of pre-revolutionary Russia — as of any peasant society, including for a long time the Soviet Union — namely, the agrarian question. Because in such a society agriculture is the major source of material (surplus food and fibres) and human resources for industrialisation, its socio-economic structure, its level of productivity, its potential for generating savings and the disposition of such savings, and, lastly, the relationship of the peasantry to the social order in a most funda-

9. Cf. Nutter [B, p. 519].

mental sense[10] — these and similar considerations help
determine the rate and course of the industrialisation process. All of these factors were, of course, profoundly affected
by the Emancipation of 1861. However, it was not the aim
of the Great Reform, as the event is known in Russian
historiography, to lay down an institutional framework for
industrialisation. If it did so at all, it did so at best only half-
heartedly and indirectly. Rather, its purpose was political
and primarily preventive: to liberate the serfs 'from above'
before they did so themselves 'from below' with much more
serious consequences for the established order.[11]

A basic premise of the Great Reform was that the land
belonged to the gentry (and other pre-Reform estate
holders), and the very intricate operation whereby a part
of the land was transferred into peasant ownership was
designed accordingly. The Reform did not give the land to
the peasants outright; instead, they had to pay for it in
fifty equal annual instalments known as 'redemption payments'. On the other hand, the gentry was given a one-time
compensation for the land it lost in the form of state bonds.
The value of the transferred land was set quite high in
relation to the market on the eve of the Reform, thereby
favouring the gentry at the expense of the peasantry. It is
true that land prices did rise steadily following the Reform,
doubling between the 1870s and the 1890s, so that with time
the redemption payments came to bear a more reasonable
relation to land values. But this was at a time when the
peasants were the chief buyers and renters of gentry land,
owing to the pressure of the growing rural population in
the densely populated regions, and when grain prices were
steadily declining. In other words, the rise in land values,
only partly accounted for by slowly rising yields, was not so
much a windfall to the peasantry as a reflection of its
desperate economic condition and a heavy burden on it.

10. For a succinct formulation of the alternative views on integrating
the peasantry into Russian society, see Professor N. V. Riasanovsky's
concluding essay in Wayne S. Vucinich, ed., *The Peasant in Nineteenth-
Century Russia*, Stanford, 1968.

11. Cf. Terence Emmons on 'The Peasant and the Emancipation' in
Vucinich, *op. cit.*

Another basic principle of the Reform was that wherever the traditional village commune existed, which is to say in the case of most of the peasants affected by the Reform, the land was transferred into the collective ownership of the commune (*mir*) and not into individual peasant ownership. At the same time the commune was made collectively responsible for the redemption payments as well as for taxes. By endowing the village commune with these rights and obligations, and by insisting on the principle of 'mutual responsibility' among its members, the Imperial government sought to bolster social stability in the rural areas (always a major problem in Russia) and at the same time to establish institutional machinery for more effective collection of fiscal dues. Naturally, social stability and fiscal efficiency are not the same thing as economic progress. Further, the Russian village commune was typically a *repartitional* one; i.e. it periodically redistributed its arable land among its households, or at least could do so at some future date. The motive for this was egalitarian, and actual land redistributions had traditionally referred to some measure of the household's need for food. But the economic implications were often negative in that they robbed the individual peasant of incentive to improve his holding or to add to it. This fact, in conjunction with the generally very low technical level in agriculture (e.g. the three-field system) tended to keep productivity very low. Lastly, the institutions of the commune tended to tie the peasant to the village by means of a double bond. On one hand, the individual was reluctant to sever his ties with the village lest he lose his right hand in a future distribution. On the other hand, the commune was reluctant to let him leave (which it could administratively prevent him from doing) lest it lost one who shared in upholding its financial burdens. As a result, the supply of rural labour to industry and related pursuits tended to be held back by the existence of the *mir*. Those who moved to town often left their families behind, and not infrequently (as late as the eve of the war) would return to the village for agricultural work in busy seasons. All this naturally affected the quality of the labour force in industry and its working-class consciousness.[12]

The story of the Great Reform and the relation between the peasantry and the Russian state during the ensuing half-century is too long and intricate to be pursued further here; for full accounts the reader is directed to other sources.[13] But we cannot fail to mention here the beginnings of a new agrarian order towards the end of that half-century. Until that time the government continued to uphold the importance of the *mir*, as implemented by the Reform, for reasons just stated. But eventually it became evident to the more perspicacious observers that it was the *mir* itself, owing to its deleterious economic effects, that was helping to undermine the very social and political stability which it was intended to bolster. This lesson was forcefully driven home by the widespread peasant disturbances at the time of the Revolution of 1905. When in the wake of that revolution P. A. Stolypin, a man of considerable astuteness and boldness, was appointed to the premiership, the result was a series of legislative acts extending from 1906 to 1911 and jointly known as the Stolypin Reforms. These measures reversed the government's emphasis on the village commune and created a relatively accessible procedure for the individual peasant's separation from the commune and for the consolidations of his often very fragmented land holdings. The purpose was not primarily economic; rather, the aim was to create a class of relatively prosperous peasants and so to shore up the social and political edifice. But the long-run economic effects might have been profound and far-reaching in raising agricultural productivity, increasing internal demand for consumer and producer goods, and augmenting the supply of labour for industry. In the event, the First World War and the Bolshevik Revolution pre-

12. Cf. Reginald E. Zelnik, 'The Peasant and the Factory', in Vucinich, *op. cit.*

13. Especially to Gerschenkron's thorough and penetrating essay in *The Cambridge Economic History of Europe* [B, 1965] and to G. T. Robinson's well-known book [B].

vented these measures from carrying out their historical mission.

It is not inappropriate to ask at this point: to what extent did the rapid industrialisation of Russia in the decades before World War I depend on prior or simultaneous development of its agriculture? More specifically, does the Russian experience fit into the schema that stresses the leading role of agriculture in the industrial development as, for example, forcefully argued by Professor Bairoch in the present collection of essays? In referring to Professor Bairoch's hypothesis we must, of course, bear in mind that the Russian experience does not fall quite into the time period that he regards relevant to his hypothesis; he seeks to demonstrate (our emphasis) 'the impossibility, *up to the middle of the nineteenth century*, of any important industrial growth without a previous, or at any rate concomitant, agricultural development',[14] and Russia's industrial spurt came, of course, somewhat later. Nevertheless, in one important respect his hypothesis is confirmed in Russia; there was indeed a 'demographic revolution' preceding and paralleling the industrial one, and this in turn was made possible by an 'agricultural revolution' (in the sense of a steady and significant rise in the total output of foodstuffs). As we have already seen, during the whole of the nineteenth century, and especially between 1860 and 1913, the population of Russia grew relatively fast, and total agricultural output grew even slightly faster. But this was achieved, it must be remembered, within the framework of farming institutions that remained very traditional and on the whole resistant to agricultural innovation until just a few years before the end of the period in question, and with very slow penetration of modern agricultural techniques into the Russian village. The 'agricultural revolution' — if any — was not a qualitative one; it relied primarily on growing inputs of both labour and land.

More difficult to discern in Russia is the active role of the pull of rising demand, generated by the agricultural revolution, for both consumer goods (chiefly, cotton) and producer

14. *Loc. cit.*, p. 24.

goods (chiefly, iron and steel), which Professor Bairoch finds to have been such an important factor in the industrial revolutions in other countries. As noted, during most of the industrialisation spurt between the 1880s and the war the peasantry was caught between falling grain prices, rising land prices and rents, and a crushing burden of taxes and redemption payments. The gentry, of course, continued to live on a much higher level, consuming part of its capital in the process. Whatever the role of the 'agricultural revolution' and the associated rapid increase of population, it is difficult to escape the conclusion — in one or another form held by much of the expert opinion — that the active and dynamic element in this industrialisation spurt was the positive role of the state. The industrial boom was deliberately promoted by the state in many ways (to some of which we have already alluded); it also created the demand that continued to feed it. True, when the boom resumed around 1907 after the pause of six-seven years, the active role of the state became more restrained, and large agglomerations of private capital, especially the German-style banks, took over much of the initiating and propelling function, until the World War changed the conditions and eventually brought the process to a halt.

In this process, agriculture's role was most important, to be sure, but in a sense mainly negative. True, it supplied manpower for industrialisation, though still in quite small numbers, and it supported the population growth, which must have had some favourable effect on internal demand for manufactures. But agriculture's primary role was to keep its belt tight so as to release resources for the boom: financially, by the peasantry's burden of payments into the Treasury, and materially, by directing a large flow of grain for export and to the cities while taking very little in return. Sooner or later, to be sure, the weakness of the country's agricultural base would begin to hinder further industrialisation and economic modernisation; it is perhaps also in this light that the importance and timeliness of the already-mentioned Stolypin Reforms should be appraised.

An alternative model to explain the well-springs and

pattern of Russian industrialisation in the three decades before World War I is offered by Professor Gerschenkron; indeed, the Russian experience more than any other has inspired his conceptualisation of industrialisation under conditions of 'economic backwardness'.[15] The model rejects both the idea that processes of development by the leader and the followers in the game of industrialisation are essentially similar and even the very concept of prerequisites for industrial revolutions. Instead, it emphasises the ideological and institutional differences that attend the industrial revolutions of the leader and of the followers — and those among the followers depending on their relative degrees of backwardness — and the corresponding differences in the suddenness of the 'spurt', the speed of industrial growth and the resultant structural patterns.

Specifically in the case of Imperial Russia, Gerschenkron sees the active role of the state, especially in the 1890s, as an expectable phenomenon under conditions of the country's relative economic backwardness, given also the 'tension' stemming from a realisation of industrial weakness in relation to the advanced countries of the time and to Russia's internal and external political aspirations. This tension, of course, need not be translated into action by the state; in Russia, however, it was thanks to the presence in power of Witte and a handful of other men of vision and determination. Gerschenkron sees the state as 'substituting' under conditions of economic backwardness for those institutions — individual entrepreneurs in the English industrial revolution, large investment banks in the intermediate ('moderately backward') case of Germany — which would in economically more fortunate countries provide the initiative and mobilise the capital for the initial phase of rapid industrialisation. Further, because of the condition of backwardness and of the active role of the state, the pressure on consumption during this phase was particularly heavy, and the role of agriculture was primarily

15. See the title essay and several others in Gerschenkron's collected essays [B, 1962]; his main thesis is summarised by him in the 'Postscript' to the volume.

passive in the sense in which we have already described it. The same institutional circumstances also tend to steer industrial development in the direction of heavy industry and towards relatively large and technologically advanced establishments.[16]

The model provides for the state's active role to recede as the industrial boom gathers its own dynamic and as the economy's resources of extra-state entrepreneurship and capital expand as a result of the initial successes. Other agents begin to assume some of the state's active role. Foremost among these are the large banks — an institution that is less centralised than the state, but more so than industry itself. Again, Gerschenkron finds a prime instance of this process of (what might be called) the changeover of substitutes in Russia, where the large banks, many of them heavily endowed with foreign capital, increasingly played this role after the turn of the century and until the war.[17]

It is a favourite game among students of modern Russian history to speculate in a 'what if' manner. What would have been the subsequent course of Russian history if there had been no World War I, no Revolution of 1917, no Soviet régime? Would Russia's industrialisation have forged on as rapidly as before? Would, indeed, the size of her industry by some later date (1940? 1960?) have been as large as under the Soviets? Would it have been the same kind of industry? What of the role of foreign capital? The banks? What of consumption levels? What makes this game unusually fascinating is the richness of contradictory evidence that the Russia of 1914 provides. Industrial progress in the

16. Some elaborations on and qualifications to the Gerschenkron model, in part with specific reference to Russia, by a leading student of West European industrialisation may be found in David S. Landes's *The Unbound Prometheus: Technological Change and Industrial Development in Western Europe from 1750 to the Present*, Cambridge, 1969, Chapter 8 (esp. pp. 542 ff.). On the whole, however, this book does not concern itself with the Russian experience.

17. Cf. Gerschenkron [B, 1962, *passim*]. A convenient survey of Russian banking before the First World War is the essay by Olga Crisp ('Russia, 1860–1914') in Rondo Cameron *et al.*, *Banking in the Early Stages of Industrialisation: A Study in Comparative Economic History*, New York, 1967.

preceding decades had been among the fastest in the world, and yet the country remained predominantly agrarian and very poor. Modern institutions and outlooks had caught on securely, but only in very limited areas. The modernisation of agriculture had just been given a start by the Stolypin Reforms, but how much effect would it have and how soon? The very successes of industrialisation rested on the continued plight of the peasantry, an explosive potential that no Russian régime could forget, and bred potential trouble in the industrial towns. At the same time the régime was rigid in its responses to social change and in-effectual in its governance. There are those historians of a deterministic bent who maintain that by 1914 the Imperial government had exhausted its historical function of indus-trialising the country, but because of the hopelessly back-ward condition only a more authoritarian and a more determined régime could push on with the task; hence the Bolsheviks.[18] As we have seen, Gerschenkron interprets the evidence rather to mean that the time had come for a less 'extreme' set of institutions to take over the job. And yet these opposite views, and others between them, agree in that they see the only likely options as being of the 'Western' variety, for in terms of Russia's traditional dilemma both Bolshevism and Capitalism — for all their inevitable Russianness in that country — are profoundly 'Western-ising' solutions.

SOVIET INDUSTRIALISATION— *The Record of the Half-Century*

The half-century of Soviet economic history may be divided into five sub-periods of almost equal length. (1) The first of these — a time of consolidation of the Soviet régime and of Stalin's dictatorship, as well as of great expectations on the economic front — is represented by the eleven years, to 1928, that witnessed the just mentioned severe economic

18. Eloquently argued by Theodore H. von Laue in *Why Lenin? Why Stalin? A Reappraisal of the Russian Revolution, 1900–1930*, Philadelphia, 1964.

setback associated with the Civil War and so-called War Communism, and recovery under the relatively liberal New Economic Policy (NEP) to the point where pre-war production and consumption levels were re-attained (and in some respects surpassed). (2) In its second decade, from 1928 to 1938, the Soviet economy underwent its biggest industrialisation spurt, and also acquired its distinctive systemic features, which in the main have persisted to this day. (3) The next decade, to 1948 or 1949, witnessed accelerated preparations for war, the War itself, and remarkably swift recovery of production to pre-World War II levels. (4) The fourth sub-period, to 1958 or 1959, saw completion of post-war reconstruction and continued very rapid industrial (and overall) growth. However, this decade in itself breaks down almost equally into (a) the last five years of Stalin's rule, to March 1953, and (b) the economy's rapid growth under his successors, especially Mr Khrushchev, thanks largely to the correction of some of Stalin's more disastrous and notorious policies, e.g. in agriculture. (5) But this sharp upswing lost momentum at the end of the 1950s. The last decade has been characterised by a significantly slower growth.[19] Looked at another way, almost half of the half-century, from 1928 to 1953, except for a loss of something like six years[20] of growth owing to the war and its immediate aftermath, is accounted for by the industrialisation spurt under Stalin's personal direction.

As we turn to look at the broad quantitative dimensions of this growth we must first answer three methodological questions. (1) From what base year shall we measure it? The Revolution took place towards the end of 1917, but that year can be quickly dismissed for the purpose at hand because it was hardly normal by any reasonable standard, economically as well as politically. The last peacetime year before that was 1913. Industrial output reached its peak before the Revolution in 1916, but data for that year are relatively scarce and it is rarely used as a base year for

19. On this much the official Soviet data and the Western recomputations generally agree.

20. This number is explained below.

growth measurement. After the Revolution the economy went downhill, reaching a low point of near-paralysis in 1920,[21] then recovering steadily in the more liberal climate of the NEP. Agricultural output re-attained the pre-war level in 1926 and industrial output in 1927 or 1928 (both in comparable territory). The First FYP formally went into operation on 1st October, 1928. Consequently, the official 'economic year' 1927/28 (which ran from October 1927 through September 1928), or the calendar year 1928, is frequently taken as the base from which Soviet economic growth is measured.

And so we must choose between 1913 and 1928 as the base year. While production levels in the two years were quite similar, the difference of fifteen years greatly affects the results when average annual rates of growth are computed. The choice of one or the other in some sense relates to the investigator's philosophy of history. Does one regard Soviet industrialisation as beginning at the end of 1928, everything coming before having been mere prologue to the story itself? Or does one consider the NEP, the Civil War and War Communism — and possibly even the First World War — to have been a necessary, integral and ineluctable part of the history of Soviet industrialisation? The latter view may appeal more to the historian, but perhaps even the economist might concede something to it. However, for present purposes we focus on the Soviet industrialising experience in its 'narrower' sense; i.e. we relate Soviet economic growth to 1928 as the base year.

We follow the record of Soviet economic growth to 1967, which happens to have been the semi-centennial of the Revolution and, as such, perhaps a fitting year at which to end our estimates. But now we arrive at our second methodological question. (2) For the purpose of computing average annual growth rates do we regard 1928–1967 as an unbroken period of 39 years, or do we subtract a number of years to allow for the setback which World War II inflicted on the Soviet economy, and therefore also on the Soviet growth effort? Again, something is to be said for either

21. Industrial production fell to a fifth of the 1913 level.

alternative, i.e. subtracting and not subtracting a number of years to allow for the effect of the war. And again we take the 'narrower' view, and assume that the war was not an organic part of the Soviet industrialisation experience (though the opposite could be argued). But how many years should we subtract? Surely more than just the four years of the war itself, for at the end of it the Soviet economy lay partly in ruins and was operating far below pre-war levels. The number we subtract is six. Naturally, no precision can be claimed for it. We arrived at it crudely by noting first that both industrial output and the national product — by both Soviet claim and most Western recomputations — approximately re-attained their pre-war (1940) levels[22] in 1948, i.e. eight years later. But we also note that — because reconstruction continued for sometime thereafter — the two magnitudes grew in the next two years (1949, 1950) at about double the rates to which they settled down in the fifties. Thus, we count the two years following 1948 as four; or, in effect, subtract two from the number of years by which the Soviet growth span is to be shortened on account of the war, which gives us the six.[23] $39 - (8 - 2) = 33$. We call the 33 years 'effective years' of Soviet growth.

Because the official Soviet series for the major economic aggregates are often seriously exaggerated, especially for the earlier decades, and in addition are at times conceptually non-comparable with analogous series for Western countries, we rely here on recomputations by Western scholars. Fortunately, by now we are well supplied with these up to the mid-sixties (though extrapolation to 1967 generally had to be made on the basis of official Soviet data). More than that, the Western recomputations provide us with a good many alternative estimates, of special importance among which are those that rest on alternative weighting systems in the construction of the index numbers. This brings us to

22. But it must be remembered that in 1940 industrial capacity was not well utilised by the standards of preceding years.

23. Reconstruction tended to push up growth rates beyond 1950, of course, so that our 'two' is possibly an understatement. This tends to offset the qualification in the preceding footnote.

our third question: (3) From what year should the prices that constitute the weights for the index numbers be drawn? Should they be drawn from an early year of Soviet industrialisation, such as 1928, or an intermediate year, such as 1937, or a relatively recent year?

This is a very important question, the answer to which seriously affects the numerical value of the findings. The reason is that the rapid technical and structural transformation of the Soviet economy, particularly during the first two FYPs (1928–1937), led to drastic changes in relative costs of production and therefore ultimately also in relative prices. Generally speaking, our measures of growth will rise very much faster if we use as weights the prices of an early year (say, 1928) than if we use those of 1937. (After 1937 the choice of the year from which prices are drawn for weighting seems to make much less difference, probably because the pace of economic transformation slowed down considerably after that year.) At times the difference is stunning. For example, in his computation of the Soviet gross national product, Bergson found, for the 1928–1937 period, an average annual rate of growth of 11·9% when the weights are 1928 prices, and 4·8% when they are 1937 prices.[24] This 'index number problem' cannot be satisfactorily analysed here. Suffice it to say that in part for simplicity of exposition, and in part for better comparability with data for other countries, the aggregate series in the tabulation that follows are those with 1937 (or sometimes later) weights. The reader will naturally bear in mind that some of the series may show considerably higher growth rates under alternative weighting procedures, as is usually amply explained and illustrated in the referenced sources.

The table on page 524 summarises the record of Soviet economic growth during the period 1928–1967, spanning as we have noted 39 calendar years and 33 years of 'effective growth'. Of course, in most cases the figures are to be taken as approximate rather than exact. To look at the most global figures first: the gross national product ('Western'

24. Bergson [B, p. 217]. For a succinct discussion of the theoretical problem the reader is referred to his Chapter 3.

definition, factor cost valuation) increased some 7- or 8-fold.[25] Averaged over a third of a century of 'effective growth' — and, unless otherwise specified, all the growth rates in the text will refer to the 'effective' period — this comes to 6–6·5% per annum overall,[26] 4·5–5% per head, and to about 3·5–4% per man-year of labour input. As readers of these volumes will no doubt appreciate, these are very high average rates of growth, especially to refer to as long a period as a third of a century, and of course very much higher than the above-cited rates for Russia during 1860–1913. Needless to say, the growth of the Soviet GNP was not uniform. We have already noted the figures for 1928–1937. The years from 1937 to 1950 were quite extraordinary — purges, preparation for war, the war itself, reconstruction, the beginnings of the Cold War. The fifties did relatively well with an average growth rate of around 7%; but considerable retardation set in at the turn of the decade, and the sixties will doubtless show a rate of GNP growth below the long-term average.

Our table also points up some of the basic contrasts in Soviet development. The favoured sectors — thanks to deliberate and determined policy — grew several times as much as the lower-priority sectors, or those sectors that at least until recently had much lower priorities. Industry (here including mining and several other activities in addition to manufacturing) increased its output as much as 17- or 20-fold,[27] at an annual average rate of 9–9·5%. Again, this compares very favourably indeed with the experience of other countries, even if it is not completely in a class by itself. It also compares very favourably with the average rate of 5% per year in Tsarist Russia during a

25. The corresponding official Soviet figure (national income produced, material output only) is 31.

26. These figures do not make allowance for the intervening expansion of territory. (See Notes to the Table.) To this extent they exaggerate the growth 'achievement'.

27. The corresponding official Soviet figure for gross output of industry is 55.

period of similar length. Steel has epitomised Soviet industrialisation; its output increased 24-fold (over 10% per year). The consumption of energy and the use of transportation and communications services are closely connected with industrial production: we are therefore not surprised to see these series rise very steeply too. As with GNP, industrial output grew relatively fast in the fifties, considerably more slowly in the sixties.

The end-uses of economic activity that have been the main object of forced growth have been those that enlarge the economy's capacity to industrialise further and that contribute to military power and related dimensions of national strength and prestige. Thus, the volume of gross fixed investment increased some 30-fold between 1928 and 1967, at an average of about 11% per year. In 1967 there was approximately twenty times as much gross fixed investment (in real terms) for every person in the country as in 1928, itself by no means a low investment year, as we have seen. Unfortunately there are no reliable comparable data on the growth of the defence effort, but it must surely have been at least equally impressive.

At the other end of the scale — still speaking of large sectors — have been agriculture and consumption. Over the four decades, agricultural output did perhaps somewhat better than double, and output per inhabitant may have increased by somewhat over 30%, while the output of foodstuffs *per capita* increased even more modestly. It must be remembered that this refers to a base year when the standard of nutrition was very low.

As for personal consumption, we must interpret the figures in the table with considerable caution. These figures show that in 1967 the volume of goods per head of population was 2·5 times as large as in 1928, implying an annual average rate of increase of some 2·5%. However, we must also bear in mind the enormous structural changes in the population and in the patterns of consumption. Thus in 1928 only 19% of the population was urban, in 1967 — 55%. When a peasant moves to the city he changes his whole mode of life, so that measures purporting to express the change in a single numerical index are likely to yield a tenuous result indeed. Moreover, as noted, there has been a great change in the structure of consumption, both rural and urban. Alongside an enormous increase in the supply of the more modern types of goods, including many kinds of consumer durables, as well as of educational, medical and 'cultural' services, the supply of the 'old' consumer goods has generally risen only modestly, if at all. Some conveniences and even necessities are still in short and irregular supply, the income-elasticity for food remains very high, many consumer services are quite inadequately provided, and the housing shortage remains acute.

Our table of necessity conceals much too. For instance, it does not show the sharp drop in agricultural production and in personal consumption that took place, contrary to plans, almost simultaneously with the launching of the Five-Year Plans, and especially in the wake of the collectivisation of agriculture in the early thirties. Aggravated anew by preparations for war and by the war itself, the setback lasted for over a quarter of a century. Only in the middle and late fifties, that is, only after Stalin's death and following Khrushchev's determined efforts to raise agricultural production and consumption levels, were the *per capita* standards of the late twenties re-attained.

Another important aspect that our table glosses over is the demographic one. To be sure, the urbanisation of the country is vividly depicted in the 45-fold increase in the urban population in the face of only a 1·5-fold increase in the total population. The latter figure — which averages to only 1·1% per year for the 39 years — is extraordinarily low for a span of four decades in a country with high rates of natural increases during normal times (at least until the onset of a steady decline in the sixties); especially if we remember that over 20 million people were added to the population of the USSR in the course of the territorial annexations of 1939–1940. The answer to this puzzle lies in two gigantic demographic disasters — the first associated with the collectivisation drive of the early thirties, the second with the Second World War and its immediate aftermath. If we define a demographic deficit incurred during a given period as the difference between the population that would have obtained if a 'normal' rate of natural increase had continued through the period and the population actually on hand at the end of the period, then the demographic deficits associated with the two events are, respectively, about 10 million and 45–50 million, a total of about 55–60 million. This figure, it should be noted, is over one-third the Soviet population in 1928, and over one-fourth the population on the eve of the war (after annexations). That such demographic catastrophies must have had enormous effects on the age, sex, regional and rural-urban structure of the population — and on the economy — is obvious, but the matter cannot be pursued here for lack of space.[28]

GOALS AND STRATEGY

The Bolshevik Revolution may not have been the first instance of a political revolution carried out for the express purpose of filling the gap between a major but relatively backward country and the industrial leaders of the world — this honour may belong to the Meiji Restoration in Japan, which occurred half a century earlier — but its historical significance in this regard is surely second to none. True, as is by now well known, Marx and his followers, until Lenin, expected the proletariat to seize power, under the leadership of its revolutionary party, in the most highly industrialised countries first. In such countries — and after the turn of the century attention tended to be focused on Germany — the proletariat would be most numerous, its class-consciousness most developed, its deprivation (compared to the bougeoisie) most glaring, and its revolutionary organisation most promising. In other words, before Lenin, Marxism was not an ideology of industrialisation under a *post-capitalist* system; rather, it predicted the demise of capitalism as a result of successful industrialisation.

28. A few thoughts on this subject may be found in my 'Thirty Years of Soviet Industrialisation', *Soviet Survey*, No. 26, October 1958, pp. 18–19.

But Russia was not such a country; and so the Menshevik branch of the Russian Marxist movement maintained to the very day of the Bolshevik Revolution that the time of a proletarian seizure of power was yet far off, that the bougeoisie still had to perform and complete its historic function of bringing Russia to a much higher level of industrialisation. In this they were good Marxists indeed. Lenin and his Bolsheviks, however, put their trust in two factors: the historical-factual one of an enormous amount of discontent and the ever-present, if latent, possibility of a peasant revolt, and the instrumental potential of a well-organised, highly disciplined, conspiratorial party to channel the popular revolt into a successful political revolution and a new social order. Their chance came with the enormous strain and discontent that the First World War inflicted on Russia, and with the social disarray and political weakness that followed the first ('February') revolution of 1917 which overthrew the monarchy. Having thus seized power as a tiny minority party speaking in the name of a minority class, and the sole 'proletarian' régime in a world of powerful capitalist states, and having survived the initial test of fire and nerve, the Bolsheviks were bound to place, sooner or later, rapid industrialisation of their country at the very top of their urgent tasks. When somewhat later, in the mid-twenties, the tenaciously held illusions of a revolution in the most advanced countries finally faded away and Stalin advanced his famous slogan of 'socialism in one country', this last phrase came to mean primarily the swiftest industrialisation with the least help from abroad and the greatest effort at home. In sum, Marxism was not at all, to begin with, an ideology of industrialisation in a *post-capitalist* setting; it became that—as Marxism-Leninism —in the minds and at the hands of the Bolsheviks themselves. Certainly, the growth of industry would simultaneously enlarge the working class, the class which provided the régime's main source of mass social support in the early years.

We need not concern ourselves here whether industrialisation (and all that goes with it) was to be a goal in itself or only a means to other ends. Certainly, the quick amassing of economic and military power to withstand what was regarded as the mortal hostility of the surrounding capitalist world — and later more specifically of the fascist powers — made rapid expansion and modernisation of heavy industry imperative in the régime's eyes. (And insofar as any historical event can do so, Stalin's military victory over Hitler confirmed the correctness of this policy.) Moreover, the prospects of communist revolutions in other countries were for a long time held to rise with Soviet 'victories' on the internal production front (as they were also expected to vary inversely with the economic fortunes of the capitalist world). And finally the building of Marxism's ultimate perfect society — full communism — was predicted on the attainment of a level of economic abundance to which industrialisation was the only road. The last, we might note parenthetically, would, however, demand something more than the mastery of highly advanced industrial technology; it would require as well both the perfection of man as a social being and the conscious dismantling of the very state apparatus that was born of the Revolution and was hyper-inflated *pari passu* with the growth of industry.

At any rate, whether an end in itself or a means to other ends, industrialisation has been at the very centre of Soviet domestic concern since the beginning of the Soviet era. Nothing underscores this more vividly than the fact that the first top-level commissions concerned with long-range industrialisation, the State Commission for the Electrification of Russia (GOELRO) and the State Planning Commission (Gosplan) itself, were established while the economy was still all but paralysed at the time of the Civil War and of War Communism, in February 1920 and February 1921, respectively.

In addition to (1) very rapid industrialisation — with pronounced emphasis on both industries and sectors that enlarge further capacity for industrial growth and military power — the following should be cited as major objectives of Soviet developmental strategy.

(2) The maintenance of a large military establishment, with heavy stress on conventional land forces since at least the mid-thirties, and also on naval and air forces, nuclear weapons and rocketry in the post-war period. The space programme should be mentioned here as well.

(3) A high degree of economic self-sufficiency (autarky) in relation to the rest of the world, the USSR being one of the very few countries that could, thanks to its size and resource endowment, seriously contemplate such an objective over the longer pull. This policy has, of course, profoundly affected both its domestic investment pattern and its foreign trade. However, the pursuit of autarky has been modified over the years owing to (a) the appearance, after the Second World War, of a dozen or so other communist-ruled countries, for whose economic progress and well-being the Soviet Union came, after a while, to feel some responsibility, and with whom some degree of international division of labour is deemed desirable; and (b) the use of foreign trade and aid, since the mid-fifties, as instruments of foreign policy vis-à-vis non-communist countries, particularly certain underdeveloped countries. (It should be noted that not all failure to trade has been due to a fundamental autarkic policy. There have also been more proximate major obstacles to trade, such as the inability to divert resources for export in the short run, the cumbersomeness of Soviet trading organisation, and politically motivated reluctance to trade with the USSR on the part of some of its partners. At the same time, longer-term pursuit of autarky may well lead to *more* trade in the short-run, specifically to the importation of equipment for the building up of industrial capacity necessary to achieve eventual self-sufficiency. Indeed, a very large part of Soviet imports has typically been of this type, as evidenced by the fact that in the early thirties imports of machinery approached and sometimes even exceeded 50% of total imports. Lastly, one might observe that even in a well-endowed country such as the Soviet Union the reaching for autarky in a changing world is not unlike reaching for the rainbow: it recedes as it is pursued, owing to progress in world technology and shifts

in domestic priorities and needs. In this regard, too, Soviet history provides many instances.)

(4) The near-complete socialisation (in the sense of de-privatisation) of the economy — which was essentially achieved with the completion of collectivisation of agriculture in the mid-thirties within the original boundaries of the USSR, and by the end of the forties in the annexed territories.

(5) The raising of consumption levels. We list this objective last not because it has had the lowest priority in the abstract — which has not been the case — but because in the event it has tended to be so treated consistently, at least until Stalin's death. We already noted the sharp fall in consumption levels during the early years of the FYP era. Since the mid-fifties consumption as a segment of the national product and those productive sectors (such as agriculture) which primarily support it, have fared relatively much better. Nevertheless, thanks chiefly to very high outlays on investment and defence, personal consumption continues to claim no more than half the national product in the USSR, one of the lowest such proportions on record.

One might list other objectives that have characterised Soviet policy: attainment of virtually complete literacy, great expansion of educational opportunities, vast training in skills, provision of massive health care, and so forth. Some of these, to be sure, have been at once objectives and means towards other aims. Yet another objective should be mentioned, one that is not economic in itself but has had profound impact on the Soviet economic system; namely, the preservation of power in the hands of the ruling party, and particularly its party-professional component, and within it that of a small group of leaders or of a single man.

INDUSTRIALISATION STRATEGY

There is no mystery about the speed of Soviet industrial growth. By way of explaining it one might begin by mentioning, again, the positive side of the country's endowment taken over by the Soviet régime, such as: the considerable industrial establishment, the large rail net, the human resources, and the rich fund of natural resources. So far so good; but there has also been a definite industrialisation strategy.

Second to none among the components of this strategy has been the massive formation of capital, together with clear priorities regarding the direction of investment. The savings corresponding to this investment were socialised, centrally accumulated, and in large measure centrally controlled through the administrative allocation of physical flows. In this regard, a key role was played by the collectivisation of agriculture, on which more presently.

Closely related to the enormous accumulation of capital has been the extensive, highly organised takeover and absorption of Western technology. In a sense, the building up of the capital stock was the process of embodiment of the technological takeover. Moreover, much of the equipment, especially of the more sophisticated kind, came and continues to come directly from abroad. Here one should also mention the large number of foreign experts that were temporarily employed by the Soviet government, especially in the twenties and early thirties. The role of imports of capital — as distinct from capital goods — in Soviet industrialisation has been relatively minor, limited mainly to short- and medium-term financing of machinery imports and to (not insignificant) reparations after World War II.

On the human side we must note the rapid transfer of the agricultural population into modern sectors (especially industry), the high rate of participation of the population in the labour force, and (as mentioned) the vast programme of education and training.

Finally, we must take cognisance of a definite hierarchy of developmental priorities at any one time — though with occasional shifts in the hierarchy. This permitted not only concentration of effort on the favoured objectives, such as the building up of heavy industry, but also provided, in the form of *low*-priority sectors and uses, at least up to a point, cushions for the absorption of the effects of mistakes, unrealistic expectations, ideological delusions, and the like.

The massive accumulation of capital is illustrated in our table by the 12-fold growth of the net capital stock (at 1937 prices) between 1928 and 1967, averaging some 9·5% per year over the 33 'effective years' of growth. This rate being considerably higher than that for the national product, a quickly rising average capital-output ratio is implied (especially in the sixties, owing to the retardation in the growth of GNP), which is contrary to the experience of at least the more rapidly growing advanced Western countries in the post-war period.[29] In any case, the growth of Soviet physical capital has been extremely fast by world standards. In 1967 there was almost eight times as much of it per inhabitant as in 1928. Its counterpart in terms of current resource flow has been the very high rate of investment maintained by the USSR at times other than preparation for the Second World War and the war itself: the gross rate has been estimated close to and over 30% in the late fifties and early sixties[30] — rates generally higher than those that obtained in the advanced capitalist countries, except Japan, at the same time.[31] Furthermore, as we have already seen, the volume of annual gross *fixed* investment grew some 30 times between 1928 and 1967.

The record in regard to the mobilisation of labour resources is equally impressive. While the population increased by 56%, the total labour input in man-years grew by 130%, and non-agricultural labour input in man-years 4·5-fold (4·7% per year on the average). This is largely accountable by rural-urban labour transfer, but in part also by the greater participation of women in employment. Of all persons working for hire (which is somewhat larger than the category of non-agricultural labour), in 1928 about

29. Cf. Denison's data as reproduced in Abram Bergson, *Planning and Productivity under Soviet Socialism*, New York, 1968, p. 93.

30. Cf. Becker [B, p. 269]; the data are at 'adjusted factor cost' following Professor Bergson's method. Moorsteen and Powell, using a different method of estimating investment, obtain appreciably lower ratios [B, Table T-50]; also, Becker-Moorsteen-Powell [B, Table T-50-X].

31. See the tabulations in Becker [B, p. 271] and Maddison [B, *passim*].

24% were women; by 1940 the figure had risen to 39, by 1950 (affected by the decimation of males in the preceding decade) to 47, and by 1967 to fully one-half. Indeed, between 1960 and 1967, some 58% of the *net* increment to the employed labour force consisted of women, in large measure housewives drawn into non-agricultural employment.

Regarding the skill level of labour, various statistics can be cited. Suffice it to point out here that according to official claims, the number of gainfully employed persons with professional, technical or vocational training, at either the secondary school or the university level, increased from 521,000 in 1928 to almost 14 million at the end of 1967. We may also note from the table that the amount of net capital stock per man-year worked rose about 5-fold over this period (12·0 ÷ 2·3).

Thus, Soviet economic growth appears to have depended chiefly on the expansion of the supply of productive factors. In current East European parlance, it has been primarily 'extensive' growth. For instance, in their very thorough analysis Moorsteen and Powell found that while, between 1928 and 1966, the gross national product increased 7·6-fold and the net national product — 6·7-fold, the volume of all inputs (capital, labour and land combined) increased 3·8–5·0 times.[32] In sum, there is little reason to believe that 'total input productivity' — the yield in national product per unit of combined inputs — rose uncommonly fast over the whole period since 1928,[33] despite the massive transfer of ready-made technology from abroad. To say that is not to belittle the Soviet achievement. The rapid increase in the supply of inputs is in itself a very impressive economic accomplishment, especially in the absence of any major inflow of capital from abroad (apart from reparations and other receipts from occupied terri-

32. Moorsteen-Powell [B, Tables T-47, T-58, T-29] and Becker-Moorsteen-Powell [B, Tables T-47-X, T-59-X]. The lower figure for aggregate inputs was obtained by the authors by assuming an 8% return on capital, the higher figure — 20%.

33. Cf. conclusions by Moorsteen-Powell [B, Ch. 9], conveniently summarised in Raymond P. Powell, 'Economic Growth in the U.S.S.R.', *Scientific American*, vol. 219, No. 6, December 1968.

tories after the war). Certainly a growth over several decades of aggregate inputs (excluding the educational stock) of between 4·5 and 5% per year, which is what the above figures imply, of the net physical capital stock at almost 8% per year (see table), and of the input of non-agricultural man-years *per capita* of $3\frac{1}{4}$% per year,[34] are all extraordinary accomplishments. With a few exceptions to be noted later, essentially the same strategy remains in effect today.

INSTITUTIONS

To translate this industrialisation strategy into day-to-day economic activity, Stalin employed a set of distinctive institutions. Surely the institution that deserves to be mentioned first in this connection is the severe political dictatorship, supported during Stalin's rule by extreme terror. The terror subsided after his death, and the dictatorship is no longer as personal as it used to be, but the political controls are still in effect, supporting the industrialisation policy and maintaining the politico-economic system. The latter should be taken to include a structure of privilege and an apparatus of rule that emerged in Stalin's day as an inevitable concomitant of his policies of industrialisation. This apparatus of rule is largely coterminous with the Communist Party, and is exercised mainly through the party's professional functionaries and the organs of coercion under the party's control.

The economy is, of course, 'socialised' in the sense that the means of production are almost without exception in the ownership of the state or of co-operative entities (such as collective farms), which in turn are under the close control of the state. This in itself does not say very much, however. What is more important is that decisions are highly centralised. The abolition of the market mechanism was completed soon after the Soviet industrialisation drive began; since then resources have been allocated primarily by administrative ('planning') decision. All major producer goods are

34. The last figure is the figure in line 4, column 4, of the table, averaged over 33 'effective years'.

physically rationed at the centre. Individual enterprises are subject to detailed targets and directives as to what and how to produce. Even the much-publicised economic reform of 1965 has modified the Soviet 'command economy' only very little. Much of the inefficiency of the Soviet economy stems from this over-centralisation, separation of production from demand, rigid management of the economy and rigid (and often not very meaningful) prices, and general bureaucratisation.

However, the command economy is closely linked to the industrialisation strategy. It is essentially an ideologically legitimated institutional response to the economy of shortages brought about by excessive pressure of goals (plans) on the disposable resources. It is a 'war economy *sui generis*', as the late Oscar Lange has characterised it, one that has continued for decades and that has been made possible by both the ideological aversion to the market and the political preference for authoritarian methods. Whether there could have been just as much growth — and more efficiency — with a substantial role played by the market mechanism is something for scholars to debate.

Beginning with 1928, and with the exception of the war years, Five-Year Plans have formally defined the pace and direction of development, the extent of structural change, and the means for accomplishing these tasks. The conformity of Soviet economic development to the FYP targets has been very uneven, and in the case of agriculture and consumption notoriously poor. The instrumental and operative roles of the FYPs should not be overstated. They have been often substantially modified in the course of their realisation by the pressure of internal and external events, and in two cases they were voided in mid-passage.[35] Moreover, it seems that since the war not a single FYP has in fact been drawn up as a completed document; instead, only summary directives have been in effect.

35. The Third FYP in 1941 (by the German attack) and the Sixth FYP in 1957. A Seven-Year Plan, 1959–1965, took the place of the remaining years of the Sixth FYP and of what would have been the Seventh FYP. It was succeeded by the Eighth FYP, 1966–1970.

A most important institution supporting the Soviet industrialisation strategy has been the collectivisation of agriculture. Launched suddenly and on a mass scale by Stalin at the end of 1929 following a decade of strained and oscillating relations between the régime and the peasantry, of sharp struggles within the party leadership on this issue, and of lively debates on how to mobilise the surplus of agriculture for the rapid industrialisation to come[36] — the operation was conducted with much coercion of the peasantry and occasional use of force. The short-term results were disastrous for agricultural production, and the negative effects continue to be felt to this day.[37] Much of the consumer's privation from 1930 on is to be attributed to this cause. But the institution of the collective farm has permitted direct physical control by the state over the produce of agriculture, and has thereby helped bring about a sharp increase in the flow of agricultural products away from the village to be devoted to industrialisation. At the same time, the economic condition of the peasantry declined sharply and remained unbelievably low until well after Stalin's death. It may well be surmised whether in the long run the negative effect on agricultural productivity may not have offset the positive resource-mobilising effect from the standpoint of the state. Be that as it may, under the circumstances collectivisation had much to do with raising the rate of investment to a high level and maintaining it there. In a sense this experience reproduced, though in a very much more violent and extreme fashion, the role that agriculture played in the later part of the nineteenth century, thanks to financial and fiscal pressure, as a major source of developmental capital *via* the coffers of the state. And just as the Tsarist régime saw fit after several decades of squeezing the peasantry for developmental purposes to take measures to create a class of prosperous private peasants

36. For a recent concise historical treatment of the 'Great Debate', the reader is referred to Nove [B, Ch. 5]. See also the monographs by Erlich and Spulber in the Bibliography.

37. Maddison estimates that 'over the years 1929 to 1936 inclusive the cumulative loss of agricultural output was around 40% of 1928 GNP' [B, p. 105].

for the sake of economic productivity and political stability (the Stolypin Reforms), so the Soviet régime, beginning in the mid-fifties, has repeatedly taken steps to improve the condition of the peasantry and to strengthen the collective farms for both economic and political reasons.

Last but not least, the Soviets have consistently relied on personal material incentives to get the work of the economy done. Although property income is rather insignificant, great inequality of material rewards has nonetheless obtained. The principle continues to be upheld and practised; it has been reaffirmed in connection with the 1965 economic reforms and the various measures to stimulate agricultural production. The principle itself and the resultant inequalities have been much criticised outside the Soviet Union as being in conflict with socialist principles, most recently and vehemently by Chinese and Cuban spokesmen. (Of course, social inequality in the USSR stems as much from differences in access to power as from income inequality.) Much of the criticism is probably well taken — not only on ethical grounds, which is a matter of first principles — but also on instrumental grounds. The use of material incentives has probably stood in the way of creating a 'communist man' and of instilling the high degree of social solidarity that the authoritarian system has demanded. But one can also seriously question whether under the given conditions the Soviets could have industrialised rapidly otherwise. In facing the basic dilemma of socialist (egalitarian) values *versus* industrial power they chose the latter, inevitably shaping society and man in the process.

CONCLUDING REMARKS

If all major industrial revolutions are dramas played out on the stage of history, then the Russian one seems to have been tinged with tragedy more than most. Interrupted twice by world wars and, in mid-passage, by a revolution for the sake of a complete break with the past, Russian industrialisation in its century-long course has exhibited as much continuity as contrast, as much persistence of problems and methods as change. The red banners of 1917 did not have 'Industry' emblazoned on them, but the Revolution turned into a drive for industrialisation-at-all-costs. It had marched to the strains of the 'International' and called for immediate Peace; it ended up by apotheosising national power and militarising the economy with much more success than the Tsars could have hoped for. Its call for Equality was followed by the greatest concentration of power; its call for Liberty, by the opposite; its promise of Land to the peasants, by the great Counter-Reform of collectivisation.

Some would speak of the curse of economic backwardness in a land justly aspiring to the fruits of material civilisation and to a rightful place in a world of great powers. Under the circumstances, the methods of industrialising had to be out of the ordinary (in Western terms), and the greater the sense of urgency, the more extraordinary the methods and the more specific the results. Both the Tsars and Soviets relied on the initiative and active intervention of the state; both squeezed agriculture dry and sacrificed the consumer's well-being on the altar of heavy industry. Only the Soviet methods were far more extreme and the human cost immeasurably more terrible. The efforts have been prodigious and the material achievements of industrialisation in both eras have been impressive, though also inevitably costly in a sheer economic sense owing to the nature of the case. In the half-century following the Revolution Russia has been greatly transformed and much more so than it was in the preceding half-century. (But so was the world in the two periods.) Today it has the second largest industry, and not the fifth as she had in 1913; and a far higher relative position in science and technology, not to speak of military power, than then. And yet in *per capita* production of industrial output or the national product overall it holds approximately the same relative place in Europe and the world as it held in 1928, 1913 and even earlier.[38] Khrushchev's famous slogan of 'catching up with and surpassing America' in *per capita* output and consumption, skilfully

38. Maddison [B, *passim*].

brandished in the optimistic days of the late fifties, has not been much heard of since the early sixties. The industrialisation drive continues as resolutely as then, of course, but the official views regarding an imminent 'victory in the competition between two systems' has been much more sober since the slowing down of Soviet growth at the turn of the decade.

Much of this talk has been for foreign consumption, of course, and especially for the benefit of those under-developed lands that are seeking ways and means of carrying out their own industrial revolutions against great odds. None of them outside full Soviet control has chosen to adopt the complete Soviet 'model' of industrialisation, and indeed, those communist countries that had some option — Yugoslavia, China, Cuba — chose to abandon or reject it as a whole. Nevertheless, many individual techniques elaborated by the Soviets for spurring industrial growth have been in various degrees and assortments taken over by other countries, communist and non-communist, less and more developed. Hardly a self-respecting country is now without its development Plan — or without its frustrations with it. Many Soviet social inventions have spread throughout the world. Yet most of the world is also well aware of the enormous human costs that accompanied the Soviet model in its native setting. At the same time, the industrialising countries of today, if usually poorer in natural and other endowments, can make much greater use of foreign capital. Insofar as the last point holds, they could do worse than study the lessons, positive and negative, of the Tsarist experience.

It has been said that

. . . the real tragedy of the Russian Revolution is subtle as well as profound. In a sense it is the tragedy of success, not the tragedy of failure. Stalin's methods of 'primitive socialist accumulation' succeeded . . . and the cruel fact is that the Russia of today, while undoubtedly a strong and in many respects a fine country, is not particularly better or worse than other countries at its stage of development. It is an illusion to think that it is a country differing in any decisive way from other recently developed countries in the world . . .

Thus we come to the bleak conclusion that the Stalinist methods were horrible, and their results commonplace . . .[39]

Well, almost commonplace. The extreme methods have tended to bring about, as they generally do, a logic of their own, including the inevitable social rigidity.

The very institutions that underpinned the development strategy now stand in the way of economic progress. The overcentralisation and the command economy are sources of waste and of technological conservatism. The mode of takeover of foreign know-how has brought about very uneven levels of technology. The maximal mobilisation of labour has also meant overemployment, disregard of cost, and waste. The resort to material incentives has tended to misdirect efforts, undermine other values, and stratify the society — perhaps one reason why, with Strachey, we may find the 'results commonplace'. Even the natural riches have been a mixed blessing, for they have spared the planners the discipline of the balance of payments, and thus also a major pressure for rationalisation of the economic mechanism.

Even more than other industrial revolutions, the Soviet one appears to have created a social order with a powerful built-in force for its own perpetuation. Rigid and authoritarian; endowed with uncommonly vast means of internal control; reserving to the top leadership all possibility of social innovation; little affected by competition in world markets; unconcerned about foreign economic penetration into its own country; secure behind its modern weaponry; untroubled by organised labour, popular suffrage or pressure groups outside the ruling stratum — this industrial society seems at this time to contain little potential for evolutionary change, which is not the same thing as industrial growth.

39. John Strachey, *The Strangled Cry*, London, 1962, pp. 192, 193.

The figures in columns (1) and (4) indicate the number of times that the given measure was greater in 1967 than in 1928.

	(1) Growth factor	(2) Average rate of growth, % per year, averaged over 39 years	(3) Average rate of growth, % per year, averaged over 33 'effective years'	(4) Per cápita growth factor Col. (1) ÷ 1.56
1. Total population a/	1·56	1·1	1·4	
2. Urban population a/	4·55	4·0	4·7	
3. Total labour input, man-years b/	2·3	2·2	2·6	1·4
4. Non-agricultural labour input, man-years b/	4·5	3·9	4·7	2·9
5. Agricultural labour input, man-years b/	1·2	0·5	0·5+	0·8
6. Capital stock, net (at 1937 prices) c/	12·0	@*6·5	7·8	7·7
7. Educational stock d/			11·2–11·8 e/ 6 f/	
8. Fuel and hydro-electricity consumed g/	@20	@ 8	@ 9·5	@13
9. Industrial output (value-added basis, 1937, and later weights) h/	17–20	7·5–8	9–9·5	11–13
10. Transportation and communications output (1955 weights) i/	27	@ 9	10·5	17
11. Agricultural output (1958 prices) j/	2+	@ 2	2+	1·3+
12. Gross national product (factor cost, 1937 and later prices) k/	@ 7–8	5–5·5	6–6·5	4·5–5

13. Consumption (1937 and later weights) l/	3·5-4	@ 3·5	@ 4	@ 2·5
14. Gross fixed investment (1937 and later weights) m/	@30	@ 9	@11	@20
15. Ingot steel production n/	24	8·5	10·1	15·4

* @ = approximately.

Note: The sources of our estimates are listed below; in these Notes they are identified by number. In all cases extrapolation to 1967 is by the present author, for which he alone bears responsibility. The territories to which these figures refer are respectively those of 1928 and 1967; i.e. some of the growth is ascribable to territorial expansion. The areas annexed by the USSR just before and after World War II contained a pre-war population equivalent to about 13% of the Soviet population of mid-1939. The corresponding addition to industrial and overall productive capacity was probably somewhat smaller (cf. Nutter in [12, pp. 167–68]). Moreover, the annexed territories were among the most ravaged during the war.

(a) The corresponding absolute figures are as follows:

	Total population	Urban population millions	Urban as % of total population	Sources estimated from
1928, mid-year	151·5	28·4	19	[6, Table 7]
1967, July 1	235·5	129·1	55	[15, p. 15]

(b) Cf. [9, pp. 365 and 643]. The figures include military personnel, but they are virtually identical for the civilian component. See also Feshbach [17, Part III], whose estimates for the post-war years differ from those of Moorsteen and Powell [9]. For agricultural labour see also [10, Table 1].

(c) Cf. [9, Table T-25; 9a, Table T-25-X]

(d) Educational stock is here defined as the cumulative investment in the human population consisting of costs of education and incomes forgone by students, at constant prices.

(e) 1926–1939. (DeWitt's estimate [5] as reproduced by Cohn [4, Table 7].) *Per capita*, the rate is 10–10·5%.

(f) 1950–1964. Cohn's extrapolation after DeWitt [17, II-A, p. 131, and 4, Table 7]. *Per capita*, about 4·3% per year.

(g) In calories, includes firewood. Estimated from [14, pp. 68 and 72].

(h) Industrial output is meant to include munitions. Cf. Shimkin-Leedy [13], Kaplan-Moorsteen [8] (who omit munitions), Powell in

[3, p. 187], Noren in [17, II-A], and Becker [1, p. 241]. Nutter's results [12, p. 196 and *passim*] follow the other Western estimates quite closely until about 1950, rise considerably more slowly thereafter [11, p. 167].

(i) [7].

(j) Cf. Johnson in [17], Nimitz [10], and Diamond in [17, II-B].

(k) After Bergson [2, pp. 93, 177], Cohn [17, II-A, and 4], Moorsteen-Powell [9, Table T-47], Becker-Moorsteen-Powell [9a, Table T-47-X], and Becker [1, p. 234].

(l) Cf. Bergson [2, p. 93], Chapman in [3, p. 238], Bronson-Severin [17, II-B], and Becker [1, p. 223].

(m) Cf. [9, p. 358].

(n) Official data.

Sources to Table

1. Abraham S. Becker, *Soviet National Income, 1958–1964*, Berkeley, 1969.

2. Abram Bergson, *The Real National Income of Soviet Russia since 1928*, Cambridge, 1961.

3. Abram Bergson and Simon Kuznets, *Economic Trends in the Soviet Union*, Cambridge, 1963.

4. Stanley H. Cohn, 'The Soviet Economy: Performance and Growth', *Studies on the Soviet Union*, vol. VI, No. 4, Munich, 1967.

5. Nicholas DeWitt, 'Costs and Returns in Education in the USSR', unpublished dissertation, Harvard University, 1962.

6. Warren W. Eason, 'Population', in Allen H. Kassof, *Prospects for Soviet Society*, New York, 1968.

7. Norman M. Kaplan, 'Growth of Outputs and Inputs in Soviet Transport and Communications', *American Economic Review*, vol. LVII, No. 5, December 1967, pp. 1154–1167.

8. Norman M. Kaplan and R. H. Moorsteen, 'An Index of Soviet Industrial Output', *American Economic Review*, vol. L, No. 3, June 1960, pp. 295–318.

9. Richard Moorsteen and Raymond P. Powell, *The Soviet Capital Stock, 1928–1962*, Homewood, Ill., 1966.

9a. Abraham S. Becker, Richard Moorsteen and Raymond P. Powell, *Two Supplements to* [9], Yale University, 1968.

10. Nancy Nimitz, 'Farm Employment in the Soviet Union', in Jerzy F. Karcz, ed., *Soviet and East European Agriculture*, Berkeley, 1967.

11. G. Warren Nutter, 'The Effects of Economic Growth on Sino-Soviet Strategy', in David M. Abshire and Richard V. Allen, eds., *National Security*, New York, 1963, pp. 149–168.

12. G. Warren Nutter, *The Growth of Industrial Production in the Soviet Union*, Princeton, 1962.

13. Demitri B. Shimkin and F. A. Leedy, 'Soviet Industrial Growth', *Automotive Industries*, January 1958.

14. TSentral'noe statisticheskoe upravlenie SSSR, *Narodnoe khoziaistvo SSSR v 1958 g.: Statisticheskii ezhegodnik*, Moscow, 1959.

15. TSentral'noe statisticheskoe upravlenie SSSR, *Narodnoe khoziaistvo SSSR v 1967 g.: Statisticheskii ezhegodnik*, Moscow, 1968.

16. TSentral'noe statisticheskoe upravlenie SSSR, *Narodnoe khoziaistvo SSSR v 1968 g.: Statisticheskii ezhegodnik*, Moscow, 1969.

17. U.S. Congress, Joint Economic Committee, *New Directions in the Soviet Economy*, Washington, 1966.

BIBLIOGRAPHY (*limited to the English language*)

Much has been published in English — not to mention Russian and other languages — on Russia since 1860, but there are very few comprehensive economic histories either for the period of rapid industrialisation before the First World War or under the Soviets, or both. Some general histories contain a good deal of significance for the student of industrialisation. One could mention Nicholas V. Riasanovsky, *A History of Russia*, second edition, Oxford, 1969 (which includes the Soviet period), and Michael T. Florinsky, *Russia: A History and an Interpretation*, Vol. II, New York, 1953 (which does not). There is no substantial comprehensive work of Russian economic history in a Western language that spans the full century of industrialisation centring on the Revolution. Coming closest to it is the primarily quantitative and in its own way useful study by Angus Maddison, *Economic Growth in Japan and Russia*, London, 1969. As the title suggests, it gives equal (though mostly separate) attention to the two countries; it also adduces many comparative data for a good number of other industrial countries.

As for the pre-1917 era, a well-known work of some vintage is James Mavor, *An Economic History of Russia*, London, second edition, 1925, 2 vols., which carries the account from earliest times to about 1907. Useful for bringing to the attention of the English reader the findings of some major pre-revolutionary Russian historians, it relies heavily for the earlier period on the work of the great Russian historian, V. Kliuchevsky, and for the rise of factory industry on that of the current economist and moderate Marxist, M. I. Tugan-Baranovsky. (The latter's classic historical work, first published in 1898, is soon to appear in English translation from the third (1907) edition as *The Russian Factory in the Nineteenth Century*, Homewood, Ill.) An important Soviet work by P. I. Lyashchenko has been translated into English as *History of the National Economy of Russia to the 1917 Revolution*, New York, 1948. The translation is of the two volumes that came out in Russian in

1939; a third volume, pertaining to the Soviet period, was published after the war but has remained untranslated. This is a good study except insofar as it reflects the historical dogmas of the time and place. As an exception (linguistically) we may list also a useful concise work in French: Bertrand Gille, *Histoire Économique et Sociale de la Russie du Moyen-Age au Vingtième Siècle*, Paris, 1949.

The last pre-war decade is surveyed by Margaret Miller, *The Economic Development of Russia, 1905–1914*, second edition, London, 1967. A classic study of the social and economic conditions in Russian agriculture before the Revolution is Geroid T. Robinson's, *Rural Russia Under the Old Regime*, New York, 1932.

Turning specifically to the question of industrialisation in late Imperial Russia, the reader will find much information assembled in the essay by Roger Portal, 'The Industrialisation of Russia', in H. J. Habakkuk and M. Postan, eds., *The Cambridge Economic History of Europe*, Vol. VI, Cambridge, 1965, pp. 801–872. The companion piece in that volume by Alexander Gerschenkron, 'Agrarian Policies and Industrialisation, 1861–1917' (pp. 706–800), is not only a skilful analysis of the provisions of the Great Reform and the complicated subsequent course of agrarian policy, but also an exposition of his theory of the relationship between agriculture and industrialisation in a backward, rapidly industrialising country. (The essay has been reprinted in the second volume of his collected essays, *Continuity in History and Other Essays*, Cambridge, Mass., 1968, Ch. 7.) For broader treatment of both Gerschenkron's conception of Russian and Soviet industrialisation and of his theory of industrialisation, the reader is referred to his first volume of collected essays, *Economic Backwardness in Historical Perspective*, Cambridge, Mass., 1965. A definitive review and summary of the available quantitative data on pre-revolutionary growth rates is Raymond W. Goldsmith, 'The Economic Growth of Tsarist Russia, 1860–1913', *Economic Development and Cultural Change*, Vol. IX, No. 3, April 1961. An inquiry into the ideas and policies of the man most responsible for promoting Russian industrialisation in the late nineteenth century is Theodore H. von Laue's *Sergei Witte and the Industrialisation of Russia*, New York, 1963, though the book is stronger on the political than the economic side. Lastly, there is V. I. Lenin's scholarly study of *The Development of Capitalism in Russia* (London, 1957), first published in 1899, which investigates the question comprehensively and in detail, and concludes — as we have noted in the text — that the process had indeed gone far by the end of the nineteenth century.

Proceeding to the Soviet period, the best general work is Alec Nove's *An Economic History of the USSR*, London, 1969. It devotes much attention to policy issues; over half the text deals with the first two decades of Soviet rule. A weakness of the work is its — deliberate — failure to cite Western recomputations of Soviet growth rates. Econometric studies apart, some of which will be mentioned presently, there is nothing for the Soviet period as comprehensive and up-to-date as Nove's economic history.

The important decade of the twenties has received much attention from historians and economists. E. H. Carr's monumental *A History of Soviet Russia*, London, is a series of many volumes that now chronologically extends to the end of the twenties. It contains a wealth of economic material. The latest volume (VIII), jointly with R. S. Davies (*Foundations of Planned Economy, 1926–29*, 1969), is of especial interest to the economic historian. Similarly, I. Deutscher's *Stalin*, Oxford, 1949, is a political biography and history that bears heavily on the economics of the time. A valuable contemporary study of the economic problems of the first decade of Soviet rule is Maurice Dobb's *Russian Economic Development since the Revolution*, London, 1928. It includes a discussion of the great industrialisation debate of the twenties, on which more specifically the reader should consult Alexander Erlich, *The Soviet Industrialisation Debate, 1924–1928*, Cambridge, Mass., 1960, and Nicolas Spulber, *Soviet Strategy for Economic Growth*, Bloomington, 1964. These debates, of course, overlapped with the issues of policy towards the peasantry, on which the fullest study is Moshe

Lewin's *Russian Peasants and Soviet Power*, Evanston, 1968 (translated from the French original of 1966).

Since the Second World War much effort and sophistication has been invested in the measurement of Soviet growth, overall and by sectors. The resulting studies tend to be very 'technical', and their findings require considerable theoretical and statistical training for proper interpretation. Since no bibliography of Soviet industrialisation would be complete without reference to this important literature, the following are cited as some of the most important exemplars. Abraham S. Becker, *Soviet National Income, 1958–1964*, Berkeley, 1969. Abram Bergson, *The Real National Income of Soviet Russia since 1928*, Cambridge, Mass., 1961. Abram Bergson and Simon Kuznets, *Economic Trends in the Soviet Union*, Cambridge, Mass., 1963. Richard Moorsteen and Raymond P. Powell, *The Soviet Capital Stock, 1928–1962*, Homewood, Ill., 1966. Abraham S. Becker, Richard Moorsteen and Raymond P. Powell, *Two Supplements* to the above, Yale University, 1968. G. Warren Nutter, *The Growth of Industrial Production in the Soviet Union*, Princeton, 1962.

9. The Failure of the Industrial Revolution in Spain 1830–1914*

Jordi Nadal

POPULATION GROWTH, A FALSE TRAIL

Leaving aside a large number of regional variations, it can be said that, in the course of the last millennium, the populations of Western Europe have experienced three major surges: the first from the end of the eleventh century to the beginning of the fourteenth; the second during the sixteenth century and, possibly, in the first years of the seventeenth; and the third from the eighteenth century on. Because of the sources available, but also for reasons of intrinsic importance, these three great leaps do not require the same treatment. A fundamental difference separates the last from the other two: whilst the latter met, or possibly provoked, a reaction in the depressions of the fourteenth, fifteenth and seventeenth centuries, the growth of population during the eighteenth century has proved to be a sustained cumulative rise, and its commencement marks a break with previous conditions of mortality, and also of fertility.

The problems arise when one tries to find some explanation of those surges, that is to establish what might have been the relationship between the demographic and the economic changes. The classic discussion attempted to resolve whether the total population was determined by economic factors or whether it was population only which determined economic changes. Today this question, which is so sweeping, has been superseded; and it is more prudently believed 'that it depended on the time and the place, that the short run was very different from the long run and that the demographic response to a change in the conditions of human life can take a great number of alternative forms, as

* This contribution has been considerably abridged by the translator, in consultation with the author, from the original text which will be published in full in Spanish.

Schumpeter suggested that the economic response to population increase may range from stagnation to innovation'.[1]

The recognition that the matter is more complex undoubtedly opens a fresh discussion of the problem, but does not resolve the problem itself. The most important point which emerges from the suggestion made in the above quotation is the recommendation to distinguish between cases, without being carried away by generalisations embracing the whole of Europe. The fact that, in general, the growth of the populations of the European countries from the eighteenth century is indeed a sustained cumulative rise does not imply the intervention of similar factors in each country. In the case of England the link between the demographic changes and the Industrial Revolution appears to be undeniable, even though 'if there is anything clear in the astonishing complexity of the relationship between demography and economics, it is precisely the impossibility of sustaining any simplist conception of that relationship'.[2] Outside England, the demographic surge which is equally evident may or may not be linked with industrialisation. The reasons for a phenomenon which appears to be generic must be individual for each country.

Disregard of this rule has sown a great deal of confusion. The demographic rise of the eighteenth and nineteenth centuries had encouraged the adoption of an over-optimistic view of the development of many European economies. In fact the cultivation of new crops brought to Europe from America explains many of the changes. Maize and potatoes saved a part of Europe from starvation. In the Danube basin the rural population doubled in a very short space of time after the introduction of maize. Without the potato many societies would have been unable to support 'modern' densities of population, as is proved by the famous

1. Ohlin, G., *Historical evidence of Malthusianism*, p. 6 in vol. *Population and Economics. Proceedings of Section V*, (*Historical Demography*) of *the Fourth Congress of the International Economic History Association*, Editor Deprez, Paul, University of Manitoba Press, 1970.

2. Wrigley, E. A., *Societé et population*, Hachette, Paris, 1969, p. 152.

Irish famine and its tragic train of victims between 1845 and 1850.

In the Spanish case analysis of the causes must be preceded by a discussion of the size of the population increase during the eighteenth century. This question has given rise to a great deal of controversy. Whilst most authors accept as trustworthy the estimates for the last third of the century (9,308,900 inhabitants in 1768, 10,409,900 in 1787, and 10,541,200 in 1797), there is a deep division of opinion about the figures produced by the first census, that of 1717–1718. For some the figure of 5,700,000 given by the census should be accepted as correct; for more, this so-called Campoflorido Census is inaccurate and its figures should be increased by 20 per cent, in accordance with the standard set by the contemporary Gerónimo de Ustariz. In the first case, the average annual rate of increase in the fifty-one years from 1717–1768 would be over one per cent; in the second case the rate would be less than a half per cent. Recently an analysis by the Italian demographer Livi Bacci has tilted the scales in favour of the argument for the more restricted increase. His reasons seem convincing, in view of the age-distribution given in the census of 1768. The acceptance of a rate of growth greater than one per cent per annum throughout the preceding fifty years would imply a life-expectancy of about forty years, a level which was not reached in Spain until the decade 1911–1920; whereas the rate of growth of 0·42 per cent, combined with the population age-pyramid of 1768, gives a life-expectancy of the order of twenty-seven years, which is most likely for that epoch.[3]

From 1768 to 1787 the rate increased to 0·59 per cent; from 1787 to 1797, a period beset by difficulties, the rate fell to 0·13 per cent. In general, comparing some stages with others, from 1717 to 1797 the population of Spain increased at the average rate of 0·42 per cent per annum, exactly the same as in the period between the first and

3. M. Livi Bacci: 'Fertility and Nuptiality Changes in Spain from the Late 18th to the Early 20th century', in *Population Studies. A Journal of Demography*, vol. XXII, No. 1 (1968) p. 84.

second censuses, from 1717 to 1768. Although much less than it would be if we accepted unquestioningly the figures of 1717, the proposed is far from contemptible. This means that the Spanish increase was lower than those of Scandinavia and England, but was outpaced by that of France, and also, it was the point of departure of a course which has never been interrupted: from 1717 each census has reported a larger number of people than the one before it.

As in England, although less spectacularly, the Spanish demographic surge of the eighteenth century accelerated during the first half of the nineteenth century and slowed down in the second half. From 1797 to 1860 the rate of increase rose to 0·63 per cent per annum, as compared with the rise in England and Wales (15,699,100 inhabitants) of 1·25 per cent per annum between 1795/6 and 1861: from 1860 to 1910 (19,944,600 inhabitants) the average rate fell to 0·49 per cent (England and Wales: 1·18 between 1861 and 1911). So that at first sight we seem to have before us yet another example of the demographic change which, in the more advanced countries, has accompanied economic change.

But in actual practice the case of Spain is untypical, and to understand it fully we must go much further. It is clear that the demographic development of Spain before the eighteenth century was not normal, and it took a different course from that followed in neighbouring countries. As far as the data can be trusted, it can be stated that from the opening of the Christian era until about 1700, the numbers of French and Englishmen quadrupled at least, Italians nearly doubled in numbers, and yet Spaniards only multiplied by 1·34. The 7,500,000 Spaniards of 1717 demonstrate that the population was much smaller than that which the territory in which it was settled could bear, even under the old economic system as it was before the great changes wrought by industrialisation. It can almost certainly be affirmed that the long-drawn-out Reconquest of Spain from the Moslems during the Middle Ages and the burdens of empire during the Habsburg period left Spain less well populated than otherwise it would have been. The theme of lack of population, as is well known, dominates the political writings of the seventeenth century, and it is almost by definition the theme of the decadence of Spain.

On the contrary, when the Treaties of Utrecht and of Rastadt (1713–1714) decreed the loss of most of Spain's European possessions, this was enough to allow the metropolis to regain strength and make evident an unwonted demographic surge. Rising above the laments of his contemporaries, one writer of that epoch realised very clearly the benefits brought about by the shedding of an unbearable burden: in contrast with the policy of preceding times, 'which demanded the depopulation of the Realm, the exhaustion of the Treasury and the extenuation of the Vassall in order to retain distant provinces', 'today Spain is smaller than her natural boundaries of the Atlantic Ocean, the Mediterranean and the Pyrenees: this is the first sign of this Monarchy's happiness!'[4] A similar interpretation should be put upon the later outburst (of late 1792 or early 1793) of Count de Cabarrús against 'the senseless expeditions to Africa, Hungary [sic] and Italy', or against the money wasted 'to maintain a two-hundred year war for the State of Milan, Naples and Parma, for what was not of the slightest importance for us.' More generally, it is worth emphasising the interest manifested towards the end of the eighteenth century in the deserted villages (the denunciations by the Asturian Campomanes, of the Aragonese Asso, of the Catalan Caresmar...) which, amounting to several thousands,[5] bore witness to the costs of a former too ambitious political alignment.

4. Romà i Rossell, 1768, quoted by Nadal, J., *La población española, Siglos XVI a XX* Ariel, Barcelona 1971, passim.
5. In a recent work are listed and located on the map a total of 1,113 deserted villages in the territories of Navarre, Aragon, Catalonia, Murcia, New Castile and Andalusia alone (cf. Cabrillana, N., *Villages desertés en Espagne* in the vol. *Villages desertés et histoire économique, XIe–XVIIIe siècles*, SEVPEN, Paris, 1965, pp. 461–512). However, the list is very incomplete; compare the 48 Catalan deserted villages in the list with the number of 288 which the Count de Cabarrús had counted about the end of 1792, or early 1793.

The important demographic rise noted between 1717 and 1860 did not spring from any industrial revolution, but it took place while the old economic system was still in full force and because of the mere removal of external obstacles which, for centuries, had kept the number of Spanish people below the level which it could have reached. There was neither industrial nor demographic revolution. As recently as 1900 Spain registered a gross birthrate of 33·8 per thousand, a death-rate of 28·8 per thousand, and a life-expectancy of less than thirty-five years—all this had been surpassed by the Scandinavian countries a hundred and fifty years before. At the end of the nineteenth century Spanish death-rate and fertility had not yet been able to make the break with old trends which is characteristic of the new development of demography.

For a century and a half, up to 1860 approximately, the waning of epidemics—which took place for no known reason, the increase of the cultivated area—to an unexpected degree aided by the very seriousness of the preceding retreat—and the adoption of maize and the potato appear to have been sufficient to support a demographic increase of 0·51 per cent per annum. Later, from 1860 to 1911, the trend slackened pace, because the breaking of new land had come up against the limit imposed by the law of diminishing returns. The lack of any agricultural revolution reveals in the end the true nature of the demographic pseudo-revolution. The 15,649,000 Spaniards of 1860 are equivalent to the figure which the country would in normal conditions have reached by about 1700, had it not been for her politically too ambitious career. Once it had reached the level permitted by the 'old' economic system without any fundamental change, the population of Spain proved unable to maintain its former advance and its growth slackened. The second half of the nineteenth century suffered once again from the old imbalance between men and resources. The recurrence of food crises—in 1857, 1868, 1879, 1887 and 1898—supplies, in my opinion, the clearest proof of the nation's incapacity to provide even for its most pressing needs.

The demographic pointer leads, in the case of Spain, to a false trail. The rise in the number of inhabitants begun in the early eighteenth century, should not be allowed to raise hopes. For at least two centuries Spain's population grew unaccompanied by any fundamental economic changes. Judging by the number of workers employed in the secondary sector, or by the latter's contribution to the national product, the true industrialisation of Spain is a contemporary phenomenon whose beginnings are in the last decade, from 1961 to 1970.[6]

The recognition of this should not, however, make us forget the existence of a long period of gestation. The Industrial Revolution very soon sank a few roots into the Hispanic field. For want of fertile soil, on the whole these roots nourished weakly plants, which relegated the old colonial Power to a secondary place. The analysis of this disappointment forms the object of this study.

The beginning of the English Industrial Revolution, which came first in time, is almost unanimously placed about 1780. From that country the Revolution spread, with more or less delay, to others. About when did it 'reach' Spain? The answer is made difficult by twin obstacles: on one hand the lack of knowledge; and on the other by asynchronism, typical of economic backwardness, and which leads to confusion of terms. In the development of England we can see a high degree of synchronisation of the technical, economic, ideological and political changes which were conducive to the triumph of capitalism. Yet this development in Spain shows ambiguous characteristics: traditional and modern economy and subsistence and capitalist economy at the same time: a century ago the Spanish economy was 'really a dual economy'.[7]

When did this dualism, still very much with us, begin in Spain? From what date can we see the emergence of clearly

6. Cf. in this connection the reflections of Vilar, P., *La Catalogne industrielle: réflexions sur un démarrage et sur un destin*, paper presented at the colloquium on *L'industrialisation en Europe au XIXe siécle. Cartographie et typologie* (Lyons, 7–10 October, 1970).

7. Cf. the book by Sanchez Albornoz, N., *España hace un siglo: una economia dual*, Ed Peninsula, Barcelona, 1968 (especially the Prologue).

capitalist forces, even though they were not yet strong enough to challenge the traditional ones? I believe that the 'leap' took place in the fourth decade of the last century, that decade which, coincident with the triumph of the bourgeoisie, witnessed the almost simultaneous beginnings of the nationalisation of lands held in mortmain, the mechanisation of the cotton industry, the pouring of cast-iron from furnaces, and mechanical constructions. In spite of inadequate planning and results, the nationalisation of lands caused an increase in agricultural production, which in turn was the support of the last phase of heavy population increase. The introduction of machinery into cotton spinning and weaving concentrated the various enterprises, reduced costs, multiplied consumption and made a decisive contribution to the formation of the national market. The firing of the first blast furnaces encouraged the use of iron, which the first foundries moulded and which finally emerged as pieces of machinery. The key date seems to be 1832, when the use of steam power was adopted by the most representative consumer industry and also when modern methods of steel production were first employed, with a first smelting to make iron, followed by a second smelting to make steel.

FOREIGN DEBT, FOREIGN CAPITAL AND RAILWAYS

The modern course of Spain and its public finances was diametrically opposite to that of Britain. Whilst in the United Kingdom overseas trade played a major role in the financing of the new industrial state, in Spain the loss of the colonies and the end of the control exercised up to then on trade between the Old World and the New, together with other factors, balked any chance of effecting by some normal method that same political evolution. As is shown in table 1 the resources of the Spanish Treasury did not rise by any substantial amount until the decade 1851 to 1860, after the bourgeois rise to power and the tax reforms of Mon-Santillán. In England, on the contrary, the leap had been made in 1801 to 1810. This placed Spain fifty years out of phase, a fact which must be borne in mind in reaching an understanding of the process which placed Britain at the head of world powers and relegated Spain to the role of a second-rate power.

TABLE 1: Ordinary Revenues of Spain and Britain from 1791 to 1880 (base 1791 to 1800 equals 100)

| | SPAIN | | UNITED KINGDOM | |
	A ordinary revenue	*B* percentage of *A* represented by customs duties	*A'* ordinary revenue	*B'* percentage of *A'* represented by customs duties
1791–1800	100·0	21·3	100·0	20·2
1801–1807	93·7	13·4[1]	210·4	19·3[1]
1814–1820	79·0	15·3[2]	336·6	19·8[2]
1821–1830	77·2	11·2	286·6	27·9
1831–1840	102·2	8·0	254·0	40·5
1841–1850	136·4	10·6	275·2	40·8
1851–1860	211·2	11·0	292·6	39·5
1861–1870	303·8	9·1	342·1	32·8
1871–1880	323·8	11·3	371·3	26·8

Notes   [1] Figures for 1801–1810.   [2] Figures for 1811–1820.

Source: *La quiebra del Estado español del Antiguo régimen (1814–1820)*, by J. Fontana, Barcelona, 1971, pp. 61 and 65.

But the table tells us even more. During the first three decades of the century the Spanish Treasury's course was not progressive, nor even stable, but clearly regressive. The fall in receipts, marked in 1811 to 1820, culminated in 1820 to 1830, when revenue scarcely surpassed three quarters of that in 1791 to 1800. The decrease occurred just at the time when the task of reconstruction was faced and when the frequently violent phase of internal dissensions opened. So there were greater expenses and less revenue, leading to the overflowing of the budget deficit. The State's finances were launched on a slippery slope up which it was impossible to climb back. Political instability and vested interests condemned the reiterated attempts at reform to still-birth or to malformation. Under these circumstances there was nothing to be done but raise loans. Resort to credit became a constant factor in Spanish policy, and all other needs of the country were ignored for its sake. Spurred by its monetary difficulties, the State did not hesitate to engage in competition with the business-men of Spain herself, establishing a policy of generous rewards for sums voluntarily deposited in its chests. The high rate of interest on government borrowing encouraged the extremely high cost of all kinds of money. The harm done in this way to the economy was enormous. The capital market, small enough already, lost its specific function of giving an impetus to productive forces, and was diverted into purely speculative investments. The process, as we shall see when we consider the iron and steel industry, discouraged the best-intentioned business-men.

The scant numerical data which we possess only confirm the truth of these assertions. In 1864, of the twenty-three stocks quoted on the Madrid Market—established in 1831—fifteen were official and only eight were private. Until its closure in September 1868 the State Deposit Fund, created in 1852, employed its entire resources in the provision of funds for the Treasury. From 1858 to 1866 the Bank of Barcelona, the second largest issuing bank in Spain, established in 1844 in the greatest industrial centre of the nation, lent an annual average of 9·2 million *reales* guaranteed by the public debt, as against an annual average of 5·08 millions guaranteed by railway stocks and bonds, and another annual average of 1·51 millions guaranteed by the shares of genuinely industrial companies. Only the Bank of Bilbao, set up in 1857 with a capital of eight million *reales*, played a truly positive part in the encouragement of production.

But what was even more serious was that the voracity of the Treasury influenced to the same extent the workings of the official bank. Instead of setting itself up as the regulator of monetary policy, the Bank of Spain, created in 1829 under the name of the Bank of San Fernando, from the outset assumed the mission of channelling funds into the Treasury, with the dual result of inhibition of the development of the economic forces when it was almost the sole financial institution in the country, and of failure in the task of consolidating itself in the position of a complete central bank. In exoneration is the plea that the function of money-lender to the State was not chosen by the Bank, but was thrust upon it. In 1829 the decree founding the Bank of San Fernando linked it with the Treasury; in 1874 the successor, the Bank of Spain, was granted the monopoly of issuing notes in exchange for a close dependence on the government. As the stipulations of the decree stated: 'With credit depressed by its abuse, loans exhausted through administrative faults, and the nationalisation of the land rendered useless for the time being, there is no alternative but to resort to other means in order to consolidate the floating debt and to sustain the enormous expenses of the war . . . In such critical circumstances . . . the undersigned Minister [Echegaray] proposes to create a National Bank which will act as a financial force in aid of the Public Treasury.'[8]

The Bank of Spain's attitude towards the private sector only began to change in any significant way in 1891, when the Bank accepted some industrial and commercial stocks as security, and in 1902, when it began to grant preferential credits to mercantile, industrial and agricultural enterprises and also allowed the opening of current accounts in gold for the payment of customs duties. These measures, the first of which should be connected with the protectionist move of the same year, show the first evidence of a wish to collaborate in the economic development of the country. But they came very late, when, owing to the final consolidation of a private banking system, they were no longer so badly needed. If it had come fifty or sixty years before, the assistance of the Bank of Spain could have been decisive. But instead of that, dealings with private individuals throughout that period were of a marginal nature, as is proved by the fact that from 1852 to 1873, the period least unfavourable to private interests, the average annual

8. Tortella, G., 'El Banca de España entre 1829 y 1929. La formación de un banco central'. in the vol. *El Banco de España. Una historia económica.* Madrid, 1970, p. 286.

amount lent to them did not rise above twenty million pesetas, whereas the average capital sum immobilised in government loans was as high as 82·1 millions.

The country's wealth flowed out through the gap of the budgetary deficit. The subjection of the official Bank to its demands allowed 'the State to proceed with the fulfilment of its obligations'[9] although not all of these. Internal resources, whether directed or not by the Bank of Spain, were insufficient to re-establish the Treasury's equilibrium. The deficit continued, with the result that it was impossible to avoid the much more onerous resort to foreign lenders and bankers. In the dramatic circumstances of the three-year period of Constitutional rule from 1820 to 1823, violently brought to an end by the armies of the Holy Alliance, or in those of the First Carlist War (1833 to 1839), or of the Revolution of September 1868, to mention only a few of the more spectacular episodes, the Treasury, exhausted and without any means of recovery, was forced to call on foreign aid. The sixteen million dollars contracted for in Paris, but in the main raised in London, during the Constitutional three years, signal the bankruptcy of the national Treasury and its delivery to foreign financiers. The facts which are known are conclusive: from 1816 to 1851 the absorption of Spanish public securities by the Paris Bourse totalled 775 million francs, including the capitalisation of interest due but not paid, a sum equivalent to 35 per cent of the whole of French investment in foreign securities;[10] during the Liberal period of 1869 to 1873 the London Stock Exchange, 'which always showed a certain sympathy for revolutionary movements in any part of the world', sold Spanish government securities to the value of £34·5 million, a figure which represented 23·8 per cent of all its loans to European countries and which placed Spain in the position of second largest debtor, after Russia.[11]

9. Ibid., p. 312.

10. Cameron, R. E., *France and the Economic Development of Europe, 1800–1914. Conquests of Peace and Seeds of War*, Princeton, 1961, p. 85.

11. Jenks, L. H., *The migration of British Capital to 1875*, 2nd ed. London & Edinburgh, 1963, pp. 422–424.

These deals were made in the very worst conditions. From the Napoleonic Wars to 1820, no financial operation could be concluded with Spain since no interest had been paid since 1806 on the two so-called 'Dutch' loans, amounting respectively to 8·86 and 240 million *reales*. In the course of thirty-three months from 1820 to 1823 the Constitutional Cortes, after laborious efforts, obtained a series of loans to the total of 2,091 millions; the first, for a nominal value of 300 millions, agreed in November 1820 with the Paris group formed by Lafitte and Ardouin, was for seventy per cent of the nominal capital, with interest of five per cent, a premium of two per cent and an advance payment of two and a half per cent to the subscribers; in fact the actual sum received by the Treasury was only 181·4 millions and the real rate of interest was as high as 11·5 per cent.[12] Again, in September 1823, after the end of the Constitutional three years, the so-called Regency of Urgel, supported by French forces in order to establish an absolute monarchy, contracted with the firm of Guebhard, also of Paris, its own loan producing sixty per cent of the nominal capital at five per cent interest on the latter. These figures, from a deflationary period, give us some idea of the price paid for foreign help. Then, when the debtor State was unable to fulfil its obligations, the demands of the lenders simply grew larger. It is enough to quote the example of the last financial operation of the reign of Ferdinand VII (died 1833), which consisted of the clandestine issue of a nominal 569 millions guaranteed by the bonds of the Constitutional period. This operation was both murky and disastrous for the Treasury, since the capital to be raised was only 26·75 per cent of the nominal sum, or in other words there was a discount of more than 70 per cent, and furthermore the deal was handled directly between the monarch and the banker Aguado (a Sevillian Jew resident in Paris since 1814), behind the back of the Treasury Minister, López Ballesteros, who managed to

12. Information from an unpublished work by M. A. Broder of Paris, concerning the documents in the Archivo Histórico Nacional (section Hacienda) of Madrid.

obtain a letter in the king's own hand-writing absolving him from all responsibility.

From its very beginning, what we can call the new Spanish foreign debt was the source of bitter and involved disputes. In 1824 the refusal of Ferdinand VII, restored as absolute monarch, to recognise the loans raised by the Cortes from the Ardouins was the reason why the London Stock Exchange adopted the rule of not allowing the bonds of insolvent states to be quoted. Three years later, in 1827, Spanish obstinacy in remaining insolvent caused the foundation in Britain of a Spanish Bondholders' Committee, an unprecedented move. The suspension of market quotations and the association of injured parties were repeated throughout the century. At last the State was forced to resort to emergency measures. The conversion of the debt (in 1851 and in 1882), a move which disguised an actual swindle, erred on the excessive side and brought unfavourable results such as London's rejection of Spanish government bonds from 1851. On the other hand, the road of indirect recompense, although more harmful to the country, appeared also to be the most speedy. In some cases, such as the cession to the Rothschilds of the mercury of Almadén (see below, pp. 577–581), the Treasury pledged its own patrimony for the benefit of some lender. This expedient, as we know, was not new. The novelty in the nineteenth century was rather in the adoption of compensations as a general rule. In response to pressure from the creditor nations freedom of investment in the private sector was offered as a recompense for investment, past or present, in the public sector.

Generally available compensations were the work of the Liberal rulers of the Progressive period (1854 to 1856) and of the Revolution of September 1868. Under the Progressives the advantages for foreign capital were granted through a system of exemptions to the regulations for limited companies. Under the so-called Glorious Revolution, these favours took the form of an almost complete liberty to found every type of company through issuing shares and, above all, of special Bases ruling mining exploitation.

The first official regulations for limited companies date from the Commercial Code of 1829, inspired by the Napoleonic Code of 1807. Under the Spanish Code the formation of any company by the issue of shares depended on the Commercial Tribunal, except in the case of issuing banks—privileged companies—which needed royal consent. This system, called 'moderately restrictive', continued in force until the financial panic of 1847 to 1848, which was attributed by contemporaries to 'excessive speculation', and was replaced by one much more strict. From then on issuing banks had to be approved by the Cortes, whilst non-issuing banks and any other kind of limited company were simply banned unless they could show that they were 'of public utility'. Driving home the nail of prohibition, a new law, of 1849, closed the door to the formation of new issuing banks.

After the difficult years from 1846 to 1849, the Spanish economy began to recover from 1850. The agricultural boom which started in 1852 gave a surplus of crops but not of cash. The Crimean War, which broke out in 1853, ceased the exportation of Russian grain—but allowed the exportation of Spanish. At once the parallel demand for credit facilities showed up the inelasticity of the financial system established in 1848 to 1849. The supply of money, which worked on the principle that the amount issued was to equal the capital available, and was limited to the New Bank of San Fernando (created in 1847 by the amalgamation of the Spanish Bank of San Fernando and the Bank of Isabella II, both of Madrid), the Bank of Barcelona (1844) and the Bank of Cadiz (founded in 1846 as a branch of the Bank of Isabella II and made independent at the amalgamation of the two Madrid banks the following year), proved to be insufficient to satisfy the growing demand for it.

The political change of 1854 allowed these deficiencies to be amended in part. In January 1856, half a year before the close of the Progressive interlude, the Cortes approved, after long debate, the bill on issuing banks and that on credit companies intimately connected with the Railway Law promulgated in June 1855. A new banking system began to replace the old. In fact, the Banking Law of 1856 adopted the standard of 'plurality of issuing banks', relieving these three banks of their sole right to make issues, extending this right to local banks or, in their default, to the branches established in the provinces by the Bank of Spain (now re-baptised after its start in life as the Bank of San Fernando); and furthermore the limit imposed on issues was raised to three times the gold reserves. For its part, the Law on credit companies brought merchant banks into the system by allowing them to issue short-term bills (for one year) which could circulate as money; and so these institutions took on the role of quasi-issuing banks. Yet the Statute of 1848 on the so-called banking and bill-clearing companies (commercial banks) was not changed, so that their situation in the future became one of marked inferiority.

From 1856 to 1864, during the period of greatest success, the circulation of notes rose constantly, from 227·9 to 499·1 million *reales*. This expansion was directly related to the increase in the number of issuing banks from three to twenty-one, even if we count the Bank of Spain and its two branches as only one such bank. In the more forward-looking towns a host of local banks took up the task of ensuring the flow of money. This fact, favourable in itself, nevertheless revealed the fragility, if not the entire lack, of a national capital market; and the great regional differences in rates of interest was another factor leading to the same conclusion. On the other hand the number of credit companies also reached its peak at the end of 1864, when there were thirty-four of them, with a total employed capital of 1,134·8 millions, 3·7 times that of the issuing institutions (306·4 millions). It is not known to what extent the issue of short-term bills by the merchant banks swelled the financial current.

In any case we must regard the development of the credit companies in the period from 1856 to 1868 as the most important attempt made in Spain in the nineteenth century to mobilise money of dispersed and obscure ownership. But what was this money, whose was it, and how was it employed? The first application to form a credit company was made on the 20th of March 1855 by Viscount de Kervegen, a deputy in the French National Assembly, and M. Millaud, the Director of the Banque Immobilière of Paris. The promoters tried to win over the authorities by offering to set aside each year the sum of one million *reales* for the purchase of Spanish public debt; but in exchange they sought the right to make issues, and it was this that brought the refusal of their scheme. The second, third and fourth applications, all successful, were also French and were put forward by groups led, respectively, by the Péreire brothers, the Rothschilds and Prost-Guilhou. The three proposals were approved by a Law of the same date as the general Law on credit companies (the 28th of January 1856), which is convincing proof that the latter was made to their measure. Lastly, the three companies forthwith subscribed four-fifths of a sizeable loan to the government (200 millions), which reinforces the notion that they had close connections with the Treasury. The Péreire brothers had already presented the government with a loan of twenty-four millions before the company was set up, doubtless hoping to ease its birth; and the draft of the document establishing the company was presented to the Cortes, in December 1855, by none other than the Treasury Minister, Bruil.

The Péreire's bank, called the Sociedad General de Crédito Mobiliario Español, was established with a capital of 465 millions, not subscribed in its entirety until 1864. The Rothschilds' bank, named the Sociedad Española Mercantil e Industrial, was authorised to raise 304 millions of capital, although it never even approached that figure, since it reached its maximum of 91·2 millions in 1857. The Prost bank, the Compañía General de Crédito de España, had an authorised capital of 399 millions, but it never issued more than a third of that sum. Even with the shortfalls noted in the last two cases, the three French banks were clearly the leaders among the long series of credit institutions born under the protection of the 1856 Law. At the end of 1864 the Crédito Mobiliario alone held two-fifths of all the funds raised by the thirty-four credit companies established in Spain. The Crédito Mobiliario Barcelonés (twelve millions) and the Crédito Castellano (11·7 millions), of Valladolid, led the native companies, but remained a very long distance behind the foreign ones. So that the mobilisation of funds during that period between 1856 and 1868 which was so crucial in various ways received its first impetus from abroad. As was to be expected, the greater part of the resources mobilised also came from abroad. At the end of 1864 'it seems unquestionable that 85 per cent, and probably even 95 per cent, of the capital of the Crédito Mobiliario was foreign'.[13] The Sociedad Española, which aimed at attracting savings from inside Spain rather than injecting French money, met little success, which explains the small proportion of capital issued and the short-fall in 1861.

It remains for us to detail the object and results of all this mobilisation of capital. The credit companies, as we have just seen, were in fact merchant banks conceived with the aim of encouraging industry. In the case of Spain the financial system set up in early 1856 showed a very marked leaning towards the promotion of railway enterprises. For a decade the railway dream stimulated the most important monetary currents. By the end of 1864, the railway concessionnaires had managed to drain off 6,212 million *reales*, whereas only 393 millions had been invested in the establishment of true manufacturing companies. The new means of transport cornered funds which normally would have gone into industry. 'Between 1856 and 1866, Spain used up all she had on railways (apart from wars, of course).'[14] This assertion seems to me to apply especially to Catalonia, the only region of Spain which at that time possessed a native capital market and a true manufacturing industry, and in consequence the only region in which the alternative 'either

13. Tortella, G., 'La evolución del sistema financiero español de 1856 a 1868' in the vol. *Ensayos sobre la economía española a mediados del siglo XIX*, Madrid, 1970, p. 102.

14. Tortella, 'Ferrocarriles, economía y revolución', in the vol. *La Revolución de 1868, Historia, pensamiento, literatura*, chosen by Clara Lida and Iris M. Zavala, New York, 1970, p. 133.

railways or industry' had full force. This fact explains why the financial crisis of 1866, an exact replica of the railway crisis, was much more violent in Barcelona than in Madrid.[15]

But this railway fever should not be regarded as anything unusual in itself, since it reflected an attitude found on all sides. The novelty in Spain lay in the very one-sided support lent by the authorities. After private initiative had constructed 500 kilometres of track between 1848 and 1855, the general Railway Law of the 3rd of June 1855 placed the concessionnaire companies at an extraordinary advantage compared with other industrial limited companies, with government encouragement in hard cash and tariff exemptions. We shall mention later the influence on the Law of the precedent set by the concession in 1849 of the line from Langreo to Gijón to the Queen's morganatic husband, the Duke of Riánsares; but now we must discuss the blossoming of the system sketched out with the aim of favouring the Duke, and to pause and examine its consequences. Thanks to the measures of 1855, railway companies were the first, before banking and credit companies, to enjoy the new regulations concerning their creation, less strict than the general system governing limited companies laid down in 1848 to 1849. Thanks to the legal dispositions of 1855 railway companies which were not Catalan (which in practice meant foreign ones) received substantial subsidies which by the end of 1863 had risen to 788·55 million *reales*[16] out of the total invested, which was considerably less than 6,000 millions. Thanks to these same dispositions railway concession companies founded before August 1864 enjoyed, during the time taken to build the line and for ten more years after its completion, a rebate of all duties on the importation into Spain of all

15. Cf. the articles of N. Sánchez Albornoz, 'La crisis de 1866 en Madrid: la Caja de Depósitos, las sociedades de credito y la Bolsa,' in *Moneda y Crédito*, No. 100, pp. 3–39 and 'La crisis finanziaria del 1866 vista da Barcellona,' in *Rivista Storica Italiana*, anno LXXX (1968) fascicolo 1, pp. 20–31.

16. Jimeno Agius, J., 'Los ferrocarriles españoles en fin del año 1863', in *Revista Minera* (as quoted in *Revista General de Estadística*) XV (1864) pp. 406–411.

capital goods, rolling stock and of fuel imported from abroad.

With these advantages railways spread rapidly throughout Spain. From 1860 to 1865 some 613·32 kilometres per year of track were opened to traffic, bringing the total to 4,828·62 kilometres. The Cía. de los Ferrocarriles del Norte de España, formed by the Crédito Mobiliario, and the Cía. del Ferrocarril de Madrid a Zaragoza y a Alicante, offspring of the Sociedad Española Mercantil e Industrial, emerged at once as the leaders of the railway enterprises. In other words, there was a close correlation between the degree of capital concentration and the volume of railway investment. When they imposed the new financial system the foreigners had railways very much in mind. The most prominent activity of the credit companies was to place enormous quantities of railway stocks and shares on the international markets and also on the internal market, although the latter operation was on a much smaller scale, but a very significant one in the conditions of the Spanish market.

Brought in from abroad and set up by the foreign resources, the pattern of rail transport in Spain soon proved to be inadequate for Spanish needs. On one hand the 'philosophy' on which it was based, 'railways are a necessary and sufficient cause of economic development', required levels of production which the country had not reached; on the other, the system built paid little attention to the convenience of internal traffic.

As for the 'doctrine', it proved to be a great mistake to confuse the means of communication with the traffic. In this respect the example of Catalonia at the end of the eighteenth century might have proved to be a useful lesson: in the opinion of the most shrewd observers it possessed the worst roads, yet also the highest development of all Spain.[17] In 1864, when the imminençe of a rail slump became perceptible, the railway engineer Martínez Alcibar put his

17. Fontana, J., 'La primera etapa de la formació del mercat nacional a Espanya', in the vol. *Homenaje a Jaime Vicena Vives.* t. 11. Barcelona, 1967, p. 151.

finger on the cause of the trouble: communications 'are of little use if there are no products to transport ... Railways help to encourage the growth of industrial production; but where the latter does not exist they do not improvise it, as is shown by experience'.[18] George Stephenson, the pioneer of railways in England, who was sent in 1845 to investigate the possibilities for railways in Spain, hit the nail on the head: 'I have been a whole month in the country, but I have not seen during the whole of that time enough people of the right sort to fill a single train'.[19]

The peculiarities of the railway system must be condemned together with the 'philosophy'. Instead of constituting a network, the system radiated from Madrid, with terminal points at the sea-ports. In this matter too the testimony of a contemporary is better than any present-day commentary: 'For the railways to be instruments of production, they should have been built with this aim, and in that case they would have acquired a life of their own ... Our railway system suffers from fundamental defects, and it is almost exclusively concerned with the notion of seeking its life at the coasts and frontiers, because it is the belief that wealth can only come to us from abroad, and unhappy is the country which does not seek prosperity within itself! With the exception of the coastal lines [in Valencia and Catalonia] which compete with coastal shipping, almost all the rest cross the Peninsula in various directions, traversing moorlands and deserts, occasionally touching some centre of production, whilst between them there are vast regions deprived of transport: in other words, our railways have been made an instrument of extraction and of international trade and not, as should have been their principal aim, an instrument of production and internal circulation.'[20]

Export, to the service of which the Spanish railway

18. 'Contestación al interrogatorio para la información sobre el plan general de ferrocarriles por el Ingeniero Jefe de minas de la provincia de Zaragoza', in *Revista Minera*, XV (1864), pp. 707–708.

19. Cameron, *France and the Economic Development of Europe*, p. 212.

20. Orellana, F. J., *Demostraciones de la verdad de la balanza mercantil y causa principal del malestar económico de España*, Barcelona 1867, pp. 114 and 111.

system was subjugated, was mainly concerned with the products of mining. Even in their reports of 1859 and 1860 the managers of the Crédito Mobiliario manifested their preference for northern railways rather than others, because of their desire 'to ensure for us the possession of coal', which they believed to be abundant in the territory of their concession, and which, in its turn, they considered essential to their ultimate aim of 'seizing the trade in metals'.[21] From its inception the greater part of the railway system was designed to be an instrument of colonisation and exploitation, much more than an instrument of true development. This was a defect of the Spanish railways which could never be corrected, but which should occasion no surprise considering the conditions and pressures under which the general Law of June 1855 was conceived.

CONFISCATION OF LANDS HELD IN MORTMAIN

We have already indicated that the decrease in revenue from the customs was the main cause of the Treasury's difficulties during the first half of the nineteenth century. In contrast was the ease enjoyed by the British Exchequer, brought about by the increasing income from foreign trade (40·8 per cent of all revenue in 1841 to 1850, as compared with 20·2 per cent in 1791 to 1800). These contrary courses give a remarkably expressive reflection of the contrary political progress of each country, and reveal the inability of Spain to provide, by normal means, for the financial needs of a modern State.

Instead of normal means, revolutionary ones were tried. At the same time as it called on foreign capital, the Madrid government, from the last years of the eighteenth century on, multiplied the issues of Royal bonds and other methods of raising internal capital. But these were marketed with ever-increasing difficulty, since no funds existed which could cover the new debts of capital and interest. In February 1824 a Sinking Fund for the National Debt was

21. Tortella, 'La evolución del sistema financiero español', p. 95.

established, mortgaging the Crown's revenue and in particular the income from certain taxes. However, the Fund must inevitably lose on the roundabouts what it gained on the swings. The growth of the snowball of the National Debt could only be halted by the creation of a 'new' national fund, over and above the traditional sources of capital. The remedy—drastic and 'in the French style'—was to be the nationalisation and sale of all property held in mortmain. According to the most reliable data (from the Land-Survey made by La Ensenada, dating back to the middle of the eighteenth century), the Church alone held 14·73 per cent of all the land in the twenty-two provinces of Castile, and took 24·12 per cent of the gross product of the agriculture of all that region;[22] the towns and cities owned even more in their municipal lands, although they made less profit; finally, the Crown possessed a not inconsiderable tract of unproductive mountain and poor quality plain. This huge expanse, to which were added the corresponding lands of the old Kingdom of Aragon, was confiscated, nationalised, and sold off at public auction, with the main, though not exclusive, aim of redeeming the excessive amount of public debt in circulation. Agrarian reform, which the enlightened thinkers of the eighteenth century had believed would act as a social and economic corrective, in practice was applied for fiscal and political reasons.

The application came late. The change in the laws relating to the land could not be made until after the death of Ferdinand VII. There were the law of 1798, which ordered the alienation of all real estate belonging to religious charities in order to obtain the funds necessary for the redemption of the first Royal bonds; the dispositions of the Cortes of Cadiz, of much wider scope, but annulled in 1814; the decrees of the three-year Constitutional period, revoked in 1823. Each time that things began to move,

22. Anes, G., 'La economía española, 1782–1829', in the vol. *El Banco de España. Una historia económica*, p. 238, note 8, and Vilar, P., 'Estructures de la societat espanyola cap al 1750. Algunes lliçons del cadastre d'Ensenada', in the new periodical *Recerques. Història, Economia, Cultura*, No. 1 (Barcelona, 1970), pp. 12 and 13.

reaction took care to put them back in their place. Yet from 1833 the wrangle over the Succession to the throne hastened events. The financing of the civil war and the need to replenish the ranks of the liberals coalesced, and brought the reigning stagnation to an end once and for all. In only two years, from July 1835 to June 1837, the ministers of the legitimate government enforced the law of 1820 which broke civil entails—an action not displeasing to the nobles, who recognised that its effect would be to increase the value of their estates, which would enter the ordinary commercial market. Further, the government laid the foundations of the alienation of Church lands, by suppressing the religious orders and awarding all their real estate to the State for confiscation. The sum produced by the sale of these lands was to be used for the redemption of the Public Debt. These measures, tempered but not annulled during the decade of Moderate government (1844–1854) served as a precedent for the wider-reaching law of the 1st of May 1855 passed by the men of the two-year Progressive government. This law decreed the sale of all property held in mortmain, including the common lands of municipalities. Although there were some modifications, confiscation and sale had become an irreversible fact.

Apparently alienation was a success. In 1845 almost three-quarters of Church real estate had been sold—indeed in some districts, such as the Balearic Islands, the percentage was as high as 99. The Church's anathemas possessed little power against the greed of the buyers. Even a region so full of religious sentiment as Navarre did not escape the general movement, and showed a very high proportion of sales. In some cases not even priests were absent from the ranks of the purchasers.

Yet, instead of serving to distribute the land and forests in small portions so as to increase the number of landowners, the enormous quantities of real estate thrown onto the market 'have passed from corporate ownership into that of individuals, which is even more discouraging to that multitude of farmers and farm-labourers without capital, without resources to obtain it, and without the understanding and knowledge to associate together and consider a matter which is so important to them'.[23] The Spanish alientation did not bring into being, as had the French, a rural society of small landowners, simply because this was never its true intention. In Spain the laws on alienation were enacted with the dual aim of rescuing the State Treasury and of ensuring the throne of Isabella II, or the power of the Liberals. In order to gain the first end, bonds of the consolidated National Debt were accepted as payment; and for the second these bonds were accepted at their nominal value, even though they had depreciated enormously. Armed with these, the speculators pushed their bids sky-high, overwhelming at the auctions the country-folk, who would have preferred to pay by long instalments, but in cash. Contrary to former opinion, the procedure was not at fault in valuations, but in the acceptance of 'paper' in lieu of cash.

The old oligarchy, rooted in the aristocracy, was superseded by a new one of bourgeois origin. The Spanish system of sale brought profit to a few, and thus accentuated the process of the concentration of land in the hands of a new class of absentee landlords, a process which made the poor dependent to some degree, in some cases even approaching serfdom. In this fashion the land, ruled by and from the city, generally did not benefit. The growing demand for agricultural produce was satisfied, in the main, by the method of increasing the area cultivated. In spite of the lack of quantitative data we can recognise the unquestionable fact that the breaking of entails and the alienation, above all that of municipal lands, was followed by a large increase in the breaking of new ground—the famous enclosures of common lands—which very considerably increased the area of land under cultivation. As a result the rural landscape underwent great changes. On the high *meseta*, the increased area was put to cereal farming; in Catalonia and Andalusia it was the grape vine. These two

23. *Manual de desamortización civil y eclesiástica. Repertorio de leyes, instrucciones, . . . desde 1° de mayo de 1855 hasta 1895*, Madrid, 1895, p. 17.

products were the most typical of Spanish farming up to the end of the nineteenth century.

The farming of wheat and other cereals grew in the shelter of rigidly protectionist laws. Nicolás Sánchez Albornoz has emphasised the apparent paradox that 'the liberals of 1820, their eyes fixed on a policy of encouragement for agriculture in order to aid new social groups did not hesitate to sacrifice upon the altars of this idea the liberties proclaimed at the beginning of the century.'[24] In fact, only a month had elapsed since the opening of the new Cortes when a decree of the 5th of August prohibited the importation into any part of Spain of wheat, barley, rye, maize, millet, oats and all other foreign grains and flours, until the price of the *fanega* (about 1·60 bushels) of wheat, which was employed as the standard, rose above 80 *reales* and that of flour rose over 120 *reales* on the principal markets, excluding the Balearics and the Canaries; whilst grains from these islands must not be exported. This decree, in fact, together with the amendments made by a Royal Decree of the 27th of January 1834, is the basis of Spanish protectionist policy with regard to cereal production until the tariff reform of 1869, and even again it was restored, although with some changes under the Restoration. It was only in 1825, 1847, 1856 and 1867 that food crises necessitated the suspension of this rigid protectionist policy. Perhaps the spread of the potato, dating back to the great famines of the Napoleonic period, contributed in some measure to this very considerable success.

During the thirty-three years between 1849 (the date of the first balance of trade figures) and 1881, there were twenty-six in which the exportation of grains exceeded the importation, as compared with seven years with the opposite result. On the other hand, from 1882 until 1913 the thirty-one yearly accounts showed an adverse balance. The balance of the first period, up to 1881, reflects the positive achievements of the breaking of new ground following the

24. Sánchez Albornoz, N., 'La legislación prohibicionista en materia de importación de granos, 1820–1868', in the vol. *Las crisis de subsistencias de España en el siglo XIX*, Rosario (Argentina), 1963, p. 16.

alienation; that of the second period reveals in part the negative effects of that change. The protectionist policy first put into effect in 1820 in accordance with the interests of the new land-owners had resulted in the country's self-sufficiency in food. However, the breaking of new land went too far, and included marginal land whose economic return was too low. Even though fertilisers—guano—were beginning to be used, the excessive growth of cultivation played a part in maintaining, and perhaps reducing, the paltry average that the crops yielded. In 1900, still, the average production of wheat was no higher than 6·92 metric quintals per hectare. As low returns imply high costs, it is easy to understand the accumulation of obstacles which faced exports from Castile. Abroad, apart from the assured markets of Cuba and Puerto Rico, there were ever fewer opportunities save in exceptional cases such as the Crimean War; inside Spain there were the constantly rising barriers against supplying the districts outside Castile, which, despite the prohibitions in force, were invaded by the smuggling of foreign grains.

The transport revolution which, to begin with, had favoured the marketing of Castilian cereals in the coastal areas ended by freezing them at their source. Railways made possible the shipment of the harvests of the American and Russian plains; steam navigation made possible their discharge in European ports. Transatlantic and trans-mediterranean competition, which had been felt in England or in France from 1875, pitilessly attacked the agriculture of Spain, Italy and Algeria about 1880. The supply by rail of grain to Barcelona fell from 72·5 thousand metric tons in 1884 to 54·4 thousand in 1885 and to 13·9 thousand in 1886; and meanwhile sea-borne grain jumped from 54·9 thousand to 76·5 thousand and to 110 thousand tons in the same period. The responsibility for the collapse of the native-grown wheat trade was apportioned, in equal shares, to the cost of production and to that of rail transport. In 1887 the Commission established especially to study the crisis was forced to recognise that: 'it costs less to bring wheat from the United States to a Spanish port than from the centre of Spain to the coastal regions and, on occasion, even less than it costs to take it from some township to the capital of its own province.'[25] Soon afterwards the Treaty of Paris and the law opening commercial relations between the USA and Cuba, were to eliminate for ever the trade in Castilian flour from Santander to the Antilles.

The slump in prices meant that many landowners were unable to maintain production in a large number of marginal areas of land. Even though this matter still needs to be investigated fully, we can presume that it led to a profound transformation in rural structures: there would probably be a decrease in the area dedicated to grain, accompanied by a search for other more profitable products. For some ten years, up to 1891, the great prosperity of viticulture acted as a palliative to part of the disaster; but after that, other remedies had to be found.

The social results of the crisis were internal flight from the land, and the formation of a common front with the industrial workers. They were made public by the National Economic Congress of 1888 held in Barcelona and they imposed the protectionist solution. For once conservative and a considerable number of liberal politicians were in agreement: Spanish production must be defended by the State whatever the cost. The tariffs of 1891 and 1906 sheltered the Castilian cereal producers behind a barrier of 110 per cent raised against the importation of foreign grains. This support helped to win back and even to surpass the lost positions. In 1901 the French Consuls estimated that the harvests in Castile and León were back to 'normal', while those in Andalusia were at about a half of normal. Up to 1930 the dry lands on which wheat was grown constantly increased in area, rising from an average of 3,459,211 hectares in the years 1903 to 1907 to an average of 4,203,868 hectares during 1928 to 1932. That is to say, in a quarter century there was an increase of 21·5 per cent over the original extent. Consequent upon this increase of cultivated area and tariff protection, which

25. Fontana, J., 'La gran crisi bladera del segle XIX', in *Serra d'Or*, *2ª* època, any II, No. 11 (Nov. 1960), pp. 21–22.

from 1922 was an absolute ban on foreign importations, Spain was once more able to supply her own needs. In 1923 and 1924, after forty-one uninterrupted years of deficit, the wheat harvest produced the first surplus since 1881. The importance of this success can be realised if one takes into account the large part played by wheat in the diet of the Spanish people. Even so, the cost of self-sufficiency became excessive once more. Yet again, the breaking of new ground was surpassing the limit imposed by the costs of production and the needs of the pastoral interests. Just as fifty or sixty years before, the most authoritative opinion had cried out against the abuses, and recommended the restoration of large areas to their original owners. This was the advice of the economist A. Flores de Lemus, in 1926, and of the road engineer Manuel Lorenzo Pardo, in 1933.

The grape was the other crop which benefited from the measures of disentailment and alienation. Yet the vineyards' prosperity has always depended on the possibility of exportation of the product, contrary to the case of wheat. The recent history of two of the great viticultural centres of the country—Catalonia and Andalusia—provides a very good illustration of this. In Catalonia, the increase in plantations of vines dates from the later years of the seventeenth century, when the English and the Dutch flocked to the coast in order to ship the local vintages and spirits. This traffic very soon became the basic factor in the early formation of capital, which led to the subsequent industrial development of the region and to the assertion that 'the decree of 1778 obeyed that inexorable law of economics, which was the need to open a foreign market for our wines and spirits.'[26] This decree permitted commerce between all the main ports of Spain and those of Spanish America. On the other hand, we have the case of Lower Andalusia, the exportation of whose sherry wines appears to date back to the late fifteenth century, and whose trade soared in the

26. Giralt Raventós, E., 'Evolució de l'agricultura al Penedès. Del cadastre de 1717 a l'època actual', in the vol. *Actas y comunicaciones de la 1ª Asamblea intercomarcal de investigadores del Penedès y Conca d'Òdena*, Martorell (Barcelona), 1950, p. 169.

eighteenth century because of the increase of English demand for them.

Although it was spread among the coastal regions, and therefore faced no serious transport difficulties, viticulture increased its rate of progress as a result of the great transferences of property which took place in the second third of the nineteenth century. As a commercial crop, the grape suited remarkably well the character of the new city-bred class of landlords. Instead of being invested insecurely in some industry with merely hypothetical returns, a part of the capital brought home from the former colonies was invested more safely in the wine and spirits trade, whose profits were certain. It was by no stroke of chance that the first Spanish railway concession, made in 1830 but ineffective until 1854, was aimed at the establishment of communications between Jerez, Puerto de Santamaría and Sanlúcar. There was also good reason why the Catalonian district of Alt Penedès in the same period between 1840 and 1860 should manifest an exceptional boom in the wine trade at the same time as an extraordinary slump in industrialisation.

Spanish exports of wine, which had been increasing for a long time, excelled even the most optimistic forecasts when phylloxera invaded the French vineyards. From the time of the introduction of the parasite in 1863, France's vineyards were inexorably destroyed. France, the largest consumer and exporter of wine in the world, was unable to meet either internal needs or external contracts. The wine-merchants were forced to resort to the massive importation of foreign vintages. Because of geographical proximity and low prices, Spanish competition won a decisive victory. Spain filled a large part of the gap left by France in the international wine trade. This export trade reached its peak in the decade 1882–1892, the period when there existed a special Hispano-French treaty which reduced tariff barriers to the minimum.

However, the euphoria (which in Catalonia resulted in a period of opulence and speculation, known as 'gold fever') did not last for ever. In Málaga the phylloxera struck in

1876, Gerona suffered in 1879, Orense in 1881. Starting from these centres, all distant from each other, the plague gradually spread into the interior, with the same perseverance as it had shown in France. In 1892, when the disease had caused great damage in the Peninsula, France, by then recuperating, rejected the 1882 treaty. No more was there easy entry for Spanish wines, whose production, in any case, had begun to decrease. In Spain, there were blighted harvests, loss of markets, a dramatic awakening to the harshest reality. The percentage of farm-workers in the total emigration figures, which had been 54·4 in 1892, rose to 73·6 in the following year. In the province of Tarragona the Priorato district, in which vines had become a monoculture, lost one-fifth of its population between the censuses of 1887 and 1900.

The expansion changed its course. In total, the 1,706,501 hectares of vines counted by the Agricultural Consultative Board in 1889, were reduced to 1,367,845 in 1907, the year in which the re-plantation with American vine-stocks immune to phylloxera came to an end. Wine, which from 1851 to 1890 'had occupied the first rank amongst all the lines of Spanish products exported',[27] was henceforth unable to recapture that primacy. American stocks, much more delicate than the European stocks destroyed by phylloxera, have a higher cost of production than had the former ones. The profit and the incentive for the producer were diminished.

Crisis in viticulture followed crisis in cereals. At the end of the nineteenth century, after a half-century of relative prosperity, the possibilities opened up by the changes in ownership of the land had been exhausted. The last-ditch defence of Spanish grains and the partial renewal of the vineyards in the hope of bringing the troubles to an end, showed that the disease was internally created, in other words that stubborn immovability ruled the agrarian scene. The only useful improvements were localised in the coastal districts of Valencia, between the rivers Mijares and

27. Vicens Vives, J., *Historia social de España y América*, t.IV, vol. II: *Burguesía, industrialización, obrerismo*, Barcelona, 1959, p. 236.

Segura, where orange trees won a massive victory over the vines, and also in a few patches here and there where sugar-beet filled the gap left, after the loss of the colonies, by Antillean sugar cane. In both these cases—oranges and sugar-beet—the crops required irrigation and brought high returns, and were urged on by exceptionally forceful groups of peasants as well as by a new-style irrigation policy (dating from the so-called Gasset plan of 1902), which at last was specifically intended to make the soil fertile.

Making things as bad as they could be, the agricultural crisis was paralleled by a crisis in stock-raising. The extension of ploughed land following on the laws of disentailment and alienation, was prejudicial to the progress of pastoral farming. In 1887 an official Commission set up to investigate both forms of farming reported: 'The fact that our pastoral farming has, since the change in our economic and political systems, gone progressively from bad to worse, is known to all. The immense quantities of real estate which civil disentailment thrust into the hands of individuals, the suppression of common and Royal lands, and the breaking of new ground have constantly and ever more insistently decreased the area of pasture and cover in which our stock-raising found sustenance and life. All the land won by agriculture, all the energy which individual initiative has expended in order to convert into arable land what beforehand had only been dedicated to pasture, have been prejudicial to the existence of our herds and flocks'.[28] At the end of the process the imbalance between agriculture and pastoral farming was so great that agriculture would finish by becoming the victim of its own expansion: 'the decrease which these practices inevitably bring to our herds contributes to the possibility that, for lack of manure and of farm-hands, some lands will gradually become barren, as has happened in some districts of Upper Aragon'.[29]

28. *La crisis agrícola y pecuaria. Actas y dictámenes de la Comisión creada por R. D. de 7 de julio de 1887 para estudiar la crisis por que atraviesan la agricultura y la ganadería*, vol. I, Madrid, 1887, p. 361.

29. Ibid., p. 366.

In this context the pastoral crisis, the fate of the sheep, deserves special attention. Sheep, the traditional symbol of Spanish pastoral farming, decreased in esteem and in numbers during the nineteenth century. This fact was to have important repercussions on foreign trade. Wool, which from the fourteenth century had become the mainstay of the country's exports, gave place to wines and minerals. Through negligence or some other reason, Spain did not succeed in maintaining exclusive possession of the ancient merino breed. In France, Piedmont, England and especially in Saxony, sheep of Spanish origin proliferated and were improved, finally to cross the seas and become naturalised in Argentina or Australia. The supply of wool for British mills, mainly Spanish in 1800 and even in 1814, had passed into German hands by 1827. The United Kingdom statistics faithfully portray the decrease of imports of wool from Spain from 1796 to 1840. Spanish statistics show that, from 1849 to 1880, the total exportation of untreated Spanish wool to all parts of the world only reached an average of 3,478 tons per year, a figure one-third less than in the second half of the eighteenth century (5,218 tons per year between 1749 and 1793). Alienation—especially of common lands—merely accentuated an already apparent decrease.

At the opposite extreme, the prosperity of mule-breeding proved to be the exception to the rule. The use of this bastard breed by Castilian farmers had ancient origins. Indeed, at the middle of the sixteenth century, scarcity of labour and extension of arable land made it a general custom to employ mules for ploughing, in part substituting, because of the greater area that these animals could plough, the slower though thorough work of oxen. In the nineteenth century the breaking of new ground made the same remedy essential. In both periods the protests of the experts were identical. In the first case Juan de Arrieta had called the use of mules 'bad, pestilential and very pernicious' as compared with the use of oxen, which was 'good, useful and admirable'.[30] Three centuries later, in 1863, Fermín

30. Cf. Alonso Herrera, G., *Agricultura general*, vol. IV, Madrid, 1819, p. 219.

Caballero denounced the mules' ploughing, shallow and hurried, as 'one of the most deadly faults of our agriculture'.[31]

The alienation of lands held in mortmain, which we have called 'revolutionary' from the Treasury's point of view appears to us, on the other hand, to have been a measure enforcing the status quo if we examine the social and economic scene. The new land-owning bourgeoisie which emerged from the sales of public lands merely maintained and prolonged former agrarian patterns.

The effect of this phenomenon on general economic development, and especially on industry, remains not yet examined. Following Gramsci's thesis on the Italian scene, one bold author[32] blamed the Catalan bourgeoisie—in Spain the only group in the nineteenth century interested in industry—for failure to carry this revolution into the fields, and for having instead come to terms with the Castilian large land-owners. If this were true, the bourgeois class would have to have decided beforehand what were to be the limits of their industrial expansion, an action which must have been contrary to their own interests. It is true that discussion of the Italian example can help to form and enrich discussion of the Spanish problem, but the example does not include all of the elements necessary for an adequate understanding of the case here. The facts which, in our case, are known, are as sparse as they are confused. We know nothing of the dimensions of the capital market, the actual sums paid for the lands, the size of investment in agricultural improvements, the use made by the nobles of the price of the disentailed lands, the size of investments in industry, the distribution of workers in the various sectors of the economy, etc. The data of Tortella concerning the formation of industrial limited companies between 1859 and 1866[33] are, in spite of their interest, unable to throw much light on the case of a country in which the small,

31. Caballero, F., *Fomento de la población rural*, Madrid, 1864, p. 83.

32. Sole-Tura, J., *Catalanisme i revolució burgesa. La síntesi de Prat de la Riba*, Barcelona, 1967.

33. 'El principio de responsabilidad limitada y el desarrollo industrial de España: 1829–1869', in *Moneda y Crédito*, No. 104 (1968), pp. 69–84.

family unit played a decisive part. The data given by Lazo concerning the reduction from 6,000 to 460 in the number of families working the old ecclesiastical lands of the province of Seville after the alienation[34] do not answer the questions of the problem of day-labourers or of possible changes in the manner of cultivation. The observations of Giralt concerning the excessive investment by the new owners in the disentailed lands of Valencia, with the consequent waning of the silk and other industries,[35] sketch out a problem of the greatest interest, but which is not typical. We definitely believe that the premises from which one must start are two which are very general and also fairly sound: on one side, that the proportion of Spanish lands held in mortmain and in entail had no parallel in Western Europe; and on the other, that native capital was scarce. The conjunction of both these elements, and the manner in which the alienation was imposed, seem sufficient to explain the fact that, in comparison with the French example, Spanish agricultural reform did not aid the formation of a numerous class of small land-owners; and also that, in comparison with the Prussian case, the large estates which were created did not adopt forms of exploitation which were truly capitalistic; and this is leaving aside subjective considerations such as lack of a spirit of enterprise in the proprietors. The mouthful represented by the lands was too big, too much for the digestive capacities of the purchasers. The later lack of financial resources among the purchasers maintained agricultural productivity at its traditional levels. We attach the greatest importance to this last finding. Without the creation of cheap surpluses, without the liberation of agricultural workers, the conditions required for the establishment of a dynamic, numerous urban proletariat were lacking. It would be interesting to know how much this fact contributed to the smallness of industrial enterprises and to the firm establishment of forms

34. *La desamortización de las tierras de la Iglesia en la provincia de Sevilla*, Seville, 1970, pp. 110–111.
35. 'Problemas históricos de la industrialización valenciana', in *Estudios Geográficos*, XXIX (1968), pp. 369–395.

of family business associations. On the other hand, the wretched condition of country people, who were too numerous for the needs of the land and were under-employed or kept on starvation wages, caused in large measure the lack of elasticity in the demand for industrial products. In our present state of knowledge it is difficult, not to say impossible, to apportion what blame should be laid on the Catalan bourgeoisie for the spectacular failure of the agricultural revolution. On the other hand, we can have little doubt about the negative effects of this failure on the activities of the bourgeoisie and on the development of the secondary sector in general.

NATIONALISATION OF SUBSOIL RIGHTS

The revolution of September 1868 found the Treasury in a parlous state. Figuerola, the new Treasury Minister, made a first calculation that the deficit amounted to 2,490 *reales*, half of which was owed to the national Deposit Fund, immediately frozen by the Provisional Government. Besides the ordinary budget revenue, within a few years almost all the income from the confiscation of lands had been consumed, as well as the considerable sums which had flowed into the Fund and the substantial amounts received as loans after the 1851 reform; the National Debt had increased by 50 per cent between 1860 and 1868, when it had reached 22,000 million *reales*, and interest had risen by 130 per cent to 590 millions.[36] Among the most urgent obligations was the need to settle at the end of the year the loans supplied by foreign companies (among them Fould and Co. of Paris), which amounted to 343 millions.

Unfortunately, the crisis was not confined to the Treasury. Four years of drought and poor harvests had ruined agriculture; the collapse of 1866 had produced financial disorder; the Cuban insurrection increased the national expenditure and at the same time reduced the money coming in from the colonies . . . Any increase in taxation,

36. *Colección legislativa de España*, vol. C (2° semestre 1868), pp. 500–511.

which was especially difficult in these circumstances, was in any case completely contrary to the political and social programme of the revolution, which had proclaimed the termination of the tax, hated as much as it was profitable, on provisions entering each municipality. Finally, the same considerations forbade the easy yet dangerous resort to monetary inflation. So that the government had no other alternative than to raise loans. At the end of October the government announced that it was offering a public loan on Treasury bonds to the value of 2,000 millions, guaranteed by foreign bankers.

The cost of this operation was heavy. Since the market quotation for the Foreign Debt stood at 35 per cent, the new bonds had to be issued at 32 per cent of the nominal value. For example, the house of Rothschild paid 100 millions in cash in exchange for bonds bearing a face value of 320 millions. Besides this there had to be the establishment of a fund to guarantee the payment of interest and of the capital borrowed. The decree which announced the loan assigned the so-called 'National property' to its repayment. Three months before, another measure had attempted to dispel the fog surrounding the position of the mines in the 'National property'. In this way, irreversibly, the continuance of the Treasury's difficulties on the one hand, and on the other the disappearance of income from the sale of lands, finally imposed the disentailment of subsoil rights.

After a long period of governmental neglect, the Mining Law of 1825 had reaffirmed the principle of royal ownership of subsoil rights stated in the regulations of 1584. In accordance with them all underground deposits were owned by the Crown, which reserved for itself the richest of them (among others those of Almadén, Arrayanes and Riotinto) and conceded to third parties the exploitation of the rest. The new laws of 1849 and 1859, however, replaced monarchical ownership by that of the State. From then on both legal texts read 'all mines belong to the Nation, whether it exploits them itself or whether it cedes them, with proper guarantees, to individuals', which was the same thing as the conversion of mines into national property. Nevertheless, the process of alienation was still incomplete while there were still restrictions imposed on the concession and, above all, while there was in existence the possibility of staking claims, which constituted an ever-present threat of deprivement. The elimination of these obstacles was the important task which gave rise to the drawing up of the 'General Bases for a New Mining Law', promulgated on the 29th of December 1868.

These Bases delegated to the civil provincial governors the power to 'make concessions' without the need for any previous proceedings (such as trials of the ore, or enquiries), and, in particular, they made the concessions in perpetuity, thereby forbidding any possibility of the staking of claims. Simply the payment of the royalty constituted a guarantee of permanent exploitation, and in practice the concession-naires became real proprietors. On the other hand, the State Treasury was willing to implement a directive of the 11th of June 1856 which allowed it, under certain conditions, to alienate mineral deposits which it had declared to be specially reserved.

The Bases of late 1868, elevated to Law by a declaration of the Cortes, and in force until July 1944, opened an era of unsuspected prosperity for the Spanish mining industry. For once, at last, the 'power to grant concessions' and the 'freedom of exploitation' had been attained after many years of loud persuasion, and financial resources teemed in to help the mining industry. The number of mining concessions—bringing a corresponding profit to the State—rose at once to dizzy heights, as if this were a new El Dorado. Spanish subsoil exploitation became the object of feverish speculation, intricately mingled in which there arrived floods of adventurers and business-men. As a result, forty-five years later, when the fever had abated, the number of mining companies had risen to 564, divided among the nations and capital investment as appears in Table 2.

The numerical inferiority of foreign companies appears to have been compensated by their greater individual

TABLE 2: Mining Companies in 1913

Those with known capital	No.	Capital (in pesetas)
Spanish	232	635,470,030
Foreign	138	593,991,445
British	52	312,245,539
French	57	152,361,739
Belgian	26	98,581,727
German	1	21,574,973
Swiss	2	9,227,467
TOTAL	370	1,229,461,475

Those without known capital		
Spanish	167	
Foreign	27	
TOTAL	194	

Source: *Anuario de minería, metalurgia, electricidad e industrias químicas en España*, publicado por la 'Revista Minera, Metalúrgica y de Ingeniería', Bajo la dirección de A. Contreras y de R. Oriol, T.XIII (1913), Madrid, 1913.

financial strength. It is true that the addition of companies whose capital was unknown might contribute to the size of the Spanish nucleus, though not greatly, since these were smaller firms. To set against this, we have frequent cases in which the actual possession of stock in Spanish mining enterprises was in the hands of foreigners. In sum, it does not appear to be too bold to affirm that in less than half a century the 1868 law placed a half of Spanish mining enterprises in the ownership of foreigners.

The results of these investments were at once evident. Once over the bad year of 1869, when political causes brought difficulties, the exportation of minerals and of metals after their first smelting reached such a high degree of success that it changed the very structure of foreign trade. Under the previous system the most valuable exportations of mining and metallurgical products had occurred in 1863 and 1864, reaching totals of 50·3 and 49·6 million pesetas. After the law of 1868–69 the value rose to 58·5, 85·5 and 102·9 millions in the years 1870, 1871 and 1872. After that the increase continued, with small fluctuations, until it reached the record figure of 338·3 million pesetas in 1910.[37] Since the other exports did not advance in the same degree, the consequence was an important climb in mining figures within the total figures for exports.

Exports of minerals and metals, which had to begin with played a secondary role, climbed to the situation of constituting almost the third part of all exports in 1899–1908. This notable increase came about mainly through the figures for minerals, which were insignificant to begin with, but which were catapulted to the summit of exports after the alienation measures decreed by the September Revolution. In fact these exports occupied the first place from 1899 to 1911. However, the quantities of metals remained fairly stable except for the slump of 1879–1888, mainly caused by the collapse of the international price of pig lead.

The great changes referred to above primarily affected lead, copper, mercury and iron.

Large-scale working of lead ores was the biggest novelty in Spanish mining and metallurgy in the nineteenth century.[38] After the Napoleonic War, the decree of the 3rd of November 1817 which freed the mineral from State control and the declaration of the Cortes, confirmed by the law of the 12th of February 1822, permitting the free working and exploitation of all mines in Spain, created the legal basis for a spectacular upsurge. Then foreign demand and the striking of very rich deposits in the coastal regions did the rest. The movement originated in the Sierra de Gador and its continuation in the Sierras of Almagrera and Cartagena: that is, in three of the mountainous spurs which shape the south-east of the Peninsula from the Alpujarras to the Cape of Palos. In 1822, the house of Reina, a firm in Málaga, established at Adra, the port nearest to the Gador

37. It should be pointed out that from 1868 the values are the tax values, and not the true statistical ones. This might constitute an important difficulty for a precise analysis of foreign trade, but it is less serious when, as in this case, we are dealing with large amounts only (cf. Andrés Álvarez, V., 'Historia y crítica de los valores de nuestra Balanza de Comercio', in *Moneda y Crédito*, No. 3, 1943, pp. 11–25).

38. I have dealt extensively with the mining and smelting of lead in my article 'Industrialización y desindustrialización del Sureste español (1817–1913)', in *Moneda y Crédito*, No. 120.

mines and the San Andrés factory, the first enterprise which merited that name. The modern lead industry was launched. At the other side of the same province of Almería, on its frontier with Murcia, the discovery of lodes in the Sierra de Almagrera, soon to eclipse the fame of Gador, came with the finding of the Jaroso vein in 1839. In Cartagena, inside the territory of Murcia, the initial smeltings of silver-bearing ores from Jaroso, effected by the Sociedad Franco-Española in 1842, spread from 1843 to include the dross of Phoenician and Roman times and from 1847 to the carboniferous seams of the neighbouring Sierra.

'The sudden development of the mining industry in the Kingdom of Granada', as Le Play wrote in 1834,[39] immediately had deep repercussions. The Andalusian ores, easy to exploit, with a metal content of 70 and even 80 per cent, were increasingly exported in pig form, thoughout the whole world, even to China, and led to a swift decline in prices on the principal markets, which caused the bankruptcy of many English and German mines. In this manner the 'lead revolution' became for Spain some sort of palliative for the crash of other products, such as wool, and already by 1827 contributed the high figure of 8·40 per cent to the total value of commercial exports. Save in exceptional circumstances, such as the Crimean War, which allowed the exportation of large quantities of Castilian grain, pig lead regularly occupied the second position after wine.

The region should have been enriched. Lead mining and smelting brought very high returns. A considerable part of the income from exports were net profits, divided between the proprietors and renters of mines and foundries—who were Spanish in the majority. High wages attracted numbers of working men, which was detrimental to agriculture. The lead from these mountains seems to have been an important factor in capitalisation. But in practice lead-smelting did not bring prosperity to other industrial sectors. From what

39. 'Itinéraire d'un voyage en Espagne, précédé d'un aperçu sur l'état actuel et sur l'avenir de l'industrie minérale dans ce pays (20 avril-15 juillet 1833)', par M. F. Le Play, ingénieur des Mines, in *Annales des Mines*, 3rd series, vol. V (Paris, 1834), p. 182.

facts we know, the blame must be placed especially on the system of exploitation of mines: stakes which were too small (normally under a hectare), which raised obstacles to all planning ahead, were made worse by the practice of letting and sub-letting for very short periods, which forced the renting firms ('assisting firms') to draw immediate profit from the deposits, against the interests of rational, long-term organisation of labour. The exploitation of the subsoil and, in the same fashion, that of the factories, was in the hands of speculators rather than in those of true industrialists.

After a long period of English dominance and a moment of equality in 1867 to 1868, Spanish production of pig lead rose in 1869 to the leadership of the world, and only lost this place in 1898 to the United States. But, in actual figures, Spanish production continued to rise until the First World War, attaining its peak in 1912. The new thrust came now from within the Peninsula, and was closely linked to the development of the railway system and the new mining laws. The provinces of Jaén and Badajoz in the last third of the nineteenth century, and those of Córdoba and Ciudad Real in the first years of the twentieth century made the greatest contributions to this success. In all cases foreign demand and—a new development—foreign capital were the decisive influences. In the province of Jaén, the district of Linares was led by English companies, with their The Linares Lead (the oldest, founded in 1852), The Alamillos, The Sopwith and especially The Fortuna, famous for its foundry, whose only competitor was the foundry of La Cruz, a French firm. Yet, in the district of La Carolina British hegemony came later, in the early twentieth century, with The Centenillo and The Guindos enlarging the field opened by Stolberg and Wesphalia of Aachen, from 1855 the greatest European producers of lead, and by the Real Cía. Asturiana de Minas. In Badajoz, the Castuera zone owed its development to Lafitte and d'Eichalt, the leading figures in the Cie Minière et Métallurgique des Asturies, and to another French company, the Société Minière et Métallurgique de Peñarroya

(1881). This firm was also very important in the zones of Azuaga and Monterrubio, as it was in the San Quintín group of mines of Villamayor de Calatrava in the province of Ciudad Real. In Córdoba the main establishment was the Minas de Villanueva del Dique Company (1904), which owned the El Soldado group, considered as the richest in Spain relative to its size, and which attracted also Peñarroya, Escombreras Bleiberg of Paris (established before in Murcia and Linares) and the Duke of Infantado.

The development of these companies and of others of lesser calibre emphasised the inferiority of the first mining exploitations in the south-east of Spain. The traditional industry of Cartagena was unable to withstand the competition. From the 1860s Adra slumped because the deposits of Gador were exhausted. The original industry was also divided among an excessively high number of companies, which in the period 1842 to 1856 alone rose from two to sixty-four. The essential concentration and modernisation came from outside, from powerful enterprises which were, in the main, French. Such were the Compagnie d'Aguilas (1880), or la Cie des mines et usines d'Escombreras Bleiberg, or the Cie Métallurgique de Mazarrón, one of whose founders, Neufville, was the president of the large Linares establishment, La Cruz. Towards the end of the century this mountain lead industry had changed into an industry of colonial type. This colonisation also spread to iron and zinc mining, other sources of wealth in the subsoil of Murcia and Almería.

In general terms copper, which had from time immemorial been employed in the manufacture of ornamental and domestic articles, was in great demand after the introduction of the use of electricity in communications. In 1853, the visit of the engineer Deligny under the sponsorship of the Marquis de Decazes (son of the founder of Decazeville, the great steel-manufacturing centre of the Aveyron, and French Ambassador to Madrid from 1846 to 1848), bore fruit in the form of the first foreign copper-mining firm. At once mining fever struck again, as is evident from the 250 claims made in the course of the same year. In 1855 the first firm was taken over by the more powerful Cie des Mines de Cuivre d'Huelva, registered in Paris, with a capital of six million francs, and which, at least in part, seems to have forestalled the Péreire brothers.

But in Spanish terms the development of electricity was of less importance in the launching of copper-mining than was the demand for sulphuric acid by the new English chemical industry. Besides copper and iron, the pyrites of Huelva contained a high proportion of sulphur, which the French technicians were unable to exploit. Very soon the inability of one side and the need of the other brought agreement between the two neighbours separated by the English Channel. The Cie des Mines de Cuivre d'Huelva ended up by leasing to a British consortium the concession it had obtained in the area of La Puebla de Guzmán and Calanas. On the 1st of December 1866 the Tharsis Sulphur and Copper Mines Ltd, registered in Glasgow with a capital of three hundred thousand pounds, raised to a million pounds in 1868, took possession of the mines of Tharsis and La Zarza.[40] Six years later the Tharsis Sulphur Company produced the largest dividend of its entire history, forty per cent, and from 1866 to 1909 the average return on capital reached twenty per cent.

The swift success of Tharsis Sulphur could not but influence the development of the neighbouring mines of Riotinto. This establishment was, together with that of Almadén, the most precious of those reserved to the Treasury. Its wealth was legendary but the legend was given the lie by the actual profit which it rendered. Sometimes exploited directly, at others subject to miserly leases with no guarantee, the mines had passed through alternate phases of semi-neglect and of pillage. The result was that in March 1870 the Treasury Minister was obliged to confess once again to the Cortes the repeated failure of State management, and to beg permission for the sale of this mining establishment. It was granted; the experts estimated the value of the mines at a hundred million pesetas—a

40. Cf. Checkland, S. G., *The Mines of Tharsis. Roman, French and British Enterprise in Spain*, London, 1967.

figure which before had not been reached at the public
auctions—and in the end the mines were leased in 1873 to
the house of Matheson and Co. of London, with the
alliance of the Deutsche National Bank of Bremen, and
Rothschild. The offer was of 92·8 million pesetas, to be paid
over a six-year period—in absolute terms a fabulous sum,
but in relative terms insufficient, if we take into account the
fact that the estimate of the mines' yield had been made in
the period of the greatest slump in the value of copper. In
any case the money—some in cash and the rest in promissory
notes vouched for by the group of purchasers—allowed the
Spanish government to stave off the pressure of the Foreign
Bondholders' Association, set up in London in 1868.

The purchasers, for their part, formed a company with
capital worth £2,500,000 in stock (£1 was then equal to
24 pesetas), and £1,000,000 in redeemable shares. The
Riotinto Co. Ltd opened in 1875 a railway to the port of
Huelva (85 kilometres), which allowed the immediate start
of mining. The business turned out to be excellent. The
mineral extracted had a proportion of sulphur of nearly 50
per cent and it opened a wide breach in both European
and American markets, rising quickly to the first place in
the world's production. Riotinto in the year 1871 to 1872,
the last year under State control, had reported a deficit
of 98,791 pesetas. But in 1879, the first of a series of substantial dividends, it produced a profit; and from 1879 to
1908 its average annual return was 70 per cent of the capital.
Already by 1884 Riotinto was considered as the greatest
producer in the world. In 1912, the record year, the iron
and copper pyrites of Riotinto constituted 44 per cent of
world production, and the district of Huelva in total
produced 66 per cent. The world leadership which these
figures imply does not signify that the Matheson and the
'Tharsis' companies were alone. From the end of the
nineteenth century an ever-increasing regiment of mining
companies tried to emulate, almost all of them in the
province of Huelva, the fruitful activities of their elder
brothers. In 1913 the companies which stood above these
others were the Peña Copper Mines Ltd (public capital of

£450,000) and the San Miguel Copper Mines Ltd (£200,000 capital), both successors of foreign firms; the first a Belgian one, and the second Portuguese.

We have spoken of the link between the mercury of Almadén, 'doubtless the most precious jewel of the Spanish nation',[41] and the credit-raising operations with the Rothschilds. This link, which had very old antecedents (from 1525 to 1645 the deposits had been leased to the house of Fugger), when it was renewed in 1835, passed through two different phases: until September 1847, the normal procedure was the sale of the mercury deposited in the Sevillian bonded store at the price raised in public auction. In theory, presence at the auction was open to anyone; but in practice the auctions were announced with such short notice that only the agents of the Rothschilds were able to attend. The average income gained by the State in this period was 792·48 *reales* per flask of 34·507 kilogrammes; the wholesalers' profits varied according to the management of the auctions and the prices on international markets; but they must have been enormous when in 1839 one of the members of the National Directory General of Mines made public the fact that the nation made a loss since the auction price at Seville was 900 *reales* per flask, whereas the market price in London rose as high as 2,250 *reales*.[42] Despite this, Spain was obliged to accept the situation because she had geared the sale to various Treasury operations, usually to loans guaranteed by the sale of mercury.

From 1848, the decrease in price of the metal caused by the discovery of mines in California, together with the decrease in its use in Mexico, brought about the failure of later contractual obligations and auction bids and opened the door to the second alternative, that of contracts for sale in which the State was a partner, or the company took commission—a method already agreed upon with the house of Rothschild. The new mercury system was in

42. Ibid., p. 287.
41. Ezquerra del Bayo, J., 'Datos sobre la estadística minera de España en 1839', *Anales de Minas* 11 (1841), p. 285.

operation from May 1852 to June 1857; and, calculated until the 31st of December 1855, the net profit for the State did not rise above 94.52 *reales* per flask, which was less than an eighth of the profits gained from 1835 to 1847. The failure was so disastrous that the government was forced to make an effort to satisfy its commissioner-creditors, and to decree, at last, that the mercury should be sold directly on the London market. From the 1st of January 1858 to the 30th of September 1866, without let or hindrance, the Spanish Treasury's Commercial Mission in London was able to sell 268,216 flasks at an average price of 788.28 *reales* each (£7 18s 0d), using a method which was so well organised that it only cost about one per cent, plus four or five per cent in freight, insurance and warehousing in London.

But such pleasing results lasted for only a short period. Since the Spanish Treasury lacked the fifteen million francs which it owed and must repay by the 6th of October 1866, it had accepted, under a Royal Order of the 22nd of September of that year, an advance of £220,000 from Rothschild and Sons of London; an advance which, as so often before, it intended to repay from the revenue resulting from the sale of Almadén mercury. This loan was offered at the initial rate of 8 per cent per year, but the rate was geared to change with the bank-rate as announced by the Bank of England so that the lender should always receive interest one per cent higher than the official Bank Rate. Furthermore, in recognition of their services in the sale of mercury, Rothschilds were to receive a commission of 3 per cent discount, 0.5 per cent for brokerage and costs: marine and fire insurance, storage at the London docks, and freight and loading costs at Seville. Soon afterwards, in May 1867, while this agreement was still in force, the chairman of the Cía del Nuevo Almadén, the most important of the mines of La California, approached the Spanish government with the proposal that it should rent the mines for a period of twenty years.[43] The proposal was

43. De Aldana, L., 'El año 1871 bajo el aspecto mineralúrgico comercial', in *Revista Minera*, XXIII (1872), p. 295.

inspired by the celebrated Jewish bankers who were the dominant firm in American mercury production and also had owned the mines of Idria, in Italy, since 1831; and by making it they openly revealed their eagerness to establish a monopoly of the valuable metal.

The Spanish government rejected the advances of 1867, but lost little time in accepting facts. The double contract of 1866 was merely the prelude to other pacts, similar yet wider in scope, negotiated by the revolutionaries of September 1866. The decree of the following 28th of October, guaranteed, among other things, by the mines owned by the State, and by the Law of the 23rd of March 1870, which expressly permitted the mortgaging of Riotinto and the cash-raising operations involving Almadén and the salt-workers of Torrevieja, were the legal instruments which allowed, in effect, the whole of the Spanish mercury production to pass into the hands of its untiring pursuers. On the 28th of May 1870, Figuerola, the Treasury Minister, signed with the Madrid representatives of Rothschild and Sons of London and Rothschild Brothers of Paris, a document of credit backed by the product of the Almadén mines and a concession granting exclusive rights of the sale of the product for thirty years. The two agreements became legal deeds on the following 20th of May. At once the price of mercury, which for several years past had been maintained at the level of £6 7s 0d, began to rise on the English market. It was £7 17s 0d on the 24th of June, and £12 0s 0d on the 31st of December.[44] This meant that the increase was 75 per cent during the first seven months of the agreement, or in other words during the first period of monopoly.

Under the first of these two agreements the Treasury was to receive, as a loan, the sum of £1,696,761 at the interest of 8 per cent, and promised to pay the creditor thirty annual instalments of £150,000. That is a total of £4,500,000 in capital and interest over the thirty years. In order to pay back the debt, in six-monthly instalments of £75,000, the whole value of Almadén was mortgaged— mines, mercury, buildings, land and so on. Under the

44. Ibid., pp. 289–290.

second agreement, which governed the sale of the mercury, the government was bound to produce an annual minimum of 32,000 flasks, to attempt to create a rise in production, and to account for these matters to the creditors, who were authorised to inspect the establishment whenever they wished. The improvements required in order to augment production were to be paid for by the government. The mercury was to be handed over in London. The creditors, declared to be the sole vendors of the mercury, were to be paid separately for the 'services' rendered. As a special concession, the Spanish State, which owned the mines, was authorised to retain 200 flasks per year, in order to meet the needs of Spain's own industries.

There is no doubt that the obligations accepted in 1870 were a great stimulus to production. Since the stipulated minimum of 32,000 flasks per year had never been reached except in 1839, there was a risk that the mines might have to be transferred into the hands of the Rothschilds, according to the agreement; and so the national budget for 1870 to 1871 allowed for a credit of 1,250,000 pesetas to be employed in the renovation of the plant, and promised further allocations later. Under this special treatment, the period from 1870 to 1900 became the most profitable of any similar periods to be found in the long history of the Almadén mines.

But the technical results were one thing, and the economic results were altogether another. Under the loan contract, the Treasury received cash to the amount of £1,628,891, which was the total sum, less 4 per cent bankers' commission; and during the thirty years' period of the contract the mines produced £4,500,000, giving the creditors a profit of £2,871,108. Yet also, the gross profit from the sale of mercury between the years 1870 and 1900 was £8,887,385 15s 9d, from which the vendors deducted £882,837 18s 2d as partners, £487,465 18s 1d as commission, discount and brokerage, and £381,889 9s 0d for freightage, insurance and warehousing.

Certainly the sale of mercury produced 239,739,150 pesetas, from which the Treasury received 40,722,278 pesetas as a prepayment (£1,628,891 at the rate of 25 pesetas per pound), and a profit of 69,309,304: a total of 110,031,582 pesetas, in contrast to the 129,707,568 taken by the house of Rothschild. From these figures it can be calculated that the Spanish State received 45·9 per cent of the profit from the sale of mercury, and paid out 54·1 per cent.

After 1900 the Treasury was obliged to renew for two further periods the rights of the sale of the mercury to N. M. Rothschild of London. Finally the Royal Decree of the 21st of December 1921 empowered the Board of the Almadén mines to sell the mercury without going through the solemn ceremony of public auction, and to organise the commerce in the manner which seemed most suitable to it. So, after eighty-six years of more or less disguised cession to private interests, the Treasury had been able to ransom Almadén.

Iron ore mining in Spain had two main centres: in the north the neighbouring provinces of Santander and Vizcaya; and in the south-east the neighbouring provinces of Almería and Murcia. The northern district has always been the more productive, since its lodes are more abundant, of higher quality, and better situated for export to the best foreign markets. Vizcaya, above all, was blessed with a beneficial situation, because of the special richness of its ores and the cheapness of them and of their extraction; and also because of their proximity to the Ría of Bilbao and the effective interest of the local public authorities. Above all, special emphasis must be placed on the mining railway from Triano, or Somorrostro, to the docks at Ortuella—a concession granted by the law of the 19th of June 1859, followed by the railway's inauguration on the 26th of June 1865—and whose existence was largely owed to the Provincial Council of Vizcaya.

But the decisive factor was the discovery and adoption of the Bessemer process for making steel, which offered a splendid opportunity for the Spanish ores. After the first trials with Cumberland hematites, the new British steel industry threw itself avidly upon the deposits in Vizcaya, which were cheaper and contained less phosphorus than did the ores from any other place.

Table 3, which gives the figures of mining, exportation and home consumption, reveals two major facts: (*a*) the close correlation between the first two variable factors; (*b*) the importance of the part of the contribution from Vizcaya, evident from the earliest years and increasing until 1900.

TABLE 3: Extraction, working and exportation of Spanish iron ore, 1861–1913 (in thousands of tons)

| | Extraction | | | Ore smelted in Spain | Ore exported |
| | I | II | III | IV | V |
	Spain	Vizcaya	(II/I 100)		(I–IV)
1861–1870	2,579	1,214	47·07%		
1871–1880	12,551	7,904	63·26%		
1881–1890	49,425	35,575	71·97%	3,789	45,636
1891–1900	66,349	49,411	74·47%	5,430	60,919
1901–1910	87,246	46,681	53·50%	7,704	79,542
1911–1913	27,769	10,992	39·58%	2,543	25,226
1861–1913	245,919	151,813	61·73%		

Source: *Estadística(s) Minera(s)*

From 1881 to 1913, in the period of its greatest prosperity, the Spanish metal industry gained a mere 8·4 per cent (19,466 thousands of tons) of all the ore extracted (230,794 thousands), which means that Spain exported the remaining 91 per cent. The United Kingdom was the most important customer, to the point that, according to Flinn,[45] it absorbed 80 per cent of Spanish exports of iron ore. If this is so, the British steel industry which, during the years of which we are writing, consumed a total of 644,678 thousand tons of ore (474,355 of native origin and 170,323 from abroad) appears to have depended on Spanish importations to the extent of 21 per cent. At all events, it is a statistical fact that from 1883 English iron mining diminished, even though the highest figures for production of iron ingots and steel came in the last year of the period under examination, 1913.

45. 'British Steel and Spanish Ore, 1871–1914', in *The Economic History Review*, 2nd series, VIII (1955), pp. 84–90.

From the 1880s the British steel industry cut short its demand for native prime materials and turned to those offered abroad, especially in Spain. The 170,323 tons of ore bought abroad by the United Kingdom between 1881 and 1913 cost that country £135,917,000 on unloading in British ports. This sum, at an average rate of 30 pesetas per pound sterling, brought 4,077 million pesetas. If we deduct one-fifth to take into account ores not imported from Spain, and the proportion of freight charges from Bilbao and other Peninsular ports, we reach a fairly reliable estimate. We must, of course, bear in mind that although transport costs fell more quickly than did the price of ore, the proportion in 1882 was 70 per cent for the price of ore at the port of loading, and 30 per cent for the transport from there to the port of unloading. We can say that about 2,283 million pesetas (gross) were earned by Spain from the market in Britain. To this sum we must add the income from exportations to other countries, and of course that from ore used by the Spanish iron and steel industry.

Foreign demand for Spanish ore might well have been a most important factor in the creation of capital; but our reply must be guarded, singling out Vizcaya from the other mining provinces. In Vizcaya the mine-owners were astute enough to associate themselves with foreign interests in order to draw profit for both parties from the wealth of the mines. Thanks to this a part of the profits remained in Spain, and indeed made possible the spectacular 'take off' of the province's industries in the last twenty years of the nineteenth century. Between 1886 and 1899 Bilbao registered 636 new companies, with a total capital of 421·9 million pesetas. In 1900, after the enormously successful year of 1899 (the best in Vizcaya's history), all records were broken, with 108 new companies, totalling 160·9 million pesetas of capital. In contrast, 1914 showed a dramatic decrease in the registrations of new companies: 58 of them, with the very small total capital of 5·8 millions. There is no exaggeration when we speak of a significant correlation between the creation of capital and the growth of exports of iron ore. Yet we must still distinguish the difference between the actual capital created and what might have been created. In other words, we should examine the relative shares of Spanish companies and foreign ones in the dividing up of profits from the mines. Most of the large companies bore foreign names (The Orconera Iron Ore Co. Ltd, The Cie Franco-Belge des Mines de Somorrostro, The Luchana Mining Co., The Parcocha Iron Ore and Railway Co. Ltd, etc.) which in itself suggests agreements made on unequal terms. Altogether foreign investment, unleashed after the visit to Bilbao in 1870 of Sir Isaac L. Bell, the great ironmaster from Middlesbrough, appears to have played the major role. The British alone formed between 1871 and 1914 a total of 64 companies for the exploitation of Spanish iron ore—not only in Vizcaya—and their investments amounted to £5,139,691. It was they who organised rational exploitation of the lodes, but on the other hand they took a very considerable share of the profits. However, it is true that The Orconera Company did spend on transport, such as railway construction, a ramp, loading facilities and wagons and engines, the sum of ten million pesetas, which was the equal of the company's original capital in 1873.

In other areas of Spain foreign domination was much greater.

THE PROBLEM OF COAL

The first attempts to encourage the coal industry were made by the Enlightened governments of the late eighteenth century. After the law of the 30th of May, 1780, which conceded a series of privileges and exemptions to any future exploiters of the mines of Villanueva del Río (province of Seville), or of any other place in Spain, in December was published a new list of Regulations: 'to encourage the extraction of coal'. These are notable since they specifically exempt coal from the general royalty levied on mines but declare the mining, commerce and exportation of coal to be free of duties. The orders introduced an innovation in the system, and were confirmed on the 24th of August, 1792. This Law also applied measures calculated to ease the exploitation of coal such as the establishment of a School of Mining in the Asturias, export subsidies to Spanish coaling ships and the promise of improvements in land and river transport. A proof of Charles III's will to go beyond strict legislative limits is that in 1789 he ordered Jovellanos to visit his homeland in the Asturias 'to encourage the coal trade'.[46]

The policy met little success. Commercial exploitation of coal was ineffective, partly on account of transport problems, but largely because of a total lack of demand. This was the history of the Arsenal at Trubia (province of Oviedo), founded in 1794 in order to compensate for the loss to French arms of the arsenals of Guipúzcoa and the munitions factories in Navarre. In 1796 'a furnace was fired with coke from Langreo coal, but whether on account of the workmen's lack of skill, or of the poor quality of the fuel, or perhaps because of lack of knowledge of the manufacture of coke, it is a fact that this attempt was not successful'.[47] The Trubia foundries were forced to use charcoal until 1808, when the French invasion put a complete stop to the work. In the years of greatest activity, 1796–1797, the amount of coal consumed never exceeded 1,561 tons. At the same period production in the basin of Espiel (province of Córdoba) was 492 tons, most of which went to the steam pump used at Almadén to drain the mercury mines. It also seems that about this period Utrillas (province of Teruel) produced the amount of lignite needed by a glass factory set up by German workers in the town. That was the total.

By the end of the Napoleonic Wars, all the coal mines were abandoned except that of Villanueva del Río. The English system, established in 1789, which 'left the most absolute and supreme dominion in the hands of the landowners', had met with complete disaster. Consequently the new mining law of the 4th of July, 1825 (together with

46. *Obras de Don Gaspar Melchor de Jovellanos*, edited and with preliminary study by Artola, M., vol. V, Madrid, 1956, p. 251.

47. 'Fábrica nacional de Trubia', unsigned article in *Revista Minera*, X (1859), pp. 519 ff.

the Royal order of the 18th of December) combined coal together with other mining, all under the regalist principle of royal ownership of mines. Very soon, in 1828, there began a regular, though small, exportation of coal from the ports of Asturias.

But this does not imply a close relationship between the new legislation and the beginnings of the coal industry of Asturias. On the contrary the law of 1825 sponsored by Fausto de Elhuyar, former president of the Royal Mining Tribunal of Mexico, who had returned to Spain in 1821, imposed very small areas for mining claims (200 by 100 *varas*).[48] It also demanded high taxes on the areas (1,000 *reales* for each concession) as well as on the gross production (5% of the value of the product); and for these reasons it was labelled as a measure with an excessively 'American' bias; that is, more interested in the exploitation of metals than of coal deposits. In practice the first two coal-mining enterprises worthy of the name only took off after the removal of these obstacles. The Real Cia Asturiana de Minas de Carbón began to prosper towards the end of 1833, after Elhuyar's death in 1833 finally permitted it to obtain the Royal Order of the 14th of November, which exempted it from all taxes for a 25-year period. There was also the Sociedad de minas de carbón de Siero y Langreo, which flourished from 1838, after the Royal Order of the 11th of November 1836 which multiplied by three the areas of coal mines, and that of the 20th of July 1837 which decreased to one fifth the exploitation tax.[49]

But the history of these companies throws light on other aspects of the problem. At its inception, the Real Cía Asturiana had been planned as a large steel enterprise in which, through the influence of the Navy Minister, some exiled constitutionalists would take part, as well as important representatives of the steel industry established in Liège. But in fact the withdrawal of John Cockerill, exasperated by the Spanish Directorate of Mines, led the

48. That is, 167·18 by 83·59 metres.
49. Schultz, G., 'Algunos datos para la historia moderna de la minería en Asturias y Galicia', in *Anales de Minas*, II (1841), pp. 254–262.

other directors to abandon metallurgical projects and to concentrate instead on the coal of Arnao, in Avilés. Lack of demand greeted the steps. Despite tax exemptions, despite the closeness of the deposits to sea transport, the Cía Asturiana de Minas de Carbón languished for fifteen years, on account of the extreme difficulty it had in finding a market for its coal. The solution only came in 1849, when the fuel began to be employed for the smelting in blast furnaces of the zinc ore which the same company mined in Guipúzcoa. To get one ton of zinc, contained in two and a half tons of ore, seven tons of fuel were needed. So that the new metallurgical industry, in the end, gave impetus to coal mining, although this brought small benefit to the country; for in 1853 the first Cía Asturiana was forced to surrender to the Compagnie Royale Asturienne des Mines. Société pour la production du zinc en Espagne, registered in Brussels and under the clear domination of foreign capital.

It is significant that the second attempt to fulfil the promise of Asturian coal ran parallel with the first. The banker Aguado was granted extensive coal mining concessions in the central coal-field of the Principality of Asturias. Enthused by the idea of providing sea transport for the fuel produced by the Sociedad de Siero y Langreo, Aguado gave new life to Jovellanos' plan for a coal road, and forthwith undertook the project. The road from Sama to the port of Gijón was finished in 1842, soon after the banker's death, but it was inadequate. Transport techniques had progressed, and the two separate tolls by which the constructor's widow attempted to retrieve the costs were too heavy. Coal from inland continued to be too expensive at the ports. At this stage a new business-man intervened to support the Aguado enterprises in the mines and the coal road. He was Fernando Muñoz, morganatic husband of the Queen Mother María Cristina, and who was created Duke of Riánsares in 1844. Muñoz 'pledged all his influence and capital in the construction of a railway which, entitled the Langreo Railway, would run from Gijón and would not go beyond his own concessions; his proposal was supported by other Spanish and foreign bankers since it would run near to theirs, and also by other private shareholders, who were ignorant of the type of speculation in which they became involved'.[50] In order to finance his enterprise the Duke asked the Treasury for a subsidy, which was granted to him in September, 1849. This subsidy, consisting of a payment of 6 per cent on capital invested in the railway, the first such made by Spain,[51] caused a bitter debate in the Senate, and appears to have had a decisive influence on the generosity of the general Railway law of 1855.

At all events the success of Riánsares and the other shareholders in the mining railways was not great. But the transport problem was not ended, as we shall see, by the cartage, since the Langreo railway was unable to overcome the obstacles. There had been no answer to the question of the utilisation of slack, which formed from 40 to 60 per cent of the coal dug, and which it was impossible to utilise away from the mine head. Once again the development of coal mining proved to be inseparable from that of a native metallurgical industry. In the end the Duke transferred his concessions to the French capitalist Adolphe d'Eichtal, a future founder-member of the Crédito Mobiliario, president of the Compagnie Minière et Métallurgique des Asturies. Just as in zinc production, it required seven parts of coal and three of ore to obtain one ton of rolled iron.

What finally created, in the central Asturian field, the demand for coal which had been vainly sought in other places were the industrial establishments of Mieres and of La Felguera. The latter (Sociedad Pedro Duro y Cía) had been active since 1859. The firm established by d'Eichtal and always maintained under French domination always held the first place among Spanish coal producers. Exactly as in the case of the Asturian firm, the enterprise created by Aguado had survived by reconversion to metallurgy; but

50. *Información sobre el derecho diferencial de bandera y sobre los de aduanas exigibles a los hierros, el carbón de piedra y los algodones, presentada al Gobierno de S. M. por la Comisión nombrada en R. D. de 10 de noviembre de 1865*, vol. III, *Carbones*, Madrid, 1867, p. 125 (report of the Commission of the 'Centro directivo de la industria carbonera de Siero y Langreo').

51. *Memoria sobre el estado de las Obras Públicas en España en 1856* Madrid, 1856, p. 70.

as in the other case, the reconversion had implied the cession of the company to foreign financiers.

This new reliance on the iron industry brought prosperity and disappointments, to the coal industry. The Mieres and La Felguera factories which took most of the coal met greater difficulties in development than had been foreseen. The railway building crisis from 1866 and the third Carlist War (1872 to 1876) pushed Spanish steel production below even the least favourable calculations. The result was that the period from 1864 to 1879, that of Asturian supremacy, coincided with the greatest stagnation of the demand, and therefore in the supply of iron. So that the two big companies on the banks of the Rivers Caudal and Nalón gave a permanent, though inelastic, market to the fuel produced in the neighbouring fields. In 1865 the Province of Oviedo produced 339,328 tons of coal, of which 80·5 per cent were burned *in situ* and a small remainder was shipped from the province's ports. In 1881 internal consumption had only risen to 364,484 tons (75·3 per cent of production) and exports accounted for 118,150, including the coaling of steamships—an insignificant advance.

After 1881 the upsurge of the market for iron might have spurred on coal mining if the logical condition had been fulfilled: that steel demand had fallen mainly on Asturias. However, in the short term logic was thwarted, as were local hopes. From the 1880s the Spanish steel industry shifted its centre of gravity from Asturias to Vizcaya: from coal country to iron-ore country. From 1883 the Oviedo factories were working at half speed, and were constantly outdistanced by the new factories established in the Bilbao estuary.

From then on, if it wished to expand, the Asturian coal industry had no alternative but to sell mainly to the Nervión valley, the major part of a production which the local factories, left without the hope of expansion, could not utilise. It is an exact replica of what had taken place in the earlier years from 1825 to 1860, when consumption was mainly outside local boundaries: in the smelting of lead and in iron-production in the south-eastern mountains of Spain, and in the cotton mills of the Catalan coastlands. On account of heavy freight costs this first opportunity was out of reach; but there remains the question of whether the passage of time and the proximity of the area of consumption did not provide an adequate promise of demand.

In order to reply, we must review the previous tariff policies, from the start of this market. Until 1832 the importation of coal had been forbidden except for lead-smelting at San Andrés, in Adra. A Royal Order of the 4th of August 1832 lifted the ban, although it imposed duties so high that in effect importation was still prohibited. The taxes were either 65·21 or 86·95 *reales* per ton, according to whether the coal was carried in Spanish or in foreign bottoms. On the 28th of October 1836, four years later, Heredia, who needed English coal for smelting iron ore in his works in Marbella and Málaga, and furthermore was in the process of buying the San Andrés factory, gained a personal rebate—a tax of only 65·21 and 43·47 *reales* instead of the graded taxes of 86·95 and 65·21 under the Order. On the 4th of August, 1837 a Royal Order extended the concession to all industrialists, thus initiating a new period. It was one of slow and steady liberalisation, culminating in the free-trade tariff of 1869 ordering a single duty, regardless of the ship's registration, of 5 *reales* per metric ton. This liberalisation marks the beginning of the dominance of British coal in Spain. The figures could not be more expressive: the jumps were from only 5,000 tons in 1838, to 128,564 in 1850, to 300,813 in 1860, to 634,496 in 1870, and to 1,023,318 in 1880. At the same time, the sale outside its province of Oviedo coal had been 12,700 tons, yet only increased to 27,600, then 66,500, later 116,000 and finally 118,000 at the dates mentioned. The coincidence in timing of the liberalisation of importations and that of the mining exploitation of the country, which went on hand in hand from 1836–37, soured the legislature's opinion of the utility of the wealth of mining and its development. Even though Asturian coal was nearest to the coast, its increased production had scarcely any outlets.

Customs barriers could do little against the competition

of foreign coal. At the mine-head, at the ports, in the freight costs, British coal possessed an irresistible advantage. From 1865 it had scarcely any handicap—more than compensated for by its better quality, and more regular sailings to the other ports of the Atlantic and Mediterranean seaboards, from Oporto round to Barcelona.[52] It was mainly the cheap transport costs which tipped the scale towards the English, as was testified before a committee of investigation in 1865:[53] 'The freight from Cardiff or Newcastle to Jamaica is even less than that from Gijón to Málaga; and the freight from Gijón to Barcelona is approximately the same as that from Newcastle to India'. Asturias imported only what was needed for its own consumption. Apart from the iron ore of Bilbao, other products were of great value as compared with their weight, and especially as compared with coal, which is heavy and costs little. On the other hand, the main feature of the trade of the United Kingdom was the certainty of a return cargo, which allowed the British to establish regular sailings. This is the reason why the great increase in the exportation of minerals following the nationalisation of subsoil deposits made the situation worse rather than better. At the beginning, in 1882, of the protectionist ebb, British coal triumphed not only in the Mediterranean, but also on the Biscay coast, which until then had been the fief of Asturian coal.

The torrent of iron ore flooding from Vizcaya and Santander to British ports made the coal and coke of Wales and Durham the ideal return cargo, so that within five years, from the end of the civil war until 1881, importations of fuel rose by 47 per cent, since a drastic reduction in freight charges shattered the previous state of affairs. In 1882, the transport costs from England to Santander equalled those from Gijón. In the case of Bilbao, more distant, the freight cost from Gijón was less, owing to the reciprocal trade, but was not low enough to defeat the

---

52. Cf. Nadal, J., 'La economía española, 1829–1931' in the vol. *El Banco de España. Una historia económica*, pp. 372–374.

53. *Información sobre el derecho diferencial de banders*, vol. III, *Carbones*, p. 192.

great advantage in price of British coal at the port of shipment. Besides, this was a general problem which affected all the Spanish ports. The change was already evident in 1865 when competition within the Bay of Biscay was established through the better quality and more regular supply of British coal; and by 1882 these advantages had become more complete because of even cheaper prices, even beyond the tip of Galicia. In actual fact, sea-borne exports of Asturian coal ended as a small coaster shipping of Lilliputian dimensions. For example, the 100,000 tons embarked in 1881 from the Gijón docks were divided between 48 ports in the Peninsula, of which 29 took less than 1,000 tons. Barcelona, heading the list, took no more than 2,568 tons. Table 4, which demonstrates the origin, Spanish or foreign, of the fuel consumed in Spain, also demonstrates the sparseness of the Spanish supply, which was only overcome towards the end of the century. In fact the troubles of the contribution from Asturias, which was always the major internal producer, (59·56 per cent of the national output between 1861 and 1913) dictated the Spanish share of the total Spanish consumption. The hopes of an axis based on Gijón and Bilbao being disappointed, and the centre of gravity of steel production shifted to Vizcaya, the further progress of the coal industry of the Principality of Asturias was small until, towards the end of the century, a policy of extreme protectionism was inaugurated and brought in a series of favourable factors. Amongst the most important of these was the success of the Hullera Española Company, created about 1884 by the Marquess of Comillas in order to ensure the regular coaling of his shipping fleet, the Transatlántica Company. Also there was the completion in July, 1894 of the railway from Ciaño–Santa Ana to Soto del Rey, linking with the main line from León to Gijón. And, above all, there was in 1896 the devaluation of the peseta, a move which formed the main bulwark in the defences against the importations of foreign merchandise.

Outside Asturias, the most important coalfield was in the province of Córdoba. There, the workings really only got

TABLE 4: Consumption and origin of coal in Spain 1851–1913 (metric tons)

| Periods | Actual Amounts | | | Percentages | | |
	I Imports	II Production	III (I/II) Consumption	I	II	III
1851–1855	787,148					
1856–1860	1,278,579					
1851–1860	*2,065,727*					
1861–1865	2,265,599	1,491,880	4,207,479	53·84	46·15	100
1866–1870	3,171,440	2,605,990	5,777,430	54·89	45·10	100
1861–1870	*5,437,039*	*4,547,870*	*9,984,909*	*54·45*	*45·54*	*100*
1871–1875	2,475,199	3,307,180	5,782,379	42·80	57·19	100
1876–1880	4,132,319	3,516,090	7,648,409	54·04	45·95	100
1871–1880	*6,607,518*	*6,823,270*	*13,430,788*	*49·19*	*50·80*	*100*
1881–1885	6,159,863	5,253,810	11,413,673	53·96	46·03	100
1886–1890	7,663,810	4,879,515	12,543,325	61·09	38·90	100
1881–1890	*13,823,673*	*10,133,325*	*23,956,998*	*57·70*	*42·29*	*100*
1891–1895	9,064,188	6,069,765	15,133,953	59·89	40·10	100
1896–1900	8,951,219	11,358,200	20,309,419	43·58	56·41	100
1891–1900	*18,015,407*	*17,427,965*	*35,443,372*	*50·82*	*49·17*	*100*
1901–1905	11,396,556	13,739,850	25,136,406	45·33	54·66	100
1906–1910	11,451,024	17,586,662	29,037,686	39·43	60·56	100
1901–1910	*22,847,580*	*31,362,512*	*54,174,092*	*42·17*	*57·82*	*100*
1911–1913	8,148,001	10,863,229	19,011,230	42·85	57·14	100
1861–1913	74,879,218	81,122,171	156,001,389	47·99	52·00	100

Sources: For imports, *Las Estadística(s) del comercio exterior de España*; for production, *Las Estadística(s) Minera(s)*

under way in the 1860s with the incentive provided by the railways, which were responsible for the establishment of the first limited companies worthy of the name: the Fusión Carbonífera y Metalífera de Belmez y Espiel, whose name indicates that in it were united the interests of several small proprietors, and especially the Houillière et Métallurgique de Belmez, a company registered in Paris in 1865 by Parent and Schaken, the famous Belgian railway constructors. To be more concrete, these hopes became fact in April 1868, the date of the opening of the line from Belmez to the castle of Almorchón, which allowed coal to be transported to the lead foundries of Linares without trans-shipment, even though the line made a great loop of 400 kilometres. This new means of transport encouraged the growth of coal production to rise from 23,709 tons in 1867 to 79,457 in 1868, definitely placing Córdoba in the second place instead of Palencia. Then in 1873 the opening of the rail link between Belmez and Córdoba reduced by almost a half the length of the route to Linares. In 1881 the establishment, in Paris of the Société Minière et Métallurgique de Peñarroya whose purpose was to smelt in Peñarroya the lead of Badajoz and Ciudad Real (and later, that of Córdoba), triggered the exploitation of new coal mines near Belmez. In 1881 too, Belmez was sending 22,000 tons of coal and 2,300 tons of coke to Madrid, then demanding 96,523 tons. But all efforts to send Córdoba coal to the coasts of Andalusia met with failure, to the prejudice of the steel-works of Málaga in particular. These, after coal had begun to be used in the iron and steel-works of the North, had placed their last hopes on Belmez coal; but the 265 kilometre rail link, completed in November 1873, did not produce the expected results. In 1882 Belmez screened coal, which cost 21·50 pesetas per ton loaded on site, cost 36 pesetas in Málaga (14·50 pesetas freight), whereas coal from Asturias cost less than 35 pesetas in Málaga, and English coal 30. Between 1861 and 1913 the province of Córdoba produced 11,167,530 tons of coal, or 13·76 per cent of the Spanish output.

THE PROBLEMS OF THE IRON AND STEEL INDUSTRY[54]

Agriculture, the textile industry and the new means of

54. See my 'Los comienzos de la industrialización española (1832–1868): la industria sidurérgica', in the vol. *Ensayos sobre la economía española a mediados del siglo XIX*, pp. 203–233; 'La economía española, 1829–1931', and 'Industrialización y desindustrialización del Sureste español, 1817–1913'.

transport form, in the most typical cases, the most important part of the market for the modern iron and steel industry.

From 1830 the demand for iron was unleashed in Spain. Although in agriculture, as we have seen, the economic results which might have been expected were not obtained, the more rational methods of farming applied by the new land-owner increased the demand for farming implements. No doubt this demand prolonged for thirty years the prosperity of the traditional foundries which produced malleable iron of first-class quality, but at too high a price. Again, the reign of Isabella II coincided, in the cotton industry, with the very rapid substitution of the native spinning *bergandanus* (a development of the mule) by more modern machines, and of the manual looms by mechanical ones, to the undoubted benefit of the expansion of the market for metal. At almost the same time the firm establishment of the copper mines, the first ships driven by steam power and the first railways were to signal the opening of a new 'iron age'. By 1883 half of the Spanish railway system had been built, and at the same date the displacement of iron ships surpassed, for the first time, that of wooden ones.

TABLE 5: Spanish Iron and Steel Production (annual averages in thousands of tons)

Years	Cast iron Spain	Forged iron (direct system) Spain
1861–1865	45·65	12·15
1866–1870	42·56	13·08
1871–1875	45·53	5·08
1876–1880	62·57	4·50
1881–1885	131·59	3·05
1886–1890	174·22	
1891–1895	185·49	
1896–1900	289·24	
1901–1905	354·69	
1906–1910	395·01	
1911–1913	412·22	

Source: *Estadistica(s) Minera(s)*.

The supply of iron, however, did not grow as rapidly as the demand. Even though it was the highest reached up to then, the production figure for pig iron was, as late as 1883, no more than 140,000 tons, a derisory amount in comparison with the production of Great Britain, which was 55·2 times as large, Germany (19·4 times) or France (12·3 times).[55] The slow increase of the Spanish figures is shown by Table 5.

The factors which led to this backwardness were varied. The lack of native capital hindered the creation of modern iron and steel plants. The pressure of foreign capital opened the door to imports of iron and machinery from abroad. For fifty years, from 1832 to 1880, the country was forced to use large quantities of imported bobbins, looms, steam engines, railway lines, steam locomotives, railway wagons and ships. Besides the slow increase in production of cast iron, the table also shows the length of the period of prosperity—until 1870—enjoyed by the open hearths, the symbol of the traditional iron and steel industry.

The greatest of the lost chances were in the building of the railway system and the conversion of the merchant navy to steam. In 1855, before the massive influx of French capital, Spain had less than 500 kilometres of track in use. Ten years later the figure had risen to 4,828, four-fifths of which were owned by companies which were mainly or wholly French. In 1866 the Stock Market crash allowed the growth of the great foreign companies involved in the Norte railway and in the Madrid, Zaragoza and Alicante system. So that 'of the 11,378 kilometres of standard-gauge track in use at the outbreak of the First World War, the companies under foreign control owned 85 per cent. In 1911 the report by the Ministry of Public Works calculated the cost of the total Spanish system at nearly 3,600 million pesetas (francs), of which the French had supplied sixty per cent, which was more than 2,000 millions.'[56]

55. The figure for England is in Mitchell and Deane at p. 132 of their *Abstract of British Historical Statistics*; the figures for Germany and France are given by Clapham, J. H., *Economic Development of France and Germany, 1815–1914*, 4th ed., Cambridge, 1963, p. 285.

56. Cameron, *France and the Economic Development of Europe*, p. 275.

This foreign dominance was both the cause and effect of the Ley General de Ferrocarriles (General Railway Law) of the 3rd of June 1855, which permitted free entry to material during the construction of lines and for ten years afterwards. Railway fever, reaching its peak in 1860 to 1865, brought with it massive importation of foreign iron products. The traditional imports of mild steel ingots (usually destined for the steel mills) and of ordinary rolled iron products (wire, tinplate, sheet iron and, above all, strip iron, hoop iron and plate iron 'for making casks and other things'), in very modest quantities, were surpassed from 1857 by imports of forged iron, wrought iron or drawn iron in bars, that is to say by common rolled iron products for the railways. Railway construction affected every sector of iron and steel products—there was an important increase in imports of cast iron, steel and ordinary rolled iron—but the influence was most apparent in the case of imports of bar iron. As in other countries, in Spain too the transport revolution introduced changes in the type of consumption. Forged iron regained its position at the beginning of the second half of the century. Furthermore, since all iron products came from pig iron produced by the first smelting in blast furnaces, we have calculated the quantity of pig iron represented by the total of all the more finished products. The result reveals that in each year of the five-year period from 1861 to 1865 (the first such period for which we have details of production) imports of iron products, without counting the innumerable consignments of steel in various forms were always greater than the whole production of the 'modern' Spanish iron and steel industry, applying 'modern' to the products of blast furnaces and not those of forges. To be more precise, the imports of iron in the quinquennium were more than double the whole production of the Spanish iron and steel works (482,171 tons as compared with 228,277). In terms of cash this state of affairs added up to a drain of 217·6 million pesetas, equivalent to 45·4 per cent of the value of the production of the entire Spanish mining industry during the same period. The lack of a market, which free-traders as well as protectionists considered to be the chief obstacle in the path of the iron and steel industry, might have been overcome if the Spanish railways had been built with native materials.

The exemption granted by the Law of 1855 remained in full operation for a decade. But then the budget of June 1864 declared 'ended the exemption from duties granted to material imported by railway companies, and instead the latter will be conceded a fixed sum'. This measure promptly encouraged the country's producers to activity. However, the first quantities obtained were small, and they were not to be continued in the future. On one hand the paltry financial return on the lines in use, restrained from 1866 the further expansion of the system. On the other hand the restrictive measures of 1864 appear not to have been applied to railways already in existence, and so the last possibilities faded away.

The United Kingdom, followed at a great distance by Belgium and France, was the principal caterer for Spanish consumption. In the quinquennium from 1861 to 1865 the respective contribution of each of these three countries to the total imports of 'drawn iron or forged iron in bars', a prominent item in the capital goods of railways, was 64·9, 24·1 and 8·2 per cent; but conversely France and Belgium were in the lead in the supply of rolling stock. The large-scale exports of rolled iron and machinery constituted the invisible item on the credit side of the foreign companies which invested their money in the construction of Spain's land communications system.

A similar failure hit the ship-building firms, utterly powerless in the face of the competition of the Scottish shipyards. After the very severe losses caused by the wars against France, Britain and the former colonies, the Spanish merchant marine only began to recover between 1850 and 1860, when the small shipyards of Vizcaya and Catalonia were working at full speed. Soon this prosperity dwindled away, owing to the adoption of steam power and iron hulls. Not even the system of subsidies for the ship-builders, nor customs barriers, nor the repayment of customs duties on material which had to be imported, could prevent the purchase of iron ships from abroad. In 1883 when, for the first time the capacity of steam ships was greater than that of sailing ships, the registrations of the former showed that 97 per cent of their tonnage was of foreign origin. From 1849 to 1868 alone, Spain imported 305 iron ships, with a total of 89,000 tons.

Yet our analysis would be incomplete if we took into account only economic policy. Without excusing in any way the burden of the importations of railway material, we must consider other factors. The iron and steel industry did not constitute an isolated sector, but formed an integral part of the more general field of the Spanish economic situation. An important enquiry made in 1866 revealed that the producers of dear iron (that is, using charcoal as fuel) pinned their hopes on the development of rail transport, which would make the new fuel available to them—the main factor, that is, in reducing costs. But the producers of cheaper iron, who used coke, thought in international terms and painted a more complex picture of the existing obstacles against their industry. Pointing out that a reduction in fuel costs was not sufficient, they posed instead the question of transport in terms of exportation, and found other elements of backwardness, from the stagnation of agriculture, which consumed scarcely any iron, to the high cost of money. The small amounts of capital in existence 'meet with more profit and ease in Stock Market operations, and their owners turn a deaf ear to proposals based on industrial establishments'. Duro y Cía was happy to borrow capital at six per cent per year. The French manager of the Hullera y Metalúrgica de Asturias was scandalised that money stood at 'four or five per cent in Paris, yet at sixteen or eighteen in Madrid', and concluded that *the sole true industry of the country nowadays is borrowing money at interest*.

Although this situation was bad, it was not equally bad for all, because there was a range of possibilities to the various firms. The stagnation of production in the period of highest consumption was a country-wide phenomenon which, however, obscured the special feature of these differences of development in the regions. Overall, the outstanding characteristic was the assumption of the leadership of the iron and steel industry by the north of Spain in place of the south.

In 1826 Manuel Agustín Heredia, president of the Merchants' Guild of Málaga, an important exporter of liquids (wines and olive oil), and whose fortune had been launched by the extraction of graphite from the Serranía de Ronda in the disturbed period of the War of Independence (1808 to 1814), set up a company to exploit the beds of magnetic iron ore at Ojén, not far from Marbella. The factory, sited on the bank of the Río Verde, set out to manufacture hoop and sheet iron for casks using the old process. Very soon, since the Ojén hematite proved very difficult to smelt by the traditional method, Heredia decided to adopt the English processes. The blast furnaces, puddling furnaces and reverberatory furnaces of La Concepción and La Constancia (in Málaga) were the first set up in Spain for civilian purposes.

Immediately, the outbreak of the First Carlist War gave them an exceptional opportunity, since it paralysed the northern works, and diverted demand to those of the south (those of Heredia and those of the El Pedroso company, in the province of Seville). From 1833 to 1840 the Andalusian firms took over the production of ordinary iron; and this movement went so far that Heredia became the greatest Spanish iron master, that his success gave rise to servile imitation of him on the part of Juan Giró (the El Ángel works, with blast furnaces in Marbella and refinement processes in Málaga), and that the Basque producers confessed their inferiority and asked Madrid for protection. In spite of the growth of El Pedroso, the renewal of activity in the old furnaces at Sargadelos (province of Lugo), now for civilian instead of military purposes, and despite the installations of new works in the north, the two Málaga iron masters, Heredia and Giró, provided in 1844 (the date of the first reliable statistics) 72 per cent of the total Spanish production of pig iron.

The dominance of the Andalusian iron industry was

maintained for thirty years. The delay imposed by the civil war on the process of modernisation of the iron works of the north lasted longer than the conflict. The La Merced factory in Guriezo (province of Santander), which had been ready to adopt the English methods in 1833, was destroyed by the Carlists and remained out of action until 1846. In Sabero (province of León), the blast furnaces installed by the Palentina-Leonesa company did not begin smelting until 1847, as was the case with similar works opened in Mieres and elsewhere. The production figures available show that there were thirty years of southern dominance: in 1844 Río Verde—Málaga, with 7,829 tons, and El Pedroso, with 1,368, were responsible for 85·5 per cent of all Spanish cast iron; in 1856 they poured 4,811 and 1,890 tons respectively out of a total of 15,227 tons of cast iron; in 1861, 17,051 and 1,981 out of 34,532. Then the Málaga figures, decisive up to that point, swiftly declined to less than 1,000 tons in 1867. Further, the production of El Pedroso, which was always by far the smaller, had already fallen away in 1865. The result was that the contribution of the provinces of Málaga and Seville to the basic product of the industry fell from 55·1 per cent in 1861 to 17·6 in 1866 and to 4·7 in 1868.

Andalusian predominance was succeeded by that of Asturias. For fifteen years, from 1864 to 1879, the province of Oviedo produced more than the other provinces, whereas its figures for forged iron were at times beaten by those of Vizcaya. The reason for this swing from south to north is found in the costs of production. In 1865 Heredia's firm had to spend 120·4 pesetas on charcoal in order to obtain one ton of cast iron, whilst the outlay of Duro y Cía, at La Felguera, was only 2·67 pesetas on coke and 5·1 on 'coal for the boilers and to heat the draught' for the same amount of iron. Although labour and some other items were slightly more expensive in Asturias, the difference in fuel costs was the decisive factor in the final price: 158·2 pesetas per ton of pig iron in Málaga, as compared with 103·8 in Oviedo. This happened in further processes also. Competition was absent. In 1862 El Ángel had shut down. In accordance with its name La Constancia, after regaining some ground during the Third Carlist War (1872 to 1876), and clinging to the dream of a railway link with the Belmez coal field, put up a heroic resistance until 1890 to 1891. Three years previously El Pedroso had fallen. Between 1860 and 1870 the change from the second to the last third of the century marked very clearly the decline of industry in the south of Spain.

The Andalusian iron industry faded away owing to lack of coal. That of Asturias was able to excel in relative terms, while its factories, sited in the coal fields, were the only ones in Spain which had coke to hand. From 1879 the arrival of Welsh coke, balancing return cargoes of iron ore, threw open the door to prosperity for the Vizcayan industry.

Traditionally, the Basque iron works had been the most active in Spain. At the end of the eighteenth century they were flourishing having become specialised in the production of anchors and other equipment for ships, which were in great demand in Portugal, France and England as well as in the Spanish naval yards of La Carraca (Cadiz), El Ferrol, Cartagena, Guarnizo and Havana. Later the loss of the colonial markets, the decay of the Spanish navy after the disaster of Trafalgar, and the introduction in other countries of indirect processes by means of blast furnaces, plunged the iron works of Navarre, Guipúzcoa and Vizcaya into a profound crisis, which was made worse by the effects of the First Carlist War. In 1840 the iron industry of the Basque provinces was backward, even by the reigning Spanish standards.

This backwardness was not easily overcome. In Vizcaya, the best endowed of these provinces, the first blast furnaces, burning charcoal, began operation at the Santa Ana works in Bolueta in 1849—that is, seventeen years later than in Málaga; also in Vizcaya the first blast furnace fuelled by coke, at the El Carmen works in Baracaldo, was fired in 1865, or seventeen years later than in Asturias. From 1861 to 1878 Vizcayan production of cast iron always fluctuated within very narrow margins and was disproportionately small. The true take-off was delayed until 1879, the date of the opening of the San Francisco works at El Desierto (Sestao). The new installation, which possessed four blast furnaces fired by coke, immediately became the most productive in Spain. In 1880, a year after its opening, it had won for Vizcaya, at the expense of Asturias, the leadership in pig iron production; and in 1884, only four years later, the 56,454 tons of cast iron poured at the San Francisco works constituted 45·4 per cent of the total national production.

Furthermore, the El Desierto factory was only the first step, since the success of its promoters acted as a stimulus to the establishment of other even more powerful enterprises. Thus in 1882 the firm of Ibarra y Cía, with mines at Saltacaballo and Guriezo (province of Santander), was transformed into a limited company, the Sociedad de Altos Hornos y Fábricas de Hierro y Acero of Bilbao, under the ownership of its former proprietors and various capitalists and credit companies. Backed by capital amounting to twenty-five million pesetas (12·5 in shares and 12·5 in bonds), the firm proposed to embark on what knowledgeable contemporaries considered 'a revolution in Spanish metallurgy',[57] which was the production of steel by modern processes. The same year saw the birth of the metallurgical and construction company La Vizcaya, with a capital of 12·6 million pesetas subscribed in the main by 'persons who owe their fortune to the mineral trade'. After having for thirty years represented the new initiative of Vizcaya, these two companies together with La Iberia, a company established in 1888 for the manufacture of tinplate, were to combine in 1902 to found the Sociedad Anónima Altos Hornos de Vizcaya. At that period the province had become the most dynamic in Spain, as the various indicators show. It had the greatest population growth, the largest railway system, the largest number of ships registered . . . ; and all this was induced by the greatest accumulation and investment of capital, a movement fostered by the heavy exportation of iron ore.

57. Alzola, B. de, *Estudio relativo a los recursos de que la industria nacional dispone para la construccion y armamentos navales*, Madrid, 1866, p. 26.

From 1861 to 1879 Vizcaya had provided 22·7 per cent of all Spanish cast iron, and from 1880 to 1913 this share rose to 65·74 per cent. The sale of minerals abroad had been doubly decisive since it provided the essential financial base and the necessary fuel, for after unloading the ore in Britain the ships overcame the lack of return cargoes by taking on, at very low freight rates, the coal and coke required by the factories around Bilbao; and in place of a Bilbao-Gijón axis, the Bilbao-Cardiff axis was created, so that, contrary to all expectations, the industrial revolution separated rather than united the destinies of the Basque provinces and Asturias.

In accordance with the scheme of 1885, the Altos Hornos firm installed the first Bessemer converter in the Peninsula, and in the period 1888 to 1899 it fired the first Martin-Siemens furnace. Thanks to steel, the industry of mechanical construction was less dependent on foreign materials. During the last two decades of the nineteenth century metal workshops multiplied in Vizcaya, Guipúzcoa, Asturias and Catalonia. In 1882 the Material para Ferrocarriles y Construcciones company, successor of the old Heredia del Remedio firm, produced the first railway wagon built in the country, and in 1884 La Maquinista Terrestre y Marítima, established like the former in Barcelona, handed over the first Spanish-built locomotive.

But the advance was not made without difficulties. From its very start the Spanish mechanical construction industry needed dedication and aid, and indeed State aid became evident on two fronts, restraining foreign competition and encouraging native production by means of special legislation. The common interests of the agricultural sector brought into being the tariff of the 31st of December 1891, which put a stop to the era of free trade which had opened in 1869; later, the tariff of 1906 merely reinforced the tendency towards strict protectionism. Furthermore, from 1907 the Conservative governments were to repeat exemptions, orders for materials and promises to native industrial firms.

These measures, of a general character, were completed

by others aimed at the protection of the two main sectors of the consumption of iron and steel. The Law of the 30th of November 1886 drove home the special tariffs of 1876 to 1877 concerning duties on materials for the railways, by establishing rates from two to four times higher than the former ones, and locomotives, till then absent from the list, were included in the new tariff. With respect to the ship-building industries, State protection assumed original characteristics. In the preamble of the Law on Construction of the Fleet (12th of December 1887), the Navy Minister expressed his desire to encourage the country's heavy industry and to strengthen it so that it would be able to satisfy all Spain's military and naval needs. Although it had aroused bitter polemics, this policy was to be renewed in 1908, with the approval of a new naval programme. It should be realised that on these two occasions the amounts of money paid out—190 and 200 million pesetas respectively—represented a substantial subvention to the infant capital goods industry. Astilleros del Nervión and the Sociedad Española de Construcción Naval, enterprises born in 1888 and 1909, in the shelter of these two programmes, are in themselves the best proof of the stimulus given by the State. Together with these two firms we should mention the Cía Euskalduna de Construcción y Reparación de Buques, working in the same field, which was set up in 1900 as an auxiliary to the Naviera Sota y Aznar, a shipping firm which specialised in the traffic between Bilbao and Britain.

Producer of steel ships and of all kinds of fixed installations and rolling stock for railways, early twentieth-century Spain may seem to present a picture of a fully industrialised country, but that does not correspond to the reality. The external trade of Spain was still in 1913 based on the sale of the products of the land and of the subsoil and on the purchase of manufactured goods from abroad. The range of industrial products offered by the country concealed a congenital weakness in the greater part of the country's factories. In the case of machinery for the cotton industry, for example, 97·81 per cent (1,705,483 out of 1,743,535) of the bobbins installed at that date were from abroad.

The problem was that of costs, which the producers always blamed on the weakness of demand, although it seems more correct to blame the excessively diversified production, which was unable to limit itself to half-manufactured goods. In 1886, when their manufacture was just beginning, Spanish ingots for making steel were produced at prices which did not compare unfavourably with those of other countries, whereas one millimetre thick Martin-Siemens steel plate cost at Altos[58] Hornos fifty per cent more than at a British works (average costs of 1886 to 1890). The Spanish advantage lay with the cost of iron ore, and the disadvantage with the cost of fuel. In those conditions it would have been reasonable for the Spanish industry to limit itself to the first smelting and to leave to others the later processes of steel manufacture, in which the costs can almost entirely be accounted for by the coal or coke used. If it had specialised in the production of cast iron it is possible that Vizcaya might have been able to export it in large quantities, replacing, at least in part, the enormous outflow of ore.

THE CATALAN COTTON INDUSTRY

Professor Pierre Vilar has reconstructed the mechanisms of the Catalan economic take-off in the eighteenth century. Supported by the cheapness of grain, the great rise in population between 1715 and 1735 resulted in a decline in agricultural wages and an increase in the seignorial dues, together with improved agricultural production and productivity. The boom affected especially viticulture, which was favoured by strong demand from abroad. The participation of the Barcelona bourgeoisie in the profits of the seignorial dues permitted the channelling towards commercial capital accumulation and was able to reinforce the original agricultural capital accumulation. But about the middle of the century a fresh imbalance between men and

58. *La reforma avancelaria y los tratodos de comercio*, vol. II, p. 404.

resources, caused by the reduction of the area occupied by cereals in favour of vines, brought back the population crisis. Some twenty years later the supply of labour bore witness to this, and contrary to what had happened in the first half of the century, wages rose, profits decreased, and capital was directed towards another activity: the manufacture of printed cottons. Industrial profits replaced income from the land, and the region's economy took other, more modern paths.[59]

The first bleach field dates from 1737, and cotton weaving began a little before 1760; the first signs of a cotton-spinning industry—still employing the traditional spinning wheel—are evident about 1765. But these facts are purely a matter of scholarly accuracy, and they have no socio-economic importance. The cotton industry does not deserve that name until the satisfaction of the demand, much of which was from Spanish America, required the adoption of English spinning techniques. The spinning jenny was introduced towards 1780, the water frame from 1791, and the mule from 1803 to 1804 on. This last machine in particular, worked by water or steam power, symbolises the transition from the traditional cottage industry to the new factory system.

From 1803 to 1808 the number of licences for the employment of water power for Crompton machines rose to fourteen, but after that this movement was interrupted, if not completely halted, by the Napoleonic Wars. Six years of fighting disorganised production and gave a remarkable opportunity for the smuggling of textiles; and furthermore, the difficulties faced by the mother country were taken advantage of by the creoles for laying the foundations of the emancipation of the colonies. In 1814, when the French troops withdrew, Catalonia had lost a considerable part of its capital goods and of its markets, so that in cotton manufacturing the scarcity of capital and the fall in demand prolonged the reign of the old spinning wheel; and this set back the mechanisation which had begun with remarkable

59. *La Catalogne dans l'Espagne Moderne. Recherches sur les fondements économiques des structures nationales*, Paris, 1962, especially vols. II and III.

speed in the early years of the century. In 1820 the manufacture of cotton prints had only returned to the 1792 level,
although there was a marked change in that local yarn had
replaced the imported ones. In 1836 water-powered mills
numbered only thirty-six, a very small figure if we recall that
between 1803 and 1808 fourteen had already been set up.

The new wave of prosperity was firmly established in the
1830s, when some of the factors became favourable. The
scarcity of labour, probably causing a rise in wages, when
the labour force was joined by the depleted generations
born during the period of calamities between 1800 and
1813,[60] and the repatriation of capital from the former
colonies, seem to have united to give a decisive stimulus to
the mechanisation of manufacturing. Driven by the
traditional water power or by the new steam engines, the
mule-jennies and also more modern equipment such as the
self-acting spinning machines (from 1844) gave the coup de
grâce to the *bergadanus*. At the same time, although not
so rapidly, the manual loom was replaced by the mechanical
loom.

The proportion of mechanical bobbins, which was 3·78
per cent in 1835 (27,220 out of a total of 719,169), had
risen to 99·04 per cent in 1861 (763,051 out of a total of
770,417), which means that spinning had been almost
completely mechanised in the course of a quarter century.
The speed is impressive. But it should be noted that at least
until 1850 the machine most employed was the mule,
already out of date and superseded. In fact, the great
advances made since 1830 were in the main no more than
a making up of the ground lost during the reign of Ferdinand
VII.

Following a tendency normal in the industry wherever
it existed, the mechanisation of weaving appears to have
been out of phase. From 1841 to 1861, in a period of time
only a little shorter than that considered in the case of

60. Cf. Nadal, J., 'Les grandes mortalités des années 1793 à 1812:
effets à long terme sur la démographie catalane', in the vol. *Problèmes de
mortalité. Méthodes, sources et bibliographie en démographie historique*, Liége,
1965, pp. 409–421.

spinning, the percentage of mechanical looms rose from 0·9 (231 out of a total of 25,111) to 44·6 (9,659 out of 21,721), which means that there was a half-mechanisation, although it was important.

The effects of the technological revolution were felt at once, with a fall in costs followed by the decrease in prices and by growth of the market. At the same time there took place a general spreading of the factory system, especially in spinning, and the specialisation of workers in the industry, who ceased to regard their activity as merely a subsidiary source of income. Printed cottons and other goods, sold ever more cheaply, displaced the consumption of other, more traditional materials on the market. To satisfy this demand cotton production soared to surprising heights. In 1860 the prosperity known at the end of the eighteenth century had been left far behind, for the Catalan mills absorbed 20,000 tons of raw cotton, ten times more than in 1820, and furthermore they held a very high place in European production, coming ahead of Belgium or Italy, for example.

All this profoundly altered the structure of the industry, for the use of machines influenced the geographical location of the mills, and yet the higher cost of the machines enforced some degree of concentration of the enterprises.

In order to liberate himself from primitive machinery, the cotton manufacturer turned to horse, water or steam power. For obvious reasons the first yielded to the other two. But surface streams were not to be found everywhere, nor was British coal, which triumphed in the market, easily transported inland. And so there was a movement of the factories to the banks of certain rivers and parts of the Mediterranean coast. The Barcelona mill of Bonaplata, Rull, Vilaregut y Cía (1832 to 1835), the first to install a Watt engine, was considered by contemporaries to be a milestone in the country's economic history. Already by 1833 it was credited with bringing about a 'complete revolution' in spinning,[61] and in 1847 it was regarded as the

61. Graell, G., *Historia del Fomento de Trabajo Nacional*, Barcelona, n. d., p. 39.

starting point of no less than 'a real industrial revolution'.[62]

The concentration of the industry is clearly reflected by the fact that a similar number of bobbins were divided among 382 firms in 1850 and among 321 in 1861 and eleven years later the establishments with more than 10,000 bobbins numbered six.

This progress implied the investment of considerable amounts of money. In some cases the capital had been repatriated from the former American colonies, but in other, perhaps more numerous cases, co-partnerships were formed which sacrificed the objective of short-term financial profit to that of the continuity of growth of the businesses. Finally, with the foundation of La España Industrial, in January 1847, the more modern resort to the limited company made its appearance. In the next eight years the number of such companies rose to nine, with a total capital of 93 million *reales*. Then, the promulgation in 1855 of the General Railway Law appeared to offer a more attractive field for the investor, with the effect that the constitution of new limited companies was brought to a halt until after 1868. It was calculated in 1862 that the Barcelona Stock Market had absorbed 45,000 railway shares. In 1866 the British Consul estimated that 'of the one hundred million dollars invested here in stocks and bonds, more than fifty are invested in railway bonds'.[63] Without doubt the difficulties met by the mill-owners in obtaining supplies of raw material—difficulties caused by the American Civil War—helped to strengthen this movement.

The cotton industry, a typical consumer industry, was directly dependent on the agricultural situation. From 1820, when the importation of foreign grain and vegetables was prohibited, the Catalan manufacturers were the staunchest defenders of the Spanish cereal producers. In 1859, a date when the railways can be considered as still non-existent, with only 1,148 kilometres open to the public, the first analysis of the balance of the coasting trade revealed, in

62. Illas y Vidal, *Memorias sobre los perjuicios que ocasionaría en España . . . La adopción del sistema del libre cambio*, Barcelona 1849, p. 50.

63. Sànchez Albornoz, *España hace un siglo: una economía dual*, p. 50.

fact, that cotton textiles (445·82 million *reales*), and wheat
and barley, other grains and flours and vegetables (409·01
million *reales*), formed the two most valuable items of this
trade.

This prosperity of agriculture, which paved the way for
that of manufactured goods, can be gauged as much by the
profits as by the possibilities of marketing the crops. In
general terms one can say that the greater area of cultivation, dating from the measures of disamortisation and
disentailment of the land, and the fall in the prices of cotton
goods drove on the penetration of these goods into the
interior of Spain. But there were short periods of fluctuation
caused by the influence of incidental factors. (*See* Table 6,
p. 615.)

Catalan manufacturing showed very rapid development
after the end of the civil war of 1833 to 1839 and, especially,
after the regency of Espartero (1840 to 1843). For speed of
growth the Moderate Decade (1844 to 1854), which saw
the lands confiscated during the preceding years brought
under cultivation, stood out above any other period.
Afterwards, the next quinquennium, 1854 to 1858, shows
a marked deceleration, caused by the food crisis of 1856 to
1857 which restricted the market for textiles and undid to
some extent the benefits of the Crimean War which had
fostered the exportation of grain from Spain, and so had
increased the purchasing power of the farmers producing
cereals. In 1857 La España Industrial made the smallest
profit of the years between its inception in 1849, and the
year 1861; whilst other factories, less well supplied with
capital, ended the year with deficits.[64] In 1861 the outbreak of the American Civil War marked the beginning
of another cycle, clearly unfavourable. Contrary to what
happened in Britain, the 'cotton famine' hit hardest in
the last years of the conflict, and its effects were prolonged beyond the peace into the second half of the
decade. This helps to explain the strong upsurge of 1869

64. Nadal, J. and Ribas, E., 'Una empresa algodonera catalana. La
fábrica "de la Rambla" de Vilanova', 1841–1861, in *Annales Cisalpines
d'Histoire Sociale*, No. 1 (1970), pp. 98ff.

to 1873 (a quinquennium favoured as well by the Franco-Prussian War) and 1874 to 1878, when Catalonia's industry returned, in part, to the trend apparent before the American Civil War. On the whole, setting aside these accidents, it is correct to speak of a long period of rapid growth which lasted almost fifty years, which coincided with great exactitude with the growth in extent and production of agriculture.

From 1880 the growth gradually slowed down until it ended in a decrease in the last quinquennium, that of 1909 to 1913. The textile industry had to march in step with agriculture which, as we know, had entered a period of difficulties. The avalanche of Russian and American cereals which descended on the Spanish coasts penned up Castilian grains in the places where they were produced. The agrarian crisis, this time one of over-production, was about to unleash a textile crisis. In 1884 to 1888 the imports of raw cotton rose only four per cent. In 1888 the two factories perhaps most representative of Catalonia, those of Güell and of La España Industrial, both situated in Sants, were forced to undertake a drastic reform of their plants and organisation to reduce costs and maintain their competitiveness. Official sources show that by 1890 capital invested in industry was bringing in smaller and smaller returns.

Faced with the dramatic inelasticity of domestic demand, the Catalan mill-owners, like the Castilian flour merchants, pinned their last hopes on the markets of Cuba and Puerto Rico. The results of the united pressure of both groups were the Law on Commercial Relations with the Antilles, of the 20th of July 1882, and the Cuban tariff of the 31st of December 1891, which obliged the last remnants of the Spanish Empire to consume the products of the mother country. The intention was neither more nor less than the extension of coastal trade to include the overseas possessions; and in consequence the exports of cotton textiles, which had been 458 tons per year in 1876 to 1880, surged to 1,069 tons in 1881 to 1885, 3,315 in 1886 to 1890, 7,859 in 1891 to 1895, and 5,265 in 1896 to 1900. The shipments reached their highest point in 1893 to 1897, when they returned an annual average equivalent to 17·2 per cent of the whole Spanish production.

The strengthening of the links with the colonies, decreed in 1882 and in full force from 1886, was a useful palliative for the internal market. As early as 1889 a Commission of mill-owners made no bones about admitting it: 'Without the Law on Commercial Relations with the Antilles, which opened an outlet for our products, it is certain that the Spanish cotton industry would have suffered a terrible catastrophe'.[65] It is easy now to conjecture that the reaction was possibly a decisive incentive to the emancipation movement in the remaining colonies. At the end of 1881, when the old tariff system, more acceptable to the creoles, was still in force, the hero of the Cuban independence movement, José Martí, strongly condemned the Spanish port of Santander, 'which lives off the flour it ships to Cuba, which is forced to accept it'.[66] On the 15th of July 1890 the guild of textile importers of Havana decided 'to form a League to oppose the high duties imposed on foreign goods'. The hypothesis that but for the crises in agriculture and cotton of the 1880s the Cuban 'disaster' of 1898 would not have come so soon has some strength.

After the Treaty of Paris that part of the products which before had been exported did not entirely disappear, since the return of soldiers and Spanish settlers meant that a considerable proportion of the consumers in the colonies was retained because they had migrated to Spain. The replacement in Cuba, Puerto Rico and the Philippines of the Spanish suppliers by those of the United States took time. The fall of the peseta on the international market, hastened by the events of 1898, had some compensatory effects since it acted as if it were a subsidy to exports. Consequently exports of cotton goods in the post-colonial period never sank below 4,068 tons—the lowest figure of all, in 1902—a quantity which was equal to 39·5 per cent of the exports in the record year 1897. This fact, together with

65. *La reforma arancelaria y los tratados de comercio*, vol. I, p. 427.
66. Martí, J., *Sobre España* (Introducción, selección y notas de A. Sorel), Madrid, 1967, p. 132.

a slight improvement in agriculture, explains the relatively high increase in cotton production in 1898 to 1903, almost equal to that of 1894 to 1898, and it brought the Catalan industry to its highest point in relation to that of the United Kingdom (10·01 per cent, a very praiseworthy figure). But from 1904 the comparative progress of the two industries suffered a change: that of Britain succeeded in clambering out of the chasm of the Great Depression, whereas that of Catalonia sank into stagnation and atrophy.

Outside Catalonia the cotton industry was of slight importance. From 1857 to 1913 the imports of raw cotton into the ports of the rest of Spain amounted to only 7·46 per cent of the Catalan imports. This is enough to allow us to measure the distance which separated Catalonia from the rest of Spain.

Yet two mills, located at Málaga, deserve mention. The firm Industria Malagueña, registered on the 23rd of May 1847, was legally the second limited company in the Spanish cotton industry, coming shortly after La España Industrial at Sants (Barcelona), which had been formed in the preceding January. But in fact this order should be reversed, because the Málaga factory had been working since September 1846, whilst the one at Sants did not start production until 1849. These firms were for some considerable time rivals for the leading place in Spanish cotton production. The southern enterprise, which had started with capital of 4·8 million *reales*, established, on land next to the La Constancia iron works, a very modern mill, 'English style', with automatic bobbins, mechanical looms, steam engines and gas lighting. In 1850 it used 690 tons of raw cotton, more than did any other Spanish factory; and in 1851 its machinery comprised 39,000 bobbins and 774 looms, a plant very nearly the size of that of La España Industrial, with its 41,748 bobbins and 1,000 looms, and markedly greater than that of the third largest Spanish plant, which belonged to another Barcelona firm, Industrial Algodonera, S. A. Furthermore the success of Industria Malagueña had prompted the establishment of a second firm, La Aurora, under the leadership of Carlos Larios, a cousin of the president of the first firm. This mill began production in 1858, with some 7,000 bobbins and 350 looms, all driven by steam power. As some contemporaries hinted, probably the development of Industria Malagueña and La Aurora had the virtue of containing within limits the contraband trade in textiles in the South of Spain. It is certain that British exports of cotton goods to Gibraltar contracted significantly from 1847.

Table 6 allows us to gauge the exact importance and the evolution up to 1913 of the Málaga cotton-producing nucleus:

TABLE 6: Ports of Entry of Raw Cotton (annual averages, in metric tons)

	I				II			
	Absolute figures				Percentages			
	1	2	3	4	1	2	3	4
		Bar-		Other		Bar-		Other
Periods	Spain	celona	Málaga	ports	Spain	celona	Málaga	ports
1857–58	19,349	17,258	731	1,360	100	89·19	3·77	7·03
1861–65	16,845	14,322	1,085	1,437	100	85·26	6·44	8·29
1866–70	21,675	18,918	1,343	1,414	100	87·28	6·19	6·52
1871–75	32,397	28,735	1,877	1,785	100	88·69	5·79	5·51
1876–80	38,124	33,721	2,158	2,244	100	88·45	5·66	5·88
1881–85	49,438	44,560	2,653	2,225	100	90·13	5·36	4·50
1886–90	49,604	45,294	2,386	1,924	100	91·31	4·80	3·88
1891–95	64,714	60,829	2,046	1,474	100	93·99	3·16	2·84
1896–1900	70,662	67,117	1,487	2,058	100	94·98	2·10	2·91
1901–05	78,055	74,589	1,422	2,043	100	95·56	1·82	2·61
1906–10	83,339	80,251	942	2,146	100	96·29	1·13	2·57
1911–13	90,507	87,321	688	2,508	100	96·46	0·76	2·77

The first data, for 1857 to 1858, years of crisis but in which the second mill began production, reveal a consumption of 612 and 850 tons of raw cotton, figures which give an average of 3·77 per cent of total Spanish imports. Then during the quinquennium 1861 to 1865, in spite of the 'cotton famine', the figure of a thousand tons per annum was surpassed and the percentage of the total rose to 6·44, the highest of all the figures for the years 1857 to 1913. After 1865 the Málaga imports continued to rise rapidly until

1881 to 1885, although not enough to keep pace with the great increase in Barcelona; and in consequence we see a rise in absolute figures, but a fall in percentage. From 1886 both these figures show the same falling trend. The difficulties of the 1880s, which in Catalonia brought industrial deceleration, caused decline pure and simple in Málaga. In 1905 La Aurora was forced to close down; and in 1913 the cotton shipped to Industria Malagueña—667 tons—was only equal to a fifth of the imports in the record year of 1884 (3,244 tons). To sum up: during the period from 1857 to 1885 Málaga had received a total of 47,047 tons, a quantity similar to that taken by all the other non-Catalan factories (48,248), and fifteen times less than that of Catalonia (735,797). During the period from 1886 to 1913 the Málaga imports fell to 41,428 tons, whilst those of other non-Catalan ports rose to 55,744 and those of Catalonia to 1,841,500. Málaga's contribution to the Spanish total, which had been 5·67 per cent in the years of prosperity, fell to 2·16 per cent in the period of decline. It is worth notice that this decline began at the same time as the southern iron and steel industry collapsed. The 1880s was the decade which saw the termination of Andalusian industrial hopes.

CONCLUSION

It has been estimated that in 1914 Spain's national income reached a total of 10,745 million pesetas, of which 4,130 (38·4 per cent) came from agriculture and stock-raising, and 2,785 (25·9 per cent) from mines, industry and crafts.[67] Again, in 1910, according to the population census, there was a total of 4,220,326 workers employed in agriculture, forestry, hunting and fishing (71·1 per cent) as against 1,034,885 employed in mines and quarries, manufacturing industry and building (17·1 per cent). These lead to the

67. Cf article by Vandellós, J. A., 'La richesse et le revenu de la péninsule ibérique', published in the journal *Metron*, V, No. 4 (1925), pp. 151–186, and, in Spanish translation, in the *Revista de Economía Política*, VI (1955), pp. 185–223.

conclusion that, at the outbreak of the First World War, Spain was still a mainly agricultural country.

Backward in comparison with the other western nations, Spain was yet ahead of those other nations whose industrialisation began only in the nineteenth century. The case of Spain is less that of a latecomer than that of an attempt, largely thwarted, to join the ranks of the first comers. It is the history of this failure that I have tried to expound in the foregoing pages. My argument laid particular emphasis on the failure of the two movements for disentailment and nationalisation of the land and of the subsoil, a failure which destroyed those agricultural and mining bases on which the industrial revolution, in the classic sense of the term, ought to have been founded. As a backcloth I presented the Treasury's difficulties, which watered down the laws of disentailment and nationalisation, restricted the market in capital for industry, and imposed an inadequate infrastructure (the railway system). Finally, the Spanish economy's vicissitudes during the nineteenth century cannot be separated from those of the imperial period, when the Treasury was nourished by the wealth of America, and the nascent bourgeoisie, satisfied with its enjoyment of the imperial market, tolerated the permanence of the seignorial régime.

But the failure of the nineteenth-century movement for industrialisation as a whole must not be allowed to conceal the partial successes. A comparison of the commercial balances of 1913 and 1850 reveals that the development of textile production was the most noteworthy of these. At the middle of the last century Spain dedicated thirty-six per cent of her importation to the purchase of textile materials and products from abroad—13·2 spent on the buying of raw materials, 4·7 on yarns, and 18 on woven goods. In 1913 the value of these imports represented no more than fifteen per cent of the total, two-thirds of which were laid out on raw cotton, and the greater part of the remaining third on other fibres likewise not processed. The dependence on foreign manufactures, so burdensome in 1850, had disappeared sixty years later. Instead, in 1913 what stood out were the large sums employed in the purchase of machinery,[68] iron and steel products, ships and coke and coal, which, totalling twenty-two per cent of all the expenditure on imports, constitute convincing proof of the backwardness of Spain's own heavy industry. Even more

TABLE 7: The principal Items of Spain's Foreign Trade in 1850 and 1913

IMPORTS			
1850		*1913*	
Items	percentages	Items	percentages
1. Raw cotton	12·7	1. Raw cotton	9·3
2. Sugar	11·7	2. Machinery	8·7
3. Cocoa	7·2	3. Coal and coke	5·9
4. Woollens	6·4	4. Chemical products	4·5
5. Cod fish	5·4	5. Timber	4·4
6. Cotton goods	4·7	6. Iron and steel (including	
7. Hemp and linen yarns	4·4	articles)	4·1
8. Silk textiles	3·8	7. Ships	3·3
9. Linen textiles	2·9	8. Cod fish	2·9
10. Hides	2·2	9. Textile raw materials	
11. Timber	2·2	(except cotton)	2·9
12. Coal	2·0	10. Wheat and flour	2·7
		11. Hides and skins	2·3
		12. Cattle	2·1

EXPORTS			
1850		*1913*	
Items	percentages	Items	percentages
1. Wines and brandy	28·3	1. Minerals	12·2
2. Wool	9·3	2. Wines	11·9
3. Pig lead	9·1	3. Metals	11·6
4. Wheat and flour	7·1	4. Fresh fruits	8·6
5. Dried fruits	7·0	5. Food preserves	4·4
6. Cork stoppers	3·8	6. Dried fruits	4·4
7. Cochineal	3·2	7. Cotton goods	3·9
8. Silver and silver coins	3·1	8. Cork stoppers	3·7
9. Olive oil	2·9	9. Vegetables	2·6
10. Raw Silk	2·6	10. Olive oil	2·5
11. Salt	1·6	11. Wool	2·2
12. Soap	1·4	12. Silver and silver coins	1·7

Source: The corresponding volumes of the *Estadística exterior de España*.

68. Yet in 1850 the imports of machinery (8·4 million *reales*) had cost less than those of cinnamon (10·0 millions)!

convincing is the fact that although the ratio between the cotton industries of Spain and the United Kingdom was as one is to ten in 1899 to 1903, the ratio between the respective iron and steel industries, calculated according to the production of cast iron, was never more than one to twenty-three, even in Spain's most favourable period, during the quinquennium 1909 to 1913.

Clearly, Spanish growth between 1830 and 1914 was unbalanced, with cotton as its leading sector; and this implied that the lack of balance was not limited to the various sectors of economic activity, but was passed on to the regions of Spain. As the leading cotton region by far, Catalonia during the major part of the period under study appeared as the sole manufacturing area, the scene of large currents of migration, the cradle of the Spanish working-class movement. Reinforcing the traditional arguments based on such things as the purchase of raw materials abroad and the lack of demand for goods and services from other sectors, Nicolás Sánchez Albornoz reduces the importance of the Catalan textile industry as the prime mover of a self-sustained growth by emphasising the merely substitutive nature of Catalonia's production. According to this view, instead of creating a new demand in the full sense, native textiles did no more than replace on the market those which before had been imported, in agreement with the old conditions of demand, and provide a firm prop for the subsistence economy.[69] In general terms, it may be retorted that the demand for goods and services made by one sector on another may very well escape the meshes which, for any particular moment, are formed by the columns of an input-output table. Further, speaking of Catalonia itself, it must be pointed out that, besides hastening the commercialisation of the products of the land, the cotton mills brought about the creation of a chemical industry and a metallurgical processing industry which were in the front rank among those of Spain. Without the first repair shop for bobbins and looms, the first Spanish-built static steam engine (before 1849), iron-hulled ship

69. *España hace un siglo: una economía dual*, Barcelona, 1868, pp. 17–18.

(1857), railway wagon (1882) and locomotive (1854) could not have been constructed in Barcelona. Finally, without that precedent there would be no explanation for the presence of Catalan firms among the most important iron and steel enterprises of Spain.

The seaboard provinces of the Basque country, Vizcaya and Guipúzcoa, constituted the second industrial island in the midst of the dominant agricultural structure. The Basque industrial take-off came much later than that of Catalonia, and was less diversified and more concentrated. The opportunity which the Bessemer converter presented to the ores of Vizcaya caused an unprecedented accumulation of capital, part of which was re-invested in the creation of a modern iron and steel industry. But this prosperity of Vizcaya rebounded to the detriment of Asturias, the coal country, whose well-founded hopes of becoming the home of the main nucleus of the whole iron and steel industry were frustrated. It is indeed true that the Asturian region was the Cinderella of the Spanish industrial revolution.

Other efforts towards industrialisation could be given up for lost by 1913. The mining and smelting of lead, in the southern half of Spain, had fallen entirely into foreign hands. Málaga, which was, after Barcelona, the second industrial province of Spain between 1850 and 1860, was half a century later completely disindustrialised. The rest of the country, with very few exceptions, remained anchored in a backward agriculture, based on cereals. Apart from the traditional centres of viticulture, not yet recovered from the ravages of phylloxera, the most interesting of these exceptions were the astonishing development of the cultivation of citrus fruits in the Valencia region and the swift establishment of the sugar beet in the basins of the Ebro and the Guadalquivir. The striking presence of fresh fruits among the exports and the notable absence of sugar from the imports in the balance of trade figures for 1913 are a faithful image of these regional agricultural advances.

BIBLIOGRAPHY

SOURCES

Collections of historical statistics are in existence only for the years after 1900: *La riqueza y el progreso de España*, published by the Banco Urquijo in 1920 and, in a fuller version, in 1924, and *Principales actividades de la vida española en la primera mitad del siglo XX. Síntesis estadística*, produced by the Instituto Nacional de Estadística, Madrid, 1952. See also *Publicaciones Estadísticas de España. Publicaciones del primer centenario de la estadística española*, Madrid, 1956, produced by the same Instituto, but which must be used with caution, and the printed results of a series of important enquiries carried out mainly with the tariff in mind, the most outstanding of which are: *Información sobre el derecho diferencial de bandera y sobre los de aduana exigibles a los hierros, el carbón de piedra y los algodones, presentada al Gobierno de Su Majestad, por la Comisión nombra al efecto en Real Decreto de 10 de noviembre de 1865*, 4 vols., Madrid, 1867; *Información sobre las consecuencias que ha producido la supresión del derecho diferencial de bandera y sobre las valoraciones y clasificaciones de los tejidos de lana, formada con arreglo a los artículos 20 y 29 de la Ley de Presupuestos del año 1878–1879, por la Comisión especial arancelaria creada por R. D. de 8 de septiembre de 1878*, 2 vols., Madrid, 1879; *La crisis agrícola y pecuaria. Información escrita y actas de las sesiones de la Comisión creada por R. D. de 7 de julio de 1887 para estudiar la crisis por que atraviesa la agricultura y la ganadería*, 7 vols. (vol. II in two parts), Madrid, 1887–1889; *La reforma arancelaria y los tratados de comercio*, 6 vols., Madrid, 1890.

BIBLIOGRAPHICAL AIDS

For agriculture, the best guide is 'Los estudios de historia agraria en España desde 1940–1961. Orientaciones bibliográficas', by E. Giralt Raventós, in pp. X to LXXIX of vol. V (1959, but completed in 1962) of the *Indice Histórico Español*, Barcelona; for mining, see the *Bibliografía minera, española*, produced by the Consejo de Minería, 2 vols., Madrid, 1946–1947, and the *Bibliografía de minería, metalurgia, geología y ciencias afines*, by J. M. López de Azcona, Madrid 1962, although they do not supplant the *Apuntes para una biblioteca española de libros, folletos y artículos, impresos y manuscritos, relativos al conocimiento y explotación de las riquezas minerales y a las ciencias auxiliares*, by E. Maffei and R. Rua Figueroa, 2 vols., Madrid, 1871, new edition by the 'Cátedra San Isidro' of León in 1970 with the addition of a third vol. entitled *Apuntes para una bibliografía minera española e tberoamericana (1870–1969)*, by J. García Morales. For the processing industries, it is advisable to consult the *Ensayo de una bibliografía de los ingenieros industriales*, by M. de Foronda Gómez. Madrid, 1948.

GENERAL WORKS

The start should be made with J. Vicens Vives': 'La industrialización y el desarrollo económico de España de 1800 a 1936', in the volume *Première Conférence Internationale d'Histoire Economique, contributions, communications*, Stockholm, 1960, pp. 129–136, *An Economic History of Spain* (with the collaboration of J. Nadal, translated by F. M. López Morillas), Princeton, 1969, and *Historia de España y América*, vol. IV, *Burguesía, industrialización, obrerismo*, Barcelona, 1961. J. Fontana, *La quiebra de la monarquía absoluta (1814–1820)*, Barcelona, 1971, provides an excellent key to the understanding of the contradictions which shaped the birth of the bourgeois state. *La política monetaria y las fluctuaciones de la economía española en el siglo XIX*, Barcelona, 1948, by J. Sardà is fundamental. *España hace un siglo : una economía dual*, Barcelona, 1968, by N. Sánchez Albornoz, gives a clear outline of the case of Spain. Recently, *Ensayos sobre la economía española de mediados del siglo XIX*, Madrid, 1970 (G. Tortella, R. Anes, C. Fernández del Pulgar, J. Nadal and G. Anes), and *El Banco de España. Una historia económica*, Madrid, 1971 (the sections relating to 1830 to 1913 are by G. Tortella and J. Nadal), show a critical approach to these questions.

P. Vilar, *La Catalogne dans l'Espagne moderne. Recherches sur les fondements économiques des structures nationales*, 3 vols., Paris, 1962, and G. Anes, *Las crisis agrarias en la España moderna*, Madrid, 1970 are invaluable for the study of the beginnings of industrialisation.

WORKS ON THE REGIONS

Most of these are concerned with Catalonia and the Basque country: *La economía de Cataluña en el siglo XIX*, by J. Carrera Pujal, offers an arsenal of data; *Industrials i polítics del segle XIX*, by J. Vicens Vives and M. Llorens, Barcelona, 1958, is a brilliant essay on Catalonia. In the second group are *Minería, industria y comercio del país vasco*, by A. de Churruca, San Sebastián, 1951, *La actividad de Vizcaya en la economía nacional*, by F. de Lequerica, Madrid, 1956, and *Un siglo de la vida del Banco de Bilbao. Primer centenario (1857–1957)*, Bilbao, 1957.

For the other regions, see the following: *El marqués de Sargadelos o los comienzos del industrialismo capitalista en España*, by J. E. Casariego, Oviedo, 1950, concerning Galicia; *Asturias industrial. Estudio del estado actual del industrialismo asturiano*, by R. Fuertes Arias, Gijón, 1902, and *El movimiento obrero en Asturias: de la industrialización a la Segunda República*, Oviedo, 1968; E. Giralt, 'Problemas históricos de la industrialización valenciana', in *Estudios Geográficos*, XXIX, 1968, pp. 369–395; J. Nadal's article 'Industrialización y desindustrialización del Sureste español (1817–1913), in *Moneda y Crédito*, No. 120, 1972, pp. 3–80, and the pamphlet by J. Senador Gómez, *Castilla en escombros. Las leyes, las tierras, el trigo y el hambre*, Madrid, 1915.

WORKS ON SECTORS

La historia de la industria catalana, by P. Romeva, 2 vols., Barcelona, 1952, *La banca a Catalunya. Apunts per a una història*, by F. Cabana, Barcelona, 1965, and *Història de l'agricultura catalana*, by J. de Camps i Arboix, Barcelona, 1969, emphasise the lack of more histories of agriculture, mining, industry, transport or banking in Spain.

For agriculture, see F. Tomás y Valiente, *El marco político de la desamortización en España*, Barcelona, 1971, *Contribución al estudio de la desamortización en España. La desamortización de Mendizábal en la provincia de Gerona*,

Madrid, 1969, and *Contribución al estudio de la desamortización en España. La desamortización de Mendizábal en la provincia de Madrid*, Madrid, 1969, both by F. Simón Segura, and particularly *La desamortización de las tierras de la Iglesia en la provincia de Sevilla (1835–1845)*, by A. Lazo, Sevilla, 1970. See also *Consideraciones sobre los factores del problema agrario en España*, by S. C. Méndez Bartolomé, Santiago, 1910 and the section by J. Nadal in the above-mentioned book *El Banco de España. Una historia económica*.

The mining sector. For lead, see *El plomo en España*, by E. Gómez Llana, Madrid, 1949, and *La minería en la Sierra Morena de Ciudad Real*, by F. Quirós Linares, Oviedo, 1970. For copper, *Memoria sobre el aprovechamiento industrial de los yacimientos de pirita ferro-cobriza de la provincia de Huelva*, by C. Guitián, F. B. Villasate and J. Abbad, Madrid, 1916, *Piritas de Huelva. Su historia, minería y aprovechamiento*, by I. Pinedo Vara, Madrid, 1963, *The Mines of Tharsis. Roman, French and British enterprise in Spain*, by J. G. Checkland, London, 1967, and the older works of R. Rua Figueroa, *Historia de las minas Río Tinto*, Madrid, 1859, and L. Aldana, *Las minas de Río Tinto en el curso de siglo y medio*, Madrid, 1875. For mercury, the splendid volume *Los almadenes de azogue (minas de cinabrio). La historia frente a la tradición*, by J. Zarraluqui Martínez, Madrid, 1934. For zinc, *La Compagnie Royale Asturienne des Mines, 1853–1953*, Paris, 1954. For iron, *Vizcaya minera. Su historia, legislación foral y derecho vigente*, by M. de Basterra, Bilbao, 1894, *Las minas de hierro de la provincia de Vizcaya. Progresos realizados en esta región desde 1870 hasta 1899*, by I. de Echevarría, Bilbao, 1900, and in particular the series *Criaderos de hierro de España*, by various authors, issued by the Instituto Geológico y Minero de España. For coal, *Consideraciones generales sobre la industria hullera de España*, by L. de Aldana, Madrid, 1862, *Carbones minerales de España. Su importancia, descripción, producción y consumo*, by R. Oriol y Vidal, Madrid, 1873, *Los carbones nacionales y la marina de guerra*, by L. de Adaro, Madrid, 1911, *La política del carbón en España*, by I. Herrero Garralda, Madrid, 1944, and the above-mentioned book by Quirós Linares.

The iron and steel industry. *Estudio relativo a los recursos de que la industria nacional dispone para las construcciones y armamentos navales*, by B. de Alzola, Madrid, 1886, *Adelantos de la siderurgia y de los transportes mineros en el norte de España*, by P. M. Clemencín and J. M. Buitrago, Madrid, 1900, the excellent volume *Criaderos de Asturias*, by L. de Adaro, 1916, in the series *Criaderos de hierro*, mentioned above, *La economía siderúrgica española*, vol. I: *Historia crítica de la historia industrial de España hasta 1900*, by F. Sánchez Ramos, Madrid, 1945, *Spain's Iron and Steel Industry*, by R. N. Chilcote, Austin (Texas), 1968, *175 años de la sidero-metalurgia asturiana*, by L. de Adaro Ruiz-Falcó, Gijón, 1968, *Los orígenes de la industrialización española (1832–1868)*, by J. Nadal, included in *Ensayos sobre la economía española de mediados del siglo XIX*, listed among the General Works.

Textile industries. *La industria algodonera española*, by L. Beltrán Flórez, Barcelona, 1943, *Aribau i la indústria cotonera a Catalunya*, by J. Fontana, Barcelona, 1963, *The Development of the Spanish Textile Industry, 1750–1800*, by J. C. La Force, Jr., Berkeley and Los Angeles, 1965, *Revolució Industrial i obrerisme. Les 'Tres Classes de Vapor' a Catalunya (1869–1913)*, by M. Izard, Barcelona, 1970, 'Una empresa algodonera catalana. La fábrica "de la Rambla", de Vilanova, 1841–1861', by J. Nadal and E. Ribas, in *Annales Cisalpines d'Histoire Sociale*, Pavia, No. 1 (1970), pp. 71–104, and 'La naissance de l'industrie cotonnière catalane: réflexions sur un démarrage', by P. Vilar, a communication presented at the Colloque International du C. N. R. S. L'industrialisation en Europe au XIXe siècle. Cartographie et Typologie, Lyons, October 1970, whose sessions are in the course of publication.

Outside the range of the 'classic' industries, two books deserve special mention: the *Historia del gremio corchero*, by R. Medir Jofre, Madrid, 1953, and *La industria eléctrica en España. Estudio económico-legal de la producción y consumo de electricidad y material eléctrico*, by F. Sintes Olives and F. Vidal Burdils, Barcelona, 1933.

For transport, the book *Transportation and Economic Stagnation in Spain, 1750–1850*, by D. R. Ringrose, Durham

(North Carolina), 1970, is a basic text for the pre-railway era. For rail transport, the *Historia de los ferrocarriles españoles* (*1830–1841*), by F. Wais San Martín, Madrid, 1967, needs to be complemented by the first three vols. of *Elementos para el estudio del problema ferroviario en España*, published by the Ministerio de Fomento, Madrid, 1918.

For money, banking and the financial system the fundamental works are those of Sardá, Sánchez Albornoz and Tortella, 'La evolución del sistema financiero español de 1856 a 1868,' pp. 17–145 of the vol. *Ensayos sobre la economía española de mediados del siglo XIX* mentioned above, and 'El Banco de España entre 1829–1929. La formación de un banco central', pp. 261–313 in the vol. *El Banco de España. Una historia económica*, both listed among the General Works.

The specialist on the working-class movement is J. Termes, the author of *Anarquismo y sindicalismo en España. La Primera Internacional* (*1864–1881*), Barcelona, 1972.

10. The Industrial Revolution in Switzerland

B. M. Biucchi

GENERAL AND HISTORICAL ASPECTS

In 1835 John (later Sir John) Bowring was sent on an official mission of inquiry to Switzerland to report to Parliament on that country's commerce, factories, and industries. His report[1] is of great interest both as a well-documented first-hand testimony (it was compiled on the basis of interviews with eminent Swiss industrialists and public authorities in the various cantons) and for its interpretation and estimate of the economic position of this staunch little country that Britain, to her astonishment, was encountering as a competitor 'in all the markets of the world'. Bowring's deductions and conclusions undoubtedly served to support the arguments of free traders in Britain's Parliament. His whole report is a panegyric of free trade. A country with a population of barely two million, in an unfavourable geographical position, had successfully striven to put into practice 'freedom of trade as a political system'.[2]

The British cotton industry probably had no particular doctrinaire or ideological motives in instituting an inquiry into the Swiss economy (two years later Bowring was sent to Germany and produced, in 1840, a report for Lord Palmerston on the Zollverein). From 1780 onwards Switzerland had been an important market for British cotton textiles; and Britain was eager to discover how, since the end of the Napoleonic wars, this little country could have become instead the most serious competitor for the British cotton industry both in Switzerland itself and in European and world markets. Our distance from those times and from the ideas then prevalent enables us today to see Bowring's re-

1. 'Report to the British Parliament on Swiss trade, factories and industry', German translation John Bowring, *Bericht an das englische Parlament über den Handel, die Fabriken und Gewerbe der Schwerz*, Zurich, 1837.
2. ibid. p. 2.

port in a more objective light, thanks also the more profound analytical studies of industrialisation as a normal concomitant of economic development that have been carried
out by economic historians from Mantoux onwards. Free
trade is undoubtedly the most characteristic element in the
structure of the Swiss economy; it appears throughout its
whole development from the sixteenth century to the present day and goes far to explain the flexibility[3] that Bowring admired in Swiss industry, and the readiness to adapt
itself to new economic situations. If today we were to add a
corollary to the conclusions of Bowring's inquiry, we might
say that early-nineteenth-century Switzerland was in a
position to meet British competition and play a role side by
side with the British textile industry in its penetration and
expansion into all the existing markets, simply because it
was prepared to accept at once from Britain the industrial
revolution.

Britain's 'industrial revolution' can be placed roughly
between 1780 and 1830; these were the years during which,
from its beginnings, the process of industrial and social
transformation became established. The corresponding
period in Switzerland can be put as between 1798 and 1830.
The coincidence of this industrial timing with the timing of
political events is not purely fortuitous. Borel d'Hauterive's
comment, in 1800—'La premiére, la plus ancienne et la plus
importante cause de la révolution francaise a été l'action
du systéme industriel et commercial sur le systéme social de
tous les peuples de l'Europe' (The first, the oldest, and the
most important cause of the French Revolution was the
repercussion of the industrial and commercial system on the
social system of all the European peoples)—is especially
valid for Britain and Switzerland, for both those countries
had by their political evolution already to a large extent
anticipated some of the fundamental principles of the
French Revolution. Industrial revolution as an economic
and social process is inseparable from the process of change,

3. See B. M. Biucchi, 'Tendenze liberiste nella storia economica
svizzera' (Free-trade tendencies in Swiss economic history), in *Rivista
internationale di Scienze sociali*, Milan, 1934, No. 4.

whether gradual or revolutionary, in political institutions and social structures. It is because of this reciprocal concatenation and interpenetration of the two phenomena that we prefer the traditional terminology of 'industrial revolution' to the more recent term, 'take-off'.

In Switzerland's case, in particular, if we seek to apply the distinctive and general characteristics of the 'take-off stage', and especially if we analyse the 'precondition stage' or try to establish the time when economic development expanded from industry to other sectors and became 'self-sustained', we have to go back to the seventeenth and eighteenth centuries. In those two centuries the cotton industry had in fact already ceased to provide the sole 'leadership-sector'.

Switzerland's other economic activities included the silk industry, watchmaking, foreign trade, international financial transactions and agriculture; and her cotton industry was technically more advanced than that of Britain (significantly, a number of terms of Swiss origin, such as Swiss mulls, Swiss books, Swiss checks and so on, were in use in British trade at that time). All this gave her industrial development a position of primacy antecedent to, or at least parallel with, industrial development in Britain. But for the fact that mechanisation represents the fundamental characteristic of an 'industrial revolution', the Swiss industrial revolution could be said to have come before the British.

Rostow's concession to the critics of his conception of 'take-off' is particularly valid as a criterion of industrial revolution in the case of Switzerland, among the first of Western countries to be 'born free'. 'Economic growth', he says (and this could equally well read 'Industrial revolution)', 'is the result of an interacting process involving the economic, social and political sectors of a society.'[4] It is no mere chance that the chronology of Switzerland's industrial revolution coincides with certain fundamental dates in her

4. W. W. Rostow, *The Economics of Take-off into Sustained Growth, Proceedings of a Conference held by the International Economic Association*, London 1963, p. xxiv.

political life. In 1798-9, just when the introduction of machine spinning began to be envisaged as an unavoidable necessity,[5] the French invasion forcibly imposed on the confederated Swiss republics a whole series of ideas and political institutions which only a small stratum of the intellectual élite was prepared to understand and accept. For those ideas were in direct contrast to the traditions of a democracy which had been in existence for several centuries but had remained fundamentally oligarchic and aristocratic in the urban cantons, bourgeois and rural in the cantons of the countryside and mountainous areas.

The 'Helvetian Republic, one and indivisible' imposed by the invading armies was politically ephemeral (1801-3) because it ignored the historical origins and essence of the Swiss state, but from the economic standpoint it accelerated and prepared the way for the integration and unification of the twenty-three cantonal economies in the federal Pact of 1848. The abolition of tithes and of all feudal landed rights, the declaration of liberty for crafts and trades, the impulse and protection given to machine spinning under the Helvetian Republic, all remained operative even when, after the fall of Napoleon, the settlement of 1815 brought Switzerland back into the orbit of the *ancien régime* restored in Vienna by Metternich's Holy Alliance.

Small-scale cantonal revolutions in 1830 succeeded in partly reviving some of the principles of the French Revolution in preparation for the federal agreement of 1848, which marked the definite creation of a new federal Helvetic state, genuinely democratic and economically unified. In the meantime, between 1803 and 1815 the Act of Mediation, dictated by Napoleon, had brought about a sensible reconciliation between tradition and revolution in the Swiss cantons. In the economic sphere, despite the obstacles to foreign trade caused by Napoleon's anti-British policy, the period of the Mediation succeeded in protecting the Swiss textile industry from British competition, gave it a useful

5. The first mention of the need to enlarge knowledge of machinery appears in pamphlets of 1764, and the first attempts to use machines were made in the canton of Appenzell in 1783.

breathing-space, and offered Swiss traders the opportunity, which they readily seized, to take advantage of the troubled situation and assert themselves by every means in continental and overseas markets. The importance of Switzerland in the development of European economy, and the fact, astonishing to the English of that day, that Switzerland at once took its place beside Britain in the industrial revolution, has passed almost unnoticed by historians of that revolution and, in general, in the economic historiography of Europe. The reason for this is simple.

Switzerland up to 1848 appeared as a little mosaic of tiny states virtually insignificant in area and population within the context of a continental economy and in relation to the major national states, France, Germany, and Italy. Behind these external appearances, however, as soon as we begin to analyse certain indications quantitatively and qualitatively we at once come upon figures and data which in terms of absolute values make nonsense of such superficial judgements. In the eighteenth century the European and world demand for so valuable a commodity as clocks and watches was met up to 90 per cent by Swiss manufacture. At the end of that century Switzerland had a population of about 1,800,000 and there were only about ten towns with over 5,000 inhabitants. The working population in the towns was mainly employed in what would now be called tertiary activities, and in the rural hillside districts, and even in certain mountainous areas like the Jura or canton Glarus, according to contemporary evidence[6] only a third of the population was dependent on agriculture, the other two-thirds being occupied in industry. At the beginning of the nineteenth century a little canton like Neuchâtel with only about 55,000 inhabitants, had about 5,000 people employed in watchmaking and exported yearly about 85,000 silver watches (average price 20 francs) and 35,000 gold watches (average price 150 francs). At the time of the industrial revolution England alone absorbed about 58% of the world production of cotton, but Switzerland took 23%. And in Switzerland, side by side with the cotton

6. J. K. Nüscheler, *Beobachtungen eines redlichen Schweizers*, Zurich 1786.

industry, there was also a flourishing silk industry, a manufacture which, technically speaking, was ahead of cotton
(as early as the eighteenth century silk mills were mechanically operated, indeed one could say 'automated', for they
worked day and night untended).

The major industry from the point of view of labour, the
cotton industry, is the only one for which we have a reliable
employment figure at the beginning of the industrial
revolution: in 1780 it employed 150,000. Adding to this the
silk and watchmaking industries, both of them possibly
superior as regards income and capital, and not forgetting
woollen and linen manufacture which largely supplied the
internal market, there seems good ground for believing the
statement of a contemporary observer that 'two-thirds of the
rural population live by industry'.[7]

Let us now see how far the timing of developments in the
industrial revolution in Switzerland bears out the assertion
that it ranked as *primus inter pares*, or at least a close second,
in relation to Britain. As to its beginnings, the 'pre-conditions' of Rostow's take-off, Swiss industrial development
can be considered to precede, or at any rate run parallel
with, the British. As an English traveller in Switzerland
towards the end of the eighteenth century remarked in
amazement, 'For a minute I thought I was in England'.[8]
But in the introduction of mechanical spinning and weaving—with the spinning jenny, the Crompton mule jenny,
and the Cartwright looms—Britain obviously was ahead of
Switzerland in technical innovations. It was these innovations that induced the Swiss cotton industry to take the first
and most important step as an essential preliminary of the
industrial revolution—the mechanisation of spinning and
weaving.

The approach of this event was clearly foreseen by the
industrialists of the day. The most striking proof of this can
be found in Lenardo's diary in Goethe's *Wilhelm Meisters
Wanderjahre*, in which he describes in detail the structure
and position of the textile industry in the rural areas of

7. J. K. Nüscheler, op. cit.
8. W. Coxe, *Travels in Switzerland*, London 1776, Vol. I, p. 3.

Switzerland on the eve of the industrial revolution. 'Mechanisation, which is making steady advances, disturbs and alarms us, and it gradually comes nearer and nearer like a storm controlled from without which is bound to come and hit us.' This pessimistic view does not prevent a clear choice of the path to be followed: 'We must take up these innovations ourselves' (*Selbst das Neue ergreifen*).[9] The other alternative, 'to seek a better fate beyond the seas', was obviously only a literary and sentimental hypothesis.

After 1780 Switzerland, who till then had been in the lead in cotton spinning and had surpassed Britain in certain special fields (fine-woven goods, embroideries, and laces), found that British textiles, cheaper and of better quality than her own, were beginning to invade the Swiss market. Swiss industry had no choice but to take a sad if courageous step: to abandon spinning for the most part and import British yarns in order to develop and expand weaving and the export of woven textiles. Sporadic attempts by the Swiss to construct their own cotton-spinning machinery produced no satisfactory results. The idea of bringing an English mechanic, John Milne and his family, to Geneva in 1788 came to nothing, both because it proved too costly and because he demanded monopolist protection. In 1794 the board of commerce in St Gall subsidised a plan for mechanised spinning which failed (an official report of the Swiss Republic said 'the thread always came out too coarse'). The first mechanised spinning-mill opened in St Gall in 1801, protected by patents of the Helvetica company,[10] and planned by Pellis, a Vaudois trader who, because of his revolutionary ideas, had taken refuge in Bordeaux in 1794 and had later returned to Switzerland in the service of Laharpe and the Helvetica. In the course of a few years mechanised spinning-mills were established in Zurich, St Gall, and Glarus, generally set up as joint-stock companies founded and directed by financially sound and commercially experienced businessmen: Escher in Zurich, Hard at Winterthur, Kunz at Uster. The first big mill in Winterthur,

9. Johann Wolfgang Goethe, *Wilhelm Meisters Wanderjahre*, book 3, ch. 13.
10. *Tageblatt der Gesetze und Dekrete*, 1800, Heft 4, p. 370 ff.

established in 1803 with a capital of 150,000 florins, by 1824 had a capital of a million florins and had installed 20,000 spindles. Heinrich Kunz, the 'king-spinner' of Uster, died in 1859 the owner of eight mills with 150,000 spindles, leaving an inheritance of 25 million francs. Escher contrived in 1823 to smuggle in a machine from England which he set up in his mill, but as soon as the first big crisis in the cotton industry developed he moved over to the construction of textile machinery. Beginning in 1826 with sixteen workers, by 1835 his factory gave employment to 400 and exported machinery to all the neighbouring countries. The turnover rose from 60,000 florins in 1830 to 588,000 in 1837. In seventeen years the company distributed dividends totalling 500,000 florins.

This was the beginning of the Swiss machine industry, and this rapid and 'spontaneous' passage from the textile to the machine industry shows how Switzerland's economic development, from watchmaking and textiles to machinery and from textiles to dyes, was already advancing 'self-sustained' by the beginning of the nineteenth century. Mechanisation extended to weaving, embroidery, and lace-making and also to silk. In 1827 the cotton-industry regions of Switzerland possessed a total of 400,000 mechanised spindles, rising in 1845 to 662,000 and in 1857 to 1,350,000.

The rapid spread of mechanisation brought the import of yarn from England to an end after 1830. Confined by the Napoleonic blockade and threatened by British competition, the Swiss textile industry rejected all temptations to go in for protection, accepted technical progress, and with astonishing skill and tenacity successfully sought new outlets overseas. The industrial revolution in textiles brought Switzerland to establish herself in world markets. One particular episode is worth recording. Napoleon in suppressing the free ports of Genoa, Trieste, and Venice cut off Switzerland from supplies of raw cotton from Brazil. Switzerland at once sought new import routes from the United States via Baltic Russia and Leipzig.

Every import, too, opened up a fresh outlet for Swiss

manufactured exports. As a contemporary document sapiently remarks: 'Even the famine of 1817-18 opened up new markets for our goods. The big imports of grain from Russia, Egypt, and the Levant supplied those countries with large amounts of European currency. And they, seeking for European manufactured goods to import, produced an intense export trade for our country both to those states and to Persia, even as far as the borders of China, to the Caspian, and to the Nile.'[11]

THE DETERMINING FACTORS OF THE SWISS INDUSTRIAL REVOLUTION

We have assigned Switzerland's industrial revolution to the period 1800-1830, and we have seen how it developed during the years when textile machinery was introduced. The rapid spread of mechanisation is clearly one of the most striking aspects and causes of the phenomenon. The other two aspects of industrial revolution—the concentration of labour in factories, and the development of antagonistic social strata or classes in the relationship between capital and labour—are less pronounced in Switzerland, although they operated gradually to modify the economic, social, and political structure of the country. In Switzerland the industrial revolution brought no fundamental change in localisation, which remained strongly decentralised, outside the towns. The industrial revolution was not accompanied by phenomena of urban agglomeration; it remained within the limits of medium and small-sized concerns (the cotton and silk weaving machines brought no appreciable change in the size of factories, given the sound organisation of trade and commerce in both home and foreign markets); and it was accompanied by a revival of agriculture, itself ready to absorb technological advance. Consequently the revolution did not cause any great social problems or upheavals,[12] because the perfect balance

11. *Verhandlungen der schweizerischen gemeinnützigen Gesellschaft* (Proceedings of the Swiss Public Utility Society), 1825.

12. There was only one case of revolt against machinery, the fire in Uster in 1832.

between town and country and the distribution of wealth among wide middle sectors of the population corrected and even attenuated, during the period 1800-1830, that 'proletarisation' (the exclusive dependence of two-thirds of the rural population on industry) that the eighteenth-century 'patriot economists' had censured. These are aspects that will be examined in greater detail when considering the effects of the industrial revolution.

The more immediate question is to explain the deeper reasons for this rapid, decisive, and widespread changeover to a modern industrial system, a change that affected every branch of all industries and that brought Switzerland in the nineteenth and twentieth centuries into the first ranks of European and world economic development.

The judgement of an acute and well-informed observer like Bowring really sums up Swiss industry's swift and almost spontaneous change-over and adaptation to the British industrial revolution, a change not passively endured but accepted in all its implications: 'I am convinced that there is no industry more solid, sound, and flexible than that of Switzerland.' Without abandoning certain constant principles of its centuries-old development and balance, the Swiss economy 'absorbed the new production functions', to use Rostow's phrase, in all its branches. Switzerland seemed at that time already to have evolved a perfect synchronisation in the rhythm of development. To conquer British competition, commerce at once opened up new sources of supply (the United States) for the textile industry and new markets for trade. Difficulties of financing for industrial investment were non-existent, in a country where industrial development had been self-financing for centuries and where foreign trade, concentrated in the towns and among a small group of businessmen, had accumulated considerable reserves of capital virtually untouched by taxation. The expansion of incomes, which at once followed the industrial revolution as soon as the period of crisis and adjustment had been overcome, gave an impetus to bank savings, already widespread in the small savings banks, and also prompted the organisation of internal and international bank credit. A good part of the wages of the numerous industrial population was reinvested in rural property (small houses and farms) throughout the country. This is one of the main factors, side by side with decentralisation, that reflects the degree of industrial (one could also say 'capitalistic') intensity in Switzerland, and which provides the key to a seeming paradox in Swiss economic policy, its strongly agrarian trend despite the prevalence of industry and commerce.

That the industrial revolution was not a purely economic phenomenon can be seen from the *political* changes that accompanied it. They modified profoundly the institutions and legislation of a traditional society jealous of its liberty and fundamentally democratic; which was divided by municipal and cantonal autonomy but nevertheless united on the general lines of an economic policy supported by a wide section of the small and medium bourgeoisie. The changes and the acceptance of the ideas of the French Revolution found their logical expression in a sequence of political events—the Helvetian Republic, the Mediation, the Restoration, and the 'revolutions' of 1830 and 1848. In the course of those events the relics of the old corporative regime were suppressed and brought to an end by deliberate legislative intervention: the abolition of feudal land ties, the distribution of common lands, freedom of domicile and of labour, industry, and commerce, all helped Switzerland to evolve easily towards free trade as an economic system, the more so since she had for centuries made free trade a basic principle of her commercial policy.

The reason for the speed and flexibility with which Switzerland adapted herself to the industrial revolution is to be sought in that whole complex of 'pre-conditions' which made her ready to absorb the necessary changes. We will now review them briefly, following Rostow's list of 'initial conditions',[13] and stressing those specifically applying to Switzerland.

13. W. W. Rostow, op. cit., p. 11 ff.

STRUCTURE OF THE POPULATION

No statistics are available to enable us to estimate population development in the present territory of the Swiss Con-
federation. It can, however, be established that there was a
big increase in population in the seventeenth and eighteenth
centuries. In the Canton of Zurich the population rose from
120,800 in 1671 to 172,200 in 1762 and to 231,576 in 1836.
In the little canton of Appenzell (Ausserrhoden) it rose
from 19,593 in 1669 to 39,571 in 1794. In the canton Glarus
the male population over sixteen years of age went up from
2,371 in 1700 to 5,797 in 1797.

The reasons for this increase of population are twofold:
demographic (decline in mortality, and the decline, especially in the countryside, in the exodus of males between the
ages of 18 and 30 for military service as mercenaries abroad)
and economic, i.e., due to industrial development, since the
increase in population occurred especially in the industrialised rural areas. The structure of the population was characterised by a balance between town and country. In the
main towns (Zurich, Basel) the population remained
stationary, because the corporative regime (the guilds) did
not allow craftsmen and the small industry of the day to
expand, and industrial development therefore lay in the
country and mountain areas where corporative restrictions
did not apply. The commercial and financial élite was
concentrated in the towns, but the higher social classes did
not contribute to the population increase to the same extent
as the small rural bourgeoisie, which provided the country
with its abundant industrial manpower ('they all work and
all find a livelihood' in the rising industries, according to
the Zurich historian Schinz, speaking of the period 1628-
1640).

The decentralisation of the expanding industries (cotton,
silk, watchmaking) in the rural areas, and the absence of
any real urban agglomeration, may give the impression
that Swiss economy in the seventeenth and eighteenth
centuries was static and traditional in character, being

based on an essentially rural society. In fact, however, in the industrial cantons two-thirds of the rural population were no longer peasants, or only seemed so superficially; they had already become involved not only in the process of industrialisation but also in ways of living and thinking which had ceased to be those of an agricultural society. The sharp division whereby trade was situated in the towns and industry in the countryside meant that the expanding industries (silk, cotton, and watchmaking) were exempt from the restrictions imposed by the corporations (which survived formally in the towns in respect of craft trades) and thus favoured industrial development. On the other hand the decentralisation and ruralisation of industrial development freed industry almost entirely from those administrative, social, and political costs which even in those days became translated into taxation. Once again we find that acute observer Bowring attributing the prosperity of Swiss industry to the fact that 'the people pays very little to the state', that 'there are no taxes on consumption', and that 'government and justice cost little'.[14] The decentralisation and ruralisation of industry also helped to mitigate the inevitable social consequences of the industrial revolution, for family incomes from industrial activities were supplemented both by the subsistence livelihood derived from small rural properties and by the investment of savings in land. In Switzerland the phenomenon of the proletariat, which accompanied the industrial revolution in other countries, was practically non-existent.

A WANING AGRICULTURAL TRADITION

On the eve of the industrial revolution the apparent prevalence of a 'rural philosophy', of an idyllic conception of agriculture as the perfect economic activity and of a physiocratic trend in economic thought, might give the impression that Switzerland was still firmly anchored to the ideas and institutions of a traditional agrarian society; so, at least, it might seem to judge by some of the rhetorical

14. J. Bowring, op. cit., p. 3.

literature of the day and by the plethora of communal agricultural societies, agricultural almanacs, and essays on rural science. In reality, however, the agrarian rural world had already undergone a profound transformation, and agriculture was no longer mainly a subsistence agriculture but had become commercialised and technically well equipped for market production. The close connection of agriculture, trade, and transport with a quite flourishing foreign trade (in livestock, wine, and salt) in the Alpine regions; the industrialisation of the countryside in the cantons of the plain and the plateaux and in the Jura; the penetration of an already highly specialised textile industry in St Gall, Glarus, Appenzell and other regions; the political weight exerted in administrative spheres by the country and mountain cantons vis-à-vis the urban cantons (Zurich and Basel in particular)—all these factors had inevitably produced a progressive rural society which in its customs and ways of living and thinking was not so very different from the small-town bourgeoisie. This rural society was increasingly prepared to accept innovations as its contacts with the outer world developed; industry brought wealth and prosperity to the country and mountain areas; and these facts, together with the ideas put about by a select band of intellectuals and writers, combined to cause the industrial changes to be accepted without difficulty. The structure of agriculture, the rural institutions, ordinances, and laws, and the political integration between town and country caused Swiss agriculture in the seventeenth and eighteenth centuries to evolve on lines parallel with the country's general economic development and, in particular, with the industrial changes.

The changes that took place in the agrarian sphere can be briefly summarised. The peoples of the Alpine cantons were the first to achieve freedom and independence. Freed from feudal burdens (tithes and other such obligations), they could then, as soon as general conditions allowed, divert their agrarian economy towards those activities (pasture and livestock-rearing, abandoning wheat cultivation since it could be easily imported) which soil, climate, and geographical proximity to foreign markets made re-munerative. The phenomenon of *enclosures*, practised on a small scale but similar to what happened in England, can be vouched for as early as the fifteenth century and from then on became more widespread as industrialisation developed. The triennial rotation of crops as a method of cultivation survived tenaciously, but intensive cultivation also made headway, especially around the towns. The Alpine cantons could be said to have a rural-bourgeois society that was already definitely pre-capitalistic in its wealth and spirit of enterprise.[15]

The exponents of physiocratic and agrarian philosophy, from the numerous agricultural societies to Pestalozzi, Fellenberg, and Hirzel, discerned clearly the predominant position of industry in the Swiss economy, and they merely sought to secure a better balance by urging agriculture towards technical and commercial progress.

FORMATION OF CAPITAL AND THE CAPITALISTIC OUTLOOK

A number of factors and fortunate coincidences combined towards the formation of capital and the spread of a capitalistic outlook which brought Switzerland, between the sixteenth and eighteenth centuries, to that stage of development that we might call, with Sombart, 'Früh-kapitalismus', or with Rostow, 'capital formation'. Mercenary service and the booty and pensions that went with it helped to create funds of capital, both private and public, in Switzerland, and the transition from war on behalf of others to trade for one's own profit merely accelerated the process. Refugees from outside (coming from Locarno to Zurich, from Lucca to Geneva, and later on the Huguenots throughout Protestant Switzerland) brought with them considerable capital, commercial experience, and that spirit of enterprise so often found in men who have to seek a

15. For a full account see C. G. Schmidt, *Der Schweizerbauer in Zeitalter des Frükapitalismus* (The Swiss Peasant in the pre-capitalist period), Berne, 1932.

new home and livelihood. The silk and watchmaking industries and foreign trade even in those days needed considerable ready capital; to establish the first silk-mills in
Zurich, on the Italian model, an enterprising refugee from
Locarno, Zanino, offered an interest of 16 to 20%, guaranteed by mortgages on his property in Locarno, and sought
the State's participation for his infant industry. The
'Grande Boutique' opened in Geneva in the eighteenth
century by the Turrettini family, from Lucca, was a holding
consisting of six trading companies with a joint capital of
421,000 gold crowns regularly distributing dividends of
from 15 to 30% of the share value. At the end of the
seventeenth century the silk mills introduced by the Locarno
refugees, run by machinery and working day and night,
numbered a hundred, but their owners gave work in spinning and weaving to some 100,000 persons in canton Zurich
and the neighbouring cantons.

Such examples could be multiplied. But the best indication of the abundance of capital is provided by the very low
rate of interest—reaching 2% in the eighteenth century—
on the investments abroad of Swiss financiers and cantons
(at the end of that century the city of Geneva, with 25,000
inhabitants, received an annual sum of 20 million *livres*
from invested capital or loans in foreign countries), and
more particularly by the wide distribution of wealth.
Waser, an eighteenth-century Swiss political mathematician, has given us a precise and reliable picture of the
distribution of wealth in Zurich which, *mutatis mutandis*,
can be regarded as typical for the whole of industrial
Switzerland at that time. He divides the 1,942 families into
five categories according to wealth, and the capital of each
category is estimated under the headings of landed property,
fixed capital, and working capital.

These statistics show, on the one hand, a certain concentration of wealth among traders' families, and on the
other a large representation—more than half the families—
of the medium bourgeoisie. That the prosperous town of
Zurich was no exception is confirmed by the distribution of
wealth (and incomes) in the mountain canton of Glarus,

No. of families	Landed property (valued in florins)	Fixed capital (in florins)	Working capital (in florins)
280	0	430	404
458	14,585	1,560	1,455
962	145,850	15,600	14,550
220	292,700	31,200	29,100
22	397,500	62,000	50,000

where the historian Trümpi in 1780 provides an estimate of the canton's patrimony: 14 million florins (Glarus at that time had a working male population over 16 years of age of about 5,000), of which a tenth was invested in trade and about a million florins was placed on loan abroad. In 1798 in the little canton of Outer Appenzell the taxable capital (which represented only 50% of the taxpayers' fortunes) amounted to 16 million francs, spread over a population of 38,000.

Public savings in the cantons and towns, accumulated through the incomes derived from mercenary service abroad, went a long way towards providing the funds for a simple, modest, decentralised administration much of which was unpaid since the offices were honorary. Taxation was so light that it furthered the private accumulation of capital, with the result that there was no need to organise bank credits (the banks developed only in the second half of the nineteenth century) because industrial expansion was able to be self-financing. The industrial and rural dependent population put their basic savings into land or real property and the rest into the small savings banks that Bowring so much admired. At the beginning of the nineteenth century Switzerland was ahead of England in savings (one in 36 of its inhabitants had savings deposits, as against one in 40 in England) and came second to it in the amount of savings per depositor—776 francs in England, 278 in Switzerland. The period of the industrial revolution coincided with a period of war and economic and commercial crises, and this, since it caused freezing, liquidation, and repatriation of capital, inevitably produced an accumulation of liquidity, which we find reflected in the savings banks statistics: in 1825 deposits totalled 4,524,385 francs, whereas in 1835 the figure had risen to 11,513,712 francs. The phenomenon of formation and circulation of capital was discernible even in rural and agricultural areas, where higher standards of living (in food, housing, and clothing) than those of a primitive and frugal rural society began to develop and so stimulated people to seek an income from the sale of agricultural produce.

Agriculture, in turn, sought to finance expansion and modernisation by obtaining credits through mortgages. Peasants sometimes found themselves running into debt and in order to meet the growing burden of interest rates had to sell their produce before the harvest came in and at a lower price. This 'financial crisis' of agriculture in the seventeenth century was a factor in promoting the transfer of large numbers of the rural population to industrial activities.

In this brief summary of developing capitalism mention must also be made of the specific role played by the Protestant attitude. It is no mere chance that industrial development arose mainly in the Protestant areas, a fact reinforced by geography: for the Catholic cantons were orientated towards a Mediterranean economy in decline, whereas the Protestant cantons shared in Atlantic development.

THE INTELLECTUAL BOURGEOISIE

In the history of European culture, in philosophy, literature, science, and the arts, Swiss names occur only rarely—among the exceptions are Paracelsus, the reformers Calvin and Zwingli, the Bernouilli family and the great architects from Ticino who, however, were more closely associated with Italy. Geneva and Basel (and Zurich in eighteenth-century literature) were the only towns open to European intellectual influences. There was, on the other hand, a large and widespread middle class which could be described as an 'intellectual bourgeoisie', on which both French Enlightenment and English Utilitarianism exercised an influence. It was this class, strong and active in all the Swiss cantons and grouped together in numerous social and educational societies, that spread the idea of economic progress in public meetings, in chambers of commerce, in the press, and throughout public opinion. It helped to widen knowledge of new techniques in agriculture and industry; and in this way it played an important part in persuading a closed and traditional society to accept the innovations and changes that were gradually revolutionising the working world.

The industrial revolution would certainly be inconceivable without French Enlightenment and English Utilitarianism. The deep penetration of Switzerland by this 'economic philosophy' (by means of the physiocratic trends in Berne and the 'Bibliothèque universelle', based on the earliest British Encyclopaedia and appearing from 1796 to 1815) was closely related to the phenomenon of industrial and technological development. The 'patriot economists' of Berne carried on a valiant work of economic enlightenment, imbued with physiocratic ideas but open to technical progress not only in agriculture but also in industry. A little work published in Berne in 1764 bore the significant title *Von der Notwendigkeit die mechanischen Kentnisse zu erweitern* (The need to extend knowledge of machinery); and in the same year a similar work appeared in Aargau. In 1767 the Berne Economic Society held a prize competition on the subject: 'In what circumstances can factories and manufacture be helpful to the population and to agriculture?' When British competition broke into the Swiss market and into Switzerland's export trade, the political decision that Goethe described as 'taking up innovations ourselves' became a principle of industrial policy unquestioningly accepted by everyone. This can be seen from the recommendations of a Zurich inquiry reporting in 1833 to the State Council on the subject of machine-weaving: 'We cannot do without these looms, just as we could not do without machine-spinning, otherwise our cotton industry would be ruined'. The university professor Christoph Bernouilli was not afraid to come down from theory to practice in his publication, of 1824, *Anfangsgründe der Dampfmaschinenlehre* (First principles of steam machinery), and in his treatise of 1829, *Rationelle oder theoretisch praktische Darstellung der mechanischen Baumwollspinnerei* (A theoretical and practical account of mechanical cotton-spinning), in which he also expressed interesting views on the economic effects of technical progress.

The flexibility and speed of Swiss industry's adjustment to the industrial and technological revolution can only be explained against the background of contemporary Swiss society—a society to all appearances rural and traditional, but within which there was a broad social stratum of intellectual bourgeoisie which, emerging simultaneously with a general diffusion of wealth and industrial activity, was prepared to accept the 'economic philosophy' of industrialisation and to play an active part, in politics, in the press, and in business circles, towards furthering its advent.

FOREIGN TRADE

Switzerland's economic development, beginning in the sixteenth century and continuing almost without interruption up to the early 1800s, might seem inexplicable or almost miraculous but for one fundamental determining factor—her foreign trade. In the sixteenth century the Swiss cantons withdrew from European politics and military affairs; in 1516 they concluded a 'treaty of perpetual peace' with France and decided, whether they liked it or not, to move over from warlike activities as a means of employing their surplus population to civilian pursuits and to peace and neutrality. Swiss industry can be said to have developed as an export industry and the trading and commercial privileges secured by the French treaty and through military capitulations with other countries (mercenary military service still went on but on a reduced scale and no longer for territorial conquests on Switzerland's own behalf) opened up the way to the markets of Europe and the world. In the seventeenth and eighteenth centuries foreign trade had already made virtually ineffective, except for municipal regulations, the mediaeval statutes governing crafts and trades. Swiss industry was born to export and born free. Corporative restrictions still survived in respect of the wool and linen trade and for the crafts and trades carried on within the town confines. But the cotton and silk industries and the Jura watchmaking industry from the outset were declared 'freies Gewerbe' (free trade) and were able to develop in conjunction with the opening of export markets in France, Italy and Germany.

Since the necessary raw materials had to be obtained from abroad, a free-trade policy, dictated by geography and the country's geophysical structure, became the normal economic practice for the Swiss cantons. Political freedom and autonomy, jealously claimed by the country and mountain cantons vis-à-vis the urban oligarchies, extended also to industry and trade. The commercial and financial élite remained concentrated in the towns, but under the stimulus of foreign trade they also sought, and readily found, room to expand their economic activities in the rural areas, thus bringing about a functional and territorial division of spheres—trade in the towns, industry in the countryside—which, in my view, affords the main reason for the balanced development of the Swiss economy from the sixteenth to the nineteenth century. Population, trade, and industry all followed in their steady development the expansion of foreign trade. Free trade, exempt in the countryside from customs and taxation burdens, was already an unquestioned rule of trade policy in the seventeenth century, accepted as normal practice by all the cantons. It is only by taking into account this centuries-long experience and tradition of 'free trade' that we can explain the intelligent and immediate reaction of Swiss industry to the English industrial revolution that came to offer stiff competition to the flourishing Swiss textile industry. Spinning was sacrificed at once, and weaving was supplied with English yarns. Mechanisation was speeded up. Harassed by Napoleonic protectionism and the continental blockade, Swiss industry had the ready intuition to seek its salvation, in the midst of the industrial revolution, in integration in the world economy.

Typical and explicit confirmation of this is provided by a contemporary source: 'Let us thank Providence for the exclusion of Switzerland from neighbouring markets; for it forced traders to enlarge their horizons. Their sons are now to be found in Persia, Astrakhan, Moscow, St Petersburg, England, New York, Rio de Janeiro, and Havana. Their thoughts no longer turn to Paris as if that city were the centre of the world.'[16]

CHARACTERISTIC ASPECTS OF THE SWISS INDUSTRIAL REVOLUTION

In Switzerland's economic history the industrial revolution, unlike the British, corresponds to a long period of crisis and general economic depression, aggravated by war conditions and political circumstances. The eighteenth century had been a century of prosperity for the towns and the countryside. What was said of Geneva was equally valid for the whole of industrial Switzerland: 'It had abandoned all low-return manufactures and paid for such goods by means of the high-return industries, jewellery and watchmaking. This was the source of its prodigious wealth, and the reason why Geneva's 25,000 inhabitants were richer than all the 800,000 in the neighbouring Departments.' Less remunerative occupations were left to foreigners. Peasants deserted agriculture, and consumption and the standard of living reflected the general prosperity and wellbeing. Competition from English textiles irrupted like a hurricane into the Swiss cantons, and the first reaction in the press and in public opinion was pessimistic and moralising in tone. 'The English machines will be the ruin of the Continent', 'Let us return to agriculture', 'We must moderate our luxury and revert to our old simple ways'—such sayings were typical of

16. *Verhandlungen* . . ., 1825, p. 273.

contemporary rhetorical exhortations and moralistic preachings.

On the economic plane the revolution was accepted with all its consequences—which were bound to be deflationary. Despite extraneous circumstances—bad harvests, food shortage, and wars—which in Switzerland as in England tended to put prices up, the period of Switzerland's industrial revolution, from 1798 to 1835, was characterised by a general decline in prices and wages. Even the price of wheat, in spite of sharp fluctuations in years of shortage (in 1818 it reached 75 francs the quintal), went down to the same level as before the industrial revolution, i.e., around 20-25 francs. Here too the 'free trade' factor played a part. The traditional suppliers of wheat for Switzerland were Italy and Swabia but in the bad years of 1816-17 the Swiss cantons sought their supplies in Russia, Egypt, and the Levant.

The phenomenon of falling prices for the products of Swiss industry was noted and acutely interpreted by contemporary observers. A report of the Swiss public utilities society in 1823 comments: 'Over the past thirty years goods have been costing about a sixth or a seventh of what they used to cost. This fall is reflected in lower prices for yarns and lower profits for the manufacturers. Wages are now a quarter of what they were, but their decline is partly compensated for by greater speeds in weaving,'[17]—In 1827 the same society's report states: 'We can expand still further the introduction of machinery, and we hope to emerge victorious from this crisis, for we are at least at the same level of civilisation as other nations, and we have the advantage of having cheap food, low taxation, and low wages.'[18] Fazy-Pasteur, presenting a paper for discussion in 1828, seems to echo even more clearly the watchword of Swiss industry: 'Cheapness, that is the principle of victory for our industry, the anchor that will save us in the storm of the

17. *Verhandlungen* . . ., 13. Bericht 1823.
18. *Verhandlungen* . . ., 1827, p. 70.

industrial revolution, the only means of combating the tariff system of the neighbouring states.'[19]

Swiss industrial policy was clear-cut and realistic: to introduce technical innovations as rapidly as possible and counter British competition by low prices. In achieving that aim, and in overcoming the difficulties and changes attendant on the industrial revolution, Switzerland was helped by a number of circumstances that made it easier for her to adapt herself. In the interval between the mechanisation of spinning and that of weaving, the unemployed workers from the spinning-mills went into the expanding cotton and silk weaving industries. When spinning became mechanised, between 1802 and 1820, the Napoleonic continental blockade offered the Swiss cotton industry ample opportunities of taking Britain's place in continental markets, both by legal trading and by means of contraband English goods. The continental blockade and the vast network of Swiss manufacturers' trading relations opened up new markets to the Swiss industries both for supply of raw materials and for export of manufactures. Switzerland, as has already been said, at the time of the industrial revolution found opportunities for expansion and integration in overseas markets. After weaving became mechanised in England, weaving in Switzerland, in the brief interval while machine looms were being introduced there, concentrated its efforts on those fine and superfine woven textiles—muslins, coloured cloth, embroideries, and lace—which had not yet been displaced by machine weaving.

Once spinning had ceased to be remunerative because of British competition, the owners of the big spinning-mills in Zurich moved over to the construction of machinery for the textile industry. Later on, the transition from the textile industry to the metallurgical and chemical industries was to seem part of a natural and spontaneous development; and in the same way now Switzerland's speed and flexibility in adapting to new situations, whether technical, structural, or commercial, aroused the admiration of acute observers such as Bowring.

19. *Verhandlungen . . .*, 1828, p. 294.

It may seem paradoxical that the industrial revolution should be accompanied by a 'return to agriculture'; but this was really simply a reversion to those factors of economic, political, and social balance which had been ingrained for centuries in Switzerland's economic development. The return to the land and the renewed emphasis on agricultural activities were not merely a rhetorical response to bad times and the industrial crisis. They also afforded the impetus for agrarian reforms, for abolishing the remaining restrictions on land tenure, and providing incentives for livestock-rearing—in short, for the decisive revival of a branch of the economy that eighteenth-century prosperity, forgetful of physiocratic teaching, had come to neglect.

The return to the land and the explicit recognition, as Schinz wrote, in 1827, that 'both together, agriculture and industry combined lead to the surest prosperity'[20] had important social repercussions. The balance, both economic and political, between town and country, and the distribution of functions and activities between them which had been in practice for more than two centuries, had given Switzerland an economic structure both free and expanding and at the same time stable, socially developed, and untouched by the ferment of social or political revolution. The return to the land as a subsidiary source of income and subsistence, together with the decentralisation and specialisation of industry which served to maintain and strengthen the industrial middle class, excluded the development of an industrial proletariat in Switzerland. A marked feature of the industrial working population of that time was their savings, which they invested in small houses and farms, and in this they were helped by their employers who advanced the necessary purchase money.

The transition to mechanised industry was faced promptly and decisively, but it came about gradually without causing sudden upheavals or unbalance in the economic structure. Viewed from this angle, Switzerland's industrial revolution was simply the natural outcome and

20. *naheren Kenut* 1827, p. 5

conclusion—in mechanisation and in the expansion and integration of her foreign trade within the world economic framework—of a long process of evolution resulting, as Franscini has said,[21] from 'the combined action of her productive forces, her traditions and her institutions'.

21. Stefano Franscini, *Nuova statistica dello Svizzera*, 1844.

MAPS

The maps that follow help the reader to understand the complex political situation before and after Napoleon.

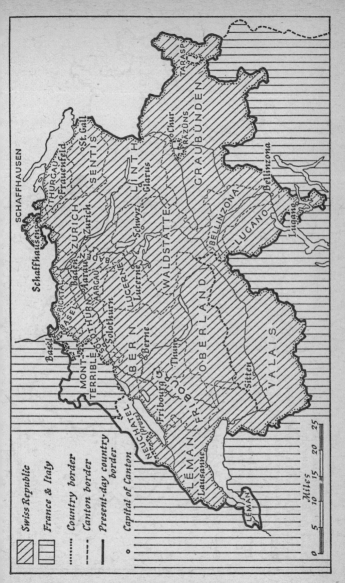

Helvetia, 1798-1803

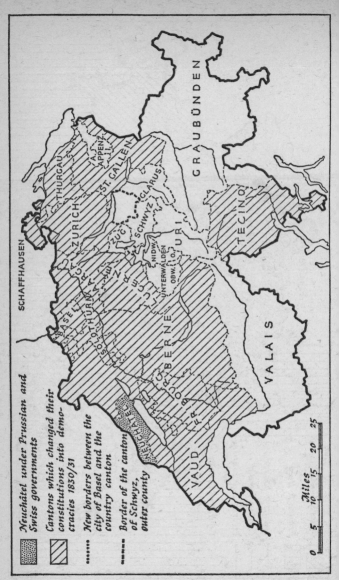

Restoration, 1814-30 and Regeneration, 1830-31

BIBLIOGRAPHY

Switzerland's economic historiography includes a number of valuable monographs on individual cantons and industries, but the industrial revolution as a whole is dealt with only in W. Rappard's *La révolution industrielle et les origines de la protection légale du travail en Suisse*. (Berne, 1914). A. Hauser's *Schweizerische Wirtschafts und Sozialgeschichte* (Zurich, 1961) gives only a superficial account of the period without going into detailed analysis. T. Geering, in his short essay *Grundzuge einer schweizerischen Wirtschafts geschichte* (Berne, 1912) provides a good outline of the basic features of Swiss economic development. A good descriptive history of the Swiss textile industry is given in Walter Bodmer *Die Entwicklung der schueizerischen Textilwirtschaft im Rahmen der ubrigen Industrien und Wirtschaftszweige*, Zurich, 1960. Rudolf Braun's *Industrialisierung und Volksleben*, Zurich, 1960, and *Sozialer und kultureller Wandel in einem ländlichen Industriegebiet im 19 and 20 Jahrhundert*, 1965, also give an excellent description of one aspect of the industrial revolution. But there is still a wide field for research, and for a thorough historical and economic investigation covering both the industrial revolution itself and Switzerland's whole centuries-long economic development.

The Emergence of an International
Economy 1700–1914

William Woodruff

When future generations look back on the European Age
they might well regard the emergence of an international
economy as one of its more remarkable achievements. For
where in history can we find a parallel to the manifold
economic relations that existed between the peoples of the
world on the eve of the First Great War? Never before had
the ties binding the world together been so closely knit or
as vital to the economic well-being of so many people as
they had become by 1914. However haphazard and fortuitous Europe's impact in the world proved to be, by the
eve of War the Europeans had succeeded in establishing a
Euro-centric world economy of the greatest complexity,
aimed primarily at serving the economic interests of the
western people.

Underlying the emergence of an international economy
was the territorial expansion of Europe in the world. In
1850 European control of overseas territories, despite Britain's loss of the North American colonies, already exceeded
the area of Europe itself. Between 1800 and 1900 the Europeans (in Eurasia and overseas) increased their control of
non-European territories eight or nine times. It was the exploitation of these territories and the growing trade done
with them that obtained for the European family wealth on
a scale never seen before. The first countries to industrialize
in western Europe (and those that did it with the least
sacrifice) were already the richest. They were rich not only
because of the wealth they had obtained from the efforts
made within their homelands, but also because of the wealth
they had obtained from outside. No group of people in world
history ever experienced such an enormous increment in its
natural wealth so quickly. It was the interaction of the
internal and external economic forces, together with the
challenge of an expanding world-wide frontier, that help to

explain the transformation of so much of western Europe's economic life, and the growing economic interdependence of Europe and the world.

Only as a result of these combined forces did Europe eventually come to hold sway over the earth; only thus did the smallest island kingdom, Britain (in 1707 the English and the Scots, conscious of their destiny, had decided to call their united countries 'Great Britain'), achieve world status and dominion. Many western Europeans came to look upon the world as a place of unlimited progress. Under European tutelage European wealth had been used to quicken and develop other lands; European science and industry had been applied to the benefit of all. Under European guidance and protection, human toil had been lessened, the serf and the slave freed, the common lot improved, distance conquered, world trade enlarged, and a system of international law established; democracy and Christianity had also triumphed in many lands. Given western leadership, there seemed to be no end to what might be achieved in the world; at least before the First Great War engulfed them, that is what many Europeans thought.

The changing nature of international trade is the most concrete evidence we have of the emergence of an international economy. In the fifteenth and sixteenth centuries the spice trade had been the chief source of wealth in European foreign commerce. As Europe expanded, this was surpassed in importance by colonial produce such as sugar, tobacco, furs and naval stores. Growing economic activity in the American colonies also stimulated the trade in slaves. Small as the profits arising out of colonial trade may appear in retrospect, they helped to provide some of the capital needed to finance the growing economic activity of parts of western Europe. By the second half of the nineteenth century, as Europe's numbers grew and its industries flourished, ever-increasing quantities of fibres, minerals, grain, timber and perishable commodities such as fruit and meat, flowed to Europe's shores. As the tide of white settlement moved across the world, as immense systems of land and sea transport were devised, as new technologies were introduced, Europe was able to draw upon the wealth of the whole world. Little wonder that international trade theory came to occupy the place it did in the writings of the British nineteenth century classical economists.

For the period 1750 to 1913 European estimates show that the value of world trade increased more than fifty-fold. Whatever credence we place on the widely differing estimates of world trade,[1] one thing does seem to emerge, namely, that world trade increased physically many more times than European or world population. In 1913, according to European estimates, almost all world trade was being done by members of the European family. However, these calculations do not show world but Euro-centric trade; they reflect the trade that came within the European orbit. Moreover, in so far as they show trade between political units, between nations, they are misleading. The development of international trade in the nineteenth and twentieth century relied upon the growing economic inter-relatedness of economic regions, not upon the will of mercantilist States.

Until well into the nineteenth century Europe could feed its increasing numbers by expanding its own resources; the growing and changing demands of Europe's industry, however, could only be met by vastly increasing the flow of industrial raw materials from abroad. None of these materials were more crucial to industrialization than fibres and minerals. Leading all other items in the commerce of the Atlantic basin in the nineteenth century was raw cotton.

1. In spite of all the work that has been done on foreign trade we can only guess at its volume and value in the hundred years before 1914. The most readily accepted guesses show world trade between 1750 and 1914 increasing from approximately U.S. $700 million to $38,150 million. In value terms, the expansion in world trade was greatest between 1820 and 1880 when it increased nearly nine times. In the first decade of the twentieth century its value doubled. Europe accounted for more than half the total of world trade (about 24 billion dollars out of a world total of 41 billion dollars). Its volume went on growing until the outbreak of the First Great War, when Europe, including Russia, took 61 per cent of the value of world imports and accounted for approximately 55 per cent of the value of world exports.

As the mechanical, factory production of textiles proceeded, Europe became particularly dependent upon the cotton crop of the Southern United States. As a result of the steep rise in Europe's demand for raw cotton, the United States crop multiplied almost sixtyfold between 1790 and 1810.[2] Fifty years later, in 1860, 'King Cotton' accounted for almost two-thirds the value of America's total exports; thanks to the huge yields of the American South, a relatively costly textile material at the beginning of the century had become relatively cheap. Although the American Civil War forced the European nations to seek alternative supplies (especially from India, Egypt and the West Indies), United States cotton exports quickly recovered in the post-war period; in 1913 they were about three times the figure for 1860. For almost a hundred years America had remained the most important source of the world supply of cotton.

The mechanization of the European woollen industry proceeded more slowly than that of the cotton industry, and it was not until the second half of the nineteenth century that the European woollen industry completely out-stripped the domestic supply of wool. By that time, sheep, brought to the grasslands of the Southern hemisphere by the Europeans, had begun to multiply extensively; wool from the Antipodes had become the mainstay of the European woollen industry.[3] In 1913 half the world's wool supply was drawn from Australia and New Zealand. Other important sources of supply were Argentina and South Africa. The economies of these countries, especially of Australia, show the extent to which the first white settlers came to depend upon European demand for the sale of their staple products. By 1913 sheep flocks in Europe were kept for their meat, not as they had been kept previously for their wool. For many Europeans it now was more economical to buy wool from the other side of the world than to produce it at home.

2. From an estimated 680 metric tons in 1790 (three years later in 1793 the use of the cotton gin tripled the amount of cotton a man could pick free from seeds), to 38,600 metric tons in 1810.

3. Of a total of 75 million pounds of raw wool imported by Britain in 1850, 39 million pounds came from Australia.

It was Europe's good fortune that for the basic ores and minerals required by the Industrial Revolution it was not as dependent for supplies on the rest of the world as it was for fibres, particularly cotton. World production of ferrous minerals between 1820 and 1910 is estimated to have increased sixty-five times;[4] a similar increase was recorded for the production of non-ferrous minerals.[5] Of the unprecedented amounts of minerals of all kinds taken from the earth during these years, most were used by the industries of the western nations. Wood began the Industrial Revolution, coal continued it, but it required iron and cheap steel, and eventually large quantities of copper and other metals for the Industrial Revolution to continue and spread in the world.

Unlike foreign supplies of raw materials, Europe's dependence on world supplies of food and drink did not become critical to its general welfare until late in the nineteenth century. In trying to meet their needs Europeans added to the world supply of food more by extending the area of stockraising and plant cultivation of known species in their newly acquired territories overseas, than by discovering new plants and animals. Also, by the gradual introduction of scientific methods, Europeans made considerable improvements upon the plants and animals they already possessed.

The changes occurring in the international grain and meat trades after 1850 reflect Europe's success in increasing its food supply from abroad. By that time the supply of wheat to Europe had become practically continuous—arriving in increasing quantities from Australia, Argentina, India, the Middle West of America, and Canada. The value of wheat exports from the United States increased more than twentyfold in the years 1850–1915.[6] The most rapid expansion of the United States wheat production occurred during 1866–

4. From about 1 million metric tons to approximately 65 million metric tons.

5. From about 48 thousand metric tons in 1810 to more than 3 million metric tons in 1913.

6. $8 million in 1850 to an annual average of nearly $173 million in the years 1911–15.

90, much of it in a period of falling prices. In the early eighties, Indian supplies had depressed prices almost as much as those from the New World. Also in the 1880's, Australian exports of wheat doubled; during the 1890's Argentine exports more than tripled. On the eve of the First Great War, as the internal demands of the United States grew, and the relative fertility of its soil declined, Russian exports of grains to the western nations came to exceed those of North America.

More remarkable was the development by the Europeans of the world meat and dairy-produce industry. The key factor here was the introduction of refrigeration, which began to be used in the meat-packing houses of the Americas and the Antipodes, as well as by the world shipping lines, at the beginning of the eighties. Thenceforth, it became increasingly profitable to raise great herds of cattle on the Texas ranges, and in the Rosario Valley of Argentina, and to establish enormous sheep stations in South Africa, New Zealand, and Australia. Live cattle had been brought from the Americas to Europe in the sixties and seventies, but it was only with the introduction of refrigeration that important quantities of meat began to enter international commerce, much of the frozen and chilled meat replacing 'live' shipments. Europe's ability to draw upon the meat supplies of the world—especially from the southern hemisphere through the tropics—strengthened the trend towards world specialization in food supply.

The United States was the leading meat supplier until the end of the nineteenth century, its exports growing at an astonishing rate between the 1870's and 1900.[7] By then, Argentina, Australia, and New Zealand had gained importance as world suppliers of meat. In 1900 European settlers in these countries were about to increase the world supply of meat as earlier on the United States had increased the supply of wheat and corn. While Europe's demands for meat in the closing decades of the nineteenth century had a considerable effect upon the development of the American

7. From an annual shipment of about 50 tons in the 1870s to about 65 thousand tons in 1900.

Midwest, the over-all impact was probably greater on the smaller and much less diversified economies of Argentina and New Zealand. In helping to lay the foundations of economies such as these, especially in making the future welfare of these countries dependent upon the willingness of Europeans to buy their products, the vastly increased world trade in meat encouraged the interdependence of the white communities of the southern and northern hemispheres.

As a result of European expansion and international specialization, food (and drink) became relatively cheap in the western world. With the great increase in the world production of grain from the 1870's until the end of the century, the price of wheat dropped from about $1.50 a bushel in 1871 to 86 cents in 1885; a decade later in 1894 the figure was about 70 cents. General business instability and the overall fall in freight charges from the Americas, Australia, and Asia in the last quarter of the century encouraged the downward trend. From the late 1890's until 1914, when prices were either rising or buoyant, the increase in the world supply of wheat meant that wheat prices lagged behind the general recovery. Other grains entering western European ports showed similar price trends. So economical to use did some of the grains become that in 1913 it was quite common for western European farmers to fatten their beasts on imported grain; an unheard of thing a century earlier. While meat prices did not fall as sharply as the price of grain, they also followed the general downward trend. In the last quarter of the century they fell by about a quarter, and in the period 1898–1913 rose less than others. This was because of growing world supplies of meat, as well as improvements in transport, and the sale of meat by-products.

The ever-growing tide of food reaching Europe's shores after the mid-century was not limited to grain and meat; it is equally true of a whole variety of products coming from the tropical and sub-tropical as well as the temperate regions. The new demands made by many Europeans for sugar, tobacco, coffee, tea, and cocoa encouraged an almost

dramatic fall in the nineteenth century prices of these commodities.

No country benefited more from the trend towards international specialization in the supply of raw materials and food than did Great Britain.

Between 1800 and 1850 British imports increased more than fourfold;[8] between 1850 and 1913, the increase was eightfold.[9] The rate of growth of these imports—even allowing for re-exports or changes in the value of money—far outstripped the rate of growth in British population, which, between 1850 and 1910, had increased from about 28 to 45 million. Equally striking were the changes experienced in the kind of trade transacted; the United Kingdom's leading import in 1800—sugar (followed by tobacco)—had given way by 1831 to raw cotton (followed by sugar and grain). The amount of raw cotton used by British industry did, in fact, increase nearly fivefold between 1800 and 1830. In the nineteenth century the supply of raw materials to British industry was completely transformed. Whereas in the eighteenth century Britain provided all the essential raw materials for its industries, especially for its staple manufacture, wool, in 1913 Britain was self-sufficient only in the supply of coal. At that time Britain depended upon foreign supplies for most of the timber, most of the wool, a growing part of the iron ore, all the cotton, petroleum and rubber needed by its industry.

However, as late as the 1860's Britain supplied most of the meat and wheat it consumed. Imports of meat rose sharply only in the last quarter of the nineteenth century. By the end of the century, Britain was dependent on foreign supplies for four-fifths of its wheat and two-fifths of its meat. Among the factors encouraging the imports of food was the increase in British population, the growth of industry and its accompanying urbanization, the improvement in the general standard of living, and the fall in world prices in the closing decades of the century.

Principal British imports by approximate percentage of total value in 1831 and 1913 were:

8. From $118 million to $485 million.   9. To $3,767 million.

1831		1913	
Cotton	19	Grain	11
Sugar	15	Cotton	9
Grain	9	Meat	7
Tea	6	Wool	4
Coffee	5	Timber	4
Flax & Hemp	5	Butter	4
Wines	3	Sugar	3
		Hides	2
		Tea	2

While Britain's trade throughout the nineteenth century was more far-flung than that of its European neighbours, most of its imports continued to come from two main sources: Europe and North America. One might say that the pace of American development—the movement of its frontier—was strongly influenced by what the British and other Europeans could absorb in the way of foreign produce.

Some of the more striking changes in the region of provenance of Britain's leading imports in the period 1831–1913 were: grain (86 per cent of total British imports in 1831 came from Continental Europe; 5 per cent in 1913; by that time the bulk of British grain imports came from North America, India, and Argentina); sugar (76 per cent from the British West Indies in 1831; 3 per cent in 1913; Europe now supplied 56 per cent); wool (between the 1830s and 1913 an almost complete switch from Continental Europe to Australasia and South Africa); meat (83 per cent from the United States in 1875; 17 per cent in 1913; when 29 per cent came from Argentina, and 23 per cent from Europe); timber (63 per cent from North America in 1850; by 1913 this figure had fallen to 13 per cent; Europe's share had risen to 83 per cent); and tea (100 per cent from China in 1831; 30 per cent in 1913; India's share had become 56 per cent).[10]

The benefits of international specialization were never as apparent to the French as they were to the British; nor in terms of population growth were they as essential (be-

10. For the region of provenance of Britain's principal imports in the period 1831–1913 see Table I, p. 718.

tween 1850 and 1910 French population grew only from 36 to 40 million). Textile raw materials remained the major item of French imports throughout the nineteenth century; coal and coke, woollen and cotton manufactures, and crude sugar were also important. French imports of grain, meat, dairy produce, and fruit grew in volume from the beginning of the twentieth century, but they never reached the same proportions as the food imports of the United Kingdom. Both in relation to employment and production, domestic agriculture occupied a much more important position in France than it did in Britain. In order of priority in 1913, imports of food ranked below raw wool and cotton, coal and coke. At this time France depended upon the other more industrialized European countries, especially Britain and Germany for imports of machinery, engineering products, metals, and chemicals. In 1913, about one-fifth of French imports of machinery was also supplied by the United States.

Principal French imports[11] by approximate percentage of total value in 1830 and 1913 were:

1830		1913	
Cotton	11	Wool	8
Sugar	9	Coal & Coke	7
Silk	6	Cotton	7
Hides & Skins	3	Grain & Flour	7
Wool	3	Oilseeds	5
Oils	2	Machinery	4
		Silk	4
		Wines	3

The important changes in the area of provenance of French imports in the nineteenth century were: the growth of the China silk trade, which by 1913 supplied 45 per cent of France's imports (the opening of the Suez Canal in 1869 increased the supplies of raw silk from China, Japan, and India); the switch from European supplies of wool (92 per cent in 1830) to those of South America and Australasia,

11. Which grew in value from $147 million in 1840 to $1,636 million in 1913.

which supplied about 66 per cent in 1913 (Europe 26 per cent); and the rise of the North African wine trade, which by 1913 supplied 55 per cent of French imports.[12]

While Germany never lost the ability to feed itself as Britain did in the nineteenth century, the German Industrial Revolution proceeded with exceptional momentum once it got under way. In 1870 only about one-third of German population was urban; by the end of the century the proportion of urban dwellers was over one-half, and on the eve of the First Great War nearly two-thirds. In these years, as the German cotton and woollen textile industries expanded, increasing quantities of raw wool and cotton were imported. In the first decade of the twentieth century Germany had the most rapidly growing cotton textile industry in Europe, relying on the United Kingdom for supplies of the finer type of yarn. With the rapid expansion of German industry since the 1880's, Germany also came to rely upon outside supplies of iron ore.

Had not the efficiency of German agriculture increased and production expanded during the nineteenth century, Germany's reliance upon eastern European and overseas areas for food would have been much greater than it was. Even so, the steep rise in German numbers between 1850 and 1910 from 36 to 65 million, coupled with the rapid transformation of Germany during the last quarter of the nineteenth century, from a predominantly rural and agricultural to a predominantly urban and industrial society, meant that Germany had to find extra food overseas. However, as the figures given below show, on the eve of War, raw materials played a larger role in German imports than food.

Principal German imports in 1880 and 1913 by approximate percentage of total value are shown on p. 667.

The major changes in the area of provenance of Germany's imports in the period 1880–1913 were the switch from European supplies of wool to those of Australia and Argentina (in 1913 Australia supplied 42 per cent and Argentina 22 per cent), and the growth of the South Ameri-

12. For the region of provenance of France's principal imports in the period 1830–1913 see Table II, p. 720.

1880			1913	
Wool, Cotton, etc.	17		Cotton	6
Grain	10		Wheat	4
Textile yarns	9		Wool	4
Cattle	6		Barley	4
Coffee, cocoa, tea	6		Copper	3
Animal feed	5		Hides	3
Hides & skins	5		Iron Ore	2
			Coffee	2
			Coal	2

can coffee trade (in 1913 Brazil supplied 64 per cent of Germany's coffee imports).[13]

There were few countries in Europe in the nineteenth and early part of the twentieth century that were not affected by the economic forces at work in the western world. Even the much smaller powers of Europe had to integrate their foreign trade within a changing world economic pattern. Thus, whereas the leading imports for the Netherlands, Belgium, and Switzerland in 1900 was food, by 1913 industrial raw materials (wool, cotton, iron, coal, timber) had come to play a greater role. Sweden was the exception, drawing less on foreign sources for food and raw materials than the others. Minerals, primarily coal, remained the principal Swedish import from 1900 to 1913, followed by metal goods and machinery. The changing situation regarding these countries is reflected in the table on p. 668.

Most of the imports of the smaller European countries came from their European neighbours. However, Belgian imports from Europe fell from 76 per cent in 1880 to 66 per cent in 1913; as they did so, imports from Argentina, India, and Australia rose. Overall figures for the imports of the Netherlands show that whereas in 1880 Europe supplied 78 per cent of all Dutch imports, by 1913 this had fallen to 38 per cent. Meanwhile, imports from Asia, North America, and Latin America had increased.

In 1914 Europe was dominant in world trade, and it was to Europe that the world's surplus of raw materials and

13. For the region of provenance of Germany's principal imports in the period 1880–1913 see Table III, p. 722.

Leading Imports of the Netherlands, Belgium, Switzerland, and Sweden.
Percentage Distribution by Value of Total Imports, 1900 and 1913

Netherlands

1900		1913	
Cereals & flour	17	Cereals & flour	17
Iron & steel	10	Iron & steel	14
Textiles, raw & manufactured	6	Textiles, raw & manufactured	6
Copper	5	Copper	4
Coal	3	Coal	4
Wood	3	Wood	4

Belgium

1900		1913	
Cereals	14	Wool	9
Raw textiles	10	Wheat	8
Resins, bitumen	4	Cotton	4
Timber	4	Rawhides	4
Crude minerals	3	Coal	3
Chemicals	3	Seeds	3

Switzerland

1900		1913	
Foodstuffs	23	Cereals	12
Silks	12	Silk goods	10
Metals	9	Cotton goods	7
Mineral substances	8	Minerals	7
Cotton	7	Colonial wares	5
Wools	5	Iron work	5

Sweden

1900		1913	
Minerals	16	Minerals	18
Metal goods, machinery etc.	15	Metal goods, machinery etc.	11
Corn & flour	10	Raw textile material & yarn	10
Textile manufactures	9	Corn & flour	8
Colonial wares	8	Textile manufactures	8

food was sent. Yet Europeans did not enjoy the benefits of international specialization without experiencing some drawbacks. The growing availability of foreign produce and the agricultural rivalry it induced, while it stimulated the trend towards industrialization and urbanization, caused a transformation of many parts of the European agricultural scene (Britain and Denmark were examples of this enforced agricultural change). It became more profitable to use land to provide standing-room for men and beasts than for cultivation. Denmark's answer to world agricultural rivalry was to concentrate on meeting the needs of Europe's breakfast table. In doing so, it greatly increased the efficiency of its dairy and animal husbandry industry. Britain's answer was to shift from arable (grain) to the more profitable pasture (milk and meat) farming.

Whatever course of action was taken by the western nations, none of them escaped a forced readjustment of their agriculture; changes on this scale in the world economy were impossible without someone's interests being sacrificed. Many of Europe's agricultural workers (peasantry and wage labour alike) made the readjustment by migrating to a nearby city or to the far-distant frontiers of the world; many of them went out of hard necessity.

For its growing imports of food and raw materials in the nineteenth century Europe paid with the products of its rapidly expanding industries. Most of these products, like textiles, were aimed at the individual buyer. As the nineteenth century progressed, however, Europe proceeded to export not only the products but the process of the Industrial Revolution. Its growing exports of steam-engines, mining equipment, textile machinery, steel mills, railways, ships, heavy engineering (heavy armaments, machine tools, ship-building and locomotive construction) and industrial chemicals (sulphuric acid, soda-ash, caustic soda, and chlorine) helped to carry the Industrial Revolution to the other continents. Those most committed to the process of industrialization, such as Britain, played the leading role.

Whether we are dealing with the exports of capital or

consumer goods, we are dealing essentially with the trade that was done by the Europeans in the world. The important exception was westernised Japan with perhaps two or three per cent of the total trade in manufactured goods in 1913. At the other end of the scale was Great Britain whose exports of manufactures and capital goods between 1800 and 1913 exceeded those of any other nation.[14]

More important than all other items in Britain's foreign trade was the export of textiles (including cottons). By the 1830's the sales of woollen cloth, hitherto Britain's most important single item of foreign trade, were far exceeded in value by the exports of cotton fabrics. In 1837, Britain sold one-third more cotton goods abroad than at home; they exceeded the exports of woollens and worsteds four times. Indeed, although we know very little about changes in the quality of British cotton manufactures, cotton textiles alone accounted for between thirty and forty per cent of all British exports during most of the nineteenth century. In 1913, by which time Britain was clothing an important part of the world's population—they were about twenty per cent of the value of all British exports.

East of Suez, India was easily the most important single cotton textile market. In 1815, before British commercial rivalry had caused the destruction of much of India's domestic textile industry, India had taken only half of one per cent of all British cotton cloth exported; by 1913 the figure was between forty and forty-five per cent.

Until the rise of the other great industrialized nations—especially the rise of the United States and Germany in the closing decades of the nineteenth century—Britain continued to supply the bulk of world cotton and woollen textiles, as it continued to supply the bulk of manufactures. In cotton manufactures and yarns, it almost had four-fifths of world trade in the early eighties. Even in 1910-13 (when the export of textile manufactures was expanding more

14. Between 1800 and 1850 British exports rose from $185 to $350 million (an increase of approximately 60 per cent). By 1913, by which time they had experienced a further seven-and-a-half fold increase, the figure was $2,573 million.

rapidly from Continental Europe and the United States than from the United Kingdom), Britain had more than half the world total. At this time (1913) four-fifths of the cotton textile production of the United Kingdom entered international trade. As a share of total exports, textiles as a whole ranged from a little more than a third in 1831, to a little less than a third in 1913. It was never to be as great again. Certain items of French and Swiss manufacture always held their own with British cottons and woollens. The inroads made into a seemingly British monopoly of the world textile trade at the end of the nineteenth and the beginning of the twentieth century, however, were along a much wider front. In addition to the growing competition provided by Continental Europe and the United States, by 1905 India and Japan had begun to supplant the British in many eastern markets. In particular, India made inroads in Britain's trade in yarns to China. Britain's sales in 1913 amounted to one-tenth the amount sold to China in the mid-eighties. Unlike Japan, which had retained political independence, the recovery of the Indian domestic textile industry depended upon how quickly it could loosen the commercial bonds that against its will and its history had bound it to Britain.

Other leading British exports in 1913 were iron and steel goods, coal, machinery, chemicals, and dyes. In contrast to the exports of textile products, which tended to decline from the end of the nineteenth century, demand for other kinds of manufactured goods and capital equipment continued to grow. Thus the rise and expansion of local manufacturing industry in other continents before the First Great War resulted, on the one hand, in a decline in the demand for certain European consumer goods, particularly for cotton textiles, and, on the other hand, in an increased demand for European equipment, especially for railway equipment and textile machinery.

The export of British iron and steel goods after 1850 was greatly dependent on the growth of the world railway network. The 2,000 miles of line opened up in the United Kingdom in 1847–48 absorbed about half a million tons of iron; a quarter of Britain's total production. There also was an ever-growing foreign demand for railway lines and equipment.

By 1875 British iron and steel exports stood at five times the 1850 level. The enormous foreign orders received in the early seventies for iron rails had, in fact, helped to produce an inflationary situation in the British iron industry. By then, however, while railways continued to be built in the world, and British iron and steel exports continued to rise in quantity, Britain's overwhelmingly dominant role in the railway industry had come under the challenge of the other industrialized western powers.

Principal British exports by approximate percentage of total value in 1831 and 1913 were:

1831		1913	
Cotton yarns & textiles	24	Cotton yarns & textiles	20
Woollen yarns & textiles	7	Iron & steel goods	8
Linens	3	Coal	8
Cutlery, hardware, etc.	2	Woollen yarns & textiles	6
Iron & steel	1	Machinery	6
		Chemicals, dyes, etc.	3

The major changes in the area of destination of Britain's exports in the period 1831–1913 were: the growth of India as a market for British cotton yarns and textiles; the increased export of woollen yarns and textiles to Europe (in 1831 25 per cent went to Europe and 43 per cent to the United States; by 1913 75 per cent went to Europe and only 3 per cent to the United States); and the increased export by 1900 of iron and steel to Asia and Australasia (exports to North America decreased from 34 per cent in 1831 to 8 per cent in 1900).[15]

In 1913, the whole complicated network of multilateral trade (that is, trade involving a third party or more) centred itself around Britain. Britain was still the largest trader and its currency the most important medium of exchange in the world. Through the fluctuations in sterling balances held in London the countries of the world were able to settle

15. For the region of destination of Britain's principal exports in the period 1831–1913 see Table IV, p. 724.

their trading accounts with each other. Britain's free trade policy (a policy that would not be adopted by other industrializing powers) and the fact that it was able to import more than it sold (the balance being met by its large 'invisible' exports: shipping, banking and other services, and interest receipts), made it the ideal creditor nation.

France, in the absence of rapid industrial change, never became as dependent on world trade as Britain did. Throughout the nineteenth century, the main items in French exports[16] were high-quality textile goods (silks, cottons, and woollens occupied the most important positions), wines and spirits, leather manufactures, articles of food such as refined sugar and dairy produce, and luxury goods. Most of France's high-quality silk, cotton, and woollen textiles were sold in Europe, particularly to Britain. The chief market for French textile products outside Europe was the United States. On the eve of War, France's best customers were its European neighbours: Britain, Germany, and Belgium. Outside Europe, the most important area for French trade was North America.

Principal French exports by approximate percentage of total value in 1830 and 1913 were:

1830		1913	
Silk cloth	25	Silk cloth	6
Cotton cloth	12	Cotton cloth	6
Wines	8	Clothing	5
Woollen cloth	6	Wool	4
Prepared hides	4	Motor vehicles	3
Linen cloth	2	Woollen cloth	3
Fancy goods	1	Chemical products	3
		Wines	3

The major changes in the area of destination of France's exports in the period 1830–1913 were the increased export of silk cloth to Europe (from 53 per cent in 1830 to 73 per cent in 1913; exports to the United States and Latin America decreased), and the growth of French North

16. French exports grew less rapidly than the British—from $119 million in 1840 to $1,324 million in 1913.

Africa as a market for cotton cloth (from 2 per cent in 1830 to 17 per cent in 1913; exports to Europe declined from 54 per cent in 1830 to 31 per cent in 1913.[17]

The foreign trade of the German States in the mid-nineteenth century[18] was modest. Although the expansion of German railways in the fifties and sixties had led to the development of the coal-mining industry, German manufacturing was still organized along traditional lines and the great majority of the population was engaged in rural occupations. During the early decades of the nineteenth century, the German States had been net suppliers of food and fine wool to other European countries, especially the United Kingdom, but as Germany's numbers grew and industrialization and urbanization progressed, Germany had no wool or grain to spare.

Like Britain, Germany's export trade between 1871 and 1913 consisted largely of factory products, sold to its industrial neighbours in Europe. By 1900 Germany had the largest iron and steel industry in Europe, and iron and steel products, together with machinery, became important items of German exports. So also were German chemical products, especially dyestuffs. To an extent unmatched by any other major German manufacture, the export markets for chemicals were outside Europe.

Principal German exports by approximate percentage of total value in 1880 and 1913 were:

1880		1913	
Textile goods	15	Iron, steel & products	13
Salt & chemicals	8	Machinery (non-elec.)	7
Textile yarns	5	Coal	5
Grain	5	Cotton goods	4
Wool, cotton, silk	4	Woollen goods	3
Metal goods	4	Sugar	3
		Paper & products	3

17. For the region of destination of France's principal exports in the period 1830–1913, see Table V, p. 726.

18. In the region of $350 million. The value of German exports increased from $1,132 million in 1900 to $2,403 million in 1913.

The major changes in the area of destination of Germany's exports in the period 1880–1913 were the increased export of iron and steel products to countries outside Europe (exports to Europe fell from 80 per cent in 1900 to 71 per cent in 1913; exports to Latin America increased from 5 to 10 per cent); and the increased export of (beet) sugar to Europe (from 58 per cent in 1900 to 87 per cent in 1913, while exports to North America declined from 37 per cent in 1900 to 2 per cent in 1913).[19]

The export trade of the smaller European powers is revealed in the table on p. 676. Between 1830 and 1913 Europe remained the largest market for Dutch, Belgian, Swiss, and Swedish exports (Europe took 89 per cent of all Dutch exports in 1880, 88 per cent in 1913; 94 per cent of all Belgian exports in 1880, 84 per cent in 1913). The exports of industrialized Belgium to Latin America, Asia, and Africa were very slight: by 1913 they had only reached 6, 4, and 2 per cent of Belgium's exports, respectively.

Western expansion and the subsequent growth of world trade in the nineteenth century were an indispensable, inseparable part of general western growth and development. The outcome for Europe was not only to have enlarged and concentrated production in the most suitable areas of the world, but also to have transmitted a degree of change to other societies (particularly in Europe's exports of capital equipment such as railroads and machinery) greater than international trade had ever done before. For some countries, depending how closely they were tied to European economic interests, while trade brought an increase in their wealth, it also brought with it a perilous dependence on the continuance of Europe's system of world trade and specialization.

The dynamic factor underlying the changes that had occurred in world trade by 1914 was the industrialization of western Europe and North America. Western industries such as mass-produced textiles, large-scale metallurgy,

19. For the region of destination of Germany's principal exports in the period 1880–1913, see Table VI, p. 728.

Leading Exports of the Netherlands, Belgium, Switzerland, and Sweden Percentage Distribution by Value of Total Exports, 1900 and 1913

Netherlands

1900		1913	
Cereals & flour	14	Cereals & flour	14
Iron & steel	11	Iron & steel	11
Textiles, raw & manufactured	6	Textiles, raw & manufactured	6
Copper	5	Copper	5
Paper	3	Paper	3
Sugar	3	Sugar	3

Belgium

1900		1913	
Raw textiles	14	Wool	8
Coal	11	Flax & flax yarns	7
Yarns, linen, etc.	6	Iron & steel	7
Railway carriages	5	Zinc	3
Glass	3	Railway carriages	3
Cereals	3	Rawhides	3

Switzerland

1900		1913	
Silk	25	Silk goods	25
Cottons	19	Cotton goods	19
Clocks & watches	14	Clocks & watches	14
Foodstuffs, etc.	12	Animal substances	12
Machinery carriages	6	Machinery	6

Sweden

1900		1913	
Timber	50	Timber	25
Live animals & animal food	14	Wood pulp, paper and products	17
Metals	12	Minerals	12
Metal goods, machinery, etc.	6	Live animals & animal food	12
Minerals	5	Metal goods, machinery, etc.	11
		Metals	10

power, and steam-driven transport could only play their full role on a world scale; the new, increasingly specialized industrial processes of the West had in fact created a productive capacity that could not be absorbed profitably within the confines of any one country. By 1914, encouraged by the increase in the material well-being of many Europeans and the growing commercialization of European life, the consumption of relatively cheap, mass-produced items of commerce was rapidly becoming the goal of western society.

No industry reflected the trend towards mass-production and commercialization as much as cotton textiles; no industry was so dependent upon foreign markets and foreign supplies of raw materials. Yet cotton had been spun and woven in the Indus Valley three thousand years before the birth of Christ; the Moors had introduced the techniques of cotton manufacture into southern Europe as early as the Middle Ages. Indeed, the later industrialization and mass-production of cotton textiles in western Europe consisted largely of the mechanization and centralization of ancient crafts—crafts that over past ages and in many parts of the world had already reached a high point of development, and in which it often required only minor changes to adopt mechanical power. The West did not teach the rest of the world how to produce textiles; what the West taught was how to produce more textiles with the aid of steam-driven machinery; at lower costs, and often of a lower quality.

Why such a relatively small industry should have come to play the crucial role it did in the industrialization of the West is not entirely clear. Of signal importance in the rise of the cotton industry was the fact that it met a growing mass-consumer demand for cheap cloth; which was partly the cause and partly the effect of western industrialization. Increasingly, as the economic position of many Europeans improved, they not only bought more clothing—they indulged themselves in changing tastes and fashions. Moreover, the Europeans were able to dispose of increasing quantities of their mass-produced wares in their colonial markets, as Britain did in India. Raw cotton also had the advantage of being far more plentiful and cheaper than raw silk, wool or flax. Yet the spinning and weaving of woollens had been carried on in Lancashire long before the rise of cottons; and wool, unlike cotton, could be obtained without the creation of an international economy. Perhaps woollens succeeded less than cottons because the manufacturing process and the marketing of woollens gave less scope to mass-production methods than did cottons.

The phenomenal increase in world demand for cheap, standardized, mass-produced, easily-transported cotton cloth and yarn was met by an equally astonishing growth of the cotton textile industry in Britain and on the Continent, as well as by the diffusion of mechanized textile production in the world; once the commercial benefits of the mechanical improvements introduced into the British textile industry had been appreciated by others, it was not long before British machines and methods were employed overseas.[20]

Although textiles were less important in the adoption of a factory system on the Continent than in Britain (and cotton until the second quarter of the century less important than wool), by the mid-century improved spinning and weaving machinery had been diffused from the United Kingdom to France, Holland, Belgium, Germany, Scandinavia, Switzerland, and Russia, as well as to the United States. By 1860 in Alsace (the most progressive continental area), and by the 1870's in Belgium and the Northern Netherlands, the power loom had ousted the hand loom. The direction of diffusion depended on the location of natural resources; on the Continent, and in the northeastern parts of the United States, the coal fields were the chief lure. Where governments encouraged the movement (especially on the Continent) through the protection of in-

20. Circumstances must have been favourable to the diffusion of technical knowledge, despite all the efforts made to prevent it, because even before the restrictions on the migration of British skilled artisans had been lifted in 1824 (the restrictions on the export of machinery and important techniques were raised in 1843), some new technology and skills had already been smuggled out of England to the Continent of Europe and America.

fant industries, by spying, or by monetary inducements to entrepreneurs, they probably did so because they felt it necessary to match Britain's industrial challenge. How could they rely on Britain alone—especially in an age of growing nationalism? Even in the early part of the nineteenth century mechanized, large-scale, industry had already become identified with a nation's wealth and power.

While the Europeans in Europe as well as overseas were the first to emulate British manufacturing methods, the profits offered by introducing the manufacture of mass-produced cotton textiles were too great to be restricted to the culturally similar, white communities of the world. Gradually, world technical progress in mechanized cotton textile production came to depend on European enterprise, capital, and technicians. In the second half of the nineteenth century, by which time the embargo on the export of technical knowledge had been lifted, European power-driven cotton textile machinery and methods had become established in India—ironical when it is remembered that it was the earlier introduction of high-quality, hand-spun and hand-woven Indian calicos that had provided the initial spur for the development of the British cotton textile industry. Indeed, the way in which great changes in the world arose from such small and unexpected beginnings in the cotton textile industry of northern England—almost fortuitous beginnings when we think of India's influence— only serves to emphasize the complexity of industrial change.

Many of the western inventions used in the mass production of cheap cottons were also adapted to woollen manufacture and diffused abroad. British machines and manufacturing methods were taken to the Continent before the onset of the Napoleonic Wars. The first woollen manufactory in the United States was begun at the end of the eighteenth century. By the 1870's British woollen textile machinery was widely used in Australia. It made its appearance in the other great wool-producing countries—New Zealand, South Africa, Argentina, Uruguay, and Chile— during the next generation.

The essential difference between the mass-production

textile industry of the West and the textile industry of the rest of the world was the extent to which western industry became dependent upon the harnessing of vast new sources of steam-power obtained from coal. Compared to wood, as a source of energy, coal was relatively plentiful, it was well-known (the Romans had used it in England), and, as the scale of production grew and the expense of transporting it was reduced, it became relatively cheap; so much so, that the Europeans in Europe and abroad proceeded to gobble up the mineral wealth of the earth as no people had ever done before. Indeed, so much production in the nineteenth century consisted of extracting this stored wealth from the earth.

Increasingly, cheap coal provided the energy for mechanical power in the mining, metallurgical, and manufacturing industries. Between 1870 and 1907, the supply of inanimate energy in Britain alone had doubled.[21] By then, the Europeans had built a world railway network of staggering proportions; with the establishment of coaling and cable stations across the world, steam had also triumphed at sea. In addition to becoming an indispensable source of power for industry and transport, by 1907 coal was also meeting the steeply rising demands for fuel made by Europe's growing cities.

In the mid-nineteenth century, Britain, the workshop of the world, produced two-thirds of the world's coal. Coal was never shipped about the world as easily as textiles, yet as the nineteenth century progressed increasing quantities of coal entered international trade. From the 1840's the growth of production elsewhere was encouraged by the diffusion of British mining technology. By then, with British

21. Despite the tremendous increase in the production of energy by converting heat into power, achieved by the West, water power remained important in western Europe—probably more so on the Continent than in Britain—until the mid-century. At that time, about one-eighth of the power available to cottons in the United Kingdom, and a third of the power available to woollen manufacture was provided by water. In the 1880's France and other European countries began to make up for their lack of coal resources by the development of hydro-electric power.

help, the Belgian coal industry had become the largest on the Continent. From the 1870's onwards, growing German demands led to the development of the large Silesian deposits. Between 1870–74 and 1900–04 Germany's coal output more than tripled.[22] The discovery and exploitation of these deposits, together with those found and worked in the United States (with the aid of British miners), encouraged world trade in coal; it also prevented the world price of coal from rising. In fact, in the last three decades of the nineteenth century, while coal did not fall in price as much as certain other items such as pig iron, it did fall about the same as most commodities. In these years (1870–74, 1900–04), British coal output had almost doubled;[23] that of the French, who imported about one-third of their coal, had more than doubled.[24] Between 1900–04 and 1910–14 the United Kingdom, Germany, and France added about one hundred million tons to their combined output,[25] which reflects the increased demands made by western industrialization for fuel and power. The peak year for British coal production was 1913. By then, however, Britain's share of world trade in coal had fallen to about a quarter of what it had been.

Stimulated by growing westernization, similar developments, assisted by European (and American) techniques, were under way in Asia from the 1860's. World coal production increased three and one-half times between 1870 and 1900, and at a little more than one and one-half times between 1900 and 1913.[26] In 1913, however, nine-tenths of world coal output was in the western (European-settled) world.

Western industrialization in the nineteenth century, could not have grown and spread in the world had not

22. From 32 million metric tons in 1870–74 to 111 million metric tons in 1900–04.

23. From about 121 to 227 million metric tons.

24. From 15 to 32 million metric tons.

25. From 369.3 million metric tons (1900–04) to 472.8 million metric tons (1910–1914).

26. From approximately 220 million metric tons to 800 million in 1900, and to 1,330,000,000 in 1913.

important changes taken place in Europe's metallurgical industries. It was in response to the demand for a stronger and more suitable material than wood for power-driven machinery that wrought iron and later steel, was first produced in large quantities. Prior to 1870 the principal metallic constructing materials were cast and wrought iron.[27] The harder, more uniform metal required for machine tools and dies had been made by the costly and limited crucible or cast steel process. Especially important was the development of the machine tools industry which substituted the machine for a human degree of accuracy.[28]

A new age began in the life of the metallurgical industry when during the 1850's Bessemer steel was made from pig iron in a blast furnace. Cheaper and stronger than wrought iron, Europe's first production of steel on a large scale quickly proved itself in railway building. By 1865 Europe was producing in the region of a quarter of a million tons of steel. World production was about three times that amount. The extent to which steel was substituted for wrought iron is reflected in certain British figures: whereas in 1833 almost three quarters of British pig iron had been made into wrought iron, in 1887 (by which time the basic improvements in steel making had been introduced)[29] wrought iron took only one twentieth. World steel production continued to rise steeply from the 1870's until the outbreak of War. As it did so European steel rails and European steamships carried the process and the products of western industrialization across the world. In 1913 steel

27. World output of pig iron grew from 1 million metric tons in 1820 to approximately 20 million tons in 1900, and about 80 million in 1913.

28. Significant was the work of John Wilkinson (whose boring mill in 1774 had permitted the boring of accurate cylinders essential for the success of the steam engine), Joseph Bramah, Henry Maudslay (whose invention, or rediscovery of the slide-rest in 1797 facilitated the cutting of metals, and with Joseph Clement's work made the screw-making machine possible), James Nasmyth, and Joseph Whitworth.

29. The Siemens-Martin (1886) gas regenerative furnace which enlarged the variety of steel produced, and the Thomas and Gilchrist basic process (1878), which allowed the use of ores with a high phosphorous content such as those of French Lorraine and the vast North American deposits.

production in the United States and Germany exceeded that of all other countries combined.[30] The enormous increase in the world supply of pig iron and steel caused a fall in prices which further encouraged their use.[31]

The adoption of modern techniques in the iron and steel industry followed closely upon British and later Continental European and American developments. The countries of Continental Europe were especially indebted to Britain, as was the United States. In determining the location of the early steel industry, coal was the chief factor.

In the nineteenth and early twentieth century, as the process of industrialization spread, Europeans (and Americans) established large-scale iron and steel works in the non-European world. The metallurgical industries were fostered abroad not only because of their importance to the general process of industrialization, but also because of what they meant to the pride and national defence of the rising parts of the world. By the outbreak of War, the output of coal and iron had become the essential criteria by which the greatness of a country could be assessed. Judged by this standard, almost all greatness rested with the western nations, for in 1913 world-wide steel production was highly concentrated in two places: Anglo-America and western Europe.

For coal and steel, the Europeans within Europe could rely upon each other. For copper, and some other non-

30. Between 1870–74 and 1900–04 the annual average world steel production rose from 1 to 27 million metric tons. Of world steel production in 1913 (76 million metric tons), the United States accounted for about (1910–14) 27 million metric tons. The average annual German, British, and French output of steel for these years (1910–14) was approximately 15, 7, and 4 million metric tons, respectively.

31. Iron that brought £10 per metric ton in Britain in 1825, sold at £3 in 1866. Steel rails that sold in the United States at $170 a long ton in 1867 (iron rails in this year were $83 a long ton) had fallen to $32 per long ton by 1884. Between 1872 and 1881 the price of European steel rails fell 60 per cent. United States steel rails in 1898 were one-fourth 1875 prices: $16–17 a ton against $69 in 1875. The railway builders were evidently prepared to pay the extra for steel's toughness, durability, and lightness, but in Britain in 1880, nine iron ships were still being built for every one of steel.

ferrous metal ores (as well as rubber, petroleum and oils), they became increasingly dependent on the outside world. In obtaining these new supplies it became necessary to diffuse European technology to the non-European parts of the world. In the 1870's Chile produced about two-thirds of the world's copper. With the development of electricity and the generation of electrical power in the last quarter of the nineteenth century, however, world output of copper increased at least ten times, and the search for copper was extended to other parts of the world. Large-scale, mechanized copper mining was introduced by Europeans (and Americans) to Japan, Canada, Australia, and Africa. Between 1900 and 1913 the world output of copper increased twofold. By then the United States supplied about sixty per cent of the world's needs. Encouraged by the growing world demand for sulphide ores of copper, lead, and zinc, a number of flotation techniques (which separated one metal from another, as well as metal from ground-up gangue) were developed towards the end of the nineteenth century. These techniques made vast deposits of low-content ores as well as complex ores containing several metals usable; much of the world-wide industrial expansion prior to and during the First Great War came to depend upon them.

Of even greater importance in its ultimate effect on international trade was the exploitation of petroleum. Only with the drilling of the Drake oil well in Pennsylvania, United States, in 1859, was petroleum produced on a commercial scale. In 1864, oil ranked sixth in United States' exports. At the beginning of the twentieth century, Russian output of crude oil equalled and for a short period exceeded American production. Between 1860 and 1914, when the demand was chiefly for lamp and lubrication liquids, the annual world crude oil production increased from approximately half a million to four million barrels. Only shortly before the First Great War, however, did the enormous demands for fuel-oil for land, sea, and air transport begin to make themselves felt.

At the end of the nineteenth and the beginning of the

twentieth century there took place what some authors have called a Second Industrial Revolution. Whereas the First Industrial Revolution depended upon the mechanization of traditional industries, the new technology increasingly depended upon scientific progress, especially in physics and chemistry. The electrical and chemical industries, for example, originated in scientific discoveries in the West. In chemicals, Germany took the lead, building up a great chemical industry on the basis of scientific discoveries. The internal combustion engine, which has come to signal a country's arrival as an industrial nation, resulted from progress in the theory of thermodynamics. In transport and communications, in textiles, in metallurgy, in aviation, in petroleum, in concrete, in rubber, in paper, in the photographic industry—in these and a score of other industries—scientific theory came to play an increasing role. Pure and applied science were brought together in an extraordinary way. So much so, that on the eve of War the western industrial nations had begun to make what they wanted out of what they had—a very different situation from that which had prevailed in the nineteenth century. International trade and development then had depended on the close inter-relatedness and reciprocity of the industrial with the primary producing parts of the world. Europe had enriched itself (none so much as Britain) from this arrangement. But Europe's new wealth, in so far as it had given rise to a Second Industrial Revolution, had weakened some of the economic ties that bound Europe to the primary producing parts of the world.

The growing need of the most advanced industrial nations in 1913 was to find markets for their manufactured goods. In sharp contrast to the relations that existed earlier between the manufacturing and the primary producing parts of the world, the world's major exporters of manufactured goods were becoming increasingly the world's major importers of manufactured goods. Yet there was no similar tendency on the part of the primary producers of the world to become the leading importers of primary produce. Indeed, for the primary producing countries of the world exactly the opposite situation prevailed. Many countries in Africa, Latin America, Asia, and Australasia—many of them part of Europe's colonial empires—had become so accustomed to meeting the demands of a particular European country, sometimes the demands of a particular European industry, that by 1913 they were unable (especially those who through intense international specialization had become committed to a system of monoculture) to deal with anybody else, least of all with their immediate neighbours.

In 1913 it was not only the nature of Europe's industries that was undergoing change; whole economies were faced with change. Britain, seat of the Industrial Revolution of the eighteenth century, and largely the cause of the great expansion of world commerce in the nineteenth century, was having to adjust to an entirely different situation than that which had witnessed its rise to power. Britain's share of world industrial output which stood at one-third in 1870, and one-fifth in 1900, by 1913 had fallen to one-seventh. The British continued to concentrate their efforts in providing the tools and equipment needed by the traditional industries: steam engines, mining equipment, textile machinery, railways, and ships. Scientifically, Britain made many contributions to the rise of the chemical, electrical apparatus, and automobile industries. But these industries—at least before 1914—were concerned primarily with home, not world, development. In any event, Britain could hardly expect to play the same role in the world economy as it had done earlier. Britain did well to press its early start in mass-produced manufactures and large-scale industry while it could; only thus did it reap the great rewards of intense international specialization. Yet its ability to win and hold three-quarters of the world markets in a commodity, as at various times in the nineteenth century it had done in cotton textiles, iron rails, galvanized iron, tinplate, locomotives, ships, coal, and other products was based on very special and changing circumstances.

In contrast to Britain, Germany's economic centre of gravity had always been in Europe, not the world. With the aid of its vast natural resources of coal and iron, its agricultural wealth, its growing numbers, its progressive business and financial organizations, and its newfound economic and political unity, Germany's star had risen rapidly in the thirty years before the War. But it had risen in a world that for most Germans was Europe.

The same was essentially true of the French. French progress in the nineteenth century proceeded at a more leisurely pace than that of either Britain or Germany. French large-scale industry had been late in developing (partly because of France's lack of coal, partly because of French antipathy to the giant corporation). Its evolution from small rural workshops and domestic industries to concentrated urban, factory industry was slow and uncertain compared to that of the other industrialized nations. Smelting iron ore with the use of charcoal, as well as the hand-spinning and weaving of textiles, persisted on a considerable scale in France long after they had been superseded in Britain by coke smelting and the use of steam-driven machinery. On the economic and industrial level, French talent and vitality were abundant (in chemical and textile manufacture alone the names of Leblanc, Jacquard and de Vaucanson spring to mind), but the dominant values of French society directed French efforts to pursuits other than the intense development of large-scale industries and the capture of world markets. The economic, political, and social climate of France (what the Germans call the 'Zeitgeist') was against it. Between 1870 and 1895 the output of the French metallurgical industries barely increased. Likewise, in the more recently developed heavy chemical industry (partly, again, because of a lack of the natural resources needed by industrialization, especially coal), by the eve of War France had become completely overshadowed by its German neighbour.

More significant for the future of the world economy in 1914 was the fact that the centre of gravity of world industrialization had begun to move across the Atlantic Ocean; Britain's dominant role in the world economy was about to pass into other hands. Industrially speaking, the

United States had come of age. It already was the industrial
and agricultural colossus of the world; soon, responding to
the challenge of the First Great War, it would become the
mightiest nation on earth. Its total output of coal, iron and
steel was far greater than that of any other country; on the
outbreak of War, it produced one-third of the world's manufactures. If we take a purely political criterion of trade,
and measure (which is how western trade figures are calculated) merely the trade entering and leaving American
ports, then, in 1913, with the United Kingdom and Germany, the United States was the third leading trading nation
in the world.[32] Its predominance was to grow. Moreover,
while America's destiny until 1914 had been largely a continental destiny, its impact on the emergence of an international economy had been no less profound than that of
Britain or any other European power. Because of this, the
histories of Europe and America in the age of European
expansion can only be understood when considered together.

Of all the industries developed by Europeans in the century
before 1914, none had a more dramatic, yet lasting effect
on the growth of a world economy than European improvements in transport and communications. Yet as late as 1800
the Europeans were using the transport provided by past
civilizations. Locomotion still depended upon human
muscle, the beasts of burden, and the wind-filled sail. The
chief improvements in transport and communications devised by Europeans until then were probably the Gregorian
calendar, the measuring of longitude at sea, and certain
innovations in naval architecture.

As the Europeans shifted their attention from the nation
to the continent and from the continent to the world, this
situation was transformed. By the First Great War, the
Europeans had built a vast network of railways around the
world; with the aid of their ocean-going steamships, they

32. If, however, we add the internal trade done between the different
American States (say, that done between the State of New York and
the State of California) to America's inter-continental trade, (as we do
in calculating continental Europe's share of world trade) then, in 1913,
the United States was probably the greatest trading nation on earth.

also had reduced the distance and the uncertainty of the high seas. Within the span of one generation, the old relation between time and distance was altered, the lull that man had known for millenia was broken.

Europe's need to improve world transport and communications extended beyond the introduction of the steam locomotive and the steamship. By the opening of the twentieth century, a network of land and sea cables encircled the globe. The Suez Canal was cut connecting the Mediterranean and the Indian Ocean. Breakwaters, ports, harbours, lighthouses and other shipping aids, were created or improved upon in every part of the world; roads, tunnels, and bridges were built in every continent. International agreements were gradually evolved by the western nations in an attempt to create a unified world economy.[33]

Of all these changes, the most significant on a world scale was the transfer of the steam engine (already in use in the mines and factories and river boats of western Europe and North America) to the early railways.

The course of railway building in the world between 1840 and 1920 is reflected in the table on p. 690.

The Europeans led the world in railway development because they were the first to experience the industrial and social changes whence came the demand for cheaper land transport; also because they possessed the human and material resources required.

At the outset, only the British had the necessary industry, technicians, the rolling-stock, the capital, and the incentive to first try to put the world on wheels. It was the growing demand of British industry for cheap coal that provided the initial impulse for the building of railways and the use

33. Including the International Telegraph Union of 1865, the Universal Postal Union of 1875, the adoption of the French gold franc as the common unit for the establishment of world telegraph tariffs, the acceptance of French as the international postal language, and English as the language of world commerce. Among the many others were agreements to regulate traffic on the high seas, the Treaty of the Meter of 1875, agreements for patents and copyrights adopted in the 1880's, and the establishment of the International Court of Arbitration at The Hague in 1899.

Development of World's Railway Mileage, 1840 and 1920[34]
(in thousand miles and in percentage of world total)

Continents and Countries with Largest Percentages	First Steam Line Opened	1840		1920	
		Mileage	%	Mileage	%
World	1825	5·49	100·0	674·89	100·0
Europe	1825	2·54	46·3	159·97	23·7
Great Britain	1825	1·48	27·0	20·33	3·0
France	1832	0·26	4·7	25·85	3·8
Germany	1835	0·34	6·2	35·85	5·3
Belgium	1835	0·21	3·8	3·05	0·5
U.S.S.R.	1837	0·02	0·4	44·49	6·6
North America	1830	2·83	51·5	292·16	43·3
U.S.A.	1830	2·82	51·4	252·87	37·4
Canada	1836	0·02	0·4	39·29	5·8
Latin America	1837	0·10	1·8	62·91	9·3
Brazil	1854	—	—	17·73	2·6
Argentina	1857	—	—	21·18	3·1
Asia	1853	—	—	62·06	9·2
India	1853	—	—	36·74	5·4
Africa	1854	—	—	27·16	4·0
South Africa	1860	—	—	10·12	1·5
Australasia	1854	—	—	26·14	3·9
Australia	1854	—	—	23·12	3·4

of steam power. The impact of the steam locomotive was so great that in the eighty years before the First Great War it is thought that it halved the cost of transport on land. It also introduced the world to an entirely new conception of speed and time. Moreover, even where canals could compete in building costs and operation, they did not have the ubiquity of the railways; a factor of great importance in the penetration of the great land masses of North America and Australasia. No other existing form of inland transport was as little affected by topography, climate, or local conditions.

Nowhere else did the steam locomotive have a greater impact than it did in North America. Construction was

34. Drawn from W. Woodruff, *Impact of Western Man* (1966), p. 253.

stimulated by the great flood of migrants, capital, and merchandise crossing the Atlantic ocean, by the vast distances of the American continent, by the rapid development of the interior, by the absence of an equally satisfactory alternative means of East-West communications, by the very newness of settlement, and the absence of long established political barriers (that hindered railway building in Europe and Africa). By 1840, North America already had about half the world total. The mileage of United States railways increased from 31,000 in 1860—when there were almost no railways west of the Mississippi[35]—to a peak of 260,000 in 1916. In 1920, the United States had almost as much mileage as the rest of the world combined; about three times the mileage available throughout Africa and Asia.

Compared to Europe and North America, railways built in other parts of the European-settled world, prior to 1914, were few. In 1920, Canada, Australia, and Argentina had only about six, three-and-a-half, and three per cent of the world total, respectively. Yet railways were of great importance in settling these countries, and in providing the means whereby their agricultural and mineral wealth could be exploited. Especially important to Canada and Australia, railways were the means whereby the opposite shores of these vast countries were bound together.

By and large, the world railway network was devised to serve western ends. Without railways, much of the economic development of the European world in the nineteenth century would have been impractical or much delayed. In the white-settled parts of the world, railways were used as an instrument of economic and political unity. The extraordinary speed with which they were built (in 1913 the predominantly European-settled areas of the world had at least four-fifths of the world's railway mileage) can only be understood in the extent to which these areas became an

35. Especially west of the Mississippi (and in Eastern Asia) nothing was so important as the railways in reversing the normal process of immigration; it was the city that stamped its identity on the land, not the land that stamped its identity on the city.

inter-related, integral, organic part of the western world. Under the influence of western demands great parts of the New World were given up to the cultivation of a single crop; European buyers stood at the doors of the newly-settled lands ready to buy whatever primary produce became available.

Railways not only helped to change the development pattern of so much of the world, in encouraging the migration of vast numbers of Europeans, they also were instrumental in changing the settlement pattern of much of the earth's surface. In North and South America they helped to people the great plains, thrusting their way westward—often in advance of European settlement—until they reached the Pacific. In Australasia and Africa they helped the Europeans to lay claim to and colonize vast territories. In eastern Europe and Asia, having pierced the Urals, they followed the bands of Russians who had preceded them, spanning the frozen wastes of Siberia until eventually, in 1897, they reached the Port of Vladivostok on the Sea of Japan.

Outside the predominantly European-settled areas of the world, there did not exist the same effective demand for improved transport as there was in the western world. Where demand existed, there was an almost complete dependence upon the enterprise, equipment, skill, and capital of western Europe and of the United States (as in some parts of Latin America). In 1920, the combined total of railway mileage for Latin America, Africa, and Asia was less than a quarter of the world total. Latin America had 62,000 miles (about nine per cent of world mileage); Asia likewise; Africa 27,000 miles (about four per cent). This in contrast to Europe's 159,000 miles (23 per cent) and North America's 292,000 miles (43 per cent).

The railways of Latin America, Asia, and Africa were not so much the implement of western colonization as of western colonialism. Their purpose, especially in the European-dominated parts of Africa and Asia, was to serve the political, military, and economic interests of western nations in Europe or North America. Even the railways of the South

American republics were built to serve external trade rather than (as in white-settled North America and Europe) to open up and unify the South American continent. Lines were concentrated in the neighbourhood of large cities, such as Buenos Aires, São Paulo, and Rio, as well as in agricultural and mining areas whose products were exported to the northern hemisphere. African developments were similarly aimed at increasing the export rather than the domestic sector of the economy. The greatest proportion of Africa's railways were grouped in localized networks along the coast, or diverged inland from the chief ports to mining regions and to assembly points and centres of agricultural production—many of them the result of competitive European colonialism. Only the white-settled area of South Africa claimed a nation-wide railway network. As for Asia, until the 1880's, British India had more mileage than almost the rest of Asia. But the Indian network was aimed at the fostering of British commercial interests and internal military security, not at the integrated development of the Indian economy.

This stress upon western commercial and political interests was apparent elsewhere in Asia, especially in China. The action of the European powers in the last quarter of the nineteenth century in China (as in parts of Africa) is fittingly described as colonial 'penetration by railways'. China never had a large mileage (approximately six thousand miles in 1913), yet all the great European powers (Britain, France, Germany, and Russia) had jockeyed for position to obtain railway concessions.

The contrast of course to China is Japan. Japan succeeded in building a railway network that met its own, not western, needs and interests. While the mileage in 1913 was small compared with parts of North America and Europe, it greatly assisted the modernization of the Japanese islands.

Growing European investments in the world in production, trade, and transport, as well as an ever-extending tide of European migration, encouraged the wider use of steam. To the Europeans, who had come to think in world rather than continental terms, and whose capital investments in large-scale industry grew hourly, time was money. To save time, and money, as well as to obtain greater regularity of shipments, the Europeans devised and improved the ocean-going steamship. Speed in the transport systems of the West of itself bred speed (insofar as it meant ever-greater quantities of capital tied up in relatively expensive transport equipment).

Yet it was not until the 1860's that steamships were either cheaper or appreciably faster than sailing vessels. All that sail needed was a favourable wind; steamship voyages had to be planned in relation to fuel. However, the greater efficiency and speed of the screw propeller, coupled with the economies obtained by the use of the compound marine steam engine (the benefits of which were beginning to be felt generally in the sixties) made the ocean steamer profitable as a cargo ship, where previously it had been confined to passengers and mails. Increasingly, the steamship was able to avoid the more circuitous routes taken by sailing vessels. Further improvements[36] in the eighties and nineties resulted in the steamship becoming more powerful and less costly.

The most striking result of European developments in ship-building was the enormous increase in world shipping tonnage from about 4 million net tons in 1800 (9 in 1850, 20 in 1880) to almost 35 in 1910, by which time steam had triumphed over sail. Between 1860 and 1910, net tonnage of sailing ships fell from about 14½ to 8 million tons, while that of steamships increased from 5½ to 26 million tons. European calculations show that world steam tonnage exceeded sailing tonnage in 1893. Sail held its own in low-value commodities (though not in the migrant trade, most

---

36. Resulting from the introduction of the triple and quadruple expansion engine (which effected still further economies), twin and multiple screw propellers (for extra speed), and turbine engines. A fundamental change, which provided an alternative means of loco-motion to steam, was the introduction of the internal-combustion engine in the early 1900's. Occupying even less space and consuming less fuel, the diesel engine gave a vessel a much greater sailing range and was more economical to operate.

of which it had probably lost to steam by the 1870's) and on the long hauls, such as to and from Australia, at least until the eighties, and in certain items, such as wool and wheat, until the end of the century.

According to European figures, most of the shipping was European and North American. Europe's share of world shipping gross tonnage in 1913 was 79 per cent; if the tonnage of the United States is added (12 per cent), the western world in 1913 accounted for nine-tenths of total world shipping.

Europe was well fitted to make the shift from sail to steam, from wood to iron, and from iron to steel. It had an abundance of the new building material—iron, a plentiful supply of the new fuel—coal, well-established, large-scale metallurgical industries, and growing reserves of engineering and maritime skills. No country was more favourably placed to take advantage of these changes than Britain whose traditions were of the sea. In the nineteenth century, Britain had possessed slightly more than half the world's shipping tonnage (Britain, after all, was the most internationally specialized of all European nations); in the twenty-five years before the First Great War the United Kingdom built not less than two-thirds of the ships launched in the world. In doing so, Britain added to the head start it already possessed in the large-scale building of steel ships. The British peak in shipbuilding was probably reached about a decade before 1914.

In contrast to the progress made by the British in the development of ocean-going shipping, which had strengthened the maritime ties that bound Britain to the rest of the western world, the American thrust, since the eighteenth century, had been westward across the continent, and southward from the Mississippi basin into the Caribbean and to Central and South America; areas whose trade—unlike that of the North Atlantic—was too small to encourage the growth of a great mercantile marine.

The effect of the increases in world shipping tonnage was to enlarge the carrying capacity of the world's ocean-going fleet. The use of cables also increased the capacity of the world's shipping fleet without another ton of shipping having been launched. Moreover, the eventual improvement in speed also meant that several times more use could be made of a steam vessel than of a sailing vessel of equal tonnage (it was calculated in 1875 that one steamship ton was roughly the equivalent of three sail ship tons). Greater regularity of service was reflected in lower insurance and interest rates.

Yet the benefits of the steamship were not as immediate or as striking as those of the steam-railways; this partly because shipping charges were usually a small element in the final cost of the item being carried; also because competition among the American and European sailing-ship companies had already greatly reduced freight rates on the major routes before steam had made itself felt. It was not until the 1870's and 1880's that steamships began to exert a downward pressure on rates. Thenceforth, until 1914 (by which time the supply of shipping facilities had more than caught up with the greatly expanded shipping demands caused by European expansion in the world), a persistent tendency towards over-expansion of the shipping industry added to this downward trend.[37]

By the early years of the twentieth century, by which time the European cable network had encircled the globe, the European trading world had become one. European fleets, now in constant touch with each other and with their homelands, were moved across the world as Europe's needs and profit opportunities dictated. London, the centre of world

37. There were many variations between different routes and commodities, but the general downward trend during the half-century before 1914 is clear. Rates on such staples as wheat from New York and cotton from Bombay to the United Kingdom fell by more than two-thirds between the 1860's and the early years of the present century. The average freight rate per bushel of wheat between New York and Liverpool fell by about 76 per cent between 1873–87. To ship a ton of flour across the Atlantic in 1880 cost 25s.; in 1886, 7s. 6d.; similar figures for pork are: 45s. to 7s. 6d.; for cheese: 50s. to 15s.; for cotton: 7s. 8d. to 3s. 8d. A general index of tramp shipping freights shows that while rates fell by about half in the period 1869–1910, general prices fell by about a fifth. Homeward freights to the United Kingdom show a similar fall between 1884 and 1910.

trade, became the centre of world communications. For the first time in history, buyers and sellers in all continents were placed in direct touch with each other.

The impact of the European steamship was also felt in the movement of people between countries and continents.[38] With railways, steamships caused a rearrangement of settlement patterns in much of the world. The speed, safety, and cheapness, if not the comfort of the Atlantic crossing by steamship encouraged migration to America from Europe. In fact, while Europeans had made their way to the rising parts of the world long before the steamship was perfected, European shipping companies under highly competitive conditions played no small part in attracting immigrants to America. The hazards and cost of the Australian run by sailing-ship were also reduced by steamship. Most dramatic of all was the effect of improved steam shipping on the South American route. Fierce competition among European steam-shipping companies in the early twentieth century fostered seasonal migration of European agricultural labourers to both Argentina and Brazil.

Two barriers that had always impeded Europe's commercial and political exploits in the world were the isthmuses of Suez and Panama.

The first of these was pierced by the French at Suez in 1869 when a sea-level canal was opened giving access from the Mediterranean to the Red Sea and the Indian Ocean. Subsequent French efforts at Panama in the 1880's proved a failure, and it was not until 1914 that the isthmus of Panama was finally breached by the Americans, and the Atlantic and the Pacific Oceans joined together.

In effect, the cutting of these canals by the Europeans and the North Americans meant that the Strait of Magellan and the Cape of Good Hope had been moved 4,800 miles northward. There now was available a new east–west water

38. Steam navigation eventually caused a considerable drop in ocean fares. Whereas in 1825 the cheapest passage from Europe to America was about $100, the rate by the 1880's had fallen to between $20–30; steerage passage from Liverpool was about $8. Steerage was important because most emigrants went out as steerage and not cabin passengers.

route around the world through the northern hemisphere —through 'the latitudes of power'—where the bulk of people and commerce lay. The opening of the Suez Canal did in fact cause a return to the trade routes that existed between Europe and the East prior to 1497. Gibraltar, Malta, Cyprus, Alexandria, and Aden returned to prominence. In the saving of distance, the cutting of Suez reduced the sea journey between London and Singapore by almost one-third and that between London and Bombay by more than two-fifths. New York was now 3,000 miles closer to Bombay. Melbourne was 1,000 miles closer to London, but dues and delays reduced the Canal's advantage over the Cape route to the Antipodes. The saving of distance achieved by the Suez Canal stimulated Asia's and Australasia's trade with Europe; it also increased the Mediterranean traffic. In providing a powerful incentive to the development of the marine engine (navigating the Canal and the Red Sea under sail was difficult), the Canal helped to bring about a premature obsolescence of sailing tonnage; in doing so it indirectly increased and cheapened the amount of sailing tonnage on other routes.

The cutting of Panama gave a tremendous stimulus to the seaborne commerce between the North Atlantic ports and the western seaboard of the American continent. The distance between Liverpool and San Francisco was cut by two-fifths; that between New York and San Francisco by three-fifths. Not least important, the Canal broke the barrier that had always impeded the flow of commerce from the Mississippi basin into the Pacific.

The interaction of improvements in steam transport, interoceanic canals, and world-wide cable networks stimulated the development of other forms of transport and communications in the period before 1914. In the opening years of the twentieth century the first faint radio message had been heard at sea; the automobile had begun to lay the basis of mass transportation for relatively rich Europeans; the telephone (with the automobile) had begun to conquer short distances; the Wright brothers had made their airborne leap at Kittyhawk; later, the Frenchman, Blériot, had flown across the English Channel. Yet amazing as these things were, none of them (certainly not before 1914) had changed the scale of the earth's regions as the European railway and the European steamship had done.

The political and economic control of much of the world was already established by the Europeans in the age of sail. Thus had Britain founded its power in the East in earlier centuries. Yet it required the introduction of steam power on land and sea (supplemented by deep-sea cables) for the Europeans to be able to colonize what they controlled. Energy, superior weapons, and ocean-going vessels may explain the Europeans' earlier ability to achieve ascendency over others, but world colonization by the Europeans, in contrast to world conquest, necessitated the development of a system of rapid world transport and communications; one was a corollary of the other. Without improved transport and communications, Europe could never have established itself as the centre of a world economy, nor could it have had the economic impact on the world that it did. The outcome for the western world was wealth on a scale never known before.

Hitherto we have sought to explain the emergence of an international economy before 1914 in terms of the changes taking place in trade, industry and transport. These changes cannot be considered apart from the growth of Europe's numbers and their migration overseas and to Russian Asia in the century before 1914. European population increased more than threefold in the period 1800–1920 (from 144 to 486 million); it grew at a faster rate than either Asian or African population. If account is taken of the number of Europeans throughout the world, including Asiatic Russia, then the increase was even greater (from 158 to 703 million). In 1750, the area of European settlement accounted for approximately 21.8 per cent of world population; in 1920, the figure was 38.9 per cent.

There is no single explanation for the rapid increase in European population in the century before 1914. The most important factor was probably the decline in the death rate.

This is usually explained as resulting from the more efficient use of labour in industry and agriculture, which made possible a rise in the general European standard of living (or at least the avoidance of famine), and from improvements, especially from the 1870's onwards, in public health, medicine, and general cleanliness. Of great significance was the fact that the Europeans—in addition to the agricultural revolution that earlier had begun to spread across western and central Europe—were able to tap the fruits of the whole earth. No civilization has ever extended its settlements and its frontier of cultivation as the Europeans did in Europe and abroad in the brief span that began in the later eighteenth century and ended with the First Great War.

World colonization by the Europeans is also one of the major factors explaining European industrialization, and the subsequent migration of Europeans to the growing towns, as well as to the white-settled areas overseas. While it would be wrong to argue that industrialization is always the cause of migration, rural exodus in nineteenth century Europe does seem to have been a corollary of western industrialization. Yet, there was a great variety in the experience of the different European nations. In the extent to which world colonization and industrialization resulted in a rural exodus and a transformation of the economy, no nation was affected as much as Britain.

Unlike earlier migrations (say, the migration of the ancient Greeks in the third century B.C.), European migration in the nineteenth century was not to civilized and relatively densely populated areas (where excess numbers might be fed and forgotten); but to the distant, relatively unoccupied, vast expanses of the Americas, Oceania and Siberia. To an extraordinary degree, these lands were used to meet the needs of the European world—not least the needs of Europe's rapidly growing urban centres. Moreover, European world colonization, and the subsequent development of industrialization, not only had its effect on the extraordinary degree of urbanization experienced within Europe, but also on the extraordinary degree of urbanization it caused outside Europe. As the tide of European migration rose in the world, great ports and cities[39] sprang up in different lands orienting themselves to Europe.

An estimate of European migration in the period 1851–1920 puts the number at more than forty million. About half of these migrated in the last three decades of the nineteenth century—a number equivalent to forty per cent of Europe's natural increase for these years. However, Europe's population was growing so rapidly that even migration on this scale did not seem to slow down the growth of Europe's total numbers. The peak of the migratory movement was reached in the early years of the present century, by which time the annual flow of emigrants had risen to approximately 1,500,000. (1909–14)

In the 1850's the largest group of migrants were the British and the Irish. They were soon joined by Germans and Scandinavians, and, from the 1880's onwards, by Italians, Spaniards, Portuguese, Greeks, Austro-Hungarians, Poles, and Russians, as well as minority groups such as the Armenians living in Turkey. France in the nineteenth century, partly because of its slow increase in numbers, was not a country of emigration; at least not on the scale of these others. By the early twentieth century, while all European countries showed an increase in emigration, the Latin and the Slav migrant had come to out-number the Anglo-Saxon. Predominant among all groups of emigrants were the young and economically active.

Approximately half of Europe's migrants went to the United States; most of the remainder went to Canada, Australia, New Zealand, South Africa, Argentina, and Brazil. Numbers of European migrants also went to other Latin American countries, as well as to parts of Africa, Siberia, and Eastern Asia. Under their influence countries such as the United States, Canada, Australia, and Argen-

39. At the end of the eighteenth century Tokyo (Edo) was the largest city in the world (which at least goes to show that industrialization is not necessarily the cause of urbanization). Until the nineteenth century, only Imperial Rome in the West had known a million inhabitants; in 1900, European-settled cities with over a million inhabitants were common. To London, Paris, Berlin, Vienna, St Petersburg and Moscow were added New York, Philadelphia, Chicago, Rio, and Buenos Aires.

tina became projections of Europe; elsewhere in Latin America, Africa, and Asia, the European identity was merged with that of other races and cultures. Overall, the Americas took, by far, most of Europe's migrants (as many as nine out of ten); Africa, despite its proximity to Europe, its size and its low density of population, took least.

The motives prompting this large-scale migration from Europe to the rising parts of the world were manifold. Some of the migrants were attracted by trade or greed or glory; some went in God's name; some doubtless went purely for the love of adventure; others because they had become infected with a desire to fulfil a crusading 'civilizing mission' (described in the eastern Europe of Czar Nicholas II as the 'oriental mission' of the Russian people). Some were forced to go because the deep social and economic changes taking place in parts of Europe had dislodged them from the land and rural employment (as with so many Europeans who had moved from the land to the towns, they were not moving towards plenty but escaping from poverty); some went to escape crop failure and famine, religious and political persecution, the arm of the law, the thumb-screw of taxation, compulsory military service and the upset of warfare (active military duty in the post-1860 period—three years in Germany and Austria, five years in France, and six years in Russia—was a powerful stimulus to emigration); still others were human tumbleweed—driven before the wind. The vast majority, we are convinced, went simply in the hope of improving their own human lot; especially their economic lot. Sometimes the State took a hand, but European emigration was more the expansion of European people than European States. The way in which Europe's numbers in the nineteenth century grew faster than the ability of Europe's economic resources and organization to absorb them, coupled with the fact that for a number of European countries the rapid increase in numbers coincided with the depression in agricultural prices in the closing decades of the nineteenth century, left very many Europeans with no other choice than to emigrate.

European emigration from the late eighteenth century to the outbreak of the First Great War was essentially the transfer of rural dwellers and agricultural workers from one part of the world to another; from areas where land was scarce and labour plentiful, to areas where land was plentiful and labour scarce. Even though, by the end of the nineteenth century the majority of emigrants were listed as townsmen, we have no means of knowing how many of them had recently come from the land. The lure of free or cheap land in providing the impulse for this movement, however, should not be exaggerated. Free land abroad provided little inducement to those who were aware of the difficulties met with on the farming frontiers of the world, including Russian Asia; it meant even less to groups like the Irish who had had their fill of famine agriculture, or who showed, for one reason or another, a proclivity for town life. Quite apart from the fact that many emigrants had no desire to settle the farming frontiers of the world, most of them were without the necessary financial resources and skills to do so. In America, these migrants had to be content to play the role of 'fillers-in'; content, that is, to hasten the American-born into his continental inheritance. Whether they acted as 'fillers-in' or went directly to settle the farming and mining frontiers of America they helped to make available to the western world the natural resources of the American continent; in doing so, they made an incalculable contribution to the development of an international economy in the period before 1914.

Of particular importance in helping to form the migrant's decision to leave Europe was the changing interaction of the economic forces of the Old World and the New. The great peaks of emigration from Europe (1844–54, 1863–73, 1881–88, and 1903–13), which coincided with the booms in the capital export sector of the European (especially Britain's) economy, cannot be separated from the total, overall impact of European man outside Europe. Some interesting conjectures[40] have been made linking the flow of migrants with business conditions in the New and the Old

40. See Bibliography.

World. However, nothing has been proved. The lure of foreign parts was always less effective as long as conditions in Europe were buoyant. Nobody migrates from prosperity. Even in the 1870's, when grain competition from the United States helped to begin what proved to be a prolonged depression of European agriculture, the inclination of most uprooted rural dwellers was to seek a living in a nearby town, rather than to move across the world. Between 1860 and 1890 the majority of farming people reaching America were coming from parts of Scandinavia and Germany where (unlike the more industrialized parts of Europe) industry had been unable to absorb those forced to leave the land. Many of these would probably not have emigrated if alternative employment could have been found in nearby towns.

In the nineteenth century, the United States took as many European migrants as the rest of the world combined; and unlike migration elsewhere, the vast majority of immigrants entering the United States stayed there. By 1914, United States population, which in 1800 had consisted of about 5 million people (chiefly of British stock), exceeded 100 million. This twentyfold increase may be compared with a fourfold increase for Russia, a threefold increase for the United Kingdom, and a twofold increase for total world population. Gross immigration into the United States relative to total population growth for the decade 1860–70 was two out of a population increase of 8 million.[41] It has been estimated that between 1880 and 1910 the inflow of migrants caused the economically active population to expand at a rate one-third faster than the total population.

The nineteenth and twentieth century European migrant provided much of the labour necessary to settle and develop the United States. The Anglo-Saxon immigrant, who predominated until the closing decades of the nineteenth century, helped to settle the farming frontier of the mid-

41. Similar figures for the next five decades were approximately: for the 1870's: three out of ten million; 1880's: five out of twelve; 1890's: four out of thirteen; 1900's (the high-water mark of European emigration): nine out of sixteen; 1910–20: six out of fourteen.

and the far-west. Large groups of Latins and Slavs, Irish and Greeks contributed to the development of the urban areas of the east and the mid-west. Arriving in a period of rapid industrial development, they found opportunities for work in the factories and mines as well as in building and public works of all kinds. Many migrants brought with them highly developed industrial skills, and the history of certain American industries is linked with European national groups. In 1890, about two-thirds of British-born were employed in industry, making the most important contribution to the technical skill required by American industrialization. The introduction of mass production techniques meant that increasing numbers of unskilled workers could find employment in manufacturing industry. The majority of these migrants were so destitute that they had no choice but to struggle to survive in the large cities of the east and mid-west. Most important, the bulk of Latin and Slav immigrants (many of them peasant farmers) did not arrive in the United States until the late nineteenth or the early twentieth century, by which time the best land had been taken, and most employment was to be found in the towns. After 1900, all immigrants, whatever their origins, found employment more readily in the industrial east rather than in the agricultural mid- and far-west.

The picture drawn of European migration to the United States, and its effects upon the development of a Euro-centric economy is true to a certain extent of other white settlements in the world. The settlement of North America and Australasia was preponderantly the work of the Anglo-Saxon, the settlement of Central and South America was the work of the Latin; the settlement of still other parts, such as Asiatic Russia, was the work of the Slav. In the colonization of parts of Africa and Asia, however, all three groups contributed. Again, in some countries of large-scale European settlement (Brazil, Chile and Mexico), the European freely mixed his blood with that of Africans, Asians, and the indigenous people; elsewhere (Argentina, Australia, and South Africa), this did not happen. Some countries were colonized much earlier than others. British influence in Australia, or Russian influence in the maritime provinces of Eastern Asia is relatively recent compared to the colonization of Latin America.

Further, while Australia and parts of Siberia originated as penal settlements, where men were sent if not to be fed then certainly to be forgotten, other migrations, such as the Dutch at the Cape, were inspired by more visionary objectives. Dutch policy elsewhere, however, like the British, seems to have been much more commercially oriented; which was in sharp contrast to the religious influences at work in Spanish and Portuguese colonization, or the political and military aims of Russian penetration of Eastern Asia.

However differently motivated, all these migrations were an integral, inseparable part of the impact of western man in the world. All of them contributed, if not in like scale then in like manner, to the development of a world economy centred on Europe. In this respect, European migration is essentially a story of world colonization based upon the growing interrelatedness, interdependence, and complementarity of relatively small, yet highly industrialized and urbanized parts of Europe and North America with the rising parts of the world. With European migrants went capital, transport systems, skills, manufactures, enterprise, and cultural traditions. In return Europe obtained an ever growing volume of fibres, food, drink and tobacco, minerals, and precious metals, timber, hides and skins, oils and rubber, indispensable for its own development.

The international economy of 1914, however, was not entirely a European achievement; Africans and Asians, as well as mixed-blooded people of the world, also contributed to its establishment. Quite apart from the nineteenth century European-induced migration of Africans within Africa, and Asians within Asia, the Europeans were responsible for the large-scale migration of Asians (especially Chinese and Indians) and Africans away from their homelands. More than ten million African slaves had been shipped across the Atlantic before the abolition of slavery in the British colonies in the 1830's. As European enterprise and European communities spread in the world, growing numbers of African and Asian labourers were sought to work in European plantations and mines, to help to establish European towns in the New World, as well as to provide some of the labour necessary to build European transport systems in all continents. The international economy of 1914, while it undoubtedly benefited the West more than the rest of the world, resulted from the combined effort and sacrifice of the whole human family.

The fact that Europeans benefited more than others in the colonization of the world is understandable. What is remarkable is that in contrast to what past civilizations have done, they should have proceeded to use their increased wealth, not to build pyramids or marble temples, but to further the economic development of the world. The profits of world colonization and European industrialization helped to provide the necessary funds; European territorial expansion provided the necessary demand. Foreign investments were in fact one of the instruments used by Europe in the nineteenth century colonization and settlement of the world.

Estimates of foreign investments in 1914[42] are as follows:

Country	Amount Invested (in millions of dollars)	Percentage of Total
United Kingdom	19,500	43
France	9,050	20
Germany	5,800	13
United States	3,500	8
Belgium, Netherlands and Switzerland	5,500	12
Other countries including Japan, Russia, Portugal and Sweden	2,200	5

42. Drawn from W. Woodruff, *Impact of Western Man*, 1966, (Tables various). These estimates should be treated with the same caution as

No country in the world was as well placed to make investments abroad or could profit from them so advantageously in the nineteenth century as Britain. Its leadership in colonization, in foreign trade (though British capital exports were not necessarily tied to merchandise sales) in industry and in railroad and shipbuilding, stimulated the accumulation of wealth. The most uneven distribution of British income at this time ensured that much of this wealth would be reinvested. Add to these things the fact that Britain was able to provide a favourable social climate for private enterprise (most of British investments were in private economic ventures), that it succeeded in devising an effective international financial mechanism, and that it was blessed by peace for almost a century after Waterloo, and it is not difficult to understand how between 1855 and 1914 British foreign holdings were able to grow from about $2,300 million to $19,500 million. On the outbreak of the First Great War Britain's foreign investments exceeded those of the rest of Europe combined.

While it is doubtful that the growth of British foreign assets in the half-century before 1914 resulted mainly from the reinvestment of the interest on its lendings, income from accumulated foreign investments were important to the British economy. Capital accumulation on this scale was in fact something new in the history of finance. In 1871–75, when Britain had an average annual deficit in foreign trade of £65 million, the income from its accumulated foreign investments (£50 million), added to the income from its invisible exports (shipping, insurance, banking, etc.), helped to tip the British balance from a foreign deficit to a foreign surplus—a matter of some consequence for the leading creditor nation of the world. Throughout the economically depressed 1870's, the British economy was bolstered up by income received from past investments (in

available figures on world trade in the nineteenth century. Odd as it may sound to the ears of those who will settle for nothing less than certainty, we simply do not know the extent of foreign investment in the period 1815–1914. We know some of it; statistics are compiled on the assumption that that which cannot be counted does not exist.

the region of £55 million per annum). Between 1891 and 1906 there was no year when Britain did not rely on the income from foreign investments to make its books balance. In 1914 about ten per cent of its national income came from this source. At that time British investments were the most widely distributed in the world; a mere nine per cent were in Europe.

No other country had even half as large a total overseas investment as Britain in 1914. France drew about five per cent of its national income from foreign investments at that time. The profits of foreign commerce (and of French industrialization) undoubtedly stimulated French investments abroad as they stimulated the British; yet it was French thrift, and especially French genius in being able to mobilize its wealth on a national scale, that enabled France to amass assets abroad. In contrast to England, more than half of France's foreign assets were distributed among its European neighbours, most often in public loans (the French were second only to the British in railway building abroad) and in financing the economic development of political allies such as Russia (which amounted to a quarter of the French total). Outside Europe, most French money was in the French African colonies, Egypt, Turkey, and the Latin world.

The German achievement in foreign lending was even more remarkable than that of the French. The German states had not enjoyed the spoils of empire or the profits of a far-flung commerce, as Britain and some of the countries of western Europe had done; they were relatively poor to begin with. Yet German foreign lending increased rapidly from almost nothing in the mid-century to almost one-third of the British total by 1914. The Frankfurt and Berlin money houses had extraordinary success in channelling the savings from agriculture and trade into foreign government loans. However, to a far greater extent than was true of Britain, Germany's limited resources were needed for its own rapid development. There simply was not enough capital to meet the growing needs of industry and urbanization, as well as to finance the German Army and Navy.

Only about two per cent of German national income in 1914 came from foreign investments, and the decline in total loans had begun before the War. On the outbreak of hostilities German foreign investments were roughly divided into two halves, one in Europe and the other in Germany's newly-won colonies and the Anglo-Saxon world. Like Britain, Germany's greatest field of foreign investment was the United States.

Compared with Britain, France, and Germany, the other European lenders were relatively unimportant. Even when taken together, Belgium, the Netherlands, Switzerland, Russia, Spain, Portugal, and Sweden provided only a small part of foreign investments. Some Europeans simply did not have the money to spare; and where the money was available the circumstances were unfavourable to the development of foreign lending. Some countries had come too late in the scramble for empires or in the move towards industrialization. Some, like Russia, were too large and too poor to have the necessary surplus resources available. Others, like Denmark, were too small to make any very great impression (money-wise) in the world. With the exception of certain Belgian investments in the African Congo, and Dutch investments in the Dutch East Indies, the investments of the other European nations were overwhelmingly in Europe and North America.

The geographical distribution of foreign investments in 1914 was:

Geographical Distribution of Foreign Investments, 1914[43]
(in millions of dollars to the nearest $50 million)

To:	From:	U.K.	France	Germany	U.S.A.	Others	Total
Europe		1,050	4,700	2,550	700	3,000	12,000
		(9%)	(39%)	(21%)	(6%)	(25%)	(100%)
Latin America		3,700	1,600	900	1,650	1,050	8,900
		(42%)	(18%)	(10%)	(18%)	(12%)	(100%)
Oceania		2,200	100	—	—	—	2,300
		(96%)	(4%)				(100%)
Asia		3,550	1,250	700	250	1,350	7,100
		(50%)	(18%)	(10%)	(3%)	(19%)	(100%)

43. Drawn from W. Woodruff, *Impact of Western Man*, (1966), p. 154.

To:	From: U.K.	France	Germany	U.S.A.	Others	Total
Africa	2,450 (60%)	900 (22%)	500 (12%)	—	200 (6%)	4,050 (100%)
North America	7,050 (63%)	500 (4%)	1,150 (10%)	900 (8%)	1,500 (15%)	11,100 (100%)

European foreign investments were overwhelmingly in the European world; indeed, foreign investment in the hundred years before 1914 is very largely a matter of the Europeans in Europe lending money to each other as well as to their kinfolk abroad. So far as overseas investments are concerned, European finance was part of the European thrust in the world. The largest investments were made in Europe and North America, where most Europeans were found and business conditions were most favourable.

Less attractive were conditions in Asia and Africa. These continents received relatively small amounts of money, and even these (with the exception of Japan) were used to serve western interests more than the interests of the native people. The money was used primarily to draw a country's export economy into the western orbit.

While European capital invested abroad in the hundred years before 1914 was not the most important factor in the development of the modern world—measured against the capital provided by foreign countries themselves, it was only a limited fraction of world gross capital formation—yet it was essential to the emergence of an international economy. In terms of the amount of money loaned, the varied nature of the investments made, the efficiency of operation, and the overall economic effect, European foreign investments, especially in the period 1850–1914, are without historical parallel.

The monies invested by Europeans abroad came primarily from the improvements made in nineteenth century European agriculture, mining, trade, commerce, transport, and industry; they were also the result of Europe's growing economic interrelatedness with other continents, particularly with the Americas. The greater part of these funds found their way to the European world and were used in almost every branch of a country's economy; the largest sums were in public works and primary industry, especially (as in South Africa) in mining. Of the investments made in public works, transport led the field; dwarfing all else were the investments in steam railways. On the outbreak of War, the larger part of Britain's approximately £4 billion invested abroad was in railway stocks and bonds (40 per cent directly in railway companies, and a good deal more indirectly through government securities). The same is true of the foreign investments of all the other European nations. Thus, in the nineteenth century, were the continents penetrated and drawn together; thus was Europe able to feed its rapidly growing numbers and its industry.

The emergence of an international economy in 1914 was the logical outcome of European expansion and settlement in the world; especially was it an expression of the dynamic nature of European civilization. Never before had anyone colonized the world as the Europeans had done in the hundred years after Waterloo; never before had the world known the degree of economic complementarity that it had achieved under European tutelage. With the help of European ideas, technology, commerce, finance, and people, it seemed as if the whole world might become the community of man held together by common ideas and interests.

Yet what had emerged was not so much an international economy based on reciprocity and the mutual goodwill of the nations of the world, but a Eurocentric world in which the Europeans had arrogated to themselves great parts of the earth and its people to be used for their ends; what had been achieved by 1914 was an inter-regional economy concerned with the establishment of European civilization and European interests outside Europe. Certainly, as regards its benefits, the international economy of 1914 left most of the people of the world outside its reckoning. Which is not to say that the wealth of the rich western nations was born simply of the ruthless exploitation of others, or that it was the exclusive creation of a single people or of a single race; it was in fact a most complex, sometimes paradoxical, process of development in which world influences crossed and intermingled. Nevertheless, the ascendency of the West over other peoples—the dominant role of Europe as the focal point of a so-called international economy—cannot be explained without taking account of the historical contribution of the peoples of other continents to the economic growth of the western nations.

The world economic community of 1914 was not only limited in extent and benefits; the success it attained sprang from an unusual degree of economic integration between the industrializing and the primary producing parts of the European world; an arrangement highly beneficial to the Europeans; and one that led British writers of the last century to exaggerate the continuing importance of international trade in economic development. In assuming that what was transitory in history was permanent, and what was particular to the West at a special point in history was general to the world at all times, the English school of economists committed no greater error than most economists are guilty of committing today. The danger now is that we shall replace international trade as the *primum mobile* in economic development with European industrial technology. Yet the wellspring of the nineteenth century economy was neither of these forces considered alone. Having overstressed trade, we now overstress technology; we read back into history the narrow technical rationalism of our own times. Yet western riches and western industrialization were not synonymous; one did not necessarily follow from the other; if anything, European industrialization was the late consequence of capital accumulation, not the cause of it. Improved technology and the creation of overhead social capital were not conditions whose pre-existence explains the acceleration of economic growth in western Europe and the subsequent development of an international economy; they were part of the acceleration in growth which can only be explained in the historical context of the total impact of western man in the world.

In the last analysis, it is the colonization of the world which gave the Europeans a temporary ascendency in wealth and power. To an extent without historical parallel, Europe exploited the human and material resources of the whole earth. Western forms of agriculture and animal husbandry were extended across the great, relatively unoccupied, temperate grasslands of the world; exhaustible, irreplaceable wealth in minerals and fuels was obtained on a scale that no age or civilization had known before; the human resources of much of the earth were redistributed to serve Europe's ends. The outcome for Europe was a special bounty which is just as reasonably explained by an uneven Providence as by an uneven technological might.

The crux in explaining the international economy of 1914 is not technology, but the use to which technology was put; which was determined, on the one hand, by the cultural and social conditions existing in the European-controlled world, and on the other by the particular stage of economic structure reached by the western nations and non-western nations at that time. The development of European technology cannot be explained without taking account of the prevailing philosophy of economic liberalism, the business ethics of the time, the relative political stability, and the growing stress placed by Europeans upon man's power to control his environment. Equally important was the social and economic framework within which these things evolved; it is easy to forget that, relative to other kinds of economy existing in the world, Europe's economic organization was already of an advanced kind in the eighteenth century. Similarly, what mattered was the kind of society into which European technical methods and goals were introduced. Where cultural affinity existed between giver and taker—as it did in the development of early British settlements overseas—the economic results were usually more satisfying. Much depended on the importance attached to economic goals and objectives.

The important thing is that the technology that was used and diffused in the world during the period of most rapid growth within Europe, as well as during the period when nations (economically speaking) were being drawn closer together, was empirical and traditional. There were important exceptions, yet the closer we look at the basic changes taking place in European agriculture, mining, industry and transport, in the nineteenth century, the more we are persuaded that Europe's Industrial Revolution and expansion in the world sprang more from the systematic and resolute use of old rather than new technology. Nothing helped to create a new economic interrelatedness in the world more than European steam railways. Yet there was nothing new about steam or railways. What mattered was the application of steam to railways. And that can only be explained in the light of the total situation.

By 1914 the indelible imprint of western man had been set upon the world; western science and industry had begun to assign to man a worldly destiny other than that which he had known. Through its expansion, its system of production, trade, and transport—above all else through its mentality—Europe, that little 'cape of Asia', had by 1914, economically and commercially unified the European-settled and European-controlled parts of the world.

We have tried to show in these pages how this was done; how interrelated these things were; how very exceptional. Yet the economic agencies through which the international economy took shape, as well as the special circumstances and conditions in which the Europeans operated, are only part of the human story. We are much less sure of our ground when we try to explain the seed of all these things. What our study of the past reveals, all that we can offer the reader (and this is as true of the process of industrialization as it is of the emergence of an international economy) is the picture of a people able and willing to adapt themselves (often unconsciously and spontaneously) to the total and changing circumstances, spiritual and temporal, in which they found themselves. The outcome was the colonization and westernization of much of the world.

Superficially at least, Europe's triumph in 1914 was practical and material. What the Europeans had excelled in was administration, organization, natural scientific knowledge and economically productive technology; they excelled in these things because, primarily, these were the things they honoured. Their achievement should not be scorned. The world had not seen the like before—nor since. If the West cannot be said to have triumphed in Christian love and humility, at least part of their material achievement was derived from the Christian doctrine of human superiority to the world of nature, and Christian universalism. Whether their worldly success—whether their powers of industry—whether the economic and commercial ties that they had drawn between the different parts of the world—whether all these things would prove any more successful or lasting than the efforts made by the Catholic Church in its search for unity in the West eight hundred years before—nay, whether, indeed, that 'Great Discontinuity' of history, the Industrial Revolution, would prove to be one of the great mutations in history, an on-going, universal process working towards the El Dorado of man, or a 'Great Abnormality', an historical moment, a man's work and hence transitory—only time would tell; only those who follow much later in the human concourse shall know if Europe's nineteenth-century promise will be fulfilled.

TABLES

TABLE I   UNITED KINGDOM
Principal Imports for Selected Years, 1831—1913
Approximate Percentage by Region of Provenance

Region of Provenance	1831						1850								1875			
	Cotton	Sugar	Grain	Tea	Flax and hemp	Wines	Cotton	Grain	Sugar	Tea	Timber	Flax and hemp	Hides	Wool	Grain	Cotton	Wool	Sugar
Europe	—	—	86	—	99	91	—	90	1	—	36	84	8	28	36	—	12	13
North America																		
Canada	—	—	12	—	—	—	—	—	—	—	63	—	—	—	7	—	—	—
U.S.A.	76	—	12	—	—	—	74	3	—	—	63	—	—	—	45	57	—	—
Latin America																		
Argentina	—	—	—	—	—	—	—	—	—	—	—	—	40	2	2	—	3	—
Brazil	11	7	—	—	—	—	5	—	5	—	—	—	27	—	—	5	—	14
Chile	—	—	—	—	—	—	—	—	—	—	—	—	—	—	—	—	—	—
Peru	—	—	—	—	—	—	—	—	—	—	—	—	1	4	—	—	—	6
British West Indies	1	76	—	—	—	1	—	—	37	—	—	—	—	—	—	—	—	22
Other	1	2	—	—	—	—	—	—	10	—	—	—	—	—	—	—	—	24
Asia																		
British India	9	3	—	—	—	1	18	—	20	—	—	14	17	5	2	26	6	7
China	—	—	—	100	—	—	—	—	—	98	—	—	—	—	—	—	—	—
Indonesia	—	—	—	—	—	—	—	—	—	—	—	—	—	—	—	—	—	7
Japan	—	—	—	—	—	—	—	—	—	—	—	—	—	—	—	—	—	—
Philippines	—	—	—	—	—	—	—	—	2	—	—	—	—	—	—	—	—	6
Other (incl. South-west Asia)	—	—	—	—	—	—	—	—	—	—	—	—	—	—	—	—	—	—
Africa																		
Egypt	3	—	—	—	—	—	3	6	—	—	—	2	—	—	4	11	—	1
East Africa	—	10	—	—	—	—	—	—	—	—	—	—	—	—	—	—	—	—
West Africa	—	—	—	—	—	—	—	—	—	—	—	—	—	—	—	—	—	—
South Africa	—	—	—	—	—	6	—	—	—	—	—	—	—	—	—	—	12	—
Other (incl. Mauritius)	—	—	—	—	—	—	—	—	14	—	—	—	—	—	2	—	—	—
Australasia																		
Australia	—	—	—	—	—	—	—	—	—	—	—	—	4	53	2	—	67	—
New Zealand	—	—	—	—	—	—	—	—	—	—	—	—	—	—	—	—	—	—
Unspecified	—	2	2	—	1	—	—	1	11	2	1	3	8	—	—	—	—	—

						1900								1913								
Meat	*Timber*	*Tea*	*Wines*	*Hides*	*Butter*	*Grain*	*Meat*	*Cotton*	*Timber*	*Wool*	*Sugar*	*Butter*	*Hides*	*Grain*	*Cotton*	*Meat*	*Wool*	*Timber*	*Butter*	*Sugar*	*Hides*	*Tea*
15	69	—	100	9	98	10	20	—	72	12	80	75	47	5	2	23	8	83	78	56	23	—
—	26	—	—	—	—	8	4	—	19	—	—	3	—	22	—	2	—	9	—	—	—	—
83	5	—	—	14	2	58	53	78	9	—	—	1	—	37	73	17	—	4	—	—	—	—
—	—	—	—	—	8	19	5	—	—	6	2	—	—	13	—	29	12	—	2	—	—	—
—	—	—	—	—	10	—	—	2	—	—	—	—	2	—	3	—	—	—	—	—	2	—
—	—	—	—	—	—	—	—	—	—	—	—	—	—	—	—	—	—	—	—	3	—	—
—	—	—	—	—	—	—	—	—	—	2	—	—	—	2	—	—	—	—	—	—	—	—
—	—	—	—	—	—	—	—	—	—	4	—	—	—	—	—	—	—	—	—	3	—	—
—	—	—	—	—	13	—	—	—	—	—	—	—	—	—	—	—	—	—	—	22	—	—
—	—	13	—	31	—	—	—	2	—	5	4	—	42	15	2	—	7	—	—	—	17	56
—	—	87	—	—	—	—	—	—	—	—	—	—	1	—	—	—	—	—	—	—	2	30
—	—	—	—	—	—	—	—	—	—	1	—	—	—	—	—	—	—	—	—	—	—	6
—	—	—	—	—	—	—	—	—	—	—	—	—	—	—	—	—	—	—	—	—	4	—
—	—	—	—	—	—	—	—	—	—	2	—	—	—	—	—	—	—	—	—	—	—	4
—	—	—	—	—	2	—	—	18	—	—	—	—	—	—	18	—	—	—	—	15	1	—
—	—	—	—	—	—	—	—	—	—	—	—	—	—	—	—	—	—	—	—	—	1	—
—	—	—	—	—	—	—	—	—	—	—	1	—	—	—	—	—	—	—	—	—	2	—
—	—	—	—	—	6	—	—	—	—	6	—	—	—	—	—	17	—	—	—	19	—	—
—	—	—	—	} 2	—	3	7	—	—	45	—	8	5	8	—	12	33	—	14	—	—	—
—	—	—	—		—	1	8	—	—	25	—	4	—	—	—	10	23	—	6	—	8	—
2	—	—	—	5	—	1	3	—	—	1	5	9	2	—	—	5	4	4	—	—	22	4

Drawn from W. Woodruff, *Impact of Western Man* (1966)

TABLE II   FRANCE
Principal Imports for Selected Years, 1830—1913
Approximate Percentage by Region of Provenance

Region of Provenance	1830						1875				
	Cotton	Sugar	Silk	Hides and skins	Wool	Oils	Wool	Silk	Hides and skins	Cotton	Oils
Europe	2	—	100	57	92	100	60	67	24	13	100
North America											
U.S.A.	79	—	—	2	—	—	—	—	4	55	—
Canada	—	—	—	—	—	—	—	—	—	—	—
Latin America											
Argentina	—	—	—	15	—	—	14	—	13	—	—
Brazil	8	—	—	16	—	—	—	—	4	1	—
Chile	—	—	—	—	—	—	—	—	—	—	—
French West Indies	—	74	—	—	—	—	—	—	—	—	—
Other	—	—	—	—	—	—	1	—	1	—	—
Asia											
British India	—	—	—	—	—	—	—	1	13	23	—
China	—	—	—	—	—	—	—	26	—	—	—
Indonesia	—	—	—	—	—	—	—	—	—	—	—
Japan	—	—	—	—	—	—	—	4	—	—	—
French East Indies	—	—	—	—	—	—	—	—	—	—	—
Other	—	—	—	—	—	—	—	—	—	—	—
Africa											
Egypt	9	—	—	—	—	—	1	—	—	6	—
French North Africa	—	—	—	3	4	—	7	—	2	—	—
French West Africa	—	—	—	—	—	—	—	—	—	—	—
South Africa	—	—	—	—	—	—	—	—	—	—	—
Other (including Mauritius and Bourbon)	—	23	—	—	—	—	—	—	—	—	—
Australasia	—	—	—	—	—	—	—	—	—	—	—
Unspecified	2	3	—	13	4	—	17	2	26	2	—

		1900								1913							
	Machinery	*Wool*	*Cotton*	*Coal*	*Silk*	*Oilseeds*	*Timber*	*Hides and skins*	*Machinery*	*Wool*	*Coal and coke*	*Cotton*	*Grain and flour*	*Oilseeds*	*Machinery*	*Silk*	*Wines*
23	92	17	7	100	26	14	81	31	69	26	100	6	39	1	80	29	41
—	4	—	80	—	—	—	16	2	29	—	—	75	6	1	18	—	—
—	—	—	—	—	—	—	—	—	—	—	—	—	1	—	—	—	—
—	—	54	—	—	—	—	2	13	—	22	—	—	27	9	—	—	—
—	—	—	—	—	—	—	—	18	—	—	—	—	—	—	—	—	—
—	—	—	—	—	—	—	—	—	—	1	—	—	—	—	—	—	—
15	—	—	—	—	—	—	—	—	—	—	—	—	—	—	—	—	—
33	—	3	—	—	—	—	—	15	—	9	—	—	—	—	—	—	—
—	—	—	2	—	3	provenance uncertain	—	3	—	3	—	7	4	33	—	3	—
—	—	—	—	—	58		—	10	—	—	—	—	—	3	—	45	—
5	—	—	—	—	—		—	—	—	—	—	—	—	8	—	—	—
—	—	—	—	—	10		—	—	—	—	—	—	—	—	—	22	—
—	—	—	—	—	—		—	1	—	—	—	—	—	9	—	—	—
—	—	—	—	—	—		—	—	—	—	—	—	3	8	—	—	—
3	—	—	10	—	—	—	—	—	—	—	—	12	—	1	—	—	—
—	—	3	—	—	—	—	—	1	—	3	—	—	12	—	—	—	55
—	—	—	—	—	—	—	—	—	—	—	—	—	—	16	—	—	—
—	—	—	—	—	—	—	—	—	—	—	—	—	—	—	—	—	—
19	—	1	—	—	—	—	—	1	—	1	—	—	—	7	—	—	—
—	—	21	—	—	—	—	—	—	—	33	—	—	6	—	—	—	—
2	4	1	1	—	3	—	—	1	2	2	—	—	2	4	2	1	4

Drawn from W. Woodruff, *Impact of Western Man* (1966)

TABLE III   GERMANY
Principal Imports for Selected Years, 1880—1913
Approximate Percentage by Region of Provenance

Region of Provenance	1880							1900	
	Wool, cotton, etc.	*Grain*	*Textile yarns*	*Cattle*	*Coffee, cocoa, tea*	*Foodstuffs (animal)*	*Hides and skins*	*Cotton*	*Wool*
Europe	74	91	100	100	79	80	87	1	24
North America	15	7	—	—	1	20	9	81	—
Canada	—	1	—	—	—	1	—	—	—
U.S.A.	15	6	—	—	—	19	9	81	—
Latin America	4	—	—	—	4	—	2	—	35
Argentina	3	—	—	—	—	—	—	—	35
Brazil	1	—	—	—	3	—	—	—	—
Chile	—	—	—	—	—	—	—	—	—
Peru	—	—	—	—	—	—	—	—	—
Venezuela	—	—	—	—	—	—	—	—	—
Other	—	—	—	—	—	—	—	—	—
Asia	5	1	—	—	16	—	1	7	—
British India	2	1	—	—	2	—	—	7	—
China	—	—	—	—	—	—	—	—	—
Indonesia	—	—	—	—	—	—	—	—	—
Japan	—	—	—	—	—	—	—	—	—
South-west Asia	—	—	—	—	—	—	—	—	—
Other	—	—	—	—	—	—	—	—	—
Africa	—	—	—	—	—	—	—	10	7
East Africa	—	—	—	—	—	—	—	—	—
North Africa	—	—	—	—	—	—	—	10	1
South Africa	—	—	—	—	—	—	—	—	6
West Africa	—	—	—	—	—	—	—	—	—
Australia	1	—	—	—	—	—	—	—	34
Unspecified	—	—	—	—	—	—	—	—	—

					1913								
Wheat	Coffee	Coal	Maize	Copper	Cotton	Wheat	Wool	Barley	Copper	Hides	Iron ore	Coffee	Coal
27	15	100	11	16	—	24	17	93	5	27	93	—	100
36	—	—	81	79	76	52	—	6	88	2	1	—	—
—	—	—	—	—	—	12	—	—	—	—	1	—	—
36	—	—	81	79	76	40	—	6	88	2	—	—	—
37	51	—	8	1	—	18	28	—	—	38	—	70	—
37	—	—	8	—	—	18	22	—	—	22	—	—	—
—	47	—	—	—	—	—	—	—	—	8	—	64	—
—	—	—	—	1	—	—	2	—	—	1	—	—	—
—	—	—	—	—	—	—	—	—	—	1	—	—	—
—	3	—	—	—	—	—	—	—	—	—	—	4	—
—	20	—	—	—	—	—	4	—	—	10	—	25	—
—	12	—	—	3	11	2	—	1	—	22	—	6	—
—	2	—	—	—	10	2	—	—	—	15	—	2	—
—	—	—	—	—	1	—	—	—	—	5	—	—	—
—	10	—	—	—	—	—	—	—	—	1	—	4	—
—	—	—	—	3	—	—	—	—	1	—	—	—	—
—	—	—	—	—	—	—	—	—	—	—	—	—	—
—	—	—	—	—	—	—	—	—	—	—	—	—	—
—	1	—	—	—	12	—	13	—	—	5	6	—	—
—	—	—	—	—	—	—	—	—	—	3	—	—	—
—	—	—	—	—	12	—	1	—	—	—	6	—	—
—	—	—	—	—	—	—	12	—	—	—	—	—	—
—	1	—	—	—	—	—	—	—	—	1	—	—	—
—	—	—	—	1	—	4	42	—	6	2	—	—	—
—	—	—	—	—	—	—	—	—	—	—	—	—	—

Drawn from W. Woodruff, *Impact of Western Man* (1966)

TABLE IV UNITED KINGDOM
  Principal Exports for Selected Years, 1831—1913
  Approximate Percentage by Region of Destination

Region of Destination	1831					1850					
	Cotton yarns and textiles	Woollen yarns and textiles	Linens	Cutlery, hardware	Iron and steel	Cotton yarns and textiles	Woollen yarns and textiles	Iron and steel	Linens	Cutlery, hardware	Coal
Europe	47	25	22	14	32	39	32	26	34	27	73
North America											
Canada	2	7	5	8	12	2	7	9	3	5	2
U.S.A.	17	43	41	61	22	9	34	44	35	40	5
Latin America											
Argentina	1	1	—	1	—	1	3	—	—	3	—
Brazil	4	2	5	2	2	5	3	1	3	3	2
Chile	3	3	1	—	—	2	3	1	2	1	—
Peru	2	2	1	—	—	1	2	—	1	1	—
British West Indies	4	1	14	4	10	2	—	2	4	2	3
Other	7	1	9	2	3	4	2	4	15	4	6
Asia											
British India	10	12	—	3	10	18	4	7	1	5	3
China	—	—	—	—	—	6	5	—	—	—	1
Indonesia	1	—	—	—	1	1	—	—	—	—	—
Japan	—	—	—	—	—	—	—	—	—	—	—
Philippines	—	—	—	—	—	—	—	—	—	—	—
Other (incl. South-west Asia)	—	—	—	—	—	1	—	1	—	—	—
Africa											
Egypt and Sudan	2	—	—	—	2	1	—	—	—	—	1
East Africa	—	—	—	—	—	—	—	—	—	—	—
South Africa	—	—	—	—	1	—	1	—	—	1	—
West Africa	—	—	—	—	1	1	—	1	—	—	—
Other (incl. Mauritius)	—	—	—	—	1	1	—	1	—	—	1
Australasia											
Australia	—	—	—	—	2	1	3	3	2	4	—
New Zealand	—	—	—	—	—	—	—	—	—	—	—
Unspecified	—	3	2	5	1	3	—	—	—	5	—

1875

Cotton yarns and textiles	Woollen yarns and textiles	Iron and steel	Coal	Linens	Machinery	Chemicals
34	63	42	78	41	59	68
2	6	7	—	3	—	1
5	13	15	—	32	2	14
1	1	2	—	—	1	—
5	2	2	3	2	2	—
1	—	1	—	—	—	—
—	—	1	1	1	—	—
}7	}3	—	1	1	1	—
		2	3	14	3	—
24	—	7	5	—	21	3
8	4	—	—	—	—	—
2	—	—	—	—	2	—
2	1	—	—	—	—	1
1	—	—	—	—	—	—
—	—	—	—	—	—	—
2	—	1	4	—	1	—
—	—	—	—	—	—	—
—	—	3	—	—	2	1
1	—	—	—	—	—	—
1	1	—	—	—	—	—
2	5	10	—	3	4	4
—	1	3	—	—	2	—
3	—	4	5	5	—	2

1900

Cotton yarns and textiles	Coal	Iron and steel	Woollen yarns and textiles	Machinery	Chemicals
23	81	39	48	56	33
2	—	3	8	1	4
5	—	5	7	4	17
3	2	4	3	2	6
2	2	2	1	2	1
2	—	1	2	—	1
—	—	—	—	—	—
}5	2	}2	}2	3	1
		2	—	2	1
32	1	13	3	11	—
7	—	2	3	—	—
3	—	—	—	—	—
3	—	4	4	3	—
1	—	—	—	1	—
—	1	1	—	1	—
—	5	1	—	2	—
—	—	—	—	—	—
1	2	5	3	3	4
3	2	—	—	—	—
2	1	1	1	—	—
4	—	11	10	5	13
1	—	3	2	2	3
1	1	3	3	4	10

1913

Cotton yarns and textiles	Iron and steel goods	Coal	Woollen yarns and textiles	Machinery	Chemicals
13	22	81	75	41	48
2	4	—	—	2	3
2	4	—	3	1	13
3	8	6	5	5	4
2	3	3	1	4	2
1	2	—	2	2	—
—	—	—	—	—	—
}5	}2	—	—	—	—
		2	—	2	1
38	20	—	—	14	5
10	1	—	2	1	1
3	1	—	1	—	—
1	4	—	4	5	4
—	—	—	—	—	—
4	—	—	—	—	—
3	1	5	—	1	—
—	1	—	—	—	—
1	6	—	4	—	6
4	1	—	—	—	—
1	—	—	—	—	—
3	12	—	—	7	5
—	3	—	—	2	2
4	5	3	4	12	6

Drawn from W. Woodruff, *Impact of Western Man* (1966)

TABLE V FRANCE
Principal Exports for Selected Years, 1830—1913
Approximate Percentage by Region of Destination

Region of Destination	1830							1875			
	Silk cloth	Cotton cloth	Wines	Woollen cloth	Prepared hides	Linen cloth	Fancy goods	Silk cloth	Woollen cloth	Wines	Silk goods
Europe	53	54	54	69	46	69	57	69	67	57	94
North America											
U.S.A.	28	11	6	9	22	7	12	21	15	5	2
Canada	—	—	—	—	—	—	—	—	—	—	—
Latin America											
Argentina	—							—	—	10	—
Brazil	3	1	4	—	7	—	—	—	2	3	—
Chile	—	1	—	2	—	—	—				
French West Indies	—	10	4	1	12	22	4	—	—	—	—
Other	4	12	5	5	—	1	—	—	2	—	—
Asia											
British India	—	—	—	—	—	—	—	—	—	—	—
China	—	—	—	—	—	—	—	—	—	—	—
Indonesia	—	—	—	—	—	—	—	—	—	—	—
Japan	—	—	—	—	—	—	—	—	—	—	—
French East Indies	—	—	—	—	—	—	—	—	—	—	—
Other	—	—	—	—	—	—	—	—	—	—	—
Africa											
Egypt	—	—	—	—	—	—	—	2	1	—	—
French North Africa	—	2	1	—	—	—	—	2	2	5	4
French West Africa	—	—	—	—	—	—	—	—	—	—	—
South Africa	—	—	—	—	—	—	—	—	—	—	—
Other	—	—	—	—	—	—	—	—	—	—	—
Australasia	—	—	—	—	—	—	—	—	—	—	—
Unspecified	12	9	26	14	13	—	27	6	11	20	—

Fancy goods	Prepared hides	Cotton cloth	1900							1913							
			Silk cloth	Wines	Woollen cloth	Wool	Fancy goods	Cotton cloth	Silk	Silk cloth	Cotton cloth	Clothing	Wool	Motor vehicles	Woollen cloth	Chemical products	Wines
72	70	54	70	65	72	95	59	35	90	73	31	55	99	64	69	76	62
5	14	2	22	5	8	1	6	13	5	13	19	10	—	—	6	10	5
1	2	2	—	3	2	—	4	4	—	1	6	14	—	8	3	—	8
—	2	4	—	1	1	—	3	2	—	—	2	1	—	4	—	—	1
1	1	1	—	—	—	—	—	—	—	—	—	—	—	—	—	—	1
—	—	—	}4		—	—	—	1	—	1	1	—	—	—	—	—	4
—	—	—	—	—	—	—	—	—	—	5	—	—	—	—	1	—	—
—	—	—	—	—	—	—	—	—	—	2	—	—	—	—	—	—	—
—	—	—	—	—	—	—	—	—	—	—	—	—	—	—	—	—	—
—	—	—	—	2	—	—	—	6	—	—	—	—	—	—	—	—	2
—	—	—	—	—	—	—	—	—	—	—	9	—	—	—	—	—	—
—	—	1	—	—	—	—	—	—	—	1	—	—	—	—	—	—	—
2	—	21	—	1	3	—	3	20	—	1	17	8	—	14	4	5	4
—	—	—	—	1	—	—	—	1	—	—	1	—	—	—	—	—	1
—	—	—	—	—	—	—	1	—	—	—	5	1	—	—	—	—	3
—	—	—	—	—	—	—	1	1	—	—	—	—	—	—	—	—	—
	11	16	8	18	14	4	23	18	5	3	9	11	1	10	17	9	9

Drawn from W. Woodruff, *Impact of Western Man* (1966)

TABLE VI   GERMANY
Principal Exports for Selected Years, 1880—1913
Approximate Percentage by Region of Destination

Region of Destination	1880						1900	
	Textile goods	Salt and chemicals	Textile yarns	Grain	Wool, cotton, silk	Metal goods	Cotton goods	Woollen goods
Europe	77	87	99	100	100	84	55	73
North America	19	13	1	—	—	6	15	6
Canada	1	—	—	—	—	—	—	1
U.S.A.	18	13	1	—	—	6	15	5
Latin America	2	—	—	—	—	2	15	6
Argentina	—	—	—	—	—	—	4	2
Brazil	—	—	—	—	—	—	3	1
Chile	—	—	—	—	—	—	4	2
Peru	—	—	—	—	—	—	1	—
Venezuela	—	—	—	—	—	—	1	—
Other	—	—	—	—	—	—	3	2
Asia	2	—	—	—	—	8	9	12
British India	—	—	—	—	—	—	3	6
China	—	—	—	—	—	—	1	2
Indonesia	—	—	—	—	—	—	—	—
Japan	—	—	—	—	—	—	3	4
South-west Asia	—	—	—	—	—	—	—	—
Other	—	—	—	—	—	—	2	1
Africa	—	—	—	—	—	—	3	1
East Africa	—	—	—	—	—	—	—	—
North Africa	—	—	—	—	—	—	1	1
South Africa	—	—	—	—	—	—	1	—
West Africa	—	—	—	—	—	—	1	—
Australia	—	—	—	—	—	—	2	1
Unspecified	—	—	—	—	—	—	—	—

Machinery	Coal	Sugar	Silk products	Iron and steel products	Clothing	1913 Machinery (non-electrical)	Iron and steel products	Coal	Cotton goods	Woollen goods	Sugar	Paper products
88	100	58	70	80	84	81	71	98	58	75	87	74
1	—	37	24	1	4	2	3	—	13	5	2	11
—	—	2	1	—	1	—	1	—	1	1	1	—
1	—	35	23	1	3	2	2	—	12	4	1	11
3	—	1	2	5	3	9	10	—	13	9	7	9
1	—	—	1	2	1	3	5	—	6	4	3	5
1	—	—	—	1	1	4	3	—	3	1	—	3
1	—	—	—	1	—	1	2	—	2	2	1	1
—	—	—	—	—	—	—	—	—	—	—	—	—
1	—	1	—	1	2	1	1	—	4	3	2	1
5	—	2	3	9	3	4	10	—	8	7	1	3
—	—	—	1	2	2	1	3	—	5	3	—	1
—	—	—	—	2	—	—	1	—	1	1	—	—
3	—	—	—	3	—	1	3	—	1	—	—	—
1	—	2	1	2	—	2	3	—	—	1	—	1
—	—	—	—	—	—	—	—	—	—	—	—	—
—	—	—	1	—	1	—	—	—	1	—	—	—
1	—	1	—	1	3	2	3	1	4	2	3	—
—	—	—	—	—	2	—	1	—	1	—	—	—
—	—	—	—	—	—	1	1	1	1	2	1	—
—	—	—	—	1	1	1	1	—	1	—	—	—
—	—	—	—	—	—	—	—	—	1	—	1	—
1	—	—	—	3	1	1	2	—	2	1	—	1
—	—	—	—	—	—	—	—	1	—	—	—	—

Drawn from W. Woodruff, *Impact of Western Man* (1966)

BIBLIOGRAPHY

Most of the existing sources tell the story of the development of an international economy only from the side of the Europeans. A really satisfactory history of the international economy—in contrast to a history of Greater Europe written by Europeans—does not exist. An inkling of what is needed is the *History of Mankind* in preparation by UNESCO. Alas, even here, results fall short of ideals. For having set out to write '. . . the first global history, planned and executed from an international point of view', Vol. 6, *The Twentieth Century*, too often becomes a verbal tug-of-war between European scholars about what are largely European points of view. One welcomes the arguments; one objects to the fact that almost all the speaking parts are held by Europeans. The global part of UNESCO's history seems to have got lost in the wings. It will be interesting to see if this is also true of Vol. 5, *The Nineteenth Century*, when it appears.

In these circumstances, I shall limit myself to indicating where the reader may find comprehensive, up-to-date bibliographies of the literature as it now stands; this will allow him to choose for himself. In addition, I shall throw out a few guide lines to the standard works, and indicate a little of the more recent research which I think is important.

GENERAL

The most useful general survey, and one containing the fullest bibliographical information is *The Cambridge Economic History of Europe*, New York, 1965, Vol. VI, parts I and II. edited by H. J. Habakkuk and M. M. Postan. The main theme of these two books is the rise and development of the industrial system in the western world since the eighteenth century. Entirely orthodox, entirely European in outlook and interpretation (eleven of the twelve contributors are Anglo-Americans), these volumes have not avoided the usual pitfalls of joint projects of this kind; certainly, they fall short of providing us with a unified vision of what has happened in the world since the Industrial Revolution. Nevertheless, the state of the literature being what it is, the individual essays are the best of their kind and indispensable for further reading.

A much earlier pioneering, general treatment, and one that influenced a great number of us in the West, is that contained in the books of the late Lillian C. A. Knowles: *The Industrial and Commercial Revolutions in Great Britain during the Nineteenth Century*, London, 1921, and *Economic Development in the Nineteenth Century: France, Germany, Russia, and the United States*, London, 1932. However, Professor Knowles wrote before American foreign aid and the 'Cold War' had transformed the study of economics and economic history. By the 1960s, at least in the United States, the study of growth economies had become almost an obsession. And as the only growth that mattered—especially as the productive contest between the U.S.A., and the U.S.S.R., grew in intensity—was the growth that could be counted, it was quite natural that an entirely new emphasis should be placed upon quantitative techniques. In economics and in modern economic history the philosopher and the historian were elbowed off the stage; the statistician and the mathematician took their place. Having neglected quantitative analysis, some economists and economic historians now swung to the other extreme; counting became confused with causation. The works of the late Lillian Knowles provide a healthy counter-poise to these trends.

So far as I know, there are only two other wide-ranging treatments of western history bearing directly on the emergence of an international economy before 1914. One is William Ashworth's *A Short History of the International Economy, 1850–1950*, London, 1952; the other is my own *Impact of Western Man; A Study of Europe's role in the World Economy, 1750–1960*, London, 1966. Ashworth's work is a modest attempt to set out the bare framework of national economic history from the Englishman's point of view.

As for my *Impact of Western Man*, the basic questions that

caused me to write this book were twofold: what led Europe to go beyond its natural boundaries and produce the effect in the world that it did; also, what was the nature of the interconnection between European expansion and the development of a world economy? In that book I made no apology for having tried to illuminate our present dramatic phase of world history in the most general way, nor for having emphasised the study of humanity as a whole. The book was a point of departure. I hope it may serve as such for others. I have provided the fullest bibliographical data. *Impact of Western Man* was not only meant to be a book of detail arising out of my research; it was also meant to be a book of interpretation.

Books containing imaginative generalisations leading to new interpretations of history and economics, that have appeared in recent times, include Joseph Schumpeter, *The Theory of Economic Development*, Cambridge, Mass., 1934 (originally published in German in 1914); Colin Clark, *The Conditions of Economic Progress*, London, 1940; Karl Polanyi, *Origins of Our Times*, London, 1945; Maurice Dobb, *Studies in the Development of Capitalism*, London, 1946; Ragnar Nurkse, *Problems of Capital Formation in Underdeveloped Countries*, Blackwell, Oxford, 1953; W. A. Lewis, *The Theory of Economic Growth*, London, 1955; Geoffrey Barraclough, *History in a Changing World*, Norman, Oklahoma, 1955; Gunnar Myrdal, *An International Economy*, New York, 1956; W. W. Rostow, *The Stages of Economic Growth*, New York, 1959. The fact that Rostow's book was assailed so strongly by experts should not dissuade the student from reading it. In any event, experts are notorious for resisting new ideas. Rostow's book gained a wide audience because it is a book of power and imagination. It would not have been quite so convincing to the world had it come from a country that, instead of achieving glittering material success, had known only poverty. Two other books of imaginative interpretation—this time much more theoretical in approach than the others—are Charles P. Kindleberger, *International Economics*, 4th ed. Homewood, Illinois, 1968; and J. R. Hicks, *A Theory of Economic History*, Oxford, 1969.

SPECIAL REFERENCES

1. INTERNATIONAL TRADE. The standard works are: J. B. Condliffe, *The Commerce of Nations*, London, 1951; Folke Hilgerdt, *Industrialisation and Foreign Trade*, League of Nations, Geneva, 1945; Hilgerdt's work is a pioneering study of the relation between international trade, manufacturing industry, and economic development; Alfred Maizels, *Industrial Growth and World Trade*, Cambridge, 1963; this is an outstanding piece of empirical analysis bringing Hilgerdt's work up to 1959. The article by K. Berrill, 'International Trade and the Rate of Economic Growth', *Economic History Review*, April, 1960, is an historical critique of the unrealistic nature of theoretical models of economic growth. That by C. P. Kindleberger 'Foreign Trade and Economic Growth—Lessons from Britain and France, 1850 to 1913', *Economic History Review*, December, 1961, is concerned with the relation between industrial growth and foreign trade. In Ch. VII of *Impact of Western Man* I have dealt with 'The Changing pattern of World Trade' and the conflicting estimates made of its value and volume. On the relation between trade and technology, see William and Helga Woodruff, *Technology and the Changing Trade Patterns of the United States*, Bureau of Economic and Business Research, University of Florida, May, 1968. A theoretical treatment is the International Economic Association's volume *International Trade Theory in a Developing World*, London, 1963.

2. TECHNICAL CHANGE AND INDUSTRIAL DEVELOPMENT. See David S. Landes, *The Unbound Prometheus*, New York, 1969. This is an enlargement of the essay to be found in the *Cambridge Economic History* mentioned earlier. Not everyone will share Mr Landes' belief that the world is engaged in a race to a western goal of industrialisation, but this book is the most scholarly effort in its field. Also H. J. Habakkuk, *American and British Technology in the Nineteenth Century*, Cambridge, 1962. This is a comparative study of the use of

human and material resources in Britain and America. It is important not for the questions it answers, but for the questions it asks. There have been many answers; see Peter Temin, 'Labor Scarcity and the Problem of American Industrial Efficiency in the 1850s', *Journal of Economic History*, September, 1966. Also Derek Aldcroft (ed.), *The Development of British Industry and Foreign Competition, 1875–1914*, London, 1968; W. O. Henderson, *The Industrialisation of Europe, 1780–1914*, London, 1969. Of world scope are: S. B. Clough, 'The Diffusion of Industry in the Last Century and a Half', *Studi in Onore Di Armando Sapori*, Milan, 1957; and John Jewkes, 'The Growth of World Industry', *Oxford Economic Papers*, February, 1951. An attempt to trace the intercontinental diffusion of technology in a particular industry is my, 'An Inquiry into the Origins of invention and the intercontinental diffusion of techniques of production in the Rubber Industry', *The Economic Record*, December, 1962. Ch. V. of *Impact of Western Man* deals with 'The Diffusion of European Technology' in the world. Alexander Gershenkron's writings about the preconditions to industrialisation are provocative and rewarding. See especially his *Economic Backwardness in Historical Perspective*, New York, 1965, and *Continuity in History and other Essays*, Cambridge, Mass., 1968. On the role of banking see: Rondo Cameron and others, *Banking in the Early Stages of Industrialisation*, New York, 1967.

3. AGRICULTURE. References to general and special works on industrialisation by western economists and economic historians, in recent times, are legion. References to agricultural change are relatively few. Now this is curious, not only because we all live by the land (and the seas), but also because—if the thesis I have set out in this essay will bear any weight—so much of the industrialisation we talk about was itself in great part the result of world colonisation by the Europeans and North Americans. I can only offer one or two general works, in English, and the emphasis in these lies more in the twentieth than the nineteenth century. See N. S. B. Gras, *A History of Agriculture in Europe*

and America, New York, 1925; H. A. Tempany and D. H. Grist, *An Introduction to Tropical Agriculture*, London, 1958; Doreen Warriner, *The Economics of Peasant Farming*, London, 1939; Royal Institute of International Affairs, *World Agriculture: an International Survey*, London, 1932. A theoretical and historical study of the adjustments made between agriculture and industry during the process of industrialisation in Pei-kang Chang, *Agriculture and Industrialisation*, Cambridge, Mass., 1949. Recent contributions aimed more specifically at British developments are: Phyllis Deane and W. A. Cole, *British Economy Growth: 1688–1959*, Cambridge, 1962, and E. L. Jones (ed.), *Agriculture and Economic Growth: 1650–1815*, London, 1967.

4. TRANSPORT. Books dealing with the history of transport and communications are more plentiful than those dealing with agriculture, yet I know of no one book providing a history of world transport and communications. There are one or two general introductions to the development of sea transport such as C. E. Fayle, *A Short History of the World's Shipping*, London, 1933; A. W. Kirkaldy, *British Shipping, Its History, Organisation, and Importance*, London, 1914; but information about land transport has to be sought in the histories of the different countries. What I know on the subject I have put in Ch. VI of *Impact of Western Man* under the heading 'The Conquest of Distance'. Interest in recent years in the United States has been concentrated on land rather than sea transport. The astonishing thing is the amount of time and labour spent by American economists and economic historians, not in trying to discover (as far as they may) what actually did happen in the past, but actually what might have happened. The literature is surprisingly large. See Robert Fogel, *Railroads and American Economic History*, Baltimore, 1964; Fritz Redlich, 'New and Traditional Approaches to Economic History and their Interdependence', *Journal of Economic History*, December, 1965; Peter McClelland, 'Railroads, American Growth and the New Economic History: A Critique', *Journal of Economic History*, March, 1968.

5. POPULATION AND EMIGRATION. Carlo Cipolla's *Economic History of World Population*, Harmondsworth, 1962 is easily the best short history on world population; the standard reference work on emigration is I. Ferenczi and W. F. Wilcox, *International Migrations*, New York, 1929 and 1931, 2 vols.; also, the relevant parts of W. S. Woytinsky and E. S. Woytinsky, *World Population and Production*, New York, 1953. Some interesting conjectures regarding the relation between the exports of capital and emigration are contained in Brinley Thomas, *Migration and Economic Growth; A Study of Great Britain and the Atlantic Economy*, Cambridge, 1954. My findings are in Ch. III of *Impact of Western Man*, 'Exodus—The Dispersal of Europeans since the Eighteenth Century'.

6. FOREIGN INVESTMENTS. Like foreign trade, we are most uncertain about the values involved in foreign investment. On this see the different estimates in my *Impact of Western Man*, 'Europe—Banker to the World; A Study of European foreign investments', Ch. IV, also the tables and detailed bibliography. See also, H. Feis, *Europe, the World's Banker, 1870–1914*, New Haven, 1930; and *The Problem of International Investment*, The Royal Institute of International Affairs, London, 1937 Important recent works on the international monetary system include: A G. Ford, *The Gold Standard: 1880–1914*, New York, 1962; Arthur L. Bloomfield, *Monetary Policy under the International Gold Standard: 1880–1914*, New York, 1959; and by the same author, *Short-term Capital Movements under the Pre-1914 Gold Standard*, Princeton, N.J., 1963.

7. IMPERIALISM AND COLONIALISM. Cupidity always has been an attractive explanation why one group is rich and another poor; never so much as in recent years. Out of a vast literature three recent important articles are: Richard Koebner, 'The Concept of Economic Imperialism', *Economic History Review*, August, 1949; Herbert Lüthy, 'Colonisation and the Making of Mankind', *Journal of Economic History*, December, 1961; and David Fieldhouse,

'Imperialism: An Historiographical Revision', *Economic History Review*, December, 1961. The reader should consult my detailed bibliography in *Impact of Western Man*, Ch. II, 'The Course of Empire'.

8. WORLD ECONOMIC GROWTH AND INCOME. For what we know in this field we are more indebted to Simon Kuznets than to anyone else. See especially his *Six Lectures on Economic Growth*, Glencoe, Illinois, 1959. Also 'Economic Growth: The Last Hundred Years', *National Institute Economic Review*, July, 1961; L. J. Zimmerman, 'The Distribution of World Income 1860–1960', Ch. II, Egbett de Vries (ed.), *Essays on Unbalanced Growth*, The Hague, 1962. An essay criticising the undue stress placed upon the political entity—the nation—as the cause of economic growth during the past hundred years is William and Helga Woodruff, 'Economic Growth: Myth or Reality: The Interrelatedness of Continents and the Diffusion of Technology, 1860–1960', *Technology and Culture*, Fall, 1966.

B. R. Mitchell

INTRODUCTION

Since there is surely no longer any need to justify the use of statistics in economic history, the purpose of this introduction will be to say something about the nature of the statistics included in this appendix, and, in so doing, to convey the necessary warnings about their indiscriminate use.

But first, a word of explanation should be given for the selection of countries for inclusion in these tables. Two general principles have been followed. First, all tables include statistics, so far as these are available, for seven countries — the six major powers of the early twentieth century (Austria-Hungary, France, Germany, Italy, Russia, and the United Kingdom) plus Sweden, which presents features of particular interest to economic historians, and is at the same time relatively rich in historical statistical material. Spain was reluctantly omitted from this group because of the opposite characteristic — great paucity of material. Second, in certain tables where figures for a country not in this group are of especial interest (as, for example, Belgian coal and iron production), these have been included. In the extreme cases — population and length of railway open — this has meant the inclusion of all countries for which information exists.

As well as excluding some of the smaller countries for which material was available, a second, more serious restriction of the coverage has been regretfully necesstiated by the amount of space available. This is the presentation of the majority of the statistics in the form of arithmetic means of groups of years, rather than showing all the annual figures that are extant. Apart from one or two tables where the figures are only available for benchmark years, there are only a few series, which seem especially useful for indicating annual fluctuation, that are not presented in this period-average form.

The experienced professional economist or historian is not likely to require any *general* warnings about the use of the statistics which follow; for when he sees, for instance, a table which purports to compare (say) the value of agricultural production in different countries at various times, or, still more, their gross national products and capital formation ratios, he will be aware of the inevitable problems which exist in attempting to make such comparisons at all accurate. Many users of this book, however, will not be experienced professionals. So that it will be well to begin with some of the broader problems in historical statistics.

At bottom practically all of these problems spring from either what one might call the mathematical limitations of statistics, or else from what can very broadly be called the lack of availability of exactly those figures which we require for international and intertemporal comparisons and for present-day analytical purposes. The two main examples of the first of these types of problem which can be found in the tables which follow are the well-known problems of index-numbers, and those which result from averaging. This is not the place to deal with the first of these in any detail. Suffice it to say that the indices must be used with caution, and with due regard for the difficulties of making meaningful comparisons over long periods of time or between countries with very different basic conditions. Indices of both agricultural and industrial production are bedevilled by problems of coverage; for example, by the lack of data on many industries, and by the fact that the more primitive the economy the lower the proportion of production that ever enters the market system and so is capable even in principle of being measured. Price indices are plagued by similar problems, and also by the gradual lessening of relevance of their commodity composition and weighting, unless subjected to revisions which mar their direct comparability over time.

The problems produced by averaging in these tables are

— apart from those inherent in index numbers — for the most part those produced by the decision to present the majority of the series in the form of means of groups of years. This tends to smooth out the picture of economic change by eliminating the sharpest discontinuities. Of course, such a smoothing is not without its advantages for some purposes, and moving averages are often used deliberately with this in mind. But it may well be objected that the choice of periods of arbitrary length (usually five or ten years) over which the averages are taken can produce its own brand of artificial movement in the series. If, for example, a decennial mean includes peak years of two trade cycles, it will give an exaggerated picture of the rate of growth from the previous ten-year period and will understate the rate of growth to the subsequent one. It is for this reason that the shorter, five-year periods were used for the output series for coal and iron, since these industries were especially affected by Juglar cycles. So far as the other series, for which decennial averages were generally used, are concerned the possibility of distortion was continually kept in mind in their compilation, and it does not seem to have occurred in any serious way. In fact it may well be that a more potent cause of distortion through the use of period-averages has been the existence of gaps in the annual statistics for some countries, especially prior to about 1880. Some of the figures shown are, therefore, averages of not ten (or five) years, but of a smaller number. If the missing year (or years) was one of exceptional conditions (from the point of view of its harvest or level of cyclical activity, for example) then the period average may well be significantly different from what it would have been had the annual series been complete. By its very nature this sort of distortion is hard to detect, unless its existence is extremely obvious. Footnotes to the tables call attention to such instances; and for the rest, one can only say that its occurrence has not *apparently* been very important.

The various problems springing from what I have called the lack of availability of statistics are numerous and largely intractable. The most obvious cases are those where statistics under certain headings were simply not collected and therefore do not exist. This *is* one of the main difficulties in the way of international comparisons, and, indeed, of economic analysis in history generally. But it is not just this obvious problem that I am thinking of when I speak of lack of availability. There is also the lack of comparability between different countries and periods in series which are on the surface the same. The cause of this may be differences or changes in definition of things which are similarly described (and this includes boundary changes). It may be the use of different units of measurement, especially in agriculture, where measures of volume were commonly used for much of the nineteenth century, and the translation of these into weight is inevitably on an arbitrary basis. It may be variations in the efficiency of the collectors of statistics (and in their printers), or in the conditions under which they work — all the things, that is, which can be summed up as variable reliability. The commentary which follows on the various sections into which the tables have been arranged is intended to point out some of the more important specific examples of these problems. But it is far from exhaustive, and the user is urged to read the footnotes to the tables carefully, and in general to tread warily when making comparisons between countries, and even for the same country over time.

NOTES ON THE SECTIONS

Population The main problem with Table 1 is the doubtful reliability of some of the figures for the earlier years. Many are estimates rather than the results of censuses; and, in any case, census-taking procedures in the early stages were often far from perfect, and in some countries there was a tendency to under-enumeration because of various fears of government action, probably the main motive being the endeavour to evade actual or potential taxation. The Scandinavian figures are almost certainly the most consistently reliable, and probably those for north-western

countries can be taken as accurate from 1820/1 onwards
and those for the rest of the continent from 1870/1 or
1880/1. Other figures must be regarded as subject to a
margin of error of up to ten per cent — perhaps more for
the first two years shown in Hungary, Italy, Russia and
Spain.

Another difficulty in the way of comparisons of population over time is produced by boundary changes, which
affected about half the countries at one time or another. So
far as possible the effect of these has been eliminated by
showing the population in the 1914 boundaries. But this is
not always possible. And in any case it should be borne in
mind when using these figures in conjunction with others.

Table 2 is straightforward, though it should be noted
that the figures relate to the city limits of the years shown,
not to uniform limits. For commentary on Table 3 the user
is referred to the source.

Agriculture There are likely to be certain inaccuracies in
many of the tables in this section as a result of conversion
from volume to weight measures, which has often had to be
done on an arbitrary basis. These are probably not all that
important, however. A greater drawback in making comparisons may well be differences in the efficiency of collection of the statistics, and of the procedures for estimating
the yields of the growing crops. Unfortunately it is impossible to say anything useful about this. Note particularly
the omission of certain years in the earlier averages for
some countries, notably Austria-Hungary. In view of quite
wide differences between harvests, these omissions may
easily have produced some distortion in the picture of
changes in output over time. These comments apply to
Tables 1 to 5; and Table 6, giving annual figures for the two
main grain crops in each country, has been inserted primarily to give some indication of the possible size of the
problem produced by harvest fluctuations.

Table 7 is straightforward, but this certainly cannot be
said of Table 8. Owing to the different bases of calculation
used for every country, direct international comparisons in

this table are impermissible, except of the trends within each country, and then only on an approximate basis. Where the figures are given in constant prices they are, of course, better indicators of change in agriculture itself — especially as the composition of agricultural output does not change enough over time to make long-period price indices impossibly hazardous to construct. Unfortunately farm price indices are not available for Sweden or the United Kingdom. It should be pointed out that the French estimates for the eighteenth century, by J-C. Toutain, which have been used here, have been subjected to considerable criticism. (See E. Le Roy Ladurie in *Annales Économies, Sociétés, Civilisations* (Sept./Oct. 1968).)

Industry This is the largest section, and the problem here has been what to leave out rather than what to include. The decision to give only tables for fuel, iron and steel, and the textile industries (apart from the overall indices in Table 1) was made on the ground that these are the only industries for which information is widely available. Probably the most important resulting omissions are engineering (for which output indicators only exist partially — e.g. for shipbuilding), non-ferrous metals, chemicals, and, especially for Sweden, the timber industries.

The indices of industrial production in Table 1 must be used with especial care, and with due regard for the choice of an end-period base. Most of the remaining tables are straightforward in a sense, though it is here (as well as in agriculture) that the main force of the earlier general warning about changes in reliability and availability applies. Except for figures derived from overseas trade statistics (and these have their own problems), all the eighteenth-century, and some of the earlier nineteenth-century figures are estimates, and should be regarded as having a margin of error of at least ten per cent.

Railways This section is straightforward, and the only comment to be made is on the diversity of figures given for most countries up to 1870 in the various sources that were examined. In view of this, the government statistical offices of those countries for which the discrepancies could not be resolved were approached for definitive figures, and where comprehensive ones were provided these have been used here.

Overseas Trade This table is reasonably straightforward, though changes in prices should be borne in mind, especially in the case of Russia. There is, of course, a far greater amount of detail available in the original sources than has been used here, for overseas trade was the aspect of economic affairs above all others about which governments collected statistics. It has to be remembered, though, that they collected them as a by-product of taxation in almost all instances. There was thus always a temptation to understate or evade, except where free trade existed. In extreme cases where tax rates were very high, the result was widespread smuggling. This is likely to have been worst — so far as figures given here are concerned — in the first half of the nineteenth century, before the mid-century relaxation of duty levels. When protective tariffs were raised again in many countries from the 1870's onwards, techniques of prevention were probably more effective. It is impossible to estimate the possible impact of smuggling on the overall figures of overseas trade. Perhaps one might guess that it resulted in a maximum understatement of ten per cent in the nineteenth century.

Literacy For commentary on these two tables the user is referred to the original source.

National Accounts The tables in this section are all 'constructs' rather than raw data — that is, they are the result of complex and elaborate calculations, for details of which the user must consult the sources. The value of Table 1, which gives national income data for five of the seven basic countries (that is excluding Austria-Hungary and Russia, for which no estimates have been made as yet), is greatly reduced by the fact that the authors who calculated the

figures used many different measures of income and investment — gross national product, net social product, gross
domestic product, and net national income; gross capital
formation, gross domestic fixed capital formation, and net
investment. Comparisons between countries, other than of
internal trends, must therefore be avoided. Such comparisons as *can* be made have been done by Professor Kuznets, and are to be found in Table 4. Tables 2 and 3 also
derive from Kuznets, and the user should consult his
Modern Economic Growth for commentary on all of them.

Price Indices Apart from the general problems of index
numbers, especially covering long periods, which were
referred to earlier, it should be noted that those given in this
table are all based on wholesale and/or import prices, and
not on retail prices. This is not in itself necessarily a disadvantage for many purposes, but it does tend to mean
that fluctuations appear to be muted. This is especially the
case with the English eighteenth-century series, which is
partly based on notoriously 'sticky' contract prices.

ACKNOWLEDGEMENTS

In compiling this appendix I have had help from a large
number of people, and I would like to thank especially
Professors Carlo M. Cipolla, Nachum Gross, Lennart
Jörberg, Richard Rudolph, and William Woodruff, and
Mr. C. A. Jewell, together with officials of the national
statistical offices of Austria, Denmark, France, the German
Federal Republic, Italy, Netherlands, Norway, Portugal,
Spain, Sweden, and Switzerland, and of N. V. Nederlandse
Spoorwegen. I am also grateful to Mr. J. M. K. Vyvyan
for translating from Russian for me.

In addition to these personal acknowledgements, we
have to thank the following for permission to publish ex-
tracts from their works:—
COLIN CLARK, *Population Growth and Land Use* (Macmillan).
CARLO M. CIPOLLA, *Literacy and Development in the West* (Pen-

guin). K. H. CONNELL, *The Population of Ireland 1750-1845* (Oxford University Press). PHYLLIS DEANE and W. A. COLE, *British Economic Growth 1688-1959* (Cambridge University Press). *Economic Journal.* G. FUA, *Notes on Italian Economic Growth 1861-1964* (Editore Giuffre, Milan). W. G. HOFFMAN, *Das Wachstum der Deutschen Wirtschaft seit der Mitte des 19 Jahrhunderts* (Springer-Verlag, Berlin). O. JOHANSSON, *The Gross Domestic Product of Sweden and its Composition 1861-1955.* S. KUZNETS, *Modern Economic Growth* (Yale University Press). O. LINDAHL, *Sveriges Nationalprodukt 1861-1951.* T. J. MARKO-VITCH, *L'industrie française de 1789 à 1964* (I.S.E.A., Paris). Scandinavian Economic History Review. J-C. TOUTAIN, *Le produit de l'agriculture française de 1700 à 1958* (I.S.E.A., Paris). W. WOODRUFF, *Impact of Western Man* (Macmillan).

POPULATION

TABLE I

Population of European Countries, 1750/1 to 1910/11

1914 boundaries except where otherwise stated (in millions)

N.B. If no figure is available for the 0/1 years, that for the nearest year available is shown, the date being indicated in brackets.

	1750/1	1800/1	1820/1	1830/1	1840/1	1850/1	1860/1	1870/1	1880/1	1890/1	1900/1	1910/1
Austria		—[2]	14·0	15·6	16·6	17·5	18·2('57)	20·4('69)	22·1	24·0	26·2	28·6
Hungary	3·5[2]	5·0[2]	—	—	—	13·2	—	15·4('69)	15·7	17·5	19·3	20·9
Bosnia-Herzegovina	—[3]											1·9
Belgium	2·2	3·1	—[3]	4·1	4·1	4·3('46)	4·5('56)	4·8('66)	5·3('76)	6·1	6·6	7·4
Bulgaria	—[3]								2·0[4]	3·3('93)	3·7	4·3
Denmark	—[3]	0·9	—	1·2('34)	1·3	1·4	1·5	1·8	2·0	2·2	2·5	2·8
Finland	0·4	0·8	1·2	1·4	1·4	1·6	1·7	1·8	2·1	2·4	2·7	2·9
France	21·0[6]	27·3[3]	30·5[3]	32·6[3]	34·2[3]	35·8[3]	37·4[3]	36·1('72)	37·7	38·3	39·0	39·6
Germany	—	—[3]	25·0	28·2	31·4	34·0	36·2	40·8	45·2	49·4	56·4	64·9
Great Britain	7·4[5]	10·5	14·1	16·3	18·5	20·8	23·1	26·1	29·7	33·1	37·0	40·8
Greece	—[3]	—[3]	—	0·8[3]	—	1·0[3]	—	1·5	2·0[3]	2·2[3]	2·4[2]('96)	2·8[2]('13)
Ireland	3·2('54)	4·8(1791)	6·8	7·8	8·2	6·6	5·8	5·4	5·2	4·7	4·5	4·4
Italy	16	19/17·2[2]	19·7('25)	21·2('33)	22·9('44)	24·4('52)	25·0	26·8	28·5	30·3	32·5	34·7
Netherlands	1·6	2·1	—	2·6('29)	2·9	3·1('49)	3·3('59)	3·6('69)	4·0('79)	4·5('89)	5·1('99)	5·9('09)
Norway	0·6	0·9	1·0	1·1	1·2	1·4	1·7('65)	1·8('75)	—	2·0	2·2	2·4
Portugal	2·3	2·9	—	—	3·7	3·5[3]	3·6('58)	—	4·2('78)	4·7	5·0	5·5
Romania	—[3]	—[3]	—	—	—	—	3·9('59)	4·8	—	5·0	6·0	7·2
Russia[9]	28	40/35·5	48·6	56·1	62·4	68·5	74·1	84·5	97·7	117·8	132·9	160·7
Poland	—	9·0	—	—	—	—	—	16·9	—	—	25·6	29·0

Serbia	—	—[a]	—	0·7[a]	—	1·1[2]('63)	1·4[3]('74)	1·9[4]('84)	2·2	2·5	2·9
Spain	8·2	10·5	14·6	—	15·7	16·2	16·6('77)	17·6('87)	18·6		20·0
Sweden	1·8	2·3	2·6	2·9	3·5	3·9	4·2	4·6	4·8	5·1	5·5
Switzerland	—	—	—	—	2·2('37) 2·4	2·5	2·7	2·8	2·9('88) 3·3		3·8

1. Germany and Austria together had the following population according to Colin Clark (op. cit. in sources): 1750 — 18·0m, 1800 — 23·0m. This presumably refers to the post 1918 boundaries.

2. Boundaries of the day, where these differ from those of 1914.

3. South-Eastern Europe had the following population according to Colin Clark (op. cit. in sources): 1750 — 8·0m. 1800 — 8·5m.

4. This excludes Eastern Roumelia.

5. Brownlee's estimate for England and Wales plus Webster's Scottish census figure for 1755.

6. This figure is for the 'old territories'. Total 1913 population, including territories added after the Balkan Wars, was 4·8m.

7. The first figure is shown on p. 64 of Colin Clark (op. cit. in sources), the second on pp. 106-7. There is no explanation of the discrepancy, but the second figure corresponds to that given in the Annuario Statistico Italiano (1878) and is comparable with those for later years.

8. This and subsequent figures do not include Madeira and the Azores, which had a population of 0·3m. in 1851.

9. It is not clear exactly what boundaries are implied here. The first two figures are attributed in the source to 'Russia in Europe', with Finland and Poland being shown separately. The later figures are probably supposed to cover the present boundaries of the Soviet Union.

SOURCES

Austria: Statistisches Jahrbuch der Österreichischen Monarchie (1881); Österreichisches Statistisches Handbuch (1915).

Hungary: COLIN CLARK, Population Growth and Land Use (London and New York, 1967), pp. 64 and 106-7 for 1750/1 to 1850/1; Ungarisches Statistisches Jahrbuch (1912) for later years.

Bosnia-Hercegovina: Österreichisches Statistisches Handbuch (1915).

Belgium: COLIN CLARK, op. cit. for 1750/1 and 1800/1; Annuaire Statistique de la Belgique (1912) for later years.

Bulgaria: The British Statistical Abstract (Foreign Countries) in Parliamentary Papers from 1874 onwards.

Denmark: Statistique Internationale du Mouvement de la Population (Statistique Générale de la France, Paris, 1907) for 1800/1 to 1900/1; the British Statistical Abstract (Foreign Countries) for 1910/1.

Finland: Suomen Tilastollinen Vuosikirja (1966).

France: COLIN CLARK, op. cit. for 1750/1; Annuaire Statistique de la France (1951) for later years.

Germany: Statistisches Jahrbuch für das Deutsches Reich (1913, modified by French census figures for 1860/1 and earlier so as to exclude Alsace-Lorraine.

Great Britain: B. R. MITCHELL and PHYLLIS DEANE, *Abstract of British Historical Statistics* (Cambridge, 1962).

Greece: COLIN CLARK, *op. cit.* for 1830/1 to 1860/1; the British *Statistical Abstract (Foreign Countries)* for later years.

Ireland: K. H. CONNELL, *The Population of Ireland, 1750-1845* (Oxford, 1950) for 1750/1 and 1800/1; B. R. MITCHELL and PHYLLIS DEANE, *op. cit.* for later years.

Italy: COLIN CLARK, *op. cit.* for 1750/1 and 1800/1; *Annuario Statistico Italiano* (1878-1914) for later years.

Netherlands: COLIN CLARK, *op. cit.* for 1750/1 and 1800/1; *Statistique Internationale du Mouvement de la Population* for 1820/1 to 1900/1; the British *Statistical Abstract (Foreign Countries)* for 1900/1.

Norway: M. DRAKE, 'The Growth of Population in Norway, 1735-1855', *Scandinavian Economic History Review*, vol. XIII, No. 1 (1965) for 1750/1 to 1850/1; the British *Statistical Abstract (Foreign Countries)* for later years.

Portugal: COLINK CLAR, *op. cit.* for 1750/1 to 1840/1; the British *Statistical Abstract (Foreign Countries)* for later years.

Romania: As for Greece.

Russia: COLIN CLARK, *op. cit.* for 1750/1 and first figure for 1800/1; P. A. KHROMOV, *Economic Development of Russia in the 19th and 20th Centuries, 1800-1917* (Moscow, 1950) for later figures.

Poland: COLIN CLARK, *op. cit.*

Serbia: COLIN CLARK, *op. cit.* for 1830/1; *Statistique Internationale du Mouvement de la Population* for 1860/1 to 1900/1; the British *Statistical Abstract (Foreign Countries)* for 1910/11.

Spain: The British *Statistical Abstract (Foreign Countries)* for 1860/1; COLIN CLARK, *op. cit.* for other years.

Sweden: *Historisk Statistisk för Sverige*, vol. I (Stockholm, 1955).

Switzerland: COLIN CLARK, *op. cit.* for 1840/1; *Annuaire Statistique de la Suisse* (1966) for later years.

POPULATION TABLE 2

Population of Major European Cities 1800–1910[1] (in thousands)

	1800	1850	1880	1910
Amsterdam	201	224	317	567
Barcelona	115	175	346	560
Berlin	172	419	1,122	2,071
Birmingham	71	233	401	526
Breslau	60	114	273	512
Brussels	—	251	421	720
Budapest	54	178	371	880
Cologne	50	97	145	516
Constantinople	600	—	—	1,200
Copenhagen	101	127	235	462
Dresden	60	97	221	547
Edinburgh	83	194	295	401
Genoa	100	120	180	272
Glasgow	77	345	587	784
Hamburg	130	132	290	932
Leipzig	30	63	149	588
Lisbon	180	240	187	436
Liverpool	82	376	553	746
London	1,117	2,685	4,770	7,256
Lyons	110	177	376	472
Madrid	160	281	398	572
Manchester	75	303	341	714
Marseilles	111	195	360	551
Milan	170	242	322	599
Moscow	250	365	612	1,481
Munich	40	110	230	595
Naples	350	449	494	723
Palermo	140	180	245	342
Paris	547	1,053	2,269	2,888
Prague	75	118	162	225
Rome	153	175	300	539
St. Petersburg	220	485	877	1,907
Stockholm	76	93	169	342
Turin	78	135	254	428
Vienna	247	444	726	2,030
Warsaw	100	100	252	856

1. Cities are shown if they had populations of 75,000 in 1800 or 500,000 in 1910. The figures are for censuses in or near to the years indicated.

SOURCES
British Cities: B. R. MITCHELL and PHYLLIS DEANE *Abstract of British Historical Statistics* (Cambridge, 1962).
Others: The French *Annuaire Statistique* (1966).

POPULATION TABLE 3

Emigration from Europe, 1861-1920 by decades (in thousands)

Country of Origin	1851-1860	1861-1870	1871-1880	1881-1890	1891-1900	1901-1910	1911-1920
Austria-Hungary	31	40	46	248	440	1,111	418
Belgium	1	2	2	21	16	30	[21][1]
Denmark	—	8	39	82	51	73	52
Finland	—	—	—	26	59	159	67
France	27	36	66	119	51	53	32
Germany	671	779	626	1,342	527	274	91
Italy	5	27	168	992	1,580	3,615	2,194
Netherlands	16	20	17	52	24	28	22
Norway	36	98	85	187	95	191	62
Portugal	45	79	131	185	266	324	402
Russia	—	—	58	288	481	911	420
Spain	3	7	13	572	791	1,091	1,306
Sweden	17	122	103	327	205	224	86
Switzerland	6	15	36	85	35	37	31
United Kingdom	[1,313][2][3]	[1,572][3]	[1,849][3]	3,259	2,149	3,150	2,587

1. Excluding 1913-18.
2. Excluding 1851-2.
3. Excluding Irish ports.

SOURCE
w. woodruff, *Impact of Western Man* (London, 1966).

AGRICULTURE

TABLE I

Output of Grain Crops—Selected Countries, Annual Averages (in million quintals)[1]

	Austria[2]	Hungary[2]	France[4]	Germany	Italy[4]	Russia[5]	Sweden	Gt. Brit.[3]	Ireland[3]
1701-10	—	—	59·1	—	—	—	—	27[6]	—
1751-60	—	—	61·5	—	—	—	—	29[6]	—
1771-80	—	—	75·6	—	—	—	—	33[6]	—
1781-90	—	—	85·3[7]	—	—	—	—	35[6]	—
1800-13	—	—	94·5[8]	—	—	268·6	5·0[9]	43[6]	—
1815-24	—	—	104·0	—	—	—	6·3[10]	49·5[7]	—
1825-34	—	—	116·3	—	—	—	7·9[11]	—	—
1835-44	49·4[13]	51·0[13]	131·4	—	—	310·1[14]	8·4[15]	—	—
1845-54	50·4[16]	50·2[17]	146·6	122·6[18]	—	363·3[21]	10·5[22]	64[19]	23·4[20]
1855-64	60·0[23]	68·1[23]	158·5	153·7	57·2[24]	381·2[25]	14·7[26]	68[19]	16·7
1865-74	56·5[27]	—	160·1	204·8	73·1	410·1[28]	15·6	70[19]	13·5
1875-84	59·3	[70·8][29]	161·8	248·4	72·8	451·0[30]	19·3	—	12·4
1885-94	66·2	102·6	160·1	304·6	63·1	515·4	21·7	56·9	11·2
1895-1904	69·0	112·8	172·1	391·0	73·2	479·3	22·4	52·5	10·8
1905-14	85·9	131·7[31]	171·9	457·9	88·8	543·1	26·1	51·7	11·3

E.I.S.

1. Where the figures were not given by weight in the sources, they were converted from the volume measure on the following basis:—Austria-Hungary — the average ratios of 1897; Great Britain and Ireland — the average ratios of 1910-39; Russia — by assuming that 1 hectolitre = 66 kilograms. Rice is not included.

2. The initial conversion to metric volume measures, where necessary, was on the basis of 1 metze = 0·615 hectolitres.

3. The initial conversion to metric measures was on the basis of 1 bushel = 0·364 hectolitres.

4. The six principal grain crops only.

5. The initial conversion to metric volume measures, where necessary, was on the basis of 1 chetvert = 0·2625 hectolitres. Figures given in poods were converted on the basis of 1 pood = 0·16388 quintals. All figures to 50 provinces of European Russia only.

6. These are very rough estimates for England and Wales only, and apply to the decades centred on the years 1710, 1750, 1780, 1790, 1810 and 1820.

7. Earlier figures exclude seed corn, and should be increased by about 15 per cent for comparison with later periods.

8. Average of 1803-12.
9. Average of 1802-14.
10. Average of 1815-22.

11. Average of 1823-32.
12. Average of 1842-4.
13. Estimate for 1844 only.
14. Average of 1834-40.
15. Average of 1833-42.
16. Average of 1845-7, 1851 and 1854.
17. Average of 1851 and 1854.
18. Average of 1846-54.
19. These are very rough estimates, based on cereal crop estimates for the United Kingdom. They were converted on the assumption that 1 hectolitre = 60 kilograms.
20. Average of 1847-54.
21. Average of 1841-8.
22. Average of 1843-55.
23. Average of 1857 and 1859.
24. Average of 1861-4.
25. Average of 1857-61.
26. Average of 1856-64.
27. Average of 1868-74 with 1872 missing.
28. Excluding 1867-9.
29. Excluding Croatia-Slavonia, the output of which amounted to approximately 7-8 million quintals.
30. Excluding 1879-82.
31. Average of 1905-15.

SOURCES

Austria: *Tafeln zur Statistik der Österreichischen Monarchie* (1842-59); *Statistisches Jahrbuch der Österreichischen Monarchie* (1863-81); *Österreichisches Statistisches Handbuch* (1880-1917).

Hungary: As for Austria, together with *Ungarisches Statistisches Jahrbuch* (1881-1915), and the British Agricultural Statistics continued in *Statistical Abstract (Foreign Countries)*, both in *Parliamentary Papers* for 1872 and 1875-80.

France: J-C. TOUTAIN, *Le Produit de l'Agriculture Française de 1700 à 1958* (Cahiers de l'I.S.E.A., 1961).

Germany: W. G. HOFFMAN, *Das Wachstum der Deutschen Wirtschaft seit der Mitte des 19 Jahrhunderts* (Berlin, Heidelberg, New York, 1965).
Italy: *Sommario di Statistiche Storiche Italiane 1861-1955*.
Russia: P. A. KHROMOV, *Economic Development of Russia in the 19th and 20th Centuries, 1800-1917* (Moscow, 1950).
Sweden: *Historisk Statistisk för Sverige*, vol. II.

Great Britain: PHYLLIS DEANE and W. A. COLE, *British Economic Growth, 1688-1959* (Cambridge, 1962) for 1700-1820; M. G. MULHALL, *Dictionary of Statistics* (4th edition, London, 1899) for 1840's to 1860's; B. R. MITCHELL and PHYLLIS DEANE, *Abstract of British Historical Statistics* (Cambridge, 1962) for later figures.
Ireland: B. R. MITCHELL and PHYLLIS DEANE, *op. cit.*

AGRICULTURE TABLE 2

Output of Potatoes—Selected Countries, Annual Averages (in million quintals)

	Austria[1]	Hungary[1]	France	Germany	Italy	Sweden	Gt. Britain	Ireland
1803-12	—	—	15·1	—	—	0·7[2]	—	—
1815-24	—	—	25·3	—	—	2·3[3]	—	—
1825-34	—	—	42·2	—	—	4·4[4]	—	—
1835-44	29·1[5]	—	63·3	—	—	5·6[6]	—	—
1845-54	27·2[7]	7·6[8]	49·8	108·7[9]	—	6·7[11]	—	42·9[10]
1855-64	31·0[12]	7·3[13]	68·8	153·7	9·4[18]	10·1[14]	—	38·5
1865-74	51·8[15]	8·9[16]	80·3	204·8	11·1	10·5[17]	—	33·1
1875-84	63·7	[23·2][18]	93·0	248·4	11·6	11·8	—	28·4
1885-94	67·7	28·2	118·0	304·6	11·5	12·5	32·3	27·6
1895-1904	102·0	40·8	106·2	391·0	16·4	12·5	32·7	26·7
1905-14	127·3	54·2[19]	117·9	457·9	26·5	16·0	36·7	31·5

1. Where the figures were given by volume, conversion was made on the basis of the 1897 overlap ratio of 1 hectolitre = 70·7 kilograms.

2. Average of 1802-14.

3. Average of 1815-22.

4. Average of 1823-32.

5. Average of 1842-4.

6. Average of 1833-42.

7. Average of 1845-7, 1851 and 1854.

8. Average of 1851 and 1854.

9. Average of 1846-54.

10. Average of 1847-54.

11. Average of 1843-55.

12. Average of 1857 and 1859.

13. Average of 1861-4.

14. Average of 1856-60.

15. Average of 1868-74, with 1872 missing.

16. 1872 only.

17. Average of 1866-74.

18. Excluding Croatia-Slavonia, the output of which was 1·4 million quintals in 1885.

19. Average of 1905-15.

SOURCES
As for TABLE 1.

AGRICULTURE TABLE 3

Output of Sugar or Sugar Beet—Selected Countries, Annual Averages (sugar in thousand metric tons, sugar beet in million quintals)

	Austria	Hungary	France		Germany		Italy	Russia	Sweden
	Sugar Beet	Sugar Beet	Sugar Beet	Sugar	Sugar Beet	Sugar	Sugar Beet	Sugar	Sugar Beet
1815-24	—	—	—	—	—	—	—	0.1	—
1825-34	—	—	—	—	—	—	—	0.5	—
1835-44	—	—	15.7[1]	26[3]	—	9[3]	—	2.7	—
1845-54	—	—	32.2[4]	52	6.7[5]	33	—	14.2	—
1855-64	21.9[7]	—	44.3[6]	102	15.8	99	—	40	—
1865-74	37.4	—	77.4	243	25.2	189	—	98	0.2[8]
1875-84	45.4	[6.7][9]	78.3	338	58.1	454	0.02[10]	213	0.2
1885-94	52.2	10.3	63.0	466	95.1	1,016	0.07	443	2.2
1895-1904		16.9	75.2	790	133.8	1,677	3.8	784	6.6
1905-14	64.3	31.0	78.8	706	160.9	1,981	14.6	1,292	9.2

SOURCES

As for TABLE 1, with the following additions:—
France: Sugar — Annuaire Statistique (1966).
Germany: Sugar — Statistisches Jahrbuch für das Deutsches Reich (1915), extended back by means of index in w. G. HOFFMAN, op. cit.

1. 1840 only.
2. Average of 1841-4.
3. Average of 1838-44.
4. 1852 only.
5. Average of 1846-54.
6. 1862 only.
7. Average of 1870-4, with 1872 missing.
8. Average of 1866-74.
9. Average of 1881-4 excluding Croatia-Slavonia, the output of which was negligible.
10. Average of 1877-84.

AGRICULTURE TABLE 4

Wine Output—Selected Countries, Annual Averages (in million hectolitres)

	Austria[1]	Hungary[1]	France	Germany[2]	Italy
1751-60	—	—	27·3	—	—
1771-80	—	—	29·8	—	—
1781-90	—	—	24·5	—	—
1803-12	—	—	35·4	—	—
1815-24	—	—	37·2	—	—
1825-34	—	—	40·2	—	—
1835-44	3·5[3]	16·4[4]	38·7	—	—
1845-54	4·1[5]	13·5[6]	47·9	1·9[7]	—
1855-64	6·2[8]	10·1[8]	48·4	2·0	21·0[9]
1865-74	2·6[10]	—	60·4	2·5	26·3
1875-84	3·7	4·6	46·0	2·5	28·1
1885-94	3·9	3·4	30·7	2·5	31·9
1895-1904	4·1	2·4	45·1	2·8	35·9
1905-14	4·7	4·5[11]	52·8	2·1	47·4

1. Converted, where necessary, on the basis of 1 eimer = 0·566 hectolitres.
2. Grape juice, not wine.
3. Average of 1842-4.
4. 1842 only.
5. Average of 1845-7, 1851, and 1854.
6. Average of 1851 and 1854.
7. Average of 1846-54.
8. Average of 1857 and 1859.
9. Average of 1861-4.
10. Average of 1868-74, with 1872 missing.
11. Average of 1905-11.

SOURCES
  As for TABLE 1.

AGRICULTURE TABLE 5

Output of Olives and Fruit—Italy, Annual Averages (in million quintals)

	Olives	Citrus Fruits	Grapes	Other Fresh Fruit
1861-4	15·8	2·5	35·7	3·9
1865-74	22·0	3·0	45·2	5·9
1875-84	19·5	4·9	48·0	6·2
1885-94	18·0	5·2	55·5	7·6
1895-1904	15·6	6·3	64·0	8·0
1905-14	11·4	9·2	79·8	10·5

SOURCES
  Sommario di Statistiche Storiche Italiane, 1861-1955.

AGRICULTURE TABLE 6

Output of Two Principal Rain Crops—Selected Countries, Annual Figures (in million quintals)[1]

	Austria		Hungary		France		Germany		Italy		Sweden[2]		Gt. Britain	
	Rye	Oats	Wheat	Maize	Wheat	Oats	Wheat	Rye	Wheat	Maize	Rye	Oats	Wheat	Oats
1815	—	—	—	—	29·6	17·1	—	—	—	—	1·7	1·1	—	—
1816	—	—	—	—	32·5	18·1	—	—	—	—	1·9	0·9	—	—
1817	—	—	—	—	36·0	19·2	—	—	—	—	1·6	1·1	—	—
1818	—	—	—	—	39·5	14·0	—	—	—	—	1·5	0·9	—	—
1819	—	—	—	—	44·9	18·5	—	—	—	—	2·0	0·9	—	—
1820	—	—	—	—	33·3	19·6	—	—	—	—	2·1	1·2	—	—
1821	—	—	—	—	43·7	20·4	—	—	—	—	—	—	—	—
1822	—	—	—	—	38·1	16·6	—	—	—	—	—	—	—	—
1823	—	—	—	—	44·0	20·4	—	—	—	—	—	—	—	—
1824	—	—	—	—	46·3	21·2	—	—	—	—	—	—	—	—
1825	—	—	—	—	45·8	15·8	—	—	—	—	—	—	—	—
1826	—	—	—	—	44·7	17·8	—	—	—	—	—	—	—	—
1827	—	—	—	—	42·6	19·9	—	—	—	—	—	—	—	—
1828	—	—	—	—	44·1	19·6	—	—	—	—	—	—	—	—
1829	—	—	—	—	48·2	19·6	—	—	—	—	—	—	—	—
1830	—	—	—	—	39·6	24·6	—	—	—	—	—	—	—	—
1831	—	—	—	—	42·3	25·0	—	—	—	—	—	—	—	—
1832	—	—	—	—	60·1	21·9	—	—	—	—	—	—	—	—
1833	—	—	—	—	49·6	20·1	—	—	—	—	—	—	—	—
1834	—	—	—	—	46·5	21·3	—	—	—	—	—	—	—	—
1835	—	—	—	—	53·8	23·2	—	—	—	—	—	—	—	—
1836	—	—	—	—	47·7	—	—	—	—	—	—	—	—	—
1837	—	—	—	—	50·9	—	—	—	—	—	—	—	—	—
1838	—	—	—	—	50·8	—	—	—	—	—	—	—	—	—

Agriculture Table 6 continued

	Austria		Hungary		France		Germany		Italy		Sweden		Gt. Britain	
	Rye	Oats	Wheat	Maize	Wheat	Oats	Wheat	Rye	Wheat	Maize	Rye	Oats	Wheat	Oats
1839	—	—	—	—	48·7	22·9	—	—	—	—	—	—	—	—
1840	—	—	—	—	60·7	—	—	—	—	—	—	—	—	—
1841	—	—	—	9·8	53·6	—	—	—	—	—	—	—	—	—
1842	16·2	12·4	12·5	—	53·5	—	—	—	—	—	—	—	—	—
1843	16·2	12·4	—	—	55·2	—	—	—	—	—	—	—	—	—
1844	16·2	12·4	—	—	61·8	—	—	—	—	—	—	—	—	—
1845	16·2	13·0	—	—	54·0	—	14·2	29·3	—	—	—	—	—	—
1846	16·1	12·7	—	—	45·5	—	19·4	63·3	—	—	—	—	—	—
1847	16·1	12·7	—	—	73·2	—	18·6	54·4	—	—	—	—	—	—
1848	—	—	—	—	66·0	—	19·0	56·5	—	—	—	—	—	—
1849	—	—	—	—	68·1	—	18·5	45·0	—	—	—	—	—	—
1850	—	—	9·3	9·6	66·0	—	17·5	43·2	—	—	—	—	—	—
1851	16·2	12·7	—	—	64·5	29·4	21·6	49·7	—	—	—	—	—	—
1852	—	—	—	—	71·4	—	18·4	47·3	—	—	—	—	—	—
1853	—	—	9·8	15·4	47·8	—	22·6	55·7	—	—	—	—	—	—
1854	17·2	12·4	—	—	72·9	—	15·2	38·9	—	—	—	—	—	—
1855	—	—	—	—	54·7	—	22·2	59·5	—	—	—	—	—	—
1856	—	—	—	—	64·0	—	24·6	60·6	—	—	—	—	—	—
1857	20·4	13·4	13·5	17·7	82·8	—	18·2	50·2	—	—	—	—	—	—
1858	—	—	—	—	82·5	—	21·1	46·9	—	—	—	—	—	—
1859	20·5	13·8	12·9	17·3	65·7	—	24·9	65·6	—	—	—	—	—	—
1860	—	—	—	—	76·2	—	23·3	53·7	32·9	14·4	4·4	5·4	—	—
1861	—	—	—	—	56·4	33·3	23·0	57·1	33·0	12·7	3·3	4·9	—	—
1862	—	—	—	—	82·4	—	25·0	65·4	34·9	16·2	4·4	6·4	—	—
1863	—	—	—	—	87·6	—	25·0	65·0	33·8	15·9	4·4	4·9	—	—
1864	—	—	—	—	83·4	—	—	—	—	—	5·0	5·9	—	—

Year														
1865	—	—	—	—	71.7	—	21.9	56.5	37.3	18.3	4.2	5.0	—	—
1866	—	—	—	—	63.8	—	22.2	52.6	39.4	20.1	4.3	6.0	—	—
1867	16.7	13.0	—	—	62.2	—	19.8	50.8	38.8	19.2	3.0	5.6	—	—
1868	16.5	12.1	—	—	87.6	—	28.5	75.0	43.1	24.0	4.0	4.0	—	—
1869	18.9	12.3	—	—	81.0	—	26.5	63.1	40.0	21.0	5.2	7.1	—	—
1870	18.2	13.9	—	—	74.2	—	24.1	62.5	40.4	18.6	5.5	7.6	—	—
1871	—	—	—	—	52.0	40.4	25.4	58.2	40.1	23.0	4.8	8.5	—	—
1872	19.4	11.6	—	—	90.6	35.7	27.5	62.5	38.6	25.0	4.3	6.3	—	—
1873	19.7	12.1	—	—	61.4	31.9	27.2	56.4	40.2	20.1	5.2	8.0	—	—
1874	16.0	11.0	—	—	99.8	33.6	32.7	70.5	39.2	25.5	5.0	4.9	—	—
1875	14.8	14.3	13.0[3]	21.0[3]	75.5	32.4	27.2	64.1	39.3	26.8	5.2	8.2	—	—
1876	19.4	13.1	13.7[3]	17.3[3]	71.6	28.7	25.6	57.7	38.1	29.7	5.0	6.9	—	—
1877	20.6	14.9	19.0[3]	15.0[3]	75.1	30.8	29.8	73.7	38.4	28.0	4.0	7.4	—	—
1878	15.5	13.1	28.7[8]	26.6[3]	71.5	36.6	35.0	81.9	36.7	23.9	5.2	9.1	—	—
1879	15.8	14.1	13.8[8]	17.1[3]	59.9	35.2	31.6	65.8	40.4	22.4	4.9	9.0	—	—
1880	19.6	14.5	21.0[3]	25.5[3]	75.5	39.9	32.4	58.6	47.0	20.9	5.7	9.2	—	—
1881	20.1	13.9	23.5[3]	21.2[3]	75.7	36.2	28.8	64.5	28.6	14.4	4.1	8.4	—	—
1882	16.7	14.5	34.8[8]	27.8[8]	98.7	40.8	34.4	71.1	42.6	18.9	5.2	10.4	—	—
1883	18.8	16.4	23.9[3]	22.6[3]	79.3	44.0	32.0	65.7	34.2	19.1	4.8	8.9	—	—
1884	19.4	14.4	28.3[6]	23.4	88.2	41.3	33.8	64.1	33.9	24.2	5.7	9.9	22.5	19.9
1885	18.7	17.2	31.6[8]	31.1[8]	85.2	40.6	35.1	68.9	32.2	21.4	5.6	8.7	21.8	19.7
1886	22.3	16.0	28.7	25.2	82.4	42.2	35.5	71.8	32.9	22.0	5.3	9.6	17.2	21.2
1887	20.0	16.0	40.0	21.8	87.1	37.6	37.5	75.4	34.7	21.2	5.8	10.1	20.8	19.5
1888	17.4	12.3	37.5	28.0	75.0	39.2	32.7	65.1	30.3	18.4	5.1	10.4	20.2	19.5
1889	19.8	15.9	26.1	29.7	83.2	39.9	30.4	63.2	29.9	20.8	5.5	7.7	20.5	20.6
1890	17.1	16.7	40.9	26.6	89.7	44.2	37.4	69.3	36.1	19.0	5.6	12.1	20.6	21.8
1891	20.5	17.1	38.6	41.8	58.8	49.7	31.0	56.4	38.9	18.4	5.8	9.6	20.2	20.4
1892	19.3	13.6	39.6	30.1	84.6	38.9	40.0	80.6	31.8	18.3	6.1	12.2	16.4	21.1
1893	—	—	44.2	38.9	75.6	28.6	39.3	89.4	37.2	21.0	6.4	9.7	13.8	20.5

Agriculture Table 6 continued

	Austria		Hungary		France		Germany		Italy		Sweden		Gt. Britain	
	Rye	Oats	Wheat	Maize	Wheat	Oats	Wheat	Rye	Wheat	Maize	Rye	Oats	Wheat	Oats
1894	20·8	16·7	39·9	20·8	93·7	42·7	38·8	83·4	34·4	15·1	4·7	11·8	16·6	24·6
1895	16·3	17·3	44·1	41·4	92·4	44·4	36·4	77·3	32·4	17·9	5·1	12·0	10·4	22·2
1896	18·8	16·0	42·2	37·9	92·6	43·0	38·5	85·3	39·9	20·3	6·3	9·4	16·0	20·7
1897	16·0	14·7	23·8	30·1	65·9	36·8	37·3	81·7	23·9	16·7	6·1	9·7	15·4	21·2
1898	20·3	18·7	38·1	37·6	99·3	46·7	41·2	90·3	37·8	20·2	5·4	12·2	20·5	21·6
1899	21·7	20·2	41·0	33·2	99·5	44·7	43·2	86·8	37·9	22·5	5·6	9·0	18·4	20·8
1900	13·9	17·1	41·5	37·2	88·6	41·4	43·1	85·5	39·0	23·6	6·7	11·9	14·8	20·8
1901	19·2	17·2	36·6	37·6	84·6	37·0	29·3	81·6	48·1	26·9	5·7	9·4	14·7	20·0
1902	21·0	18·2	49·8	30·4	89·2	46·4	43·7	94·9	39·9	19·0	5·8	9·6	15·9	23·7
1903	20·6	18·6	48·1	40·5	98·8	50·0	40·0	99·0	53·8	23·9	6·2	10·8	13·4	22·6
1904	23·3	15·9	40·0	18·0	81·5	42·2	42·6	100·6	49·0	24·3	5·4	8·7	10·3	23·1
1905	24·9	18·0	46·4	28·6	91·1	44·4	41·9	96·1	46·8	26·1	6·5	10·6	16·5	21·1
1906	25·2	22·4	56·5	46·6	89·5	42·8	44·0	96·3	51·5	24·9	6·9	11·9	16·6	22·4
1907	22·0	24·8	35·6	44·1	103·8	51·2	39·4	97·6	51·8	23·7	5·3	11·4	15·5	24·4
1908	28·8	20·9	45·0	42·3	86·2	47·5	42·1	107·4	44·5	25·7	6·7	12·7	14·7	22·4
1909	29·1	25·0	34·0	46·6	97·8	55·6	42·5	113·5	50·4	26·7	6·5	11·8	17·2	22·3
1910	27·7	20·6	49·3	54·2	88·8	48·2	42·5	105·1	40·6	27·3	6·2	12·9	15·4	22·1
1911	26·4	22·7	51·7	41·0	87·7	50·7	44·7	108·7	51·0	25·1	6·2	11·0	17·6	20·7
1912	29·7	24·3	50·3	51·0	91·0	51·5	47·7	115·5	43·9	26·5	5·9	12·7	15·7	19·9
1913	27·0	26·8	45·8	46·2	86·9	51·8	50·9	122·2	56·9	29·1	5·9	14·0	15·5	20·1
1914	18·9	19·2	28·6	43·8	—		43·4	104·3	44·9	28·2	6·8	8·1	17·1	20·6

3. These figures exclude Croatia-Slovenia.

1. See footnote 1 to TABLE 1.
2. Earlier Swedish figures are as follows:—

	Rye	Oats
1802	1·40	1·05
1803	1·67	0·85
1804	1·55	1·01
1805	1·58	1·00
1806	1·35	1·00
1807	1·60	0·93
1808	1·57	0·76
1809	2·06	1·05
1810	1·93	1·13
1811	1·56	1·00
1812	1·79	0·82
1813	1·81	0·83
1814	1·76	1·04

SOURCES

As for TABLE 1, except France — *Annuaire Statistique* (1951).

AGRICULTURE TABLE 7

Numbers of Farm Livestock—Selected Countries (in thousands)

The dates, especially up to 1870, are generally approximate

CATTLE	Austria	Hungary	France[1]	Germany[2]	Italy	Russia	Sweden[3]	Gt. Brit.[4]	Ireland[4]	Denmark[4]	N'lands
1840	4,984	5,607	11,762	—	—	—	1,700	—	1,863	828	—
1850	5,126	5,085	11,911	—	—	—	1,807	4,200	2,918	—	—
1860	8,013	5,647	11,813	14,999	3,230	—	1,987	—	3,606	1,121	1,252
1870	7,425	5,279	11,284	15,777	3,606	20,966	1,966	5,403	3,800	1,239	1,411
1880	8,584	5,311	11,446	—	4,505	22,122	2,228	5,912	3,922	1,470	1,470
1890	8,644	5,593	13,562	17,556	5,014	25,528	2,399	6,509	4,240	1,460	1,533
1900	9,511	6,738('95)	14,521	18,940	5,415	31,661	2,583	6,805	4,609	1,745	1,656
1910	9,160	7,153	14,532	20,159	6,337	31,315	2,748	7,037	4,689	2,254	2,027

SHEEP	Austria	Hungary	France[1]	Germany[2]	Italy	Russia	Sweden[3]	Gt. Brit.[4]	Ireland[4]	Denmark[4]	N'lands
1840	6,745	—	32,151	—	—	—	1,453	—	2,106	1,645	—
1850	5,639	10,688	33,282	—	—	—	1,547	—	2,122	—	—
1860	5,285	11,290	29,530	28,017	8,038	—	—	—	3,542	1,749	866
1870	5,026	15,077	24,590	—	6,975	44,171	1,595	28,398	4,337	1,842	900
1880	3,841	9,838	22,516	—	8,436	45,529	1,457	26,619	3,562	1,549	848
1890	3,187	—	21,658	13,590	6,900	46,052	1,351	27,272	4,323	1,225	819
1900	2,621	8,123('95)	20,180	9,692	7,478	47,628	1,261	26,592	4,387	1,074	881
1910	2,429	7,805	17,111	5,788	11,841	40,734	1,004	27,103	3,980	727	889

Agriculture Table 7 continued

PIGS	Austria	Hungary	France	Germany	Italy	Russia	Sweden	Gt. Britain	Ireland	Denmark	N'lands
1840	—	—	4,911	5,245	—	—	514	—	1,413	237	—
1850	2,156	4,959	5,246	5,735	—	—	555	—	928	—	271
1860	—	—	6,038	5,995	2,092	—	379	—	1,271	304	271
1870	2,551	4,443	5,377	8,549	1,618	9,391	354	2,171	1,461	442	329
1880	2,722	4,160	5,566	11,047	1,983	9,265	419	2,001	850	527	335
1890	3,550	—	6,017	12,174	1,800	9,554	654	2,774	1,570	771	579
1900	4,683	7,330('95)	6,740	16,807	2,008	11,761	806	2,382	1,269	1,168	747
1910	6,431	5,496	6,900	21,885	2,541	12,049	957	2,350	1,200	1,468	1,260

1. Earlier estimates for France include the following:—

	Cattle	Sheep	Pigs
circa 1780		32,000	—
circa 1790		20,000	4,000
circa 1810		35,190	3,900
circa 1830		29,030	—

		Cattle
England and Wales	1774	2,850
United Kingdom	1812	5,500
United Kingdom	1831	5,220
United Kingdom	1855	7,955

	Pigs	
	3,000	(original source — Campbell),
	4,050	(original source — Colquhoun).
		(original source — McCulloch),
	3,686	(original source — McCulloch),

2. Earlier estimates for Germany are as follows:—

	Pigs
1816	3,243
1822	3,593
1831	4,037

3. Earlier figures for Sweden are as follows:—

	Cattle	Sheep	Pigs
1805	1,468	1,214	—
1810	1,516	1,243	—
1818/22	1,510	1,341	471
1828/32	1,658	1,413	525

4. Earlier estimates derived from M. G. MULHALL, *Dictionary of Statistics* (4th edition, London, 1899) are as follows:—

SOURCES

As for TABLE 1, with the following additions:—
France: *Annuaire Statistique* (1917/19, 1951, 1966).
Germany: *Statistisches Jahrbuch für das Deutsche Reich* (1915).
Great Britain: BRAITHWAITE POOLE, *Statistics of British Commerce* (London, 1852).

AGRICULTURE TABLE 8

Value of Agricultural Output—Selected Countries, Annual Averages

	France[1]		Germany[2]		Italy[3]		Sweden[4]	U.K.[5]
	in million current francs	in million constant francs of 1905-14	in million current marks	in million constant marks of 1913	in million current lire	in million constant lire of 1938	in million current kroner	in million current pounds Sterling
1701-10	1,138	2,697	—	—	—	—	—	[19·3][6]
1751-60	1,333	3,187	—	—	—	—	—	[58·2][7]
1771-80	2,305	4,168	—	—	—	—	—	—
1781-90	2,497	4,411	—	—	—	—	—	75·5[8]
1803-12	3,294	5,054	—	—	—	—	—	107·5[8]
1815-24	3,758	5,065	—	—	—	—	—	76·0[9]
1825-34	4,335	5,692	—	—	—	—	—	79·5[8]
1835-44	4,494	6,550	—	—	—	—	—	99·9[8]
1845-54	5,287	7,212	2,623[9]	4,402	—	—	—	106·5[8]
1855-64	7,363	8,094	3,369	5,068	3,596[10]	19,769[10]	212[12]	118·8[8]
1865-74	8,387	7,887	4,538	5,997	5,208[11]	24,465[11]	261	130·4[8]
1875-84	7,821	7,705	5,331	6,898	5,399[11]	25,905[11]	326	109·1[8]
1885-94	7,212	8,000	5,887	8,051	5,158[11]	26,075[11]	320	110·8[8]
1895-1904	7,536	9,149	7,382	9,908	5,743[11]	29,539[11]	426	104·6[8]
1905-14	10,266	10,266	9,427	11,241	7,745[11]	34,948[11]	648	—

1. Gross agricultural output, less seed, fodder, expenses, etc.
2. Gross agricultural output, less seed, fodder, and wastage. 1913 boundaries throughout.
3. Gross saleable production of agriculture.
4. Gross agricultural output less products used in agriculture for further production.
5. Contribution of agriculture, forestry and fishing to gross national income.
6. Based on Gregory King's estimates for England and Wales for 1688 which are believed to understate the true figures — See Source, pp. 156-7.
7. Based on Arthur Young's estimates for England and Wales for *circa* 1770, which are believed to overstate the true figure — See the Source pp. 156-7.
8. Figures are for 1801, 1811, 1821, etc., to 1901.
9. Average of 1850-54.
10. Average of 1861-65.
11. Average of 1866-75, 1876-85, 1886-95, 1896-1905, 1906-15.
12. Average of 1861-4.

SOURCES

France: J-C. TOUTAIN, *Le Produit de l'Agriculture Française de 1700 à 1958* (Cahiers de l'I.S.E.A., 1961).

Germany: W. G. HOFFMAN, *Das Wachstum der Deutschen Wirtschaft seit der Mitte des 19 Jahrhunderts* (Berlin, Heidelberg, New York, 1965).

Italy: *Annali di Statistica*, serie VIII, vol. 9.

Sweden: O. JOHANSSON, *The Gross Domestic Product of Sweden and its Composition 1861-1955* (Stockholm, 1967).

United Kingdom: PHYLLIS DEANE and W. A. COLE, *British Economic Growth, 1688-1959* (Cambridge, 1962).

INDUSTRY

TABLE I

Indices of Industrial Production—Periodic Figures—1905-13=100

	Austria	France	Germany	Italy	Russia	Sweden[1]	United Kingdom
1751-60	—	—	—	—	—	—	2·3
1761-70	—	—	—	—	—	—	2·4
1771-80	—	—	—	—	—	—	2·7
1781-90	—	10·9	—	—	—	—	3·8
1791-1800	—	—	—	—	—	—	5·1
1801-14	—	12·3[a]	—	—	—	—	7·1
1815-24	—	16·3	—	—	—	—	9·5
1825-34	—	21·5	—	—	—	—	13·8
1835-44	—	28·5	11·7[4]	—	—	1·4[3]	19·8
1845-54	—	33·7	15·0	34·6[5]	—	2·2	27·5
1855-64	—	42·6	24·2	42·9	9·7[6]	4·1	36·6
1865-74	—	49·8	33·0	50·2	13·5	6·6	49·2
1875-84	39·1[7]	58·6	45·3	54·6	22·9	10·7	60·6
1885-94	52·5	68·2	68·9	64·8	38·7	16·8	70·5
1895-1904	74·4	82·7	—	—	72·7	58·4	85·2
1905-13	100	100	100	100	100	100	100

1. This is an index of the *value* of manufacturing production.

2. Average for 1803-12.
3. Average for 1836-44.
4. Average for 1850-4.
5. Average for 1861-4.
6. Average for 1860-4.
7. Average for 1880-4.

SOURCES

Austria: RICHARD L. RUDOLPH, 'The Role of Financial Institutions in the Industrialization of the Czech Crownlands, 1880-1914,' unpublished doctoral dissertation, Department of History, University of Wisconsin (1968), p. 23.

France: T. J. MARKOVITCH, *L'Industrie Française de 1789 à 1964* (Cahiers de l'I.S.E.A., 1966). Original base: 1938 = 100.

Germany: W. G. HOFFMAN, *Das Wachstum der Deutschen Wirtschaft seit der Mitte des 19 Jahrhunderts* (Berlin, Heidelberg, New York, 1965). Original base: 1913 = 100.

Italy: *Annali di Statistica*, serie VIII, vol. 9. Original base: 1938 = 100.

Russia: R. W. GOLDSMITH, 'The Economic Growth of Tsarist Russia, 1860-1913', *Economic Development and Cultural Change* (April 1961). Original base: 1900 = 100.

Sweden: *Historisk Statistisk för Sverige*, vol. III.

United Kingdom: W. G. HOFFMAN, *British Industry, 1700-1950* (Oxford, 1955). Original base: 1913 = 100.

INDUSTRY TABLE 2

Output of Coal and Lignite—Selected Countries, Annual Averages (in million metric tons)

	Austria	Hungary	France	Germany	Italy	Russia	Sweden[1]	U.K.	Belgium
1800	—	—	—	—	—	—	—	11.2	—
1811	—	—	0.8	—	—	—	—	—	—
circa 1815	—	—	0.9	1.2	—	—	—	16.2	—
1820-4	0.1	—	1.1[2]	1.2[2]	—	—	—	17.7[2]	—
1825-9	0.2	—	1.5[2]	1.6[2]	—	—	—	22.3[2]	—
1830-4	0.2	—	2.0	1.9	—	—	—	22.8[2]	2.4[3]
1835-9	0.3	—	2.9	3.0	—	—	—	28.1[2]	3.1
1840-4	0.5	—	3.5	4.4	—	—	—	34.2[2]	4.1
1845-9	0.8	0.02[4]	4.4	6.1	—	—	—	46.6[2]	5.1
1850-4	1.2	0.02[5]	5.3	9.2	—	—	—	50.2[2]	6.8
1855-9	2.2[2]	0.2[6]	7.6	14.7	—	—	—	67.8	8.6
1860-4	3.6	0.3[7]	10.0	20.8	0.04[8]	0.4	—	86.3	10.2
1865-9	5.3	0.5	12.7	31.0	0.05	0.5	—	104.7	12.5
1870-4	9.2[10]	0.7[9]	15.4	41.4	0.1	1.0	0.05	123.2	14.7
1875-9	12.3	—	17.0	49.9	0.1	2.2	0.09	135.7	14.7
1880-4	15.9	1.1	20.2	65.7	0.2	3.7	0.15	158.9	17.5
1885-9	19.8	1.3	21.5	78.1	0.3	5.0	0.18	167.9	18.4
1890-4	25.7	1.8	26.3	94.0	0.3	7.1	0.20	183.2	19.9
1895-9	30.6	2.5	30.6	120.1	0.3	11.0	0.24	205.1	21.5
1900-4	33.5	3.3	33.0	157.3	0.4	17.3	0.31	230.4	23.3
1905-9	38.7	4.0	36.4	201.2	0.5	23.7	0.29	260.2	24.8
1910-13	41.1	9.6	39.9	247.5	0.6	30.2	0.36	275.4	24.8

1. Figures are for 1871-5, 1876-80, etc.
2. Applies to beginning year of period indicated.
3. Average of 1831-4.
4. Average of 1842-4.
5. Average of 1845-7.
6. Average of 1851-4.
7. Average of 1855-7 and 1859.
8. Average of 1861-4.
9. Average of 1865-7.
10. Average of 1870-4 excluding 1872.

SOURCES

Austria: *Tafeln zur Statistik der Österreichischen Monarchie* (1842-59); *Übersichtstafeln zur Statistik der Österreichischen Monarchie für 1861 und 1862; Statistisches Jahrbuch der Österreichischen Monarchie* (1863-81); *Österreichisches Statistisches Handbuch* (1880-1915).

Hungary: *Tafeln zur Statistik der Österreichischen Monarchie* (1842-59); *Statisches Jahrbuch der Österreichischen Monarchie* (1863-81); *Ungarisches Statistisches Jahrbuch* (1881-1915).

France: T. J. MARKOVITCH, *L'Industrie Française de 1789 à 1964* (Cahiers de l'I.S.E.A., 1961) for 1811 and 1816; *Annuaire Statistique* (1951 and 1966) for later figures.

Germany: *Statistisches Jahrbuch für das Deutsches Reich*

Italy: *Sommario di Statistiche Storiche Italiane 1861-1955* (Rome, 1958).

Russia: P. A. KHROMOV, *Economic Development of Russia in the 19th and 20th Centuries, 1800-1917* (Moscow, 1950).

Sweden: *Historisk Statistisk för Sverige*, vol. III for figures to 1870; L. JÖRBERG, *Growth and Fluctuations of Swedish Industry, 1869-1912* (Lund, 1961) for 1870-1912 figures; British Iron & Steel Federation *Statistical Year Book* (1936) for 1913 figure.

United Kingdom: B. R. MITCHELL, forthcoming publication for figures to 1850; B. R. MITCHELL and PHYLLIS DEANE *Abstract of British Historical Statistics* (Cambridge, 1962) for later figures.

Belgium: A. WIBAIL, 'L'Évolution Économique de l'Industrie Charbonnière Belge depuis 1831', *Bulletin de l'Institut des Sciences Économiques*, vol. VI, no. 1 (1934).

INDUSTRY TABLE 3

Coal and Coke Imports—Selected Deficient Countries, Annual Averages (in thousand metric tons)

	France (net)	Italy (gross)	Sweden (gross)
1827-34	599	—	—
1835-44	1,298	—	51[1]
1845-54	2,748	—	63
1855-64	5,620	408[2]	263
1865-74	7,025	749	470
1875-84	9,007	1,764	904
1885-94	10,256	3,791	1,567
1895-1904	12,681	4,858	2,766
1905-13	18,392	8,892	4,401

1. Average of 1840-4.
2. Average of 1861-4.

SOURCES

France: *Annuaire Statistique* (1966).

Italy: *Sommario di Statistiche Storiche Italiane 1861-1955*.

Sweden: The British *Statistical Abstract* (*Foreign Countries*) and its predecessors, except for 1913, which comes from League of Nations, *International Trade and Balance of Payments*.

INDUSTRY TABLE 4

Output of Pig Iron—Selected Countries, Annual Averages (in thousand metric tons)

	Austria	Hungary	France	Germany[1]	Italy	Russia	Sweden	U.K.	Belgium
1781-90	—	—	141	—	—	—	—	69[2]	—
1791-1800	—	—	—	—	—	—	—	127[3]	—
1800-14	—	—	200[4]	—	—	200[5]	—	248[6]	—
1815-19	—	—	150	—	—	—	—	330[7]	—
1820-24	73[10]	—	212	75[8]	—	164[11]	—	418[9]	—
1825-29		—	244	90	—	167	—	669[12]	—
1830-34	103[15]	—	327	111	—	177[16]	—	700[13]	95[14]
1835-39		—	395	146	—	—	113[17]	1,142[18]	126
1840-44	118[19]	27[19]	488	160	—	184[20]	118[17]	1,465	97
1845-49	146	36[31]	561	184	—	200[28]	134[17]	1,784[31]	176
1850-54	173	48[23]	900	245	—	231	155[17]	2,716[34]	201
1855-59	226[35]	80[35]	1,065	422	—	254	171[17]	3,583	312
1860-64	216	93	1,262	613	25[26]	297	205[17]	4,219	366
1865-69	227	98[27]	1,211[38]	1,012	20	310	268[17]	4,984	469
1870-74	305	146	1,462	1,579	24	375	322	6,480	594
1875-79	283	135	1,918	1,770	19	424	346	6,484	484
1880-84	440	151	1,626	2,893	23	477	418	8,295	699
1885-89	540	217	1,998	3,541	13	616	452	7,784	766
1890-94	664	313	2,386	4,335	11	1,096	470	7,402	758
1895-99	888	420	2,665	5,974	11	1,981	505	8,777	966
1900-04	996	429	3,391	7,925	47	2,773	526	8,778	1,070
1905-09	1,359	467	4,664	10,666	142	2,799	554	9,855	1,388
1910-13	1,655	549		14,836	366	3,870	667	9,792	2,171

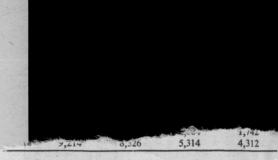

... 9,214   8,526   5,314   4,312

... Average of 1860, 1864 and 1865.
... Average of 1871-4.

... URCES

... weden output: *Historisk Statistisk för Sverige*, vol. **III**.
... weden exports and Spain output and exports: The British *Statistical* ...racts (*Foreign Countries*), except 1913 figure which came from the ...sh Iron and Steel Federation *Statistical Year Book* (1936).

	U.K.	Belgium
	—	—
	0.49[1]	0.09
	0.90	0.17
	1.82	0.21
	2.86	0.28
	3.19	0.61
	4.33	0.79
	5.04	1.37
	6.09	2.28
	6.93	

... *Reich* for later figures.

...istisk för Sverige, vol. **III** for ...wth and Fluctuations of Swedish ...d, 1961) for 1870-1912 figures; ...ure. ...S.F. *op. cit.*

1. 1914 boundaries throughout.
2. 1788 only.
3. 1796 only.
4. Average of 1803-12.
5. Average of 1800-13.
6. 1806 only.
7. 1818 only.
8. Average of 1823-24.
9. Average of 1820 and 1823.
10. Average of 1819-28.
11. 1825 only.
12. Average of 1825, 1827, and 1828.
13. Average of 1830 and 1833.
14. Average of 1831-34.
15. Average of 1829-38.
16. Average of 1835, 1836 and 1838.
17. Averages for 1836-40, 1841-5, etc., up to 1866-70.
18. Average of 1835 and 1839.
19. Average of 1841-44.
20. Average of 1841 and 1844.
21. Average of 1845 and 1847.
22. Average of 1846-49.
23. Average of 1851-54.
24. Average of 1850, 1852 and 1854.
25. Average of 1855-57 and 1859.
26. Average of 1861-64.
27. Average of 1865-67.
28. Alsace-Lorraine excluded after 1870.

SOURCES

Austria: *Tafeln zur Statistik der Österreichischen Monarchie* (1842-59); *Statistisches Handbüchlein für die Österreichische Monarchie* (1861); *Übersichtstafeln zur Statistik der Österreichischen Monarchie für 1861 und 1862*; *Statistisches Jahrbuch der Österreichischen Monarchie* (1863-81); *Österreichisches Statistisches Handbuch* (1808-1915).

Hungary: As for Austria, plus *Ungarisches Statistisches Jahrbuch* (1881-1915).

France: T. J. MARKOVITCH, *L'Industrie Française de 1789 à 1964* (Cahiers de l'I.S.E.A., 1966) for first three figures; *Annuaire Statistique* (1966) for later figures.

Germany: *Statistisches Jahrbuch für das Deutsches Reich.*

Italy: *Sommario di Statistiche Storiche Italiane 1861-1955.*

Russia: P. A. KHROMOV, *Economic Development of Russia in the 19th and 20th Centuries, 1800-1917* (Moscow, 1950).

Sweden: *Historisk Statistisk för Sverige*, vol. III for figures up to 1870; L. JÖRBERG, *Growth and Fluctuations of Swedish Industry, 1869-1912* (Lund, 1961) for 1870-1912 figures; British Iron and Steel Federation *Statistical Year Book* (1936) for 1913 figure.

United Kingdom: B. R. MITCHELL and PHYLLIS DEANE, *Abstract of British Historical Statistics* (Cambridge, 1962).

Belgium: A. WIBAIL, 'L'Évolution Économique de la Sidérurgie Belge de 1830 à 1913,' *Bulletin de l'Institut des Sciences Économiques*, vol. V, no. 1 (1933).

INDUSTRY TABLE 5

Output of Steel—Selected Countries, Annual Averages (in million metric tons)

	Austria-Hungary	France	Germany	Italy	Russia	Swede[n]
1867-9	—	—	—	—	—	0·03
1870-4	—	—	—	—	—	0·06
1875-9	—	0·26	—	—	0·08	0·1
1880-4	0·34	0·46	0·99	0·15[2]	0·25	0·20
1885-9	0·55	0·54	1·65	0·24	0·23	0·3
1890-4	0·96	0·77	2·89	0·22	0·54	
1895-9	1·16	1·26	5·08	0·24	1·32	
1900-4	1·74	1·70	7·71	0·32	2·35	
1905-9	2·45	2·65	11·30	0·65	2·63	
1910-13		4·09	16·24	0·98	4·20	

1. Average of 1871-4.
2. Average of 1882-4.

SOURCES

Austria-Hungary: British Iron and Steel Federation *Statistical Year Book* (1937).

France: *ibid* for figures to 1889; *Annuaire Statistique* (1966)

[Germany:] *Jahrbuch für das Deutsches...*

Italy: B.I.S.F. *op. cit.*

Russia: *ibid.*

Sweden: *Historisk Statistisk...* 1867-9; L. JÖRBERG, *Growth... Industry 1869-1912* (Lund...); B.I.S.F. *op. cit.* for 1913 fi[gure].

INDUSTRY TABLE 6

Output and Exports of Iron Ore—Spain and Sweden, Annual Averages (in thousand metric tons)

	Spain		Sweden	
	Output	Exports	Output	Exports
1836-45	—	—	255	—
1846-55	—	—	306	—
1856-65	207[1]	—	413	—
1866-74	635[2]	—	648	—
1875-84	2,667	2,256	797	—
1885-94	5,026	4,633	1,123	—
1895-1904	7,705	7,077	2,684	236
1905-13	9,214	8,3__	__4_	1,_1_

1.
2.

SOURCES
Sw...
Sw...
Abs[tract...]
Brit[ish...]

INDUSTRY TABLE 7

Output of Crude Oil—Selected Countries, Annual Averages (in thousand metric tons)

	Austria-Hungary	Germany[2]	Italy	Russia	Romania
1860-4	—	—	—	8[1]	3
1865-9	—	—	—	15	7
1870-4	—	—	—	44	13
1875-9	25	—	—	245	15
1880-4	45	6	—	764	19
1885-9	59	12	—	2,673	29
1890-4	96	16	2	4,799	71
1895-9	272	29	2	7,514	134
1900-4	554	65	3	10,794	362
1905-9	1,292	124	7	8,292	1,058
1910-13	1,367	131	8	9,120	1,675

1. Average of 1863-4.
2. Figures are for 1881-5, 1886-90, etc. to 1911-13.

SOURCES

Austria: The French *Annuaire Statistique* (1916-18).

Germany: *Statistisches Jahrbuch für das Deutsche Reich.*

Italy: *Sommario di Statistiche Storiche Italiane, 1861-1955* (Rome, 1958).

Russia: P. A. KHROMOV, *Economic Development of Russia in the 19th and 20th Centuries, 1800-1917* (Moscow, 1950).

Romania: As for Austria.

INDUSTRY TABLE 8

Imports of Petroleum—Selected Countries, Annual Averages (in thousand metric tons)

	Austria-Hungary[1]	France	Germany	Italy	Sweden	U.K.[2]
1855-64	—	16·9	—	[1·2][3]	[0·7][3]	7·6
1865-74	—	22·7	93·6	30·6	4·5	33·1
1875-84	103·7[4]	67·4	284·2	56·2	14·5	169·3
1885-94	133·6	193·2	623·6	80·3	37·0	431.3
1895-1904	316·3	232·2	914·0	80·4	74·9	935.5
1905-13	−3,504·3	121·7	1,015·4	103·7	138·5	1,397·6

1. Net imports or exports (–).
2. Converted from gallons on the basis: 1 ton =256 gallons.
3. 1864 only — none before.
4. Average of 1877-84.

SOURCES
Austria-Hungary: *Österreichisches Statistisches Handbuch* (1800-1917) and the British *Statistical Abstract* (*Foreign Countries*).
France: T. J. MARKOVITCH, *L'Industrie Française de 1789 à 1964* (Cahiers de l'I.S.E.A., 1966).
Germany: *Statistisches Jahrbuch für das Deutsches Reich.*
Italy: *Sommario di Statistiche Storiche Italiane, 1861-1955.*
Sweden: The British *Statistical Abstract* (*Foreign Countries*).
United Kingdom: *Annual Statement of Trade.*

INDUSTRY TABLE 9

Output of Electric Energy—Selected Countries, Annual Figures (in million kilowatt hours)

	France	Germany	Italy	Sweden	U.K.
1900	—	960	160	40	—
1901	340	1,280	220	80	—
1902	370	1,360	300	90	—
1903	425	1,600	400	120	—
1904	475	2,240	450	160	—
1905	530	2,640	550	160	—
1906	600	2,720	700	230	—
1907	670	3,200	950	330	1,432[1]
1908	750	3,920	1,150	360	—
1909	850	4,800	1,300	550	—
1910	1,020	5,370	1,500	780	—
1911	1,230	6,010	1,800	840	—
1912	1,480	7,370	2,000	1,230	—
1913	1,800	8,010	2,200	—	2,500[1]

1. Public supply only.

SOURCES

France: *Annuaire Statistique* (1966).

Germany: W. G. HOFFMAN, *Das Wachstum des Deutschen Wirtschaft seit der Mitte des 19 Jahrhunderts* (Berlin, Heidelberg, New York, 1965). The index was converted to output figures on the basis of *Statistisches Jahrbuch für das Deutsches Reich* (1926).

Italy: *Sommario di Statistiche Storiche Italiane 1861-1955*.

Sweden: L. JÖRBERG, *Growth and Fluctuations of Swedish Industry, 1869-1912* (Lund, 1961). The figures given are of capacity. These were converted on the basis of 1000 h.p. capacity = 2·993 million kwh.

United Kingdom: Census of Production for 1907; *Encyclopedia of Social Sciences* for 1913.

INDUSTRY TABLE 10

Raw Cotton Consumption—Selected Countries, Annual Averages (in thousand metric tons)

	Austria-Hungary	France	Germany	Italy	Russia	Sweden	U.K.
1751-60	—	—	—	—	—	—	1·3
1761-70	—	—	—	—	—	—	1·7
1771-80	—	—	—	—	—	—	2·3
1781-90	—	4·0	—	—	—	—	8·1
1791-1800	—	—	—	—	—	—	13·9
1801-14	—	8·0[1]	—	—	0·9[1]	—	31·8
1815-24	—	18·9	—	—	1·0	—	54·8
1825-34	6·8[2]	33·5	3·9[4]	—	1·8	—	105·6
1835-44	14·3	54·3	11·1[5]	—	6·1	1·1[6]	191·6
1845-54	26·5	65·0	21·1[5]	—	21·5	3·1	290·0
1855-64	32·7	74·1	42·0[7]	[1·8][8]	34·3	5·1	369·4
1865-74	40·8	85·9	85·6	11·2	53·1	6·4	475·8
1875-84	67·1	99·5	134·3	30·7	109·6	9·1	605·0
1885-94	96·9	127·0	208·2	73·2	158·3	12·7	691·8
1895-1904	135·4	174·0	309·3	125·7	251·7	16·7	747·7
1905-13	191·4	231·1	435·4	186·0	352·2	20·4	868·8

INDUSTRY TABLE 5

Output of Steel—Selected Countries, Annual Averages (in million metric tons)

	Austria-Hungary	France	Germany	Italy	Russia	Sweden	U.K.	Belgium
1867-9	—	—	—	—	—	0·03	—	—
1870-4	—	—	—	—	—	0·06	0·49[1]	—
1875-9	—	0·26	—	—	0·08	0·13	0·90	0·09
1880-4	—	0·46	0·99	0·15[2]	0·25	0·20	1·82	0·17
1885-9	0·34	0·54	1·65	0·24	0·23	0·30	2·86	0·21
1890-4	0·55	0·77	2·89	0·22	0·54	0·39	3·19	0·28
1895-9	0·96	1·26	5·08	0·24	1·32	0·45	4·33	0·61
1900-4	1·16	1·70	7·71	0·32	2·35	0·49	5·04	0·79
1905-9	1·74	2·65	11·30	0·65	2·63	0·55	6·09	1·37
1910-13	2·45	4·09	16·24	0·98	4·20	0·62	6·93	2·28

1. Average of 1871-4.
2. Average of 1882-4.

SOURCES

Austria-Hungary: British Iron and Steel Federation *Statistical Year Book* (1937).

France: *ibid* for figures to 1889; *Annuaire Statistique* (1966) for later figures.

Germany: B.I.S.F. *op. cit.* for 1880-4 figures; *Statistisches Jahrbuch für das Deutsche, Reich* for later figures.

Italy: B.I.S.F. *op. cit.*

Russia: *ibid.*

Sweden: *Historisk Statistisk för Sverige*, vol. III for 1867-9; L. JÖRBERG, *Growth and Fluctuations of Swedish Industry 1869-1912* (Lund, 1961) for 1870-1912 figures; B.I.S.F. *op. cit.* for 1913 figure.

United Kingdom: B.I.S.F. *op. cit.*

Belgium: *ibid.*

INDUSTRY TABLE 6

Output and Exports of Iron Ore—Spain and Sweden, Annual Averages
(in thousand metric tons)

	Spain		Sweden	
	Output	*Exports*	*Output*	*Exports*
1836-45	—	—	255	—
1846-55	—	—	306	—
1856-65	207[1]	—	413	—
1866-74	635[2]	—	648	—
1875-84	2,667	2,256	797	—
1885-94	5,026	4,633	1,123	236
1895-1904	7,705	7,077	2,684	1,742
1905-13	9,214	8,326	5,314	4,312

1. Average of 1860, 1864 and 1865.
2. Average of 1871-4.

SOURCES

Sweden output: *Historisk Statistisk för Sverige*, vol. III.

Sweden exports and Spain output and exports: The British *Statistical Abstracts* (*Foreign Countries*), except 1913 figure which came from the British Iron and Steel Federation *Statistical Year Book* (1936).

SOURCES

Austria: *Tafeln zur Statistik der Österreichischen Monarchie* (1842-59); *Statistisches Handbüchlein für die Österreichische Monarchie* (1861); *Übersichtstafeln zur Statistik der Österreichischen Monarchie für 1861 und 1862; Statistisches Jahrbuch der Österreichischen Monarchie* (1863-81); *Österreichisches Statistisches Handbuch* (1808-1915).

Hungary: As for Austria, plus *Ungarisches Statistisches Jahrbuch* (1881-1915).

France: T. J. MARKOVITCH, *L'Industrie Française de 1789 à 1964* (Cahiers de l'I.S.E.A., 1966) for first three figures; *Annuaire Statistique* (1966) for later figures.

Germany: *Statistisches Jahrbuch für das Deutsches Reich*.

Italy: *Sommario di Statistiche Storiche Italiane 1861-1955*.

Russia: P. A. KHROMOV, *Economic Development of Russia in the 19th and 20th Centuries, 1800-1917* (Moscow, 1950).

Sweden: *Historisk Statistisk för Sverige*, vol. III for figures up to 1870; L. JÖRBERG, *Growth and Fluctuations of Swedish Industry, 1869-1912* (Lund, 1961) for 1870-1912 figures; British Iron and Steel Federation *Statistical Year Book* (1936) for 1913 figure.

United Kingdom: B. R. MITCHELL and PHYLLIS DEANE, *Abstract of British Historical Statistics* (Cambridge, 1962).

Belgium: A. WIBAIL, 'L'Évolution Économique de la Sidérurgie Belge de 1830 à 1913,' *Bulletin de l'Institut des Sciences Économiques*, vol. V, no. 1 (1933).

1. 1914 boundaries throughout.
2. 1788 only.
3. 1796 only.
4. Average of 1803-12.
5. Average of 1800-13.
6. 1806 only.
7. 1818 only.
8. Average of 1823-24.
9. Average of 1820 and 1823.
10. Average of 1819-28.
11. 1825 only.
12. Average of 1825, 1827, and 1828.
13. Average of 1830 and 1833.
14. Average of 1831-34.
15. Average of 1829-38.
16. Average of 1835, 1836 and 1838.
17. Averages for 1836-40, 1841-5, etc., up to 1866-70.
18. Average of 1835 and 1839.
19. Average of 1841-44.
20. Average of 1841 and 1844.
21. Average of 1845 and 1847.
22. Average of 1846-49.
23. Average of 1851-54.
24. Average of 1850, 1852 and 1854.
25. Average of 1855-57 and 1859.
26. Average of 1861-64.
27. Average of 1865-67.
28. Alsace-Lorraine excluded after 1870.

INDUSTRY TABLE 4

Output of Pig Iron—Selected Countries, Annual Averages (in thousand metric tons)

	Austria	Hungary	France	Germany[1]	Italy	Russia	Sweden	U.K.	Belgium
1781-90	—	—	141	—	—	—	—	69[2]	—
1791-1800	—	—	—	—	—	—	—	127[3]	—
1800-14	—	—	200[4]	—	—	200[5]	—	248[6]	—
1815-19	—	—	} 150	—	—	—	—	330[7]	—
1820-24	} 73[10]			75[8]	—	—	—	418[9]	—
1825-29			212	90	—	164[11]	—	669[12]	—
1830-34	} 103[15]		244	111	—	167	—	700[13]	95[14]
1835-39			327	146	—	177[16]	113[17]	1,142[18]	126
1840-44	118[19]	27[19]	395	160	—	184[20]	118[17]	1,465	97
1845-49	146	36[21]	488	184	—	200[22]	134[17]	1,784[21]	176
1850-54	173	48[23]	561	245	—	231	155[17]	2,716[24]	201
1855-59	226[25]	80[25]	900	422	—	254	171[17]	3,583	312
1860-64	216	93	1,065	613	25[26]	297	205[17]	4,219	366
1865-69	227	98[27]	1,262[28]	1,012	20	310	268[17]	4,984	469
1870-74	305	146	1,211[28]	1,579	24	375	322	6,480	594
1875-79	283	135	1,462	1,770	19	424	346	6,484	484
1880-84	440	151	1,918	2,893	23	477	418	8,295	699
1885-89	540	217	1,626	3,541	13	616	452	7,784	766
1890-94	664	313	1,998	4,335	11	1,096	470	7,402	758
1895-99	888	420	2,386	5,974	11	1,981	505	8,777	966
1900-04	996	429	2,665	7,925	47	2,773	526	8,778	1,070
1905-09	1,359	467	3,391	10,666	142	2,799	554	9,855	1,388
1910-13	1,655	549	4,664	14,836	366	3,870	667	9,792	2,171

1. Average of 1803-12.
2. Average of 1812-14.
3. Average of 1828-34.
4. Average of 1832-4.
5. Average of 1836-45 and 1846-55.
6. Average of 1840-4.
7. Average of 1856-64.
8. Average of 1862-4, which were affected by the American Civil War. M. G. MULHALL, *Dictionary of Statistics* (4th edition, London 1899) gives the following annual averages for earlier decades: 1821-30 = 1·0, 1831-40 = 3·0, 1841-50 = 5·0, and 1851-60 = 90.

SOURCES

Austria-Hungary: Based on annual figures compiled by DR. NACHUM T. GROSS from *Tafeln zur Statistik der Österreichischen Monarchie*, *Statistisches Jahrbuch der Öster-reichischen Monarchie*, and *Österreichisches Statistisches Handbuch*. The original units were converted on the basis 1 Wiener centner = 0·56 metric centner, and 1 Zoll centner = 0·5 metric centner.

France: T. J. MARKOVITCH, *L'Industrie Française de 1789 à 1964* (Cahiers de l'I.S.E.A., 1966).

Germany: *The Cambridge Economic History of Europe*, vol. VI, part I, p. 394 for 1832-4 figures; *Statistisches Jahrbuch für das Deutsches Reich* for other figures.

Italy: The British *Statistical Abstract (Foreign Countries)* for figures up to 1912; *International Yearbook of Agricultural Statistics 1909 to 1921* for 1913 figure.

Russia: P. A. KHROMOV, *Economic Development of Russia in the 19th and 20th Centuries, 1800-1917* (Moscow, 1950).

Sweden: As for Italy.

United Kingdom: B. R. MITCHELL and PHYLLIS DEANE, *Abstract of British Historical Statistics* (Cambridge, 1962).

INDUSTRY TABLE II

Cotton Spindles—Selected Countries, Annual Figures (in thousands)

	Austria-Hungary	France	Germany	Italy	Russia	Gt. Brit.[1]	Belgium	Switz'land
1834	800	2,500	626('36)	—	700('40)	10,000	200	580
1852	1,400	4,500	900	—	—	18,000	400	900
1861	1,800	5,500	2,235	—	1,00('57)	31,000	612	1,350
1867	1,500	6,800	2,000[2]	450	—	34,000	625	1,000
1877	1,558	5,000[2]	4,700[2]	880	2,500	39,500	800	1,850
1882/3	1,950	4,800	4,800	1,150	4,400	42,800	840	1,900
1891/2	2,400	5,040	6,071	1,686	6,000	40,500	930	1,722
1904	3,450	6,150	8,434	2,435	6,000	43,900	880	1,600
1913	4,909	7,400	11,186	4,600	9,212	55,700	1,492	1,398

1. Doubling spindles included up to 1867.
2. Alsace-Lorraine transferred from France to Germany in 1871.

SOURCES

1834 to 1867: D. S. LANDES in The Cambridge Economic History of Europe, vol. VI, part I, except 1840 Russia from M. G. MULHALL, Dictionary of Statistics (4th Edition, London, 1899), 1857 Russia from S. J. CHAPMAN, The Cotton Industry and Trade (London, 1905), and 1867 Italy from L'Industria Tessile Cotoniera in Italia dai suoi Inizi ad Oggi (Rome, 1952).

1877: Annali di Statistica series II, vol. 13.

1882/3: T. ELLISON, The Cotton Trade of Britain (London, 1886).

1891/2: F. MERTTENS, in Transactions of the Manchester Statistical Society (April, 1894).

1904: S. J. CHAPMAN, op. cit., except Great Britain, which came from Reports of H.M. Inspectors of Factories for 1903.

1913: J. A. TODD, The Cotton World (London, 1927).

Woollen and Worsted Industry Indicators—Selected Countries, Annual Averages (in thousand metric tons except where otherwise indicated)

| | Austria-Hungary | | France | | | Germany | | | Italy | | United Kingdom[a] | | |
	Output Raw Wool[b]	Net Imports of Raw Wool	Output Raw Wool	Net Imports of Raw Wool	Output of Wool Hosiery and Cloth	Output Raw Wool	Net Imports of Raw Wool	Index of Wool Cloth Output 1913=100	Output Raw Wool	Imports of Raw Wool	Output Raw Wool	Net Imports of Raw Wool	Index of Wool Cloth Output 1913=100
1751-60	—	—	—	—	—	—	—	—	—	—	—	—	9·8
1761-70	—	—	—	—	—	—	—	—	—	—	—	—	10·2
1771-80	—	—	[48]	—	—	—	—	—	—	—	36[3]	0·1[3]	11·0
1781-90	—	—	—	6·0	7·8	—	—	—	—	—	—	—	12·3
1791-1800	—	—	[351/30·0]	—	—	—	—	—	—	—	{41[4]}	1·3[4]	13·7
1801-14	—	—	38·0	6·0	9·9	—	—	—	—	—	45[5]	4·6[5]	16·2
1815-24	—	—	48·0	5·8	13·8	12·7[6]	—	—	—	—	50[7]	7·8[7]	18·7
1825-34	—	—	58·1	8·4	17·1	18·1	2·0[8]	7·9[9]	—	—	53	13·1	22·7
1835-44	(31)	−4·8[10]	64·3	17·4	22·8	25·3[9]	3·0[8]	12·1	—	—	56	20·3	26·2
1845-54	(27)	−1·6[11]	66·6	24·0	26·9	28·2[8]	5·1[8]	16·3	—	—	60	28·8	29·5
1855-64	(29)	−2·2	60·0	50·4	34·8	31·1[6]	7·1[8]	25·5	7·3[13]	5·1[12]	65	42·4	33·2
1865-74	(35)	1·7	47·3	99·5	44·9	35·2[13]	15·2	37·1	7·1	5·4	72	73·1	48·3
1875-84	(22)	10·0	45·7	138·2	55·2	30·1[14]	42·7[8]	49·3	9·6	8·2	66	89·6	59·2
1885-94	(20)	17·5	52·3	177·2	72·2	23·8[15]	123·2	78·8	9·9	9·9	64	129·6	65·0
1895-1904	(19)	25·5	40·1	203·0	74·4	17·1[16]	154·7	93·0	10·8	13·3	62	154·1	71·1
1905-13	(19)	35·2	34·4	219·3	79·2	15·0	175·7	100·3	14·6	21·7	52	180·6	89·1

1. Rough estimates based on figures in the sources and on the number of sheep and the average yield per sheep. The 1905-13 figure is from 'The Textile Mercury's' *Wool Year Book* (1908-14).

2. England and Wales to 1780, Great Britain from 1782 to 1819. The Hoffman index of cloth output is based up to 1820 solely on Yorkshire production.

3. 1755 only.

4. Average of 1776-99.

5. Average of 1800-19.

6. Average of 3 or 4 years in each period, at intervals of 3 years.

7. Average of 1820-4.

8. Averages of 1821-30, 1831-40, etc. to 1871-80.

9. Average.

10. Average of 1831-40.

11. Excluding 1849.

12. Average of 1861-4.

13. Average of 1867 and 1872.

14. 1882 only.

15. 1892 only.

16. Average of 1900 and 1904.

SOURCES

Austria-Hungary: *Tafeln zur Statistik der Österreichischen Monarchie* (1842-59); *Statistisches Jahrbuch der Österreichischen Monarchie* (1863-81); *Übersichtstafeln zur Statistik der Österreichischen Monarchie für 1861 und 1862*; *Österreichisches Statistisches Handbuch* (1880-1917); *Ungarisches Statistisches Jahrbuch* (1881-1915).

France: Figures in brackets from 1771-80 and 1781-90 from J-C. TOUTAIN, *Le Produit de l'Agriculture Française de 1700 à 1958* (Cahiers de l'I.S.E.A., 1961); others from T. J. MARKOVITCH, *L'Industrie Française de 1789 à 1964* (Cahiers de l'I.S.E.A., 1966).

Germany: Net imports from M. G. MULHALL, *Dictionary of Statistics* (4th edition, London, 1899) and *Statistisches Jahrbuch für das Deutsche Reich*; other figures from W. G. HOFFMAN, *Das Wachstum der Deutschen Wirtschaft seit der Mitte des 19 Jahrhunderts* (Berlin, Heidelberg, New York, 1965).

Italy: *Sommario di Statistiche Storiche Italiane 1861-1955*.

United Kingdom: Index of cloth output from W. G. HOFFMAN, *British Industry 1700-1950* (Oxford, 1955); other figures from B. R. MITCHELL and PHYLLIS DEANE, *Abstract of British Historical Statistics* (Cambridge, 1962).

INDUSTRY TABLE 13

Linen and Jute Industry Indicators—Selected Countries, Annual Averages (in thousand metric tons)

	Austria-Hungary		France			Germany	United Kingdom	
	Flax and Hemp Input	Jute Input	Flax and Hemp Input	Jute Input	Linen and Hemp Cloth Output	Linen Yarn Output	Flax and Hemp[1] Input	Jute Input[1]
1761-70	—	—	—	—	—	—	40.0	—
1771-80	—	—	—	—	—	—	47.5	—
1781-90	—	—	77.5	—	46.2	—	54.8	—
1791-1800	—	—	73.0[3]	—	44.6[3]	—	72.4	—
1801-14	—	—	80.0	—	48.4	—	86.4	—
1815-24	—	—	96.5	—	57.8	—	92.7	—
1825-34	—	—	104.4	—	69.3	—	101.8	—
1835-44	—	—	—	0.2	—	—	137.4	—
1845-54	148.5[2]	—	97.8	1.4	63.7	358[4]	156.8	13.5[5]
1855-64	147.4[5]	—	109.7	11.6	74.3	351	148.6	45.2
1865-74	160.4[6]	—	103.2	23.2	83.4	349	177.6	118.9
1875-84	137.3	9.1	91.4	32.4	81.5	327	165.7	180.0
1885-94	141.4	23.3	61.3	54.3	64.6	285	156.0	215.5
1895-1904	153.2	40.2	39.5	79.8	61.9	263	158.3	223.6
1905-13	166.3	50.8	32.7	98.8	65.3	224	175.6	224.7

1. Small quantities of jute were included with flax and hemp before 1851.
2. Average of 1803-12.
3. Average of 1851 and 1854.
4. Average of 1850-54.
5. Average of 1857, 1859 and 1863.
6. Average of 1866 and 1867. This figure includes a small amount of jute.

SOURCES
Austria-Hungary: *Tafeln zur Statistisk der Österreichischen Monarchie* (1851-59); *Statistisches Jahrbuch Österreichischen Monarchie* (1863-80); *Österreichisches Statistisches Handbuch* (1880-1917); *Ungarisches Statistisches Jahrbuch* (1881-1915); the *British Statistical Abstract (Foreign Countries)*.

France: T. J. MARKOVITCH, *L'Industrie Française de 1789 à 1964* (Cahiers de l'I.S.E.A., 1966).

Germany: The 1913 figure of flax consumption (production plus net imports) was taken from the *Statistiches Jahrbuch für das Deutsches Reich*, converted to yarn by the method described in W. G. HOFFMAN *Das Wachstum der Deutschen Wirtschaft seit der Mitte des 19 Jahrhunderts* (Berlin, Heidelberg, New York, 1965), p. 367 and then extended backwards by the index on pp. 368-370.

United Kingdom: The 1913 figure of flax consumption (production plus net imports) was taken from the *Annual Statement of Trade* and *Agricultural Statistics*, and extended backwards by means of the linen yarn (= flax consumption less a fixed proportion) index in W. G. HOFFMAN, *British Industry 1700-1950* (Oxford, 1955). Hemp and jute consumption (i.e. net imports) were taken from E. B. SCHUMPTER, *English Overseas Trade Statistics 1697-1800* (Oxford, 1960), the *Return Relating to Flax and Hemp* in P.P. 1854 LXV and similar previous returns, and the *Annual Statement of Trade*.

INDUSTRY TABLE 14

Silk Industry Indicators—Selected Countries, Annual Averages (in thousand metric tons unless otherwise indicated)

	France			Germany	Italy	United Kingdom[1]
	Output of Raw Silk	Net Imports of Raw and Thrown Silk	Output of Silk Hosiery and Cloth	Index of Silk Industry Output 1913 = 100	Output of Raw Silk	Net Imports of Raw and Thrown Silk
1751-60	6·6	—	—	—	—	0·3
1761-70	—	—	—	—	—	0·4
1771-80	6·6	—	—	—	—	0·4
1781-90	6·2	0·5	0·9	—	—	0·5
1791-1800	—	—	—	—	—	0·5
1801-14	5·0[a]	0·2	0·6	—	—	0·6
1815-24	5·0	0·5	1·2	—	—	1·0
1825-34	7·8	0·9	1·5	—	—	1·8
1835-44	13·3	1·2	2·4	7·6[b]	—	2·6
1845-54	18·6	2·5	4·0	11·6	—	3·0
1855-64	11·9	3·3	4·4	15·9	16·6[c]	3·6
1865-74	11·8	4·8	4·8	28·0	39·5	3·1
1875-84	7·7	3·7	4·9	40·4	33·7	3·2
1885-94	7·8	4·0	5·6	56·0	45·1	4·0
1895-1904	7·9	1·7	5·7	78·5	53·6	3·8
1905-13	6·8	1·1	6·5	103·7	43·5	4·1

1. England and Wales to 1780; Great Britain from 1781 to 1814.
2. Average of 1803-12.
3. Average of 1837-44.
4. Average of 1861-4.

SOURCES

France: 1751-60 and 1771-80 — J-C. TOUTAIN, *Le Produit de l'Agriculture Française de 1700 à 1958* (Cahiers de l'I.S.E.A., 1961); later periods, T. J. MARKOVITCH, *L'Industrie Française de 1789 à 1964* (Cahiers de l'I.S.E.A., 1966).

Germany: W. G. HOFFMAN, *Das Wachstum der Deutschen Wirtschaft seit der Mitte des 19 Jahrhunderts* (Berlin, Heidelberg, New York, 1965).

Italy: *Sommario di Statistiche Storiche Italiane, 1861-1955*.

United Kingdom: B. R. MITCHELL and PHYLLIS DEANE, *Abstract of British Historical Statistics* (Cambridge, 1962).

RAILWAYS

TABLE I

Length of Line Open at Decennial Intervals—All European Countries 1914 boundaries except where otherwise indicated (in kilometres)

	1840	1850	1860	1870	1880	1890	1900	1910
Austria-Hungary	144	1,579	4,543	9,589	18,507	26,519	36,330	43,280
Belgium	334	903	1,730	2,897	4,112	4,526	4,591	4,679
Bulgaria[1]	—	—	223	223	534	803	1,565	1,931
Denmark	—	30	109	770	1,584	2,005	2,914	3,445
Finland[1]	—	—	107	483	885	1,928	2,931	3,651
France	497	2,915	9,167	15,544[3]	23,089	33,280	38,109	40,484
Germany	469	5,856	11,089	18,876[3]	33,838	42,869	51,678	61,209
Great Britain	2,390	9,797	14,603	21,558[4]	25,060	27,827	30,079	32,182
Ireland	21	865	2,195	3,201[4]	3,816	4,496	5,125	5,476
Italy	20	620	2,404	6,429	9,290	13,629	16,429	18,090
Netherlands	17	176	335	1,419	1,846	2,633	2,776	3,215
Norway	—	—	68	359	1,057	1,562	1,981	2,976
Portugal	—	—	67	694	1,144	2,118	2,168[5]	2,888[6]
Romania	—	—	66	316	1,384	2,494	3,100	3,437
Russia[1]	27	501	1,626	10,731	22,865	30,596	53,234	66,581
Serbia	—	—	—	—	—	541	570	929
Spain	—	28	1,917	5,442	7,490	10,002	13,214	14,675
Sweden	—	—	527	1,727	5,876	8,018	11,303	13,829
Switzerland	—	25	1,051	1,426	2,575	3,243	3,867	4,716

1. All figures are for 1861, 1871, 1881, etc.

2. Excluding Alsace-Lorraine. The 1869 figure including Alsace-Lorraine is 16,465 km.

3. Excluding Alsace-Lorraine. The 1871 figure including Alsace-Lorraine is 21,471 km.

4. 1871 figure.

5. This figure, given in the source, does not seem to be compatible with a figure of 2,362 km. for 1899 which was supplied to me by the Institute Nacional de Estatistica.

6. 1911 figure.

SOURCES

Austria-Hungary: Information for Austria supplied by Österreichisches Statistisches Zentralamt; Hungary from *Statistisches Nachrichten über die Eisenbahnender Öster-reichisch-Ungarischen Monarchie* (1890-1) and the British *Stasical Abstract (Foreign Countries)*.

Belgium: G. STÜRMER, *Geschichte der Eisenbahnen* (Bromberg, 1872) for 1840; the British *Statistical Abstract (Foreign Countries)* for later years.

Bulgaria: The French *Annuaire Statistique*, 1951.

Denmark: Information supplied by Danmark Statistik.

Finland: As for Bulgaria.

France: 1840 figure from information supplied by the Institut National de la Statistique et des Études Economiques, others from *Annuaire Statistique* (1951).

Germany: G. STÜRMER, *op. cit.* for 1840-1860; information supplied by Statistisches Bundesamt for later years.

Great Britain: B. R. MITCHELL and PHYLLIS DEANE *Abstract of British Historical Statistics*.

Ireland: As for Great Britain. 1840 figure derived from U.K. total by B. R. MITCHELL.

Italy: *Sommario di Statistiche Storiche Italiane 1861-1955*.

Netherlands: Information supplied by N. V., Nederlandse Spoorwegen.

Norway: Information supplied by Statistisk Sentralbyrå.

Portugal: The British *Statistical Abstract (Foreign Countries)*.

Romania: As for Bulgaria.

Russia: P. A. KHROMOV, *Economic Development of Russia in the 19th and 20th Centuries 1800-1917* (Moscow, 1950).

Serbia: *Statesman's Year Book*.

Spain: G. STÜRMER, *op. cit.* for 1850; the British *Statistical Abstract (Foreign Countries)* for later years.

Sweden: Information supplied by Statistiska Central-byrån.

Switzerland: As for Portugal.

RAILWAYS TABLE 2

Length of Line Open at End of Each Year—Selected Countries 1914 boundaries except where otherwise indicated (in kilometres)

	Austria-Hungary	France	Germany	Great Britain	Ireland	Italy	Russia	Sweden
1825	—	—	—	43	—	—	—	—
1826	—	—	—	61	—	—	—	—
1827	—	—	—	66	—	—	—	—
1828	—	17	—	72	—	—	—	—
1829	—	17	—	82	—	—	—	—
1830	—	31	—	157	—	—	—	—
1831	—	31	—	225		—	—	—
1832	—	52	—	267		—	—	—
1833	—	73	—	335		—	—	—
1834	—	141	—	480		—	—	—
1835	—	141	6	544		—	—	—
1836	—	141	6	649		—	—	—
1837	14	159	21	870		—	—	—
1838	32	159	140	1,196		—	27	—
1839	144	224	240	1,562		8	—	—
1840	144	410	469	2,390	21	20	—	—
1841	351	548	683	2,858		20	—	—
1842	378	645	931	3,122		49	—	—
1843	378	743	1,311	3,291		82	—	—
1844	473	822	1,752	3,600		133	—	—

Railways Table 2 continued

	Austria-Hungary	France	Germany	Great Britain	Ireland	Italy	Russia	Sweden
1845	728	875	2,143		3,931[1]	152	144	—
1846	935	1,049	3,281		4,889[1]	259	278	—
1847	1,209	1,511	4,306		6,352[1]	286	368	—
1848	1,249	2,004	4,989	8,022	585	379	382	—
1849	1,428	2,467	5,443	8,918	795	564	—	—
1850	1,579	2,915	5,856	9,797	865	620	501	—
1851	1,748	3,248	6,143	10,090	1,005	702	1,004	—
1852	1,748	3,654	6,605	10,673	1,140	705	—	—
1853	1,806	3,954	7,141	10,958	1,343	808	1,049	—
1854	1,912	4,315	7,571	11,525	1,444	1,081	—	—
1855	2,145	5,037	7,826	11,744	1,589	1,207	—	—
1856	2,448	5,852	8,617	12,318	1,702	1,360	1,170	66
1857	2,929	6,868	8,991	12,919	1,725	1,580	—	209
1858	3,653	8,094	9,650	13,452	1,913	1,777	—	326
1859	4,030	8,840	10,593	14,069	2,037	2,236	1,336	447
1860	4,543	9,167[a]	11,089	14,603	2,195	2,404[a]	1,626	527
1861	5,018	9,626	11,497	15,210	2,291	2,773	2,238	571
1862	5,263	10,522	12,048	16,027	2,573	3,109	3,516	908
1863	5,461	11,533	12,651	17,038	2,803	3,725	3,521	1,014
1864	5,499	12,362	13,114	17,704	2,889	4,162	3,616	1,143
1865	5,858	13,227	13,900	18,439	2,960	4,591	3,842	1,305
1866	6,125	13,915	14,787	19,234	3,074	5,258	4,573	1,567
1867	6,430	15,000	15,679	19,837	3,105	5,559	5,038	1,687
1868	7,166	15,835	16,316	—	—	5,933	6,786	1,687

1869	8,009	16,465	17,215	—	—	6,124	8,166	1,727
1870	9,589	15,544	18,876	—	—	6,429	10,731	1,727
1871	11,752	15,632	21,471[a]	21,558	3,201	6,710	13,641	1,817
1872	13,883	17,438	22,426	22,097	3,367	7,044	14,360	1,935
1873	15,597	18,139	23,890	22,513	3,383	7,223	16,206	2,321
1874	16,110	18,744	25,487	23,062	3,425	7,707	18,220	3,361
1875	16,753	19,357	27,970	23,365	3,459	8,018	19,029	3,679
1876	17,479	20,034	29,305	23,695	3,473	8,422	19,623	4,298
1877	18,016	20,534	30,718[5]	23,951	3,547	8,664	21,092	4,837
1878	18,201	21,435	31,471	24,273	3,638	8,755	22,371	5,193
1879	18,432	22,249	33,250	24,815	3,679	8,898	22,680	5,677
1880	18,507	23,089	33,838	25,060	3,816	9,290	22,865	5,876
1881	18,914	24,249	34,381	25,336	3,931	9,506	23,091	6,170
1882	19,724	25,576	35,081	25,751	3,969	9,753	23,429	6,305
1883	20,579	26,692	35,993	26,052	4,029	10,149	24,145	6,400
1884	21,867	28,722	36,780	26,309	4,066	10,591	25,007	6,600
1885	22,351	29,839	37,571	26,720	4,146	11,003	26,024	6,890
1886	22,984	30,696	38,525	26,891	4,238	11,823	27,345	7,277
1887	24,296	31,446	39,785	27,220	4,306	12,277	28,240	7,388
1888	25,205	32,128	40,827	27,501	4,401	13,037	29,428	7,527
1889	25,981	32,914	41,793	27,619	4,494	13,537	29,933	7,888
1890	26,519	33,280	42,869	27,827	4,496	13,629	30,596	8,018
1891	27,543	33,878	43,424	27,902	4,610	13,964	30,723	8,279
1892	27,810	34,881	44,177	28,067	4,662	14,487	31,202	8,461
1893	28,500	35,350	44,340	28,429	4,816	15,004	32,870	8,782
1894	29,436	35,971	45,462	28,765	4,902	15,492	35,206	9,234
1895	30,341	36,240	46,500	28,986	5,109	15,970	37,058	9,756
1896	31,600	36,472	47,433	29,144	5,117	16,053	39,546	9,896
1897	33,060	36,934	48,449	29,411	5,101	16,243	41,585	10,226

Railways Table 2 continued

	Austria-Hungary	France	Germany	Great Britain	Ireland	Italy	Russia	Sweden
1898	34,486	37,255	49,830	29,762	5,114	16,352	44,622	10,360
1899	35,708	37,494	50,702	29,828	5,114	16,407	49,870	10,708
1900	36,330	38,109	51,678	30,079	5,125	16,429	53,234	11,303
1901	36,795	38,274	52,933	30,385	5,166	16,451	56,452	11,574
1902	37,346	38,547	53,843	30,495	5,175	16,723	57,599	11,951
1903	38,072	39,105	54,775	30,860	5,266	16,825	58,362	12 362
1904	38,438	39,363	55,817	31,139	5,307	16,912	59,616	12,543
1905	39,124	39,607	56,739	31,456	5,333	17,078	61,085	12,647
1906	40,270	39,775	57,584	31,722	5,415	17,380	63,623	13,088
1907	40,645	39,963	58,291	31,796	5,414	17,583	65,500	13,248
1908	41,556	40,186	59,241	31,951	5,415	17,723	65,919	13,364
1909	42,632	40,285	60,389	32,026	5,460	17,913	66,345	13,604
1910	43,280	40,484	61,209	32,184	5,476	18,090	66,581	13,829
1911	43,729	40,635	61,978	32,223	5,478	18,394	68,027	13,942
1912	44,335	40,838	62,734	32,266	5,480	18,632	68,954	14,171
1913	44,748	40,770	63,378	32,623	5,491	18,873	70,156[6]	14,377

1. At 30 June.
2. 104 km. of Savoy railways transferred from Italy to France.
3. Excluding Alsace-Lorraine.
4. Including Alsace-Lorraine.
5. This and subsequent figures are for 31 March in the year following that indicated.
6. By this date there was a further 1,590 km., the exact date of construction of which was (and is) unknown.

SOURCES

As for TABLE 1, with French figures to 1841 from information supplied by the Institut National de la Statistique et des Études Économiques.

OVERSEAS TRADE

TABLE I

Values of Imports and Exports (excluding transit trade)—Selected Countries

	Austria-Hungary (in million kronen)		France (in million francs)		Germany (in million marks)		Italy (in million lire)		Russia (in million paper roubles)		Sweden (in million kronor)		United Kingdom (in million £)		
	Imports	Exports	Imports	Exports	Imports	Exports	Imports	Exports	Imports	Exports	Imports	Exports	Imports	Domestic Exports	Re-exports
1796	—	—	—	—	—	—	—	—	—	—	—	—	39·6	30·1	8·5
1797	—	—	—	—	—	—	—	—	—	—	—	—	34·4	27·5	9·3
1798	—	—	—	—	—	—	—	—	—	—	—	—	49·6	32·2	11·3
1799	—	—	—	—	—	—	—	—	—	—	—	—	50·9	36·8	9·4
1800	—	—	—	—	—	—	—	—	—	—	—	—	62·3	37·7	14·7
1801	—	—	—	—	—	—	—	—	—	—	—	—	68·7	40·6	12·9
1802	—	—	—	—	—	—	—	—	45·8	63·3	—	—	54·7	45·9	12·9
1803	—	—	—	—	—	—	—	—	44·5	67·1	—	—	53·9	36·9	9·1
1804	—	—	—	—	—	—	—	—	42·7	59·0	—	—	57·3	38·2	11·0
1805	—	—	—	—	—	—	—	—	46·1	72·4	—	—	61·0	38·1	10·0
1806	—	—	—	—	—	—	—	—	43·3	62·6	—	—	53·3	40·9	9·2
1807	—	—	—	—	—	—	—	—	33·2	53·6	—	—	53·8	37·2	8·3

Overseas Trade Table 1 continued

	Austria-Hungary (in million kronen)		France (in million francs)		Germany (in million marks)		Italy (in million lire)		Russia (in million paper roubles)		Sweden (in million kronor)		United Kingdom (in million £)		
	Imports	Exports	Imports	Exports	Imports	Exports	Imports	Exports	Imports	Exports	Imports	Exports	Imports	Domestic Exports	Re-exports
1808	—	—	—	—	—	—	—	—	—	—	—	—	51·5	37·3	6·5
1809	—	—	—	—	—	—	—	—	—	—	—	—	73·7	47·4	14·3
1810	—	—	—	—	—	—	—	—	—	—	—	—	88·5	48·4	12·5
1811	—	—	—	—	—	—	—	—	—	—	—	—	50·7	32·9	6·7
1812	—	—	—	—	—	—	—	—	76·4	139·3	—	—	56·0	41·7	9·1
1813	—	—	—	—	—	—	—	—	121·5	132·4	—	—	—	—	—
1814	—	—	—	—	—	—	—	—	113·1	194·1	—	—	80·8	45·5	24·8
1815	—	—	—	—	—	—	—	—	113·8	219·4	—	—	71·3	51·6	16·8
1816	—	—	—	—	—	—	—	—	129·3	200·2	—	—	50·2	41·7	12·6
1817	—	—	—	—	—	—	—	—	167·2	294·6	—	—	61·0	41·8	10·1
1818	—	—	—	—	—	—	—	—	181·2	255·9	—	—	80·7	46·5	12·3
1819	—	—	—	—	—	—	—	—	177·1	215·1	—	—	56·0	35·2	10·2
1820	—	—	—	—	—	—	—	—	245·2	222·5	—	—	54·2	36·4	10·4
1821	—	—	—	—	—	—	—	—	208·0	200·1	—	—	45·6	36·7	9·5
1822	—	—	—	—	—	—	—	—	156·5	188·2	—	—	44·6	37·0	7·8
1823	—	—	—	—	—	—	—	—	160·4	197·7	—	—	52·0	35·4	7·2
1824	—	—	—	—	—	—	—	—	178·7	205·3	—	—	51·2	38·4	7·5

Year											Average		Average			
1825	—	—	—	—	—	—	—	—	191·3		244·6			73·6	38·9	8·2
1826	—	—	—	—	—	—	—	—	193·5		190·3			50·4	31·5	7·3
1827	—	—	414	507	—	—	—	—	207·9		238·3			58·8	37·2	6·8
1828	—	—	454	511	—	—	—	—	200·9		206·4			57·3	36·8	6·5
1829	—	—	483	504	—	—	—	—	215·9		226·8			54·1	35·8	6·6
1830	—	—	489	453	—	—	—	—	198·1		272·3			55·9	38·3	5·6
1831	131	152	374	456	—	—	—	—	177·0		244·2			62·0	37·2	6·7
1832	151	170	505	507	—	—	—	—	196·0		261·0			52·5	36·5	7·3
1833	155	174	491	560	—	—	—	—	193·1		249·3			58·9	39·7	6·9
1834	154	164	504	570	—	—	—	—	218·1		228·9			64·7	41·6	8·0
1835	175	169	520	577	—	—	—	—	222·8		226·7			68·0	47·4	9·2
1836	190	184	565	629	—	—	—	—	237·3		282·4		⎧	84·4	53·3	9·3
1837	186	171	569	514	—	—	—	—	251·8		263·5		⎪	70·1	42·1	9·0
1838	197	201	657	659	—	—	—	—	247·7	26·0	312·9	26·8	⎨	80·1	50·1	9·2
1839	197	202	651	677	—	—	—	—	249·2 ⎱		341·2 ⎱		⎪	90·8	53·2	10·2
1840	212	206	747	695	—	—	—	—	78·1 ⎰		85·4 ⎰		⎩	91·2	51·4	10·0
1841	203	214	805	761	—	—	—	—	80·8		89·3		⎧	83·9	51·6	9·9
1842	212	207	847	644	—	—	—	—	84·6		85·0		⎪	76·4	47·4	8·4
1843	224	208	846	687	—	—	—	—	75·0	27·5	82·2	30·6	⎨	71·0	52·3	7·8
1844	230	219	867	790	—	—	—	—	78·5		93·4		⎪	78·9	58·6	8·0
1845	233	215	856	848	—	—	—	—	83·2		92·2		⎩	88·4	60·1	9·3
1846	253	212	920	852	—	—	—	—	87·0		102·4		⎧	87·3	57·8	9·2
1847	256	224	956	720	—	—	—	—	89·2		148·3		⎪	112·1	58·8	11·7
1848	167	93	474	690	—	—	—	—	90·8	33·6	88·0	37·6	⎨	88·2	52·8	8·4
1849	176	119	724	938	—	—	—	—	96·2		95·9		⎪	101·4	63·6	12·1
1850	307	252	791	1,068	—	—	—	—	93·9		98·1		⎩	103·0	71·4	12·0
1851	301	260	765	1,158	—	—	—	—	103·7		97·4		⎱	109·5	74·4	12·5
1852	399	373	989	1,257	—	—	—	—	100·9		114·8		⎰	110·0	78·1	13·0

Overseas Trade Table 1 continued

	Austria-Hungary (in million kronen)		France (in million francs)		Germany (in million marks)		Italy (in million lire)		Russia (in million paper roubles)		Sweden (in million kronor)		United Kingdom (in million £)		
	Imports	Exports	Imports	Exports	Imports	Exports	Imports	Exports	Imports	Exports	Imports	Exports	Imports	Domestic Exports	Re-exports
1853	466	498	1,196	1,542	—	—	—	—	102·3	147·7	53·3	60·5	148·5	98·9	16·8
1854	418	436	1,292	1,414	—	—	—	—	70·4	65·3			152·4	97·2	18·6
1855	473	465	1,594	1,558	—	—	—	—	72·7	39·5			143·5	95·7	21·0
1856	574	503	1,990	1,893	—	—	—	—	122·6	160·3			172·5	115·8	23·4
1857	558	483	1,873	1,866	—	—	—	—	151·7	169·7	79·8 (Average)	73·2 (Average)	187·8	122·1	24·1
1858	617	551	1,563	1,887	—	—	—	—	149·4	151·2			164·6	116·6	23·2
1859	536	585	1,641	2,266	—	—	—	—	159·3	165·7			179·2	130·4	25·3
1860	462	610	1,897	2,277	—	—	—	—	159·7	181·4			210·5	135·9	28·6
1861	472	615	2,442	1,926	—	—	791	478	167·1	177·2	109	68	217·5	125·1	34·5
1862	430	668	2,199	2,243	—	—	800	577	152·9	180·4	99	77	225·7	124·0	42·2
1863	525	606	2,426	2,643	—	—	865	634	154·7	154·5	99	85	248·9	146·6	50·3
1864	545	703	2,528	2,924	—	—	941	574	175·3	186·7	98	85	275·0	160·4	52·2
1865	558	730	2,642	3,088	—	—	925	558	164·3	209·2	107	95	271·1	165·8	53·0
1866	490	761	2,794	3,181	—	—	836	617	205·3	222·9	114	93	295·3	188·9	50·0
1867	589	815	3,027	2,826	—	—	849	740	265·3	244·8	136	110	275·2	181·0	44·8
1868	775	858	3,304	2,790	—	—	858	787	260·9	226·6	137	103	294·7	179·7	48·1
1869	841	876	3,153	3,075	—	—	893	792	342·0	264·4	136	112	295·5	190·0	47·1

1870	872	791	2,867	2,802	—	857	756	335·9	360·0	143	129	303·3	199·6	44·5
1871	1,082	935	3,567	2,873	—	924	1,076	368·5	369·3	163	144	331·0	223·1	60·5
1872	1,228	776	3,570	3,762	—	1,131	1,166	435·2	327·0	207	187	354·7	256·3	58·3
1873	1,166	847	3,555	3,787	—	1,229	1,133	443·0	364·4	261	207	371·3	255·2	55·8
1874	1,255	1,006	3,508	3,701	—	1,244	980	471·4	431·8	297	208	370·1	239·6	58·1
1875	1,099	1,102	3,537	3,873	—	1,516	1,024	531·1	382·0	260	196	373·9	223·5	58·1
1876	1,069	1,190	3,989	3,576	—	1,273	1,211	477·6	400·7	281	209	375·2	200·6	56·1
1877	1,111	1,333	3,680	3,436	—	1,107	936	321·0	527·9	298	208	394·4	198·9	53·5
1878	1,104	1,309	4,176	3,180	—	1,021	1,027	595·6	618·2	230	179	368·8	192·8	52·6
1879	1,113	1,368	4,595	3,231	—	1,208	1,087	587·7	627·8	212	172	363·0	191·5	57·3
1880	1,227	1,352	5,033	3,468	2,923	1,147	1,112	622·8	498·7	270	217	411·2	223·1	63·4
1881	1,284	1,463	4,863	3,561	3,029	1,192	1,165	517·7	506·4	280	208	397·0	234·0	63·1
1882	1,308	1,563	4,822	3,574	3,224	1,188	1,152	566·8	617·8	292	241	413·0	241·5	65·2
1883	1,250	1,500	4,804	3,452	3,259	1,239	1,188	562·2	640·3	324	240	426·9	239·8	65·6
1884	1,225	1,383	4,343	3,232	3,190	1,275	1,071	536·9	589·9	317	222	390·0	233·0	62·9
1885	1,116	1,344	4,088	3,088	2,854	1,403	951	435·4	537·9	332	227	371·0	213·1	58·4
1886	1,078	1,397	4,208	3,249	2,974	1,401	1,028	426·5	484·1	291	212	349·9	212·7	56·2
1887	1,137	1,346	4,026	3,246	3,137	1,526	1,002	399·6	617·3	286	226	362·2	221·9	59·3
1888	1,066	1,458	4,107	3,247	3,207	1,117	897	386·1	784·0	317	253	387·6	234·5	64·0
1889	1,178	1,532	4,317	3,704	3,165	1,317	954	432·0	750·9	367	270	427·6	248·9	66·7
1890	1,221	1,543	4,437	3,753	3,327	1,261	899	406·7	692·2	371	267	420·7	263·5	64·7
1891	1,226	1,573	4,768	3,570	3,176	1,073	879	371·6	707·4	361	280	435·4	247·2	61·9
1892	1,244	1,445	4,188	3,461	2,954	1,120	959	399·5	475·6	346	279	423·8	227·2	64·4
1893	1,340	1,611	3,854	3,236	3,092	1,139	967	449·6	599·2	318	290	404·7	218·3	58·9
1894	1,400	1,591	3,850	3,078	2,961	1,042	1,033	553·6	668·8	341	294	408·3	216·0	57·8
1895	1,445	1,484	3,720	3,374	3,318	1,131	1,047	526·1	689·1	339	307	416·7	226·1	59·7
1896	1,412	1,548	3,799	3,401	3,525	1,125	1,057	585·5	688·6	357	324	441·8	240·1	56·2
1897	1,511	1,532	3,956	3,598	3,635	1,114	1,096	560·0	729·7	399	344	451·0	234·2	60·0
1898	1,640	1,615	4,472	3,511	5,081	1,311	1,210	617·5	732·7	446	323	470·5	233·4	60·7

Year															
1899	1,609	1,862	4,518	4,153	5,483	1,407	4,207	1,436	660·5	627·0	503	346	485·0	264·5	65·0
1900	1,696	1,942	4,698	4,109	5,766	1,592	4,611	1,348	626·4	716·2	526	375	523·1	291·2	63·2
1901	1,653	1,886	4,369	4,013	5,421	1,631	4,431	1,385	593·4	761·6	460	335	522·0	280·0	67·8
1902	1,720	1,914	4,394	4,252	5,631	1,633	4,678	1,467	599·2	860·2	502	364	528·4	283·4	65·8
1903	1,877	2,130	4,802	4,252	6,003	1,730	5,015	1,490	681·7	1,001·2	530	398	542·6	290·8	69·9
1904	2,048	2,089	4,502	4,451	6,354	1,787	5,223	1,573	651·4	1,006·4	572	374	551·0	300·7	70·3
1905	2,146	2,244	4,779	4,867	7,129	1,938	5,732	1,704	635·1	1,077·3	574	407	565·0	329·8	77·8
1906	2,341	2,380	5,627	5,265	8,022	2,396	6,359	1,902	800·7	1,094·9	638	457	607·9	375·6	85·1
1907	2,502	2,457	6,223	5,596	8,749	2,751	6,846	1,938	847·4	1,053·0	674	470	645·8	426·0	91·9
1908	2,398	2,255	5,640	5,051	7,667	2,790	6,399	1,731	912·6	998·3	598	444	593·0	377·1	79·6
1909	2,746	2,319	6,246	5,718	8,527	2,976	6,594	1,878	906·3	1,427·7	614	435	624·7	378·2	91·3
1910	2,853	2,419	7,174	6,234	8,934	3,117	7,475	2,089	1,084·4	1,449·1	669	542	678·3	430·4	103·8
1911	3,192	2,404	8,066	6,077	9,707	3,222	8,106	2,187	1,161·7	1,591·4	690	605	680·2	454·1	102·8
1912	3,557	2,734	8,231	6,713	8,957	3,462	8,957	2,307	1,171·8	1,518·8	783	682	744·6	487·2	111·7
1913	3,407	2,770	8,421	6,880	10,770	3,432	10,097	2,441	1,374·0	1,520·1	847	731	768·7	525·2	109·6

1. The value of one paper rouble in terms of silver kopeks was raised by approximately four times.

SOURCES

Austria-Hungary: *Tafeln zur Statistik der Österreichischen Monarchie* (1842–59); *Statistisches Handbüchlein für die Österreichischen Monarchie* (1861); *Statistisches Jahrbuch der Österreichischen Monarchie* (1861–81); *Österreichisches Statistisches Handbuch* (1882–1915/17).

France: *Annuaire Statistique* (1966).

Germany: W. G. HOFMANN, *Das Wachstum der Deutschen Wirtschaft seit der Mitte des 19 Jahrhunderts* (Berlin, Heidelberg, New York, 1965).

Italy: *Annali di Statistica*, serie VIII, vol. 9.

Russia: P. A. KHROMOV, *Economic Development of Russia in the 19th and 20th Centuries, 1800–1917* (Moscow).

Sweden: 1861 onwards from O. LINDAHL, *Sveriges Nationalprodukt, 1861–1951* (Stockholm, 1956); earlier averages from *Historisk Statistisk för Sverige*, vol. III.

United Kingdom: B. R. MITCHELL and PHYLLIS DEANE, *Abstract of British Historical Statistics* (Cambridge, 1962).

LITERACY

TABLE I

Illiteracy in Europe, *circa* 1850 (Approximate percentage of adult illiterates is indicated where known)

Countries with less than 30% illiterate	Countries with 30 to 50% illiterate		Countries with over 50% illiterate	
Denmark[1]	Austrian Empire[2]	40-45%	Bosnia-Hercegovina	
Finland	Belgium	45-50%	Bulgaria	
Germany (Prussia 20%)	England and Wales	30-33%	Gibraltar, Malta	
Iceland	France	40-45%	Greece	
Netherlands	Ireland		Hungary	
Norway	Luxembourg		Italy	75-80%
Scotland 20%	Monaco, Andorra, Liechtenstein		Montenegro	
Sweden 10%			Portugal	
Switzerland			Romania	
			Russian Empire	90-95%
			Serbia	
			Spain 75%	

1. Including the Faroes.
2. Excluding Lombardo-Veneto.

SOURCE
CARLO M. CIPOLLA: *Literacy and Development in the West* (Harmondsworth, 1969).

LITERACY TABLE 2

Decline of Illiteracy

	Percentage of Bridegrooms who signed with marks	Year in which rate was attained	Percentage of recruits who could not write	Year in which rate was attained
France	—	—	50	1835
	—	—	40	1848
	30	1860	30	1863
	20	1875	20	1873
	10	1888	10	1890
Prussia	10	c.1850		
Italy	50	1878		
	40	1892		
	30	1905		
	20	1919		
Russian Empire			70	1888
			60	1896
			50	1901
			40	1907
England and Wales	30	1853-5		
	20	1868-70		
	10	1886		
Scotland	10	1859		
Ireland	20	1890		
	10	1901		
Belgium			50	1844
			40	1859
			30	1869
			20	1881
			10	1904

SOURCE
  As for TABLE 1.

NATIONAL ACCOUNTS

TABLE I

National Income and Capital Formation at Fixed and Current Prices

I. *France*—Gross National Product and Gross Capital Formation

	G.N.P. Current Prices (million francs)	G.N.P. 1905-13 Prices (million francs)	G.C.F. Current Prices (million francs)	G.C.F. 1905-13 Prices (million francs)
1781-90	7,700	6,949	1,299	1,172
1803-12	9,755	7,324	2,147	1,612
1815-24	10,503	8,969	1,724	1,472
1825-34	12,503	10,977	2,031	1,783
1835-44	14,894	12,929	2,630	2,283
1845-54	17,407	14,628	3,041	2,555
1855-64	22,824	17,972	4,675	3,681
1865-74	26,499	21,199	5,097	4,078
1875-84	27,235	23,418	5,401	4,644
1885-94	27,321	27,541	5,275	5,318
1895-1904	29,095	30,788	6,208	6,569
1905-13	38,035	38,035	7,972	7,972

II. *Germany*—Net Social Product and Net Investment

	N.S.P. Current Prices (million marks)	N.S.P. 1913 Prices (million marks)	N. Inv. Current Prices (million marks)	N. Inv. 1913 Prices (million marks)
1850	6,070	10,534	(500)	(700)
1851	6,431	10,568	570	740
1852	7,296	11,121	990	1,300
1853	7,189	10,630	470	600
1854	8,203	10,961	920	920
1855	7,882	10,316	260	370
1856	9,139	11,553	1,190	1,200
1857	8,581	11,845	560	680
1858	8,334	12,053	670	750
1859	8,134	12,219	710	880
1860	9,630	13,604	1,260	1,530
1861	9,379	13,002	720	890
1862	10,050	13,731	1,320	1,670
1863	10,372	14,639	1,500	1,970
1864	10,207	14,677	1,220	1,630
1865	10,279	14,858	1,050	1,440

National Accounts Table 1 continued

II. Germany

	N.S.P. Current Prices	N.S.P. 1913 Prices	N. Inv. Current Prices	N. Inv. 1913 Prices
1866	10,714	15,106	1,060	1,460
1867	11,558	15,108	850	1,070
1868	12,967	16,621	1,920	2,270
1869	11,750	15,660	860	1,040
1870	12,876	16,706	1,590	1,870
1871	14,013	17,395	1,480	1,520
1872	16,627	19,133	2,600	2,440
1873	17,950	19,768	2,370	2,120
1874	19,544	21,316	3,370	3,180
1875	18,242	21,070	2,480	2,570
1876	17,966	20,890	2,390	2,750
1877	17,414	20,705	1,830	2,240
1878	17,874	21,803	1,820	2,310
1879	16,678	21,193	1,210	1,820
1880	16,902	20,576 [1] / 19,874	1,330	1,860
1881	17,330	20,616	1,590	2,160
1882	17,489	20,444	1,530	2,110
1883	18,014	21,909	1,810	2,460
1884	18,540	22,712	1,960	2,730
1885	18,731	23,452	1,960	2,740
1886	18,935	24,142	1,980	2,830
1887	19,280	24,558	2,230	3,030
1888	20,716	25,840	2,400	2,960
1889	22,249	26,478	2,940	3,600
1890	23,676	27,754	3,360	4,050
1891	22,624	26,822	2,080	2,900
1892	24,061	28,390	3,140	3,980
1893	24,357	30,606	2,930	4,080
1894	24,361	30,196	2,530	3,710
1895	25,254	32,179	2,830	4,010
1896	26,979	33,377	3,590	4,860
1897	28,714	34,739	4,150	5,360
1898	31,028	36,813	5,330	6,650
1899	31,761	36,860	5,390	6,010
1900	32,448	36,466	5,100	5,330
1901	31,617	36,197	3,890	4,470
1902	31,928	36,918	3,520	4,060
1903	34,402	40,132	4,960	5,890
1904	36,284	42,263	5,630	6,630
1905	38,878	43,346	6,050	6,710
1906	40,643	44,299	6,680	7,040
1907	42,976	46,181	7,610	7,740

National Accounts Table 1 continued

II. *Germany*

	N.S.P. Current Prices	N.S.P. 1913 Prices	N. Inv. Current Prices	N. Inv. 1913 Prices
1908	42,441	46,410	5,610	6,020
1909	44,358	47,512	6,040	6,700
1910	45,785	47,457	6,100	6,610
1911	48,106	49,648	7,270	7,830
1912	51,563	51,914	8,570	8,590
1913	52,440	52,440	8,170	8,170

III. *Italy*—Net National Income and Gross Domestic Fixed Capital Formation

	N.N.I. Current Prices (million lire)	N.N.I. 1938 Prices (million lire)	G.D.F.C.F. Current Prices (million lire)	G.D.F.C.F. 1938 Prices (million lire)
1861	8,980	47,262	688	3,622
1862	10,076	47,982	762	3,629
1863	9,224	47,302	711	3,647
1864	8,995	49,151	683	3,733
1865	9,524	52,327	712	3,911
1866	10,122	53,276	754	3,966
1867	9,555	48,259	746	3,766
1868	10,414	50,308	781	3,775
1869	9,739	51,256	733	3,859
1870	9,962	51,616	669	3,466
1871	10,099	51,264	730	3,704
1872	10,696	50,932	791	3,768
1873	12,052	52,859	903	3,960
1874	12,824	53,213	881	3,654
1875	12,200	55,706	927	4,234
1876	10,795	55,074	843	4,303
1877	11,822	54,756	988	4,553
1878	12,115	55,067	1,069	4,859
1879	11,143	55,715	1,070	5,351
1880	11,715	56,321	1,179	5,669
1881	10,680	54,212	1,163	5,906
1882	11,648	56,542	1,278	6,205
1883	11,449	56,399	1,295	6,381
1884	10,388	57,391	1,226	6,771
1885	15,401	57,680	1,894	7,094
1886	12,013	58,317	1,552	7,646
1887	10,367	58,903	1,397	7,936
1888	10,519	58,438	1,367	7,596
1889	6,688	56,682	816	6,912

National Accounts Table 1 continued

III. Italy

	N.N.I. Current Prices	N.N.I. 1938 Prices	G.D.F.C.F. Current Prices	G.D.F.C.F. 1938 Prices
1890	11,229	60,372	1,117	6,003
1891	13,512	60,865	1,225	5,519
1892	11,779	58,601	1,117	5,556
1893	10,569	60,394	1,007	5,753
1894	8,864	59,892	865	5,845
1895	8,220	61,345	786	5,869
1896	10,562	62,868	954	5,676
1897	10,715	60,534	976	5,512
1898	11,625	64,227	1,015	5,605
1899	12,809	65,353	1,246	6,359
1900	14,030	70,148	1,388	6,938
1901	14,600	74,488	1,440	7,346
1902	14,151	73,703	1,406	7,323
1903	13,465	75,648	1,399	7,861
1904	14,916	75,333	1,661	8,389
1905	14,938	79,037	1,887	9,984
1906	16,095	81,700	2,299	11,671
1907	18,430	87,763	2,824	13,449
1908	18,709	87,837	3,067	14,401
1909	19,004	92,700	3,006	14,665
1910	18,329	88,547	3,116	15,054
1911	20,049	93,687	3,158	14,755
1912	21,058	94,857	3,337	15,030
1913	21,517	99,616	3,161	14,635

IV. Sweden—Gross Domestic Product and Gross Domestic Fixed Capital Formation

	G.D.P. Current Prices (million kronor)	G.D.P. 1913 Prices (million kronor)	G.D.F.C.F. Current Prices (million kronor)	G.D.F.C.F. 1913 Prices (million kronor)
1861	794	924	50	88
1862	841	944	76	131
1863	826	984	64	110
1864	779	974	71	126
1865	805	1,006	54	97
1866	829	999	76	138
1867	872	991	63	115
1868	891	979	39	73
1869	830	966	66	121
1870	954	1,163	67	120

National Accounts Table 1 continued

IV. *Sweden*

	G.D.P. Current Prices	G.D.P. 1913 Prices	G.D.F.C.F. Current Prices	G.D.F.C.F. 1913 Prices
1871	1,001	1,192	72	124
1872	1,124	1,276	98	145
1873	1,294	1,362	155	205
1874	1,408	1,436	188	234
1875	1,295	1,335	178	232
1876	1,441	1,470	170	206
1877	1,396	1,440	168	208
1878	1,280	1,407	144	197
1879	1,247	1,467	123	181
1880	1,334	1,482	126	167
1881	1,415	1,538	137	187
1882	1,351	1,501	122	163
1883	1,405	1,579	133	177
1884	1,368	1,591	147	205
1885	1,370	1,671	135	189
1886	1,285	1,647	144	212
1887	1,253	1,670	103	157
1888	1,321	1,693	125	196
1889	1,456	1,798	146	208
1890	1,511	1,821	149	209
1891	1,605	1,888	122	175
1892	1,571	1,870	126	185
1893	1,558	1,923	113	172
1894	1,620	2,104	132	198
1895	1,595	2,045	173	260
1896	1,783	2,315	179	252
1897	1,892	2,365	226	296
1898	1,996	2,376	249	316
1899	2,122	2,439	288	336
1900	2,261	2,569	300	333
1901	2,260	2,628	262	316
1902	2,210	2,540	257	316
1903	2,474	2,811	316	376
1904	2,485	2,856	332	399
1905	2,543	2,890	329	380
1906	2,911	3,234	386	430
1907	3,077	3,238	411	426
1908	3,131	3,262	357	400
1909	3,166	3,333	324	354
1910	3,366	3,543	366	387
1911	3,464	3,685	401	420
1912	3,603	3,603	418	431
1913	4,128	4,128	509	508

National Accounts Table 1 continued

V. *United Kingdom*—A. Great Britain, Gross National Income

	G.N.I. Current Prices (million pounds)
1801	232
1811	301
1821	291
1831	340
1841	452
1851	523
1861	668

B. United Kingdom, Net National Income and Domestic Fixed Capital Formation

	N.N.I. Current Prices (million pounds)	N.N.I. 1900 Prices (million pounds)	Gross D.F.C.F. Current Prices (million pounds)	Net D.F.C.F. Current Prices (million pounds)	Net D.F.C.F. 1900 Prices (million pounds)
1855	636	508	—	—	—
1856	665	531	44	28	33
1857	645	502	42	27	30
1858	635	545	42	28	32
1859	656	553	39	25	29
1860	694	559	43	27	31
1861	727	591	50	33	39
1862	741	597	61	41	49
1863	759	600	68	46	51
1864	795	629	79	54	57
1865	822	662	82	56	61
1866	846	675	89	61	68
1867	840	670	66	45	50
1868	836	673	57	39	43
1869	867	711	56	38	40
1870	936	774	74	51	56
1871	1,015	817	86	59	64
1872	1,072	813	98	68	65
1873	1,149	857	96	68	59
1874	1,126	891	110	80	70
1875	1,113	912	114	83	81
1876	1,099	909	121	88	90
1877	1,089	901	120	87	91
1878	1,059	927	108	75	80

National Accounts Table 1 continued

V. United Kingdom B.

	N.N.I. Current Prices	N.N.I. 1900 Prices	G.D.F.C.F. Current Prices	N.D.F.C.F. Current Prices	N.D.F.C.F. 1900 Prices
1879	1,032	930	91	65	72
1880	1,076	932	94	67	70
1881	1,117	987	91	63	68
1882	1,160	1,035	95	64	66
1883	1,153	1,029	98	64	66
1884	1,124	1,054	88	57	64
1885	1,115	1,115	79	49	57
1886	1,136	1,162	66	39	46
1887	1,185	1,225	65	39	47
1888	1,259	1,302	72	43	51
1889	1,350	1,380	82	48	54
1890	1,385	1,416	86	50	55
1891	1,373	1,404	91	52	59
1892	1,335	1,350	98	58	69
1893	1,339	1,369	91	56	67
1894	1,418	1,518	96	61	74
1895	1,447	1,587	93	62	77
1896	1,484	1,627	105	72	88
1897	1,538	1,647	131	91	108
1898	1,618	1,673	156	111	127
1899	1,700	1,799	173	125	135
1900	1,750	1,750	190	141	141
1901	1,727	1,746	191	142	148
1902	1,740	1,759	196	146	158
1903	1,717	1,717	192	141	154
1904	1,704	1,685	185	134	147
1905	1,776	1,757	173	123	136
1906	1,874	1,834	164	113	122
1907	1,966	1,883	150	100	105
1908	1,875	1,835	120	77	83
1909	1,907	1,846	121	75	81
1910	1,984	1,881	124	81	86
1911	2,076	1,947	120	78	84
1912	2,181	1,985	129	84	84
1913	2,265	2,021	157	105	100

1. Figures before this do not include the 'saldo der Leistungsbilanz'.

SOURCES
France: T. J. MARKOVITCH, *L'Industrie Française de 1789 à 1964* (Cahiers de l'I.S.E.A., 1966).

National Accounts Table 1 continued

Germany: W. G. HOFFMAN, *Das Wachstum der Deutschen Wirtschaft seit der Mitte des 19 Jahrhunderts* (Berlin, Heidelberg, New York, 1965).

Italy: G. FUA, *Notes on Italian Economic Growth, 1861-1964* (Milan, 1966).

Sweden: O. JOHANSSON, *The Gross Domestic Product of Sweden and its Composition 1861-1955* (Stockholm, 1967).

United Kingdom: A. PHYLLIS DEANE and W. A. COLE, *British Economic Growth, 1688-1959* (Cambridge, 1962).

B. C. H. FEINSTEIN, 'Income and Investment in the United Kingdom, 1856-1914' *Economic Journal* (1961).

NATIONAL ACCOUNTS TABLE 2

Percentage Distribution of National Product between Sectors

	Agriculture		Industry		Services (incl. Transport)	
	Initial Date	Terminal Date	Initial Date	Terminal Date	Initial Date	Terminal Date
France						
1789/1815 to 1825/35	50	50	20	25	30	25
1825/35 to 1872/82	50	42	25	30	25	28
1872/82 to 1908/10	42	35	30	37	28	28
Germany						
1860/9 to 1905/14	32	18	24	39	44	43
Italy						
1861/5 to 1896/1900	55	47	[20 includes transport]	22	[25 excludes transport]	31
Sweden						
1861/5 to 1901/5	39	35	17	38	44	27
Great Britain						
1801 to 1841	32	22	23	34	45	44
1841 to 1901	22	6	34	40	44	54

SOURCE

SIMON KUZNETS, *Modern Economic Growth* (Yale University Press, 1966) pp. 88-93.

NATIONAL ACCOUNTS TABLE 3

Percentage Distribution of G.N.P. by Final Use

	Private Consumption	Government Consumption	Gross Domestic Capital Formation	Capital Exports Capital Imports (—)	Gross National Capital Formation
Germany					
1851-70	81·6	4·0	13·7	0·7	14·4
1871-90	73·1	5·9	18·9	2·1	21·0
1891-1913	68·7	7·1	23·0	1·1	24·1
Italy					
1861-80	87·3	4·2	10·0	—1·5	8·5
1881-1900	84·4	4·8	10·8	0	10·8
1901-10	78·4	4·2	15·9	1·4	17·3
Sweden					
1861-80	85·3	4·4	10·8	—0·5	10·3
1881-1900	85·0	5·4	11·2	—1·6	9·6
1901-20	81·6	5·8	13·1	—0·5	12·6
United Kingdom					
1860-79	82·7	4·8	9·4	3·1	12·5
1880-99	81·9	5·8	8·4	3·9	12·3
1900-14	78·6	7·4	8·7	5·3	14·0

SOURCE
ibid. pp. 236-239.

NATIONAL ACCOUNTS TABLE 4

Capital Formation Proportions

	N.D.F.C. as % of N.D.P. or N.N.P.	Net National Savings as % of N.D.P. or N.N.P.
Germany		
1851-70	8·5	9·2
1871-90	11·4	13·8
1891-1913	15·0	16·1
Italy		
1861-80	4·6	3·1
1881-90	5·0	5·0
1901-10	9·9	11·5
England and Wales		
1740-70	—	5·5
1770-1800	—	6·5
United Kingdom		
1801/11 to 1821/31	—	7·5
1821/31 to 1851/61	7·4	9·0
1860-79	7·7	10·9
1880-99	6·9	11·0
1900-14	7·5	13·2

SOURCE

SIMON KUZNETS, *Modern Economic Growth* (Yale U.P., 1966) pp. 248-250 and 'Quantitative Aspects of the Economic Growth of Nations: VI', *Economic Development and Cultural Change* (July, 1961).

PRICE INDICES

TABLE I

	England Consumer's Goods (1770 = 100)		England Consumer's Goods (1770 = 100)
1750	95	1770	100
1751	90	1771	107
1752	93	1772	117
1753	90	1773	119
1754	90	1774	116
1755	92	1775	113
1756	92	1776	114
1757	109	1777	108
1758	106	1778	117
1759	100	1779	111
1760	98	1780	110
1761	94	1781	115
1762	94	1782	116
1763	100	1783	129
1764	102	1784	126
1765	106	1785	120
1766	107	1786	119
1767	109	1787	117
1768	108	1788	121
1769	99	1789	117

Price Indices continued

	Austria-Hungary (1867-77 = 100)	France[1] (1901-10 = 100)	Germany (1846 = 100)	Italy (1913 = 100)	Sweden (1900 = 100)	England Consumer's Goods (1770 = 100)	Great Britain (1821-5 = 100)	Great Britain (1867-77 = 100)	Great Britain (1900 = 100)
1790	—	—	—	—	—	124	89·3	—	—
1791	—	—	—	—	—	121	89·7	—	—
1792	—	—	112	—	—	122	88·1	—	—
1793	—	—	112	—	—	129	96·6	—	—
1794	—	—	115	—	—	136	98·5	—	—
1795	—	—	139	—	—	147	114·9	—	—
1796	—	—	130	—	—	154	116·1	—	—
1797	—	—	123	—	—	148	106·2	—	—
1798	—	—	132	—	—	148	107·9	—	—
1799	—	—	150	—	—	160	124·6	—	—
1800	—	—	154	—	—	212	151·0	—	—
1801	—	—	153	—	—	228	155·7	—	—
1802	—	—	149	—	—	174	122·2	—	—
1803	—	—	158	—	—	156	123·6	—	—
1804	—	—	155	—	—	161	124·3	—	—
1805	—	—	178	—	—	187	136·2	—	—
1806	—	—	179	—	—	184	134·5	—	—
1807	—	—	169	—	—	186	131·2	—	—
1808	—	—	201	—	—	204	144·5	—	—
1809	—	—	178	—	—	212	155·0	—	—
1810	—	—	150	—	—	207	153·4	—	—
1811	—	—	140	—	—	206	145·4	—	—

Price Indices continued

	Austria-Hungary (1867-77 = 100)	France (1901-10 = 100)	Germany (1846 = 100)	Germany (1913 = 100)	Italy (1913 = 100)	Sweden (1900 = 100)	England Consumer's Goods (1770 = 100)	Great Britain (1821-5 = 100)	Great Britain (1867-77 = 100)	Great Britain (1900 = 100)
1812	—	—	156	—	—	—	237	163·7	—	—
1813	—	—	137	—	—	—	243	168·9	—	—
1814	—	—	125	—	—	—	209	153·7	—	—
1815	—	—	128	—	—	—	191	129·9	—	—
1816	—	—	141	—	—	—	—	118·6	—	—
1817	—	—	169	—	—	—	—	131·9	—	—
1818	—	—	148	—	—	—	—	138·7	—	—
1819	—	—	117	—	—	—	—	128·1	—	—
1820	—	153	103	—	—	—	—	115·4	—	—
1821	—	143	97	—	—	—	—	99·7	—	—
1822	—	138	96	—	—	—	—	87·9	—	—
1823	—	143	93	—	—	—	—	97·6	—	—
1824	—	133	82	—	—	—	—	101·9	—	—
1825	—	146	87	—	—	—	—	113·0	—	—
1826	—	136	82	—	—	—	—	100·0	—	—
1827	—	134	88	—	—	—	—	99·3	—	—
1828	—	129	89	—	—	—	—	96·4	—	—
1829	—	130	88	—	—	—	—	95·8	—	—
1830	—	130	89	—	—	—	—	94·5	—	—
1831	—	124	93	—	—	—	—	95·3	—	—
1832	—	125	81	—	—	—	—	91·5	—	—
1833	—	126	87	—	—	—	—	88·6	—	—

Year										
1834	—	—	86.5	—	—	—	—	87	128	—
1835	—	—	84.5	—	—	—	—	88	132	—
1836	—	—	95.2	—	—	—	—	89	135	—
1837	—	—	94.3	—	—	—	—	84	126	—
1838	—	—	97.8	—	—	—	—	89	131	—
1839	—	—	104.3	—	—	—	—	92	130	—
1840	—	—	102.5	—	79.3	—	—	91	135	—
1841	—	—	97.7	—	80.5	—	—	89	134	—
1842	—	—	88.8	—	81.5	—	—	89	131	—
1843	—	—	79.7	—	77.7	—	—	88	121	—
1844	—	—	81.1	—	72.5	—	—	87	118	—
1845	—	—	83.3	—	75.6	—	—	93	121	—
1846	—	89	86.0	—	79.1	—	—	100	129	—
1847	—	95	96.8	—	80.8	—	—	111	136	—
1848	—	78	81.8	—	78.5	—	—	87	112	—
1849	—	74	73.9	—	77.6	—	—	80	111	—
1850	—	77	73.5	—	77.4	—	58.2	81	111	—
1851	—	75	—	—	78.9	—	61.7	85	110	—
1852	—	78	—	—	81.4	—	65.5	93	119	—
1853	—	95	—	—	84.0	—	68.3	105	139	—
1854	—	102	—	—	89.8	—	75.6	114	148	—
1855	—	101	—	—	96.3	—	76.5	120	154	—
1856	—	101	—	—	106.2	—	79.0	120	156	—
1857	—	105	—	—	106.4	—	73.0	115	151	—
1858	—	91	—	—	95.3	—	69.6	104	137	—
1859	—	94	—	—	89.7	—	66.8	101	137	—
1860	—	99	—	—	93.7	—	71.1	107	144	—
1861	—	98	—	—	97.6	97.6	72.5	107	142	—
1862	—	101	—	—	100.3	91.2	73.4	107	142	—

Price Indices continued

	Austria-Hungary (1867-77 = 100)	France (1901-10 = 100)	Germany (1846 = 100)	Germany (1913 = 100)	Italy (1913 = 100)	Sweden (1900 = 100)	England Consumer's Goods (1770 = 100)	Great Britain (1821-5 = 100)	Great Britain (1867-77 = 100)	Great Britain (1900 = 100)
1863	—	143	105	70·9	87·2	95·3	—	—	103	—
1864	—	141	104	69·7	87·2	91·2	—	—	105	—
1865	—	132	101	69·1	85·8	91·1	—	—	101	—
1866	—	134	103	71·0	89·7	94·0	—	—	102	—
1867	104·1	131	111	74·1	90·2	99·9	—	—	100	—
1868	97·7	132	111	78·4	95·8	103·3	—	—	99	—
1869	99·6	130	105	75·1	89·3	97·4	—	—	98	—
1870	102·4	133	—	77·4	88·5	93·4	—	—	96	—
1871	105·6	138	—	81·7	91·3	95·8	—	—	100	135·6
1872	105·1	144	—	86·6	99·1	99·8	—	—	109	145·2
1873	103·5	144	—	92·2	105·1	107·5	—	—	111	151·9
1874	99·0	132	—	91·7	104·9	111·4	—	—	102	146·9
1875	91·2	129	—	86·6	92·9	110·6	—	—	96	140·4
1876	94·5	130	—	85·9	90·0	111·0	—	—	95	137·1
1877	97·8	131	—	84·0	102·1	110·4	—	—	94	140·4
1878	89·2	120	—	81·9	98·9	103·2	—	—	87	131·1
1879	84·5	117	—	78·4	92·8	96·8	—	—	83	125·0
1880	89·3	120	—	82·4	93·3	101·8	—	—	88	129·0
1881	87·1	117	—	81·2	87·3	104·3	—	—	85	126·6
1882	86·0	114	—	81·9	89·6	101·5	—	—	84	127·7
1883	86·1	110	—	79·8	83·9	101·0	—	—	82	125·9
1884	84·5	101	—	79·0	80·4	97·3	—	—	76	114·1

Year										
1885	79.8	99	—	77.1	84.7	92.7	—	—	72	107.0
1886	76.9	95	—	76.6	85.2	88.2	—	—	69	101.0
1887	76.7	92	—	76.8	79.4	85.0	—	—	68	98.8
1888	77.1	96	—	78.2	80.8	88.1	—	—	70	101.8
1889	77.0	100	—	80.6	85.4	92.0	—	—	72	103.4
1890	77.0	100	—	82.3	87.6	94.0	—	—	72	103.3
1891	78.0	98	—	81.9	85.3	96.9	—	—		106.9
1892	74.1	95	—	80.8	81.0	95.2	—	—		101.1
1893	75.2	94	—	77.4	76.0	91.3	—	—		99.4
1894	72.0	87	—	76.0	73.8	86.7	—	—		93.5
1895	72.4	85	—	77.1	77.6	88.3	—	—		90.7
1896	70.5	82	—	78.6	78.2	87.6	—	—		88.2
1897	72.1	83	—	80.3	76.6	90.4	—	—		90.1
1898	74.7	86	—	80.6	78.7	94.7	—	—		93.2
1899	76.4	93	—	83.5	80.8	98.9	—	—		92.2
1900	81.5	99	—	86.5	84.5	100.0	—	—		100.0
1901	79.8	95	—	85.1	84.1	97.6	—	—		96.7
1902	77.9	94	—	84.7	81.3	98.4	—	—		96.4
1903	80.0	96	—	85.1	80.6	100.1	—	—		96.9
1904	81.8	94	—	85.4	77.0	98.8	—	—		98.2
1905	85.3	98	—	88.1	80.3	101.0	—	—		97.6
1906	90.5	104	—	92.5	83.3	103.1	—	—		100.8
1907	94.5	109	—	93.1	89.8	108.4	—	—		106.0
1908	91.0	101	—	91.8	87.4	110.0	—	—		103.0
1909	94.4	101	—	93.8	88.1	109.0	—	—		104.1
1910	—	108	—	97.3	88.2	109.0	—	—		108.8
1911	—	113	—	97.1	95.3	107.4	—	—		109.4
1912	—	118	—	99.5	102.8	114.6	—	—		114.9
1913	—	116	—	100.0	100.0	114.9	—	—		116.5

1. General French Price Index, 1905-13 = 100 (Source: T. J. Markovitch, *L'Industrie Française de 1789 à 1964* (Cahiers de l'I.S.E.A., 1966).

1781-90	110·8	1855-64	127·0
1803-12	133·2	1865-74	125·0
1815-24	117·1	1875-84	116·3
1825-34	113·9	1885-94	99·2
1835-44	115·2	1895-1904	94·5
1845-54	119·0	1905-13	100

SOURCES

England:
  E. B. SCHUMPETER
  Britain 1821-5 =100
  GAYER, ROSTOW &
  SCHWARZ
  1867-77 =100
  A. SAUERBECK
  1900 =100
  Board of Trade

all from B. R. MITCHELL and PHYLLIS DEANE, *Abstract of British Historical Statistics* (Cambridge, 1962).

Germany: 1846=100 A. JACOBS and H. RICHTER, *Die Grosshandelpreise in Deutschland von 1792 bis 1934*, Sonderhefte des Instituts fur Konjuncturforschung No. 37 (Berlin, 1935) — originally on 1913 =100 basis; 1913 =100 W. G. HOFFMAN, *Das Wachstum der Deutschen Wirtschaft seit der Mitte des 19 Jahrhunderts* (Berlin, Heidelberg, New York, 1965).

France: *Annuaire Statistique de la France* (1966).

Italy: *Cento Anno di sviluppo economico e sociale dell' Italia.*

Austria-Hungary: B. VON JANKOVICH in *Bulletin de l'Institut Internationale de Statistique*, XIX No. 3 (1911).

Sweden: Cost of Living (Budget B. of Myrdal), quoted in JEAN MARCZEWSKI, *Introduction à l'Histoire Quantitive* from G. MYRDAL, *The Cost of Living in Sweden 1830-1930* (London, 1933).

Notes on the Authors

LENNART JÖRBERG
is Associate Professor of Economic History at Lund University, Sweden. He received his doctorate at Lund University and studied economic history and economics at Harvard University and the University of California, Berkeley in 1957–58. He was visiting professor at Institut für Weltwirtschaft, Kiel in 1964 and at the University of California, Berkeley in 1965–66. He is the author of *Growth and Fluctuations of Swedish Industry 1869–1912; Studies in the Process of Industrialisation*, Lund 1961 and of articles and reviews in American, German and Swedish journals.

GREGORY GROSSMAN
was born in 1921 and obtained his Ph.D. in Economics at Harvard University. Since 1953 he has been at the University of California (Berkeley), where he now holds the position of Professor of Economics. He was a Research Fellow at the Russian Research Centre, Harvard University in 1956, and a Guggenheim Fellow in 1964–65. Among his publications are *Soviet Statistics of Physical Output of Industrial Commodities*, Princeton 1960, and *Economic Systems*, Prentice Hall, 1967.

JORDI NADAL
was born in 1929. In 1968 he became Professor of Economic History at the University of Valencia and since 1970 has held the same position at the University of Barcelona. Among his publications are *La population catalane de 1553–1717. L'immigration française et les autres facteurs de son développement*, Paris 1960 (with E. Giralt); *La poblacion espanola (siglos XVI a XX)*, Barcelona 1966; and, in collaboration with the late Professor J. Vicens Vives *Manual de historia economica de Espana*, Barcelona 1959.

B. M. BIUCCHI

is Professor of Economic History at the University of Fribourg. His publications include a number of articles on the economic history of Switzerland.

WILLIAM WOODRUFF

is a graduate of Oxford, London, Nottingham and Melbourne (Australia), and is presently the Graduate Research Professor in Economic History at the University of Florida at Gainesville. His research is concerned with global development—particularly the role of Europeans and North Americans in the world economy during the past two centuries. During 1966 he was a member of the Institute for Advanced Study at Princeton, where he completed his recently published *Impact of Western Man, a Study of Europe's role in the world economy: 1790–1960*. The second volume of *Impact of Western Man, American Odyssey: 1760–1970*, on which he is currently engaged, treats American history as a focal point of world history since the mid-eighteenth century.

B. R. MITCHELL

was born in 1929 and received his M.A. from Aberdeen University and his Ph.D. from Cambridge. He was sometime Senior Research Officer in the Department of Applied Economics at Cambridge University and is at present University Lecturer in Economics there and a Fellow of Trinity College. He is the editor of the *Abstract of British Historical Studies* and co-editor of the *Second Abstract of British Historical Statistics*.

Index of Persons

Index of Places

General Index

The Fontana History of Europe

Praised by academics, teachers and general readers alike, this series aims to provide an account, based on the latest research, that combines narrative and explanation. Each volume has been specially commissioned from a leading English, American or European scholar, and is complete in itself. The general editor of the series is J. H. Plumb, lately Professor of Modern History at Cambridge University, and Fellow of Christ's College, Cambridge.

Fontana History

Fontana History includes the well-known History of Europe, edited by J. H. Plumb and the Fontana Economic History of Europe, edited by Carlo Cipolla. Other books available include:

Lectures on Modern History Lord Acton

The Conservative Party from Peel to Churchill
Robert Blake

A Short History of the Second World War
Basil Collier

American Presidents and the Presidency
Marcus Cunliffe

The English Reformation A. G. Dickens

The Norman Achievement David C. Douglas

The Practice of History G. R. Elton

Politics and the Nation, 1450-1660 D. M. Loades

Ireland Since the Famine F. S. L. Lyons

Britain and the Second World War Henry Pelling

Foundations of American Independence J. R. Pole

A History of the Scottish People T. C. Smout

The Ancien Regime and the French Revolution
Tocqueville

The King's Peace 1637-1641 C. V. Wedgwood

The King's War 1641-1647 C. V. Wedgwood

Fontana Politics